MICHAEL DILLON was founding Director of the Centre for Contemporary Chinese Studies at the University of Durham, where he taught Modern Chinese History. He is a Fellow of the Royal Historical Society and the Royal Asiatic Society and was Visiting Professor at Tsinghua University in Beijing in 2009. He is the author of *China: A Modern History* (I.B.Tauris).

'A well-paced, and judicious account, well written and very easy to read. Its strength is in giving equal weight to the various phases of Deng's career, rather than focussing too much on the post-1978 period. It also captures something of the complexity and contradictoriness of Deng.'

Kerry Brown, author of *The New Emperors*

'Through this fascinating and clearly written biography of Deng Xiaoping, Michael Dillon shows us how different Chinese power politics works from our economic and political world. Economic liberalisation that seems capitalist to the extreme, is combined with state interference and ideological conservatism. In this respect Xi Jinping can be seen as a straight continuation of Deng Xiaoping's reform agenda.'

Barend Ter Haar, Run Run Shaw Professor of Chinese, University of Oxford

DENG XIAOPING

The Man who Made Modern China

MICHAEL DILLON

I.B. TAURIS
LONDON · NEW YORK

Published in 2015 by I.B.Tauris & Co. Ltd
6 Salem Road, London W2 4BU
175 Fifth Avenue, New York NY 10010
www.ibtauris.com

Distributed in the United States and Canada Exclusively by Palgrave Macmillan
175 Fifth Avenue, New York NY 10010

ISBN: 978 1 78076 895 3
eISBN: 978 0 85773 539 3

A full CIP record for this book is available from the British Library
A full CIP record is available from the Library of Congress

Library of Congress Catalog Card Number: available

Printed and bound in Sweden by ScandBook AB

CONTENTS

LIST OF PLATES

ACKNOWLEDGEMENTS

In Montargis I am grateful to Mme. Dr. Peiwen Wang, President of the Association Amitié Chine Montargis; M. Stéphane Poisson, Chef de Cabinet du Maire; and the staff of the secretariat and office of the Mairie for assistance with material on the presence in the town of Deng Xiaoping and other Chinese students on the work–study programme. Joyce Dillon shared the search for traces of Deng in France and prepared the index. Jan van der Made, of Radio France International, very kindly made available to me his reports from Beijing for Dutch radio on the death of Deng.

In addition to having one of the best collections of recently published academic books in Beijing, All Sages Books (*Wansheng shuyuan*) on Chengfu Road in Wudaokou was the perfect place to read and reflect on modern Chinese history and the life of Deng Xiaoping and his contemporaries over lunch or coffee. The advice and assistance of staff at Xinhua Books in Wangfujing was also invaluable. In Sichuan, material relating to Deng and local history came from the Deng residence (*Xiaoping guju*) museum in Paifang and Xinhua Books in Shapingba, Chongqing. As always the British Library and the Brotherton Library at the University of Leeds were valuable sources of older material.

At I.B.Tauris I am once again grateful for the assistance of the editorial, production and marketing staff and the anonymous readers. Lester Crook's encouragement and constructive criticism since the inception of the project, and Joanna Godfrey's support and advice are much appreciated.

PREFACE

'Deng's China' has never achieved the currency that 'Mao's China' enjoyed in the 1960s and 1970s, but there is little doubt that the resurgence of the Chinese economy that began in the 1980s could not have taken place without the commanding presence of Deng Xiaoping. Mao was never the sole dictator of 'Mao's China', as is sometimes suggested (although he may well have wished that he could be), and neither were the reforms that followed his death in 1976 solely the work of Deng. Deng had been one of Mao's greatest supporters for many years, both before and after the Chinese Communist Party (CCP) came to power in 1949, but it is for his differences with Mao that he will be remembered rather than for the common ground that they shared. Deng was far from being the 'onlie begetter' of China's post-Mao reforms: other senior communists, notably Zhou Enlai, Chen Yun and Zhu Rongji, played important supporting roles, but Deng secured the political support of the Communist Party and, without this, the economic reforms could not have begun. An understanding of Deng's life and work is essential if we are to comprehend the reasons behind both the success of the economic reform programme that he promoted so vigorously, and the impact on China of the limitations of his political vision, especially his obstinate resistance to any meaningful political reform.

The age of revolution and civil war, in which Deng Xiaoping's personality and political views were formed, may have ended, but the age in which he came to exert a powerful influence on China, the age that began in 1976 with the end of the Cultural Revolution and the death of Mao Zedong, is still a work in progress. Deng Xiaoping's long and eventful life began in 1904 in the rural depths of Sichuan, a populous but isolated province in south-western China, in the dying years of the

Qing dynasty. It took him finally to Beijing and the leadership, in fact if not in name, of the Communist Party and the Chinese state at a time when he was able to bring about historic changes to the economy and society of his country, changes that are still determining its direction well into the twenty-first century. Deng's status in the party and the government was never precisely articulated, and foreign observers began to refer to Deng as the 'paramount leader' of China. This was not a title used by the government or the Chinese Communist Party, but a form of words which recognised the fact that he appeared to rule China although he had not replaced Mao Zedong as chairman. Even if he was acknowledged to be the most senior political figure, Deng never had absolute control of policy, as is demonstrated by his tour of the south in 1992, at the age of 88, to defend his economic reforms.

He formally retired from active politics in the autumn of 1989 and spent much of his time playing bridge, one of his lifelong passions. He insisted that his only remaining position of authority was as honorary chairman of the Chinese Bridge Association – one of the few instances where he used the title of chairman. In reality, as an honoured elder statesman, he continued to be consulted and exercised a degree of influence from behind the scenes – although to what extent is debatable – until his death in Beijing in 1997.

This account of Deng focuses on the most significant periods of his life and his career as a revolutionary, a political soldier and a politician in and out of power; it emphasises the experiences that formed his character, attitudes and beliefs and the periods in which he had the greatest opportunity to influence the course of modern Chinese history. In outline, the main phases of his eventful life were: his upbringing and education in a Hakka family in Sichuan at the end of the Qing dynasty and the beginning of the Chinese Republic; the momentous decision almost immediately after the end of World War I to leave China and embark on a period of study and manual labour in northern France in the early 1920s, during which he came into contact with European and Chinese Marxists; soldiering on the Long March from 1934 to 1935, which eventually established the CCP as a political force in the years before World War II; the civil war with the nationalists between 1945 and 1949; the practical experience of government after 1949 and the creation of the new state of the People's Republic of China (PRC); serving as secretary-general of the CCP under Mao Zedong during the 1950s; a period of rejection and internal exile during the Cultural Revolution in the 1960s; and finally his triumphal return to power in the 1970s and the opportunity and the determination to alter the course of China's history, which he accomplished between 1978 and his death in 1997.

This is a political biography, but where possible the emphasis is as much on the biography as on the political. In Deng's life it is impossible to separate them as his was almost exclusively a political life, but it is essential to try to understand him as an individual operating in the political world of China in revolution, rather than just as he appears in official documents. If it is to be of any value, the biography of a political figure, especially one of such significance as Deng, must avoid hagiography and demonology (which are all too prevalent in discussions of the leaders of the Chinese communist movement by both Chinese and foreigners) and the devil will be, as always, in the detail.

Deng Xiaoping is a far more complex figure than the way he is usually portrayed in contemporary China would indicate. He transformed China in the 1980s and without him it is unlikely that the country would have enjoyed the economic growth and the relationship with the outside world that it benefits from today. Supporters of Deng's more open-minded approach to economic development and international relations, which is usually compared favourably – and accurately – with the introverted and isolationist attitudes of Mao Zedong, have often glossed over the less laudable part that he played in restricting pressure for greater openness and democracy at critical points of his career.

In 1956–7, when he was secretary-general of the CCP, he acquiesced in a nationwide political campaign that was designed to bring to heel educated Chinese who had vented their criticisms of maladministration, corruption and especially of the senseless and grandiose policies of Mao Zedong that were to lead to the Great Leap Forward. This 'Anti-Rightist Campaign' cost many writers, academics, journalists and other professionals their careers, their families and, in some cases, their lives. In later life Deng would concede that the campaign had gone too far and affected far too broad a swathe of the intelligentsia who were labelled as 'rightists', but he did not distance himself from the need to launch the campaign in the first place. However, in Deng's defence, it has to be acknowledged that the victims would have remained marked for life as 'rightists' if he had not ordered that this designation be formally removed when he returned to power in the 1970s.

The Anti-Rightist Campaign had ensured that even the limited political opposition that had been permitted during the early 1950s came to an end. Deng did nothing to allow it to return and, in spite of reversing the policy on 'rightists', he was still not prepared to tolerate the criticisms of the Party that appeared on the Democracy Wall in Xidan Street during the 'Beijing Spring' of 1978–9. This was a wave of popular demands for the 'fifth modernisation' – democracy – which led to the imprisonment of, among others, one of the leading dissidents of the period, Wei Jingsheng.

Deng has also been accused of a degree of culpability for the military onslaught that ended the Democracy Movement in June 1989 and caused the deaths of hundreds, if not thousands, of unarmed Chinese citizens in and around Tian'anmen Square in Beijing. At the time he was effectively retired and, although he retained the formal chairmanship of the Central Military Commission, his authority was limited and it is not clear to what extent he was able to use his remaining influence to stop the repression. It is, however, an issue that must be investigated.

If Deng Xiaoping is given the credit he deserves for the success of the economic reforms, he must also shoulder some of the blame for China's failure to implement political reform. He was certainly no liberal in the Western sense, but neither was he simply a crude and brutal Stalinist. He was a complex man who operated successfully within the parameters available to him and the organisations in which he chose, or was chosen, to work. He also developed as a man, a political leader and a statesman, but he had his limitations as well as his talents. One of his limitations was that, although he was prepared to tolerate far more internal discussion and disagreement than many of the other leaders of the Chinese Communist Party, particularly Mao Zedong, he was not prepared to permit dissent if he were persuaded that the CCP's hold on power was threatened by it. A different leader might have had different priorities, but that does not mean that he (it is improbable that at that time it could have been a she) would have been able to carry the Party forward with a programme of political democracy in addition to the economic reforms. Even as China's fifth-generation leadership took power under Xi Jinping and Li Keqiang in the autumn of 2012 and the spring of 2013, that conundrum had not been resolved.

Fang Lizhi (1936–2012), the distinguished astrophysicist and supporter of democracy protests from the mid-1980s, has complained that previous biographers did not consider Deng's attitude towards human rights and that the term was not even indexed in Ezra Vogel's monumental *Deng Xiaoping and the Transformation of China*.[1] The concept of human rights as it is understood in the twenty-first century does not figure in Deng Xiaoping's political thinking. He was of the generation of old-fashioned Marxists who were trained in the Stalin period and accepted the argument that social problems could ultimately be solved only by revolution. In his later years he focused on economic reforms, convinced that development would provide everything that China needed. He did not understand the need for China to address issues of human rights and for this he was criticised during his lifetime, although not always publicly, by many Chinese democrats including some of his erstwhile protégés.[2]

Could Deng have taken any other path after his exposure to Marxism in the 1920s and 1930s? After rising through the ranks of the CCP and its military formations during the Long March and the civil war of 1946–9, could he have become anything other than a loyal and tough senior cadre who could be trusted to eliminate any serious opposition to the party that had brought itself and him to power in China? But then, as an experienced senior cadre at the centre of political decision making, what was it that enabled him to see the impasse in which China was trapped during the 1960s, and doggedly pursue a course that was opposite to the one that had been insisted on by Mao, in spite of intense opposition and even persecution from his one-time comrades? What was there in his makeup or his background that enabled him to realise that a different course for China was not only necessary but was possible within the framework of the Communist Party and the government that it had created? And equally, when he had realised this, what prevented him from deciding that political reform and greater democracy was just as important? China today is largely of his making.

It is striking that among the senior leadership of the Chinese Communist Party that took power in 1949, the two who were among the most amenable to international links and economic reform, Deng and Zhou Enlai, had both spent part of their youth in France, sojourns that left profound impressions on both men. In contrast, the political leader who was most intransigent in insisting that China should follow its own course and avoid contamination from the outside world was Mao Zedong, who had not travelled outside China at all before 1949 and then embarked only on two fraught, and ultimately fruitless, visits to Stalin's Moscow, excursions that would hardly give him a balanced and positive view of the outside world. It is unlikely that overseas experience was solely responsible for the more open-minded political outlooks of Deng and Zhou, but Deng's experience in northern France in the 1920s played an important part in the construction of his view of the world.

NEW SOURCES FOR THE LIFE OF DENG XIAOPING

The 'opening up' (*kaifang*) of China since the start of Deng Xiaoping's reform programme has included a phenomenal expansion of publishing, and many more books on his life and thought are now available in Chinese, published in the People's Republic or Hong Kong. Most of these concentrate on his final 20 years and especially his skill and persistence in forcing through the reforms in 1978, his crowning achievement, but there are also several that deal with his Southern Tour of 1992, during which he managed to defuse fierce political opposition. Writing about Deng Xiaoping has become a minor industry and the number of Deng biographies is equalled only by those written about his contemporary, friend and sometime political collaborator, Zhou Enlai.

Is there anything new to say about Deng Xiaoping? Since Deng came to prominence in the 1970s a number of biographies have appeared in English. The most recent of these, Ezra Vogel's *Deng Xiaoping and the Transformation of China*, is a substantial study but it deals almost entirely with Deng's career after the Cultural Revolution. His formative period, including his childhood in Sichuan, work and studies in France, revolution and war and his successful political career up to 1969, are covered in only 30 pages. Vogel has used source material published as late as 2009 (although it is difficult to be sure as there is no full bibliography) but other source material has been rendered obsolete by the avalanche of new Chinese-language publications. Until recently the accounts of Deng's life published in Chinese in China have been political, but political in the narrow sense that they were designed to assign him to the correct niche in the pantheon of the Chinese

Communist Party. One interesting exception is the account of his life in several volumes written by his youngest daughter, Deng Maomao, known more formally as Deng Rong. These books (only one of which is available in English at the time of writing) are both fascinating and infuriating. Not only are they motivated by filial duty and affection, as might be expected, but Deng Maomao has also had a career in China's diplomatic and military establishment, so it is hardly surprising that what she has written is not an objective assessment of her father's life and work. The English version of the first volume was translated by a team in China and that is how it reads: it also desperately needed the services of a competent editor. Nevertheless, it contains details and insights that are valuable when they can be weighed against information and assessments provided in other sources.[3]

As with all political lives it is possible, and indeed necessary, for Deng's contribution to the development of China to be re-evaluated with the passing of time and the availability of new information. Confidential material in the Communist Party archives remains unavailable and Deng is still too recent a senior leader for those who knew him well to be willing to give candid interviews. However, the most recent biographical material, published in China in the early twenty-first century, is much stronger on detail, and is therefore more useful, than most of the hagiographical and highly censored material that was previously available.

In particular, three books published in 2011 attempt to encapsulate his entire life and career for different readerships. They are Zhao Xiaoguang and Liu Jie, *Deng Xiaoping de san luo san qi* (*The Three Falls and Three Rises of Deng Xiaoping*), the two volumes of *Shihua shishuo Deng Xiaoping* (*Straight Talking about Deng Xiaoping*) edited by Shi Quanwei, and especially the extraordinarily detailed Liu Jianhua and Liu Li, *Deng Xiaoping jishi* (*Chronicle of the Life of Deng Xiaoping*). The last of these is an invaluable sourcebook and a compendium of accounts of various periods and aspects of Deng's life and career by different writers and includes reminiscences by former colleagues. These accounts overlap and this assists in assessing their usefulness as sources. Some of the authors of these reminiscences were senior political figures in their own right; others were aides, members of staff and journalists who encountered him in the course of their work. The tone of the memoirs in these books is almost entirely positive, and many of the accounts contain warm memories of a man who was in many cases a friend as well as a colleague; they are, however, remarkably free from sycophancy. The judgements expressed in these contributions, if not the factual details, must be used with caution, but some of the anecdotes that are included contain telling, and at times revealing, detail that is not available elsewhere. It is not easy to corroborate them but neither is it apparent why factual information at this level of detail would be falsified.

There are significant gaps in the narrative or at least areas that are not treated in the same level of detail. This is particularly the case for the difficult years of the Anti-Rightist Movement and the Great Leap Forward when the material is much thinner. It is difficult to pin down Deng's political role, and especially to determine with any degree of confidence how much political influence he was able to exercise. For the Cultural Revolution (roughly 1966–76), especially for the period of Deng's exile in Jiangxi Province, there is far more informative material. After 1975, as Deng gradually took command and his 'reform and opening' policies were generally accepted, the written record begins to expand significantly. The official chronology of Deng's activities in the last 22 years of his life can be found in the two volumes compiled by Leng Rong and Wang Zuoling (chief editors): *Deng Xiaoping nianpu 1975–1997* (*Chronicles of Deng Xiaoping 1975–1997*).

These accounts, and others that have been published in Chinese and are not readily available outside China, are the foundation for this new political biography of Deng. They provide a view of Deng's career from the inside, from those who worked with him and observed him at close quarters in the hothouse of Chinese politics, and not just as he appeared to the foreign dignitaries who met him and could not fail to be impressed by this small, tough character who seemed to be the antithesis of everything that Mao Zedong had stood for.

The detail recorded in conversations with Deng, and speeches made by him that are quoted in these books, adds to their credibility, although in many cases there are no published texts to corroborate the recollections. Although it is reasonable to be suspicious of what might appear to be the verbatim recall of conversations after many decades, it is important to remember that it has always been the normal practice for officials of the Chinese Communist Party and its government to take notes in meetings, and especially at briefings by senior visiting leaders: these could be used later in the case of local disputes over the implementation of policies. Anyone who has sat through meetings in China will be familiar with the constant, furious scribbling in notebooks backed with plastic (often red). Sources used in this biography do not specifically claim that they are based on such notes but this is not surprising in a society where caution always has to be exercised, in the knowledge that political fortunes can change suddenly and unexpectedly. During the Cultural Revolution, the possession of notes of Deng's speeches could have been viewed by Red Guard activists as clear evidence of anti-Mao activity or sentiment.

DENG XIAOPING: AN OUTLINE CHRONOLOGY

1904:	22 August, born Paifang, Sichuan
1915:	Higher-level primary school in Guang'an
1918:	Guang'an middle school
1920:	Leaves Sichuan for France
1921:	Schneider factory, Le Creusot
1922:	Hutchinson factory, Montargis
1922:	Chinese Youth Communist Party founded in Paris
1922:	Chatillon-sur-Seine, brief period as a student
1924:	Elected to executive Chinese Communist Youth League in Europe at 5th Congress.
1925:	Moves to Paris, police order arrest of Chinese revolutionaries
1926:	Travels to Moscow by train with other young Chinese communists
1926:	Moscow, Sun Yat-sen University
1927:	Returns to China, Xi'an and Wuhan
1927–9:	Underground political work in Shanghai
1929–31:	Guangxi failed uprisings
1931–4:	Jiangxi Soviet political roles at county level
1934:	Long March
1937–8:	Eighth Route Army in north China
1939:	Marries Zhuo Lin in Yan'an
1939–49:	Second Field Army
1949:	First secretary South-western China Bureau in Chongqing

1952: Beijing as deputy premier and minister of finance

1956: Secretary-general of CCP Central Committee and director of Organisation Department

1958–67: Economic development work with Liu Shaoqi to counter disastrous results of Great Leap Forward

1966: Cultural Revolution, criticised as opponent of Mao

1969: Exiled to Jiangxi Province

1974: Returns to Beijing as first deputy premier

1976: Purged again after Tian'anmen Incident

1977: Deputy chairman of Central Committee and Central Military Commission and chief of the General Staff of the People's Liberation Army

1978: Third Plenum of CCP Central Committee accepts Deng's reform programme

1980: Resigns as deputy premier and PLA chief-of-staff to secure political demise of Hua Guofeng

1989: Tian'anmen Democracy Movement crushed

1992: Southern Tour

1993: Publication of *Selected Works of Deng Xiaoping 1982–1992*

1997: 19 February, dies aged 92

FAVOURED SON OF SICHUAN: GROWING UP IN PAIFANG (1904–20)

I have always had a clear conscience. Let history judge me.[1]

Sichuan (formerly spelled Szechuan) is a landlocked province in south-western China. It is renowned for its highly spiced cuisine: in popular local restaurants, sliced meat is cooked in the middle of the customers' tables in vats of simmering oil laced with red-hot chillies. Even Chinese visitors from other regions find the level of spices in Sichuan difficult to handle (with the possible exception of travellers from Mao Zedong's home province of Hunan, which is Sichuan's neighbour to the east), let alone foreigners. The province savours its differences from the rest of China and archaeological discoveries that have reinforced accounts of an .independent prehistoric civilisation in the region have only increased the pride of the population in their distinctive local culture.

SICHUAN: A PROVINCE APART

Sichuan lies hundreds of miles to the west of the economically powerful coastal provinces of Guangdong, Fujian, Jiangsu and Zhejiang: these were the first parts of

China to benefit from the Central Committee's decision in 1978, after much bitter argument, to adopt Deng Xiaoping's proposal that China should change course in the direction of 'reform and opening' (*gaige kaifang*). It was China's most populous province until the vast metropolis of Chongqing was detached in 1997. Although it is not by any means a poor region in Chinese terms, Sichuan was included in the group of western provinces that were to benefit from the programme for Great Western Development (*Xibu da kaifa*), a strategy that was launched in 1999 to confront the problems of poverty and under-development in China's west. There are many poor rural areas in Sichuan as in other parts of western China, particularly in the mountainous border regions, many of which are home to Tibetan and other ethnic minority communities, but on the whole Sichuan is not as under-developed as its near neighbours in Gansu, Guizhou and Tibet. Part of the credit for this belongs to Zhao Ziyang who became the Communist Party secretary of the province in 1975 and introduced market reforms even before they were formally enshrined in national policy. Indeed the success of Zhao's reforms in Sichuan gave Deng Xiaoping valuable assistance in persuading recalcitrant members of the CCP leadership that they should turn their backs on the over-centralised economy of the 1960s and 1970s. The province has every reason to regard itself as a pioneer in the modernisation of the Chinese economy.

Sichuan is a province apart. The majority of the population, like most Chinese, consider themselves to be part of the Han ethnic group, but there are great differences between them and the Han of other parts of China. The Sichuanese, who all live within sight of a belt of high mountains that surround the settled areas, speak a language that is officially a south-western version of Mandarin, but it is difficult for outsiders to comprehend. Sichuan people may be conversant with Standard Chinese (*putonghua*), but, like Deng Xiaoping, they retain a distinctive local accent.

The people of Sichuan trace their ancestry back to the two ancient kingdoms of Ba and Shu, which had developed independently of the central states of the northern plains and the Yangtze Valley in the period before China's unification in 221 BC; some archaeologists argue that the Sichuan Basin was a separate cradle of Chinese civilisation. Migration and development over the centuries, and particularly during the war-torn 1940s when officials, soldiers and refugees from all over China flocked to Chiang Kai-shek's temporary capital of Chongqing (Chungking as it was then known), have blurred the differences, but the Sichuanese remain proud of their regional culture. They are even prouder that one of their own, Deng Xiaoping, has become celebrated as the creator of the modern Chinese economic miracle. Even though Deng's political and military career took him away from Sichuan at a very early age, by way of France and the Long March to the centre of power in the Zhongnanhai leadership complex in Beijing, he retained not only his accent but much of the toughness and independence of his upbringing in the farming villages of central Sichuan.

The provincial capital of Sichuan is Chengdu, which is also the current headquarters of the Chengdu Military Region, an important command that includes responsibility for the troops operating in Tibet. As a city it has been eclipsed by the growth of Chongqing, one of twenty-first-century China's mushrooming metropolises, vying with its rival Shanghai for recognition as China's largest city. During World War II, Chongqing was the headquarters of the Guomindang (GMD) National Government of Chiang Kai-shek (alternatively transliterated as Jiang Jieshi) after it was forced out of Nanjing by the Japanese military. It was also the site of a notorious massacre of communist prisoners by the nationalists on 27 November 1949. The exploits of the underground communist organisation in wartime Chongqing and the massacre are commemorated in an impressive and much visited museum and also in a novel, *Red Crag* (*Hongyan*). The novel was first published in 1961, has recently been reprinted by the Communist Youth League's publishing arm, and is displayed prominently in the museum shop.[2]

Chongqing expanded rapidly during the early reform period and in 1997 was declared an independent municipality directly responsible to the central government, with a status equivalent to that of a province: it is one of only four in China, the others being Beijing, Tianjin and Shanghai. Still regarded as something of a backwater because of its remoteness from the booming cities of the east, Chongqing began to attract nationwide attention in 2011 under its party secretary Bo Xilai, who had been making a political reputation for himself with a ruthless campaign against organised crime and an attempt to revive the 'red culture' of the Cultural Revolution period in his city. Fame turned to notoriety when Bo and his wife Gu Kailai became implicated in the death of a British businessman, Neil Heywood. Gu was convicted of Mr Heywood's murder and sentenced to death, suspended for two years, also effectively imprisonment for life. In September 2013 Bo was found guilty of corruption, bribery and the abuse of power and imprisoned for life. Chongqing, under a new party secretary, returned to its over-riding interest in commerce and attracting tourists to the Yangzi Gorges.

PAIFANG AND THE DENG FAMILY SEAT

Deng Xiaoping's home village can be reached by taking the train north from Chongqing: the express from Guiyang in Guizhou Province to Xi'an in Shaanxi ploughs northwards across Sichuan, stopping at Chongqing, and in less than two hours stops at Guang'an Station, a halt with a few restaurants and shops and still some 30 kilometres distant from the town of Guang'an, 100 kilometres north of Chongqing and 200 kilometres east of Chengdu. A further 10 kilometres outside the town is the village of Paifang, part of the rural township of Xiexin. Paifang means 'memorial arch' and the village takes its name from an arch erected by local people to honour the scholarly achievements of an ancestor of the Dengs who lived in the early Qing dyansty and was said to have been a member of the elite Hanlin Academy that served the imperial court. In the early 1960s the name was changed to Weiren (Great Man) by a sycophantic official to commemorate Deng Xiaoping. However, as the Cultural Revolution unfolded and Deng became a target, Red Guards renamed it Fanxiu (Anti-Revisionism) village. It then reverted to its original name of Paifang, which the local people had continued to use anyway.

Paifang was the home of three generations of the Deng family. Deng Xiaoping was born there on 22 August 1904 and lived there until he was about 15. Today the modest village has been eclipsed by a theme park dedicated to Deng Xiaoping. The centrepiece is a museum at the family's former home that commemorates both his early life in Sichuan and his political achievements towards the end of his life. A remark that he made on a visit, 'We must improve Guang'an', is repeated frequently in the captions and the literature in the museum and, judging from the development of industry and private housing in the area, some of this at least has come to pass. Deng and his immediate family lost touch with their relatives as a result of decades of war and revolution. Deng left at the age of about 15 to work and study in France and the Soviet Union and never lived in Paifang again, but he did visit his hometown after coming to national prominence and never forgot his origins.[3]

The Deng residence (*Xiaoping guju*) in Paifang was originally a simple and unadorned single-storey building, a traditional wooden courtyard house with a tiled roof, and typical of the houses of wealthy farmers in that part of Sichuan. Simple it may have been but it was not small; its 17 rooms occupied a space of 800 square metres. When Deng was appointed to lead the Communist Party in south-western China at the end of the 1946–9 civil war, his base was in Chongqing, and during the early 1950s he persuaded his stepmother to move from the old house and live with him and his family in the city; the house was handed over to the local government. When he returned to power in the 1970s, officials in Chongqing and Guang'an wanted to build a museum on the site to honour him. Deng resisted this suggestion and insisted that it should be left for local people. It remained in the hands of the village authorities and at least nine families occupied its 11 buildings – there had been some additions and extensions since Deng had left home. Three rooms were set aside for visitors: these contained photographs of Deng with foreign leaders (including eventually two presidents of the United States, Nixon and Carter); a Qing dynasty bed which was said to have belonged to the Deng family; and mementoes of Deng's early life. They were the beginnings of a simple museum in honour of Deng. However, Deng saw none of this as he had not been back to the house since he left in 1920: he occasionally heard from the Guang'an local officials, and his wife, Zhuo Lin, was in touch with surviving relatives of his mother's family, the Dans, who still lived in part of the old house. The number of visitors increased, and scrolls bearing couplets in literary Chinese in honour of Deng hung on either side of the main entrance. At the Spring Festival of 1994, new laudatory scrolls were provided by a member of the Sichuan Scroll Association and thousands of people filed past them. Guang'an officials decided that this was the time to restore Deng's birthplace, which was badly in need of repair. In 2001 the local government began to construct Paifang New Village close to the Deng family home: this included hotels and restaurants to support the increase in tourism and has brought a new prosperity to many of its residents. A nearby shopping centre provides souvenirs and other merchandise for tourists.

Since Deng's death in 1997, the whole site has been thoroughly renovated as a memorial park. Today the Deng family house is set in spacious grounds planted with trees to shade it from the sun and surrounded by thick clumps of bamboo. It is not clear to what extent the current size of the grounds represents the size of the family's original landholdings. The ultra-modern exhibition building dominates the complex, but it is still possible to see the old house, including the public area where the family entertained visitors, and the rooms used by members of the family: a desk and writing materials said to have belonged to Deng Xiaoping are still on display. The exhibition hall alone, which was opened to the public on 13 August 2004, occupies 3,800 square metres and has six sections devoted to the main phases of Deng's military and political career. It is packed with photographs, relics, documents and mementoes of Deng's life and constantly shows archive film of his role in China's revolution. The formal opening ceremony on 13 August 2004, which also commemorated the centenary of Deng Xiaoping's birth, was conducted by President Hu Jintao, who unveiled a bronze statue of Deng sitting in a chair: the inscription below the statue, which simply reads 'bronze statue of Deng Xiaoping' (*Deng Xiaoping tongxiang*) was written by the previous president, Jiang Zemin. The involvement of these two successive heads of state indicates the importance that subsequent leaders of the CCP have attached to Deng's legacy.

The bronze statue has become the focal point of ceremonies to commemorate Deng. On 19 February 2009, the twelfth anniversary of his death, local people and visitors placed wreaths and bouquets of flowers around the statue. In August 2011 a large crowd of people gathered to remember Deng and to acknowledge the progress the area had made, which was not unconnected with the flood of tourists. Bai Ping, a local government official, led hundreds of villagers who laid flowers in front of the bronze statue, bowing as they did so. One group of friends from Chongqing make the journey to Deng's birthplace every year; and a celebrated actor, Pu Shuxian, who had played Deng in a television series, had come from Sichuan's Renshou County. Su Xiaoyong, the manager of a small hotel in Paifang, confided that he burned incense in front of a portrait of the leader mounted on his living room wall because Deng's reform policies had pulled his community out of poverty and they would always be grateful to him. The memorial was turning into a shrine.[4]

GROWING UP IN PAIFANG

Deng's boyhood in Paifang was unremarkable. Millions of village children, who were born in modest circumstances as the Qing dynasty and the Chinese Empire declined, experienced a similar childhood. There was nothing to indicate that he would make such an indelible mark on China in later years. Deng's daughter devotes only two pages of her filial account to these 16 years, and the accounts of other Chinese biographers are not much longer.

The Deng family had lived in Sichuan for three generations and, according to family tradition, had arrived in Sichuan from Jiangxi Province in the early years of the Ming dynasty, perhaps in the fifteenth century. Their distant origins, however, may have been in Meizhou, a county in the east of Guangdong Province. Meizhou had, and still has, a large Hakka population and that community has a longstanding tradition of migration in search of work both within China and overseas. The Deng family were Hakkas, an unusual ethnic group in China. Hakkas (the standard Chinese term is *Kejia* which translates as 'guest families') are considered to be part of the majority Han population but are also separate. The Hakka language is a variation of a northern form of speech that is thought to have been brought to Guangdong in a twelfth-century migration, and this distinguishes Hakkas from their neighbours who speak various southern forms of Chinese. What made them stand out even more was that Hakka women, unlike women in other Han communities, did not have bound feet. Hakkas have a reputation for being exceptionally hardworking and adept at business, and have often played a major role in China's military and political life, including radical political movements. Whether or not the reputation for industry and business acumen is justified, it was how Hakkas were perceived, but they were also marginalised and knew that they had to make their own way in life. Among other well-known twentieth-century political figures of Hakka ancestry are Sun Yat-sen, the first president of the Chinese Republic; the Song (Soong) family who were connected by marriage to both Sun and Chiang Kai-shek; Lee Kuan Yew of Singapore, who was later to inspire Deng's drive for economic growth; Hu Yaobang, the reform-minded premier of the PRC during the 1980s; and two presidents of Taiwan, Lee Tenghui and Ma Ying-jeou.

Family tradition maintains that in the remote past some of their ancestors had been graduates of the highest level of the imperial examination and one was the member of the Hanlin Academy commemorated by the village's eponymous ceremonial arch. The family fell into decline and Deng's grandfather was desperately poor, but he worked hard and earned enough money to acquire a little land which he later managed to extend. His son, Deng Xiaoping's father, Deng Shaochang (also known as Deng Wenming), was born in 1886 and died in 1936 – his tomb has also been preserved in Paifang. He had some elementary education and there are suggestions that he had also studied at a school of law and politics in Chengdu, but the farm was his life and he was sufficiently prosperous to be able to afford to hire labourers for the most backbreaking work. In the classification that was later drawn up by the CCP, he would have been a minor landlord or at least a 'rich peasant'. Although Deng Shaochang was neither an intellectual nor a radical and his attitudes were in many ways typical of those of his time and his social background, he had become utterly discontented with the state of China at the turn of the century. He became a member, and possibly an official, of the Elder Brother Society (*Gelaohui*), a secret organisation devoted to the overthrow of Manchu rule. He joined one of the revolutionary armies that were created to fight against the forces of the Qing dynasty and when Sichuan seceded from the Empire in the early days of the 1911 Revolution he was a junior non-commissioned officer in a unit based in Guang'an. Deng Xiaoping, who was seven years old at the time of the revolution, visited his father in the barracks and stayed with him for two days, an early introduction to the military life. Deng Shaochang served the new Republic as the head of a local guards unit established by the country magistrate and later as the head of their township.

Deng Xiaoping was the eldest son (but the second child as his older sister Deng Xianlie had been born in 1902) of Shaochang and his second wife, who came from a more prosperous Guang'an family, the Dans. His mother, whose name is not recorded, was intelligent but illiterate and it is not clear whether she was a second wife or a concubine. There were two younger sons and, much later, two more sons and a daughter when Deng Shaochang married for a third time after Deng Xiaoping's mother died in 1926.

It was a large but not atypical rural family and, as the eldest son, Xiaoping had both status and privileges, but there were also great expectations. From the age of five he went to school, initially to a traditional private school (*sishu*) that operated on strict Confucian principles of education and was built on the site of a house once owned by the illustrious Deng ancestor who had been in the Hanlin Academy. Deng Xiaoping had been named Xiansheng at birth, but as that can be construed to mean 'sage' (perhaps a reference to the scholar in the family's distant past) it seemed rather presumptuous to the school's old-fashioned teacher and was changed to Xixian ('aspire to wisdom', which is more appropriate for a five-year-old) and this was his name for his first 20 years. At this infants' school the main preoccupation was the painstaking and often painful task of learning to write and remembering the thousands of Chinese characters that are necessary to read traditional documents and literature. Homework was routine and Deng and his school friends competed to see who would get the most circles, which indicated that a character was correctly written, and the fewest crosses to mark an error. When Deng came home from school with his exercises covered with circles his mother would reward him with special chicken meals.

When Deng was six he moved to the local primary school, in the nearby and larger village of Xiexin, where the curriculum was based on memorising and learning to recite aloud the Confucian classics. Like every other small boy in China (but only the occasional girl), Deng Xiaoping began by committing to memory the *San zi jing* (*Three Character Classic*), the simplest of primers for classical Chinese, before moving on to the more complex *Qian zi wen* (*Thousand Character Classic*), the *Bai jia xing* (*Hundred Surnames*) and then the basic texts of the Confucian canon – the Four Books of Confucian philosophy and the Five Classics, which added history and poetry. Deng would never have claimed to be a scholar or an intellectual but he did acquire a sound traditional education in calligraphy, literary Chinese and Confucian culture.

There are many anecdotes about Deng's childhood but one about his education is very telling. His parents had invited a highly educated member of a local landlord family to write New Year couplets for them to hang outside the main entrance. This man was known for his old-fashioned and reactionary views and it is not clear why he was their choice, but he used the opportunity to write couplets that ridiculed the progressive ideas of Deng's father, Deng Shaochang, who had become involved in radical organisations opposed to the Qing regime. The reactionary scholar assumed that no-one in the household would understand what he had done as Deng Shaochang was intelligent and literate but not well educated and Deng's mother could not read at all. When Xiaoping returned home and saw the couplets he was outraged at the dirty trick that had been played on his parents. He tore down the couplets, went out to buy new paper and wrote his own: he would have been about ten years old at the time and his writing was not perfect but the sentiments were at least more in tune with the values of the Deng family. Deng's calligraphy improved and the mature version is admired even though (or possibly because) it is so different from the dramatic, bold and unconstrained flourishes that characterise much of Mao Zedong's calligrapy.

By the age of 11 Deng had mastered the Confucian set texts sufficiently to be allowed to move to the only higher-level primary school in Guang'an County. Admission was by examination and as he was both able and conscientious he was able to move up in 1915. The new school extended the range of classical texts that the students studied and included some modern subjects, but its teaching methods were just as antiquated. Deng had no difficulties with the academic demands of the school, but the cost of keeping him in education was a considerable burden to the family which was often short of ready cash even though they owned land. Deng Shaochang had invested all his hopes in his son's future so he supported him throughout his school career, even selling off part of the family property to raise the necessary funds. In 1918, at the age of 15, Deng Xiaoping progressed to the Guang'an middle school but did not stay there for long: it looked as if he was not going to live up to his father's expectations that he would become a great scholar and official. However, these were turbulent and unusual times: the lure of travel abroad beckoned and the opportunity to study in France arose.[5]

À LA RECHERCHE DU DENG PERDU: THE ROOTS OF CHINESE COMMUNISM IN PROVINCIAL FRANCE AFTER WORLD WAR I (1920–6)

I did all kinds of work in France but it was all unskilled labour.[1]

Montargis is a small town of some 15,000 inhabitants in the Loiret region of central France; it lies to the south of Paris and east of Orléans and nestles in the valley of the River Loing, which is a left-hand tributary of the Seine. It is a rural and agricultural area, known for its honey. The town is celebrated as the place where sweet nutty pralines were invented, probably in the seventeenth century, and a shop which may have sold the confectionery since that time still stands in the centre of the town. The Canal de Briare, which connects the valleys of the Loire and Seine, was constructed between 1604 and 1642; it passes through Montargis and played an important part in the industrial development of the town and its region.

In the 1920s this quintessential French provincial town became the focus of a group of enterprising and idealistic young Chinese attracted by the opportunity to study abroad and earn their keep by working. While many local people prefer to think of their town as 'la Venise du Gâtinais', the Venice of its region, and praise its mediaeval atmosphere, for the newly-arrived Chinese it looked oddly familiar. On the face of it the journey from China to a small town in rural France should have resulted in an immense culture shock, but even in the twenty-first century Montargis is strangely reminiscent of the towns and villages of southern China. The town centre is ringed by canals, the old course of the River Loing and the ancient town moats; these are crossed by a total of 131 bridges, many of them gently arching in a way that in a summer haze or an autumn mist could persuade a tired labourer that he was still in China somewhere south of the Yangzi River. One prominent Montargoise who is originally from China is constantly reminded of the vista of waterways and bridges of her birthplace, Hangzhou, and the countryside that surrounds it.[2]

WORK–STUDY MOVEMENT

The Work–Study Movement (*qingong jianxue yundong*) that drew young educated Chinese to Montargis was the brainchild of Li Shizeng (1881–1973), the scion of a wealthy and well-connected family and the son of an adviser to the Tongzhi Emperor. He was a political thinker and a writer with anarchist sympathies, but he eventually persuaded himself that he should work with the nationalist Guomindang and died in Taiwan at the age of 92. When he arrived in Paris in 1902, Li originally intended to study botany and agriculture, but he yearned for a more peaceful rural environment and felt that he had found it when he chanced upon Montargis, and enrolled in what was then known as the École Pratique d'Agriculture du Chesnoy in the Loiret.[3] Li studied at Chesnoy from 1904 to 1906 and then continued his work at the Pasteur Institute in Paris where he devoted his energies to the development of soybean products, intending to transfer this knowledge to China. From this evolved the idea of a soy food manufacturing plant at Colombes to the north-west of Paris, which he opened in 1908 and staffed entirely with Chinese labourers. This was the beginning of the Work–Study Movement. Li's base in Montargis was 31, rue Gambetta, where he was visited by, among others, Sun Yat-sen and the future Minister of Education, Cai Yuanpei; a plaque outside the house today marks his association with the town. Another address in Montargis which has close associations with the Chinese students is 15, rue Tellier (at the time known as 15, rue du Pont de l'Ouche). Several of its rooms were rented to Chinese students; these included Li Weihan, who took part in the Long March, headed the CCP's Party School and became deputy chairman of the Chinese People's Political Consultative Conference; Li Fuchun, later deputy premier and chairman of the State Planning Commission; and his wife Cai Chang. For male students, the College Gambetta provided both education and an upstairs dormitory in which they lived. The school, dating back at least to the sixteenth century, when it was rebuilt after a fire, became the Town Hall in 1988. Its Chinese alumni also included Chen Yi, a future minister of foreign affairs, who signed the agreement on diplomatic relations between France and China with President de Gaulle in 1964 and Cai Hesen, a close associate of Mao Zedong, who was executed by Chinese police in Guangzhou in 1931. Most of the female Chinese students studied and lived at the College de Chinchon, the first secondary school for girls in Montargis. These included Cai Hesen's wife, Xiang Jingyu, who was also executed in 1928.

Montargis was easily accessible from Paris by the rail network that was inaugurated when the first train on the Moret–Nevers line stopped at Montargis station on 14 August 1860. The capital could now be reached in four hours by train, whereas the old stagecoaches had taken 12 hours. On 16 November 1912 Li Shizeng had a private meeting with Thierry Falour, the mayor of Montargis, and suggested a scheme for bringing young Chinese to the town. His idea was that they would study, work in local industries and live either in the schools or with local people. This scheme was welcomed by the members of the town council who appreciated the economic benefits that it would bring to the town, as well as the educational opportunities for the young Chinese. The first Chinese students to benefit from this forerunner of the Work–Study Movement arrived in Montargis in 1913. Over 2,000 young Chinese travelled to France to study and work in the 1910s and 1920s, and at least 300 of them spent their time in Montargis. Many formed lasting links with the local community: they also found a degree of freedom which they had not enjoyed in China and used this to debate ideas of reform and revolution, the future of their motherland and their part in that future. Many of them, including Zhou Enlai (the future premier of the People's Republic of China) and Deng Xiaoping, returned to China and were active in the Chinese revolution between 1927 and 1949.

In March 1921, a clandestine communist group was established in Paris. It included Zhang Shenfu (1893–1986), a philosopher who became China's leading expert on the thinking of Bertrand Russell; Liu Qingyang, who may well have been the first female member of the Chinese Communist Party; and two emerging student leaders, Zhou Enlai and Zhao Shiyan (1901–27), like Deng a Sichuanese and an able organiser who was executed when the Guomindang nationalists wiped out the communists in Shanghai in 1927. This embryonic group expanded rapidly after the formal establishment of the Chinese Communist Party in China in July 1921. In June 1922, representatives of this group and others from elsewhere in France, Belgium and Germany met in the Bois de Boulogne in Paris to create the CCP's European Branch. The moving spirit at this time was Zhao Shiyan, who acted as secretary and was based in a small hotel at 17, rue Godefroy, but Zhou Enlai became a member of the executive committee and was well established in the organisation by the summer of 1922 when Deng Xiaoping was introduced to the Communist Party, which he joined the following autumn.[4]

DENG SETS SAIL FOR FRANCE

In the summer of 1919 Deng's father had returned home after visiting Chongqing and had brought with him information about the Work–Study Movement and a course in Chongqing to prepare young Chinese who wished to participate in it. Deng Shaochang was unusual in supporting his son's interest in an overseas education but he had benefited from a modern education in Chengdu, was dissatisfied with traditional methods of education and was deeply critical of the warlord government that ruled Sichuan. Deng, together with cousins and school friends, travelled to Chongqing to prepare for the great expedition to France. Deng returned home to Guang'an in August 1920 to take his leave of his mother, for whom it was a difficult parting as she realised that she might never again see her son who was barely 16 years old. She was resolutely opposed to his travelling to France and it took weeks for her to be persuaded that she should bless the enterprise.

Deng's journey to France began on 27 August 1920 when, with 82 other students from eastern Sichuan, he boarded the 3pm steamer *Jiqing* (*Auspicious*) from the Yangzi River port of Wanxian, in what is now the Chongqing municipality, and sailed downriver, eastwards via Yichang, Hankou and Jiujiang to Shanghai. At 11 am on 11 September he and his fellow students, who now numbered about 90 and had never before left their homeland, set sail from Shanghai for France on the French liner *André Lebon*, which had been berthed on the Huangpu River. On 19 October, after 39 days at sea, the liner docked in Marseilles and Deng and 21 of his companions travelled overland by road to Paris, a journey of 16 hours. They reached Bayeux in Normandy on 21 October and were immediately impressed by the contrast between France and poor and backward China. Like many of this 'May Fourth generation' – those who had grown up in the nationalist upsurge that followed the 4 May 1919 demonstrations against Japan's acquisition of Chinese territory after World War I – Deng was acutely conscious of the need for China to develop and prosper, and he had come to believe that travelling to the West to learn from their experience was essential if they were to succeed in this momentous task.

However, Deng's experience of life in France was not entirely positive. He was exposed to a developed society and economy but his exposure was as an immigrant and a casual labourer. In later life he would recall that he could only find work as a general labourer and that, in common with the other work–study students, money was always a problem. He had to live extremely frugally and was unable to pay the tuition fees that the schools required. His studies were self-financed, whereas some better-connected students had loans or even scholarships from the Chinese government. His family circumstances were very restricted at the time that he left Sichuan and he had brought very little money with him. Some of his better-off fellow students had between 30 and 50 francs a month at their disposal but Deng started with only 18. His capital did not last long even at this rate and within a few months he was penniless. His dreams of a study programme with work to support it soon evaporated and he found himself working as a full-time labourer to support himself. This was not what he had imagined when he left China and it contributed to his moving towards the emerging young communist movement in France. It is interesting to reflect on his dissatisfaction with his treatment as an overseas student and his long-term attitude toward the West and its economic system as a model for China. In the mid-1970s, when he finally achieved a position in which he could influence China's future direction, he pressed strongly for economic reform. However, he resolutely resisted demands from some political thinkers, including members of the CCP, for China to move away from the one-party system that had been in place since 1949 and create a multi-party democracy on the Western model. He was profoundly influenced by his early experience in France and the realities of life for the poorest of the poor in a Western democratic industrial society.

LE CREUSOT AND THE SCHNEIDER WORKS

To resolve their financial problems, Deng and other students from Sichuan found temporary work in Le Creusot, as labourers at the industrial plant operated by the firm of Schneider and Co. in the town. The Schneider plant, which is at the top of a hill on the main road that leads into the town, looks more like an aristocratic country residence than a factory: it was originally the Chateau de la Verrerie, an eighteenth-century crystal glass factory that had developed under the patronage of Marie Antoinette. The Schneider enterprise was largely responsible for the transformation of Le Creusot from a village to an industrial town; it had been a major armaments firm before and during World War I but, by the time Deng arrived, had diversified into general steel production and electrical engineering. Schneider's was famous for the great Creusot steam hammer that was constructed in 1877 and is now a tourist attraction at the site of the factory. Deng worked in the steel rolling mill between 2 April and 23 April 1921 with the works number of 07396; the mill where he laboured is now part of an industrial museum. The labourers toiled for long hours, over 50 a week, which often included night shifts, and worked at a temperature of 40° Celsius, which is normal for a steel mill. They constantly fed the rollers under the watchful eye of supervisors who cursed any of them found slacking. The work was dangerous with the ever-present risk of burns and broken bones and was tough for a small youth of 17, but Deng needed the wage, low as it was. It was barely enough for food and warmth as the normal wage for Chinese labourers was only 10 francs a day. For lunch they had tap water and bread. When Deng left Le Creusot not only did he not receive his final wage, he was asked to refund an overpayment of 100 francs – whether he did so is not recorded.

Although this first experience of employment was a short one, it had a profound effect on a young man more used to the schoolroom. It brought him into contact with modern industrial machinery and processes but also taught him about the lot of the poorest workers in an industrial economy. It put into perspective all that he had heard about prosperity, freedom, democracy and brotherhood in the West. It also brought him into contact with radical young Chinese, including Zhao Shiyan (the uncle of future premier Li Peng) who later took part as a labour organiser in the Northern Expedition and was executed by the nationalist Guomindang in Shanghai in 1927. The radicals offered a powerful and attractive theoretical and organisational solution to the practical problems he had encountered, in the shape of the nascent Chinese Communist Party. In later life he frequently referred to his experience of the 'dark side of capitalism' in his emerging political consciousness.[5]

PARIS AND ARTIFICIAL FLOWERS

Deng left Le Creusot for Paris and after over five months without work took a job at the Chambrelen factory in the 10th arrondissement by the banks of the River Seine. This could not have been a greater contrast with the steel mill as his new employer specialised in the manufacture of fans and artificial flowers and Deng was classified as a 'flower maker', creating imitation blooms out of muslin and silk fabric fastened to metal wires. Once again the wages were low and many of the workers were women who were able to earn only 2 francs in a day by making 100 flowers: faster workers who could make more might take home as much as 10 francs. Deng was also concerned that the job was not secure and indeed within two weeks he and other Chinese staff were laid off, 'once again joining the great army of the unemployed', where he remained for another three months.

MONTARGIS AND THE HUTCHINSON FACTORY

On 14 February 1922 Deng finally reached Montargis where he found his third job, a relatively secure position making waterproof footwear in the shoe manufacturing workshop of the Hutchinson rubber plant at Châlette-sur-Loing. At the time the factory employed several thousand workers, mostly women and young people, and it is still in operation today. Châlette is a short distance outside the town centre of Montargis and Deng lived in the village in a small flat (a 'shack' they called it) behind the factory. The American industrialist Hiram Hutchinson had set up this rubber factory at Châlette in 1853 on the site of the former Langlée royal paper mill and he began to hire foreign labourers after World War I as the French economy began to improve after a period of retrenchment. The workforce included Indians, Vietnamese, White Russians and Chileans and between 1920 and 1927 there were 214 Chinese, including Wang Ruofei, an early member of the CCP who would die in an air crash in 1946. Most of the labourers worked an eight-hour shift and devoted their evenings to their studies, although Deng recalls that his shifts lasted ten hours and he worked as many as 54 hours each week. The work was lighter than at the steel plant, but the pace was fast and the labourers had to be nimble and precise. The factory operated a piece-work system; Deng adapted well and was able to make at least ten and sometimes as many as 20 pairs of shoes a day. This earned him approximately 15 or 16 francs per day and after deducting his living expenses he had a surplus of over 200 francs a month; just as importantly, the work was secure. Recollections of his fellow workers give a glimpse of the life that the Chinese labourers led in Châlette. The two hours between their evening meal and bedtime were the most precious. Although they were all theoretically students, very little reading took place and the atmosphere in their 'wooden shack' was lively. They 'chatted, cracked jokes, teased and argued with each other but fortunately never came to blows'.

> There was a lad from Sichuan, small and rather stout and only about eighteen years old. Every day at this time he would come bouncing in, going over to one corner to tell a joke, laugh and then to another to play a trick.

The Sichuan lad was of course Deng Xiaoping.

He may not have studied formally – in later years Deng would recall that, of the five years and two months that he spent in France, he spent four years working – but at the Hutchinson factory he was systematically exposed to radical ideas. Some of the other Chinese working there were already committed revolutionaries and he read copies of the radical May Fourth period journal *Xin Qingnian* (*New Youth*) that circulated among their group.

PARIS: RENAULT AT BILLANCOURT

Still anxious to pursue the dream of an education funded by work, Deng left Hutchinson's on 17 October 1922 to study at the College de Châtillon-sur-Seine. He enrolled on 3 November but could not afford the fees and went back to the rubber factory on 2 February 1923: he was always conscious of never having completed his education. He continued at Hutchinson's for a little over a month but then decided to leave for good. The management at Hutchinson's recorded his reason for leaving as 'refusal to work': they were not aware that he had joined the Chinese Youth Communist Party (*Zhongguo shaonian gongchandang*) and had decided that radical politics was to be his life's work. According to his younger brother, Deng Xianzhi, he wrote a long letter to his family in Sichuan informing them, in one brief paragraph, of this momentous change of direction and telling them that as he was now 'taking the revolutionary road' he would not be able to return home. Not surprisingly this caused great consternation and his mother was particularly distressed and wanted him home immediately. Deng sent home several copies of the magazine *Red Light* (*Chiguang*) that he and Zhou Enlai were producing, but Deng Xianzhi was too young to understand the political terminology or the significance of what his brother had embarked on.

Deng Xiaoping left Montargis on 30 July 1925 and moved back to Paris where the Chinese radicals were based. He registered at the Boulogne-Billancourt police station and signed up to work as a labourer at the Renault car factory, a colossal enterprise that employed over 10,000 people, of whom some 600 were Chinese. Deng was assigned to work as a trainee fitter helping with the maintenance of tools and machines, the most technically-advanced work that he had undertaken since arriving in France. The Renault factory still retains his work card numbered 82409A with the name Deng Xixian spelled in the fashion that he had also used in Montargis, Teng Hei Hien. It also included in Chinese characters the name Deng Xiaoping that he was now using, his address at 27, rue Traversiere and a note that his wage in the polishing workshop was 1 franc 5 centimes. Forty years later during the Cultural Revolution, Deng was to find his experience at Renault unexpectedly useful when he was banished to Jiangxi Province and worked in a tractor-fitting plant in Xinjian on the outskirts of Nanchang.[6]

EVOLUTION OF CHINESE COMMUNISM IN FRANCE

In Montargis there had been endless political discussions: in the students' lodgings after work; at the female students' house where Deng and others would go to eat authentic Chinese noodles; in the nearby park on their days off; or while walking to and from the public bathhouses near the river. There was, however, no political organisation in Montargis: the focus for activist Chinese students in France was, perhaps not surprisingly, Paris. In addition to his work at Renault, Deng became involved in a scheme proposed by Zhou Enlai. Zhou suggested that Deng should manage a *doufu* (tofu) shop to benefit the many work–study students who found themselves in straitened circumstances; the shop also brought him into close contact with the wider Chinese student community in Paris. By this time Deng's dream of an education for its own sake had evaporated, his initial plan of studying to benefit China was metamorphosing into a revolutionary vocation, and he became more deeply involved in the creation of a communist group within the Chinese community. In true Parisian style the activities of this group revolved around a small café, in this case one close to the Place d'Italie in the 13th arrondissement, which also happened to be near Zhou Enlai's lodgings at 12, rue

Godefroy. The building in which Zhou lived now sports a plaque to mark his stay there between 1922 and 1924.

In June 1922 the activist group that had been established by 18 Chinese students, including Zhao Shiyan, Zhou Enlai and Li Weihan transformed itself into the Chinese Youth Communist Party in Europe (*Lü Ou Zhongguo shaonian gongchandang*) at an open air meeting in the Bois de Boulogne on chairs that they had hired from a cafe owner. On 1 August of the same year, the first issue of their journal, *Youth* (*Shaonian*), was published from a room above a café at 17, rue Godefroy. According to Cai Chang, the production of this duplicated paper was a collaborative effort. Zhou Enlai was in overall charge; Deng, who had become a member of the group at a provisional congress in February 1923, and Li Dazhang cut the stencils and Li Fuchun distributed it. In February 1924 *Youth* changed its name to *Red Light* (*Chiguang*) to indicate a shift from a theoretical orientation to a more militant and activist role; it appeared irregularly although it was intended to be bi-monthly. The group worked during the day and carried out their duties for the paper and the Party in the evenings. Deng often worked well into the night to try to ensure that the paper appeared every two weeks and he became so skilled at the mimeograph production process that he was known as the 'Doctor of Duplication'. Zhou Enlai did not have to work as a labourer because he was a full-time organiser for the new Party. In June 1923 the group held its Second Congress, by which time it had changed its name to the Chinese Communist Youth League in Europe (*Lü Ou Zhongguo gongchanzhuyi qingniantuan*). Zhou Enlai became secretary and Deng was involved in 'branch work' (*zhibu gongzuo*), the nature of which is not specified. It presumably involved organising and coordinating the work of different branches, but even at this early stage Deng was recognisably taking responsibility for the organisation of the group.

CHINESE IDEOLOGICAL BATTLES IN EUROPE

The political struggle in China between radicals who supported the nationalist Guomindang and those whose primary allegiance was to the Chinese Communist Party was also fought in the émigré community in France. The ideological weapon of the young communists was *Red Light*, which was formally launched under its new name in February 1924 and appeared bi-monthly in sextodecimo (16mo) format with at least ten pages in each issue until it ceased publication in 1925. Its readership included work–study students but also Chinese labourers and other

Chinese living in France. Deng wrote many articles for *Red Light* under a number of different names. He later recalled that these were in support of a national revolution in China and attacked the representatives in France of one of the rightwing factions of the Guomindang, notably Zeng Qi and Li Huang, who had founded the Young China Party (*Zhongguo qingnian dang*). That group was nationalist, anti-communist and anti-fascist, but its members were also wary of the leadership of Chiang Kai-shek (Jiang Jieshi). Zeng was for a time the Paris correspondent of the Shanghai newspaper *Xinwenbao* and, although favouring a 'third way' that was neither nationalist nor communist, eventually threw in his lot with Chiang Kai-shek after Japan invaded China in 1937. Zeng and Li were nationalists and opposed the class struggle approach of the communists and the participation of the CCP in the United Front, the period of political cooperation with the GMD during the Japanese occupation. However, in the complex and confused politics of the time, Zeng had worked with Zhou Enlai in creating an Association of Chinese Clubs in France. Among the most important polemical articles that Deng wrote for *Red Light* at this time were in issues 18 and 21, in which he castigated the counter-revolutionary nature of the Young China Party.

DENG TAKES A LEADERSHIP ROLE

By the time that the Chinese Communist Youth League in Europe held its Fifth Congress from 13 to 15 July 1924, Deng had become a fixture in the leadership. He was elected to the executive committee and at the first meeting was one of the three chosen to operate as the secretariat. Deng was responsible for copying, duplicating and printing and for managing the financial affairs of the executive. He was still only 20 but he had demonstrated a flair for inserting himself into a position of influence – albeit one that called for hard work and attention to detail – that foreshadowed his later roles in the Chinese Communist Party, culminating in his work as general secretary of the CCP in the 1950s. Working in a secretariat of one kind or another would become a recurring feature of his political life. He was also deployed to work with trade unions in the factories and in the spring of 1925 was sent to carry out propaganda and organisational work in the Lyon area.

Perhaps the most important legacy of Deng's time in France, apart from his exposure to Marxism and the organisational experience that he gained, was the close political friendship that he forged with Zhou Enlai. Fifty years later, he recalled Zhou as having been a diligent and conscientious party worker whose working day all his life was at least 12 hours and often 16 and who never shirked the difficult jobs. Zhou was, he said, like an elder brother to him. Zhou was six years older and that was enough to put him well ahead of Deng in terms of the family hierarchy, which is often used by analogy in school, universities and employment to indicate seniority and precedence. Zhou was already highly regarded in the emerging Chinese communist leadership and was a full-time Party worker in Paris. Deng learned a great deal from him, both in terms of factual knowledge and style of working, and seems to have accepted Zhou's leadership without any reservation. The group of Chinese radicals in Paris had originally coalesced around the philosopher Zhang Shenfu, who together with Liu Qingyuan (the first woman member of the CCP) had introduced Zhou as a member of the CCP. Personal animosity and the divisive personality of Zhang had created tensions between his group and the Montargis radicals with whom Deng was associated. Zhou succeeded in forging an alliance between the two groups, demonstrating tact and organisational skills even at this early stage in his career.

Deng retained a great affection for the café in the 13th arrondissement which had made such an impression on him as a teenage activist. Many years later when he passed through Paris en route for a meeting at the United Nations in 1974 he asked staff at the Chinese embassy to take him to the Place d'Italie, but the area had changed beyond all recognition and he was not able to revisit the café of his youth and drink coffee there. Nevertheless, he got the staff to fetch him coffee from the little cafés on the nearby street and liked to compare Parisian cafés with the teahouses that he recalled from his childhood in Sichuan.

POLICE SURVEILLANCE AND EXPULSION

The activities of these youthful communists inevitably brought them to the attention of the French police. All of Europe was alert to the possibility of insurgency in the wake of the October Revolution that had overthrown the Tsarist regime in Russia in 1917. An atmosphere of near paranoia accompanied the failure of the Western intervention in the Russian civil war, and 'red scares', including the fake Zinoviev letter calling for communist agitation in Britain that appeared in 1924 just before the general election, were commonplace.

The date of the foundation of the French Communist Party is usually taken to be the Tours Conference of December 1920, when socialists and communists went their separate ways, the latter supporting the Bolshevik Revolution in Russia and backing the establishment of the Committee for the Third International. This split took place during a period of industrial unrest and a growing labour movement and in the words of its daily newspaper *L'Humanité*, the French Communist Party perceived itself to be 'in daily conflict with the bourgeois state'. For the historian of France, Rod Kedward, 'This was more than polemic. Sackings and arrests for Communist activities were commonplace,' and party officials frequently found themselves in prison.[7]

Chinese student activists were also under constant surveillance and on 22 June 1925 an order was issued to track down and arrest the most prominent of them. Within a few days over 20 of the most active had been rounded up and imprisoned and 47 work–study students were expelled from France. The Chinese Communist Youth League decided to continue its activities under the name of the Guomindang, which was not quite as bizarre as it sounds since the CCP and the GMD were theoretically co-operating in a United Front. Deng Xiaoping was still in Lyon, alone and isolated from the Youth League leadership in Paris. There was no news from the capital, but it was clear that the central organisation no longer existed. He returned to Paris and established what later became known as the Extraordinary Executive, taking the lead in re-creating an organisation that had collapsed. In June 1925, with two other members he also created a new secretariat. The new body met at a café in Billancourt on 1 July 1925 but had to disperse after the proprietor warned them that the police were about to carry out a raid. The League could still muster between 30 and 70 members at meetings, but it was increasingly under surveillance and obliged to operate clandestinely. The underground members concentrated on whether the League could survive and how to rebuild its organisation.

Deng became an individual of particular interest to the police. In August 1925 they discovered where he was living and in the French archives there is a police report of meetings that he chaired in September and October. He was named in a detailed intelligence report of 7 January 1926, but the police complained that they had been unable to discover the location of meetings or the identity of the organisers in advance, which suggests a high degree of security within the Chinese Communist Youth League and the Chinese community in France. The exclusiveness of the Chinese organisation and the language barrier made the task of the police difficult, but it was noted that Deng received an unusually large number of letters from China along with communist pamphlets and newspapers. Zhou Enlai returned to China in July 1924 to undertake other duties for the CCP and many of the activists realised that France was no longer safe for them and left for China. In November and December Deng Xiaoping received letters from the European branch of the CCP, instructing him and another four or five members to leave France and travel by rail to Moscow for further training. They left Paris for Moscow on 7 January 1926; their rooms were searched the following evening but the birds had flown. According to Deng's daughter, Maomao, as they boarded the train they were served with an official order from the French police, marked 'to be delivered in person', expelling them from the territory of France in perpetuity. That story provides a wonderfully dramatic ending to Deng's sojourn in France, but police files indicate that the order was not in fact made until the following day, 8 January, when the room above the rue Godefroy café was searched and their printing press and radical library, which included *The ABC of Communism* by Bukharin and Preobrazhensky, books on Sun Yat-sen and copies of the group's newspaper, the *Chinese Worker* (*Zhongguo gongren*), were seized. By then the revolutionaries had already left the country. Fifty years later Deng returned to Paris as the rising political leader of post-Mao China but it did not seem politic to enquire whether the permanent expulsion order was still in force.

Thus ended Deng's five years in France, a period which he was to remember with great affection and in which he made political contacts that he would maintain for the rest of his life. His experiences in France were the basis for the political attitudes (never really a fully-fledged philosophy) that he would retain until his death.[8]

3

MOSCOW AND THE CHINESE REVOLUTION (1926–31)

No other ideology has ever intruded.[1]

For aspiring communist cadres anywhere in the world in the 1920s, a sojourn in Russia, the home of the October Revolution and the emerging epicentre of the world communist movement, was a *sine qua non*. The revolution was still a novelty and its future was by no means secure but its supporters were convinced that it would expand internationally from its base in Russia. The Bolshevik government in Moscow was determined to extend its influence in the European part of the former Russian Empire and throughout Asia.

In December 1922, representatives of four new Soviet republics controlled by the Bolsheviks – Russia, Ukraine, Byelorussia and Transcaucasia – proclaimed the foundation of the Union of Soviet Socialist Republics. Further east in those regions of Asiatic Russia that were populated largely by non-Russians – speakers of Turkic and Iranian languages – civil war between the Red and White Armies continued to rage across the steppes. The Asian territories of Russia and the countries on its borders, including China, became a high priority for agents of the new government in Moscow. Lenin had established himself as the leader of the Bolsheviks in the wake of the 1917 revolution, but by 1922 he was a sick man and factions within the Communist Party of the Soviet Union (Bolshevik) – CPSU (B) – manoeuvred furiously to replace him. He died on 21 January 1924 and the political conflict became a personal battle between Stalin and Trotsky. Stalin isolated his opponents, forced Trotsky into exile, consolidated his own position and would remain in power until his death in 1953. In spite of these bitter and destructive internal disputes, Moscow and the CPSU (B) retained their authority as the main source of legitimacy for foreign communists. Training and political education were developed to ensure that emerging communist parties operated on the Soviet model and, as far as possible, under Moscow's control.

SUN YAT-SEN UNIVERSITY

The decision to send Deng to Moscow had been taken by the European branch of the CCP as early as 1925: a letter dated 29 May sent to the Party's executive in Moscow included his name (as Deng Xixian) in a list of students to be sent to the USSR for study. In November an exchange of letters listed Deng as one of a group of five. On 7 January 1926 the executive of the European branch of the Chinese Communist Youth League issued a circular announcing that 'it has been decided this evening that the 20 comrades going to Russia have set off from Paris and will probably be back in China before long'. Liu Mingyan of the committee wrote that 21 comrades, including Deng Xiaoping, Fu Chong and Deng Shaosheng, Deng's Uncle who had worked with him in France, were on their way to Moscow. Deng broke his journey for a brief stopover in Germany where he stayed with the family of an old working man who gave up his bed for Deng.

Deng arrived in Moscow in the middle of January and enrolled in the Communist University of the Toilers of the East (known also as Far Eastern University and to the Chinese as the University of the East, *Dongfang Daxue*). This academy had been established in 1921 to train communist cadres from the Asiatic regions of the Soviet Union and other parts of the developing world and it operated until the end of the 1930s. Deng soon transferred to the Sun Yat-sen University of the Toilers of the East, which had been created as an independent institution in 1925 based on the department of the Communist University of the Toilers of the East that had specialised in training Chinese communist and nationalist cadres. Chinese students had first travelled to Moscow in 1923 at the express wish of Sun Yat-sen himself during the first period of cooperation between the newly created Guomindang and the CCP.

Sun Yat-sen University was in a four-storey building at 16, Volkhova Street and was run by Karl Radek until he was replaced by Pavel Mif in 1927. It provided its Chinese students with two years of education and training in revolutionary theory and practice that would serve them and the international communist movement. Students had to learn Russian as their instructors were mainly from the Soviet Union and in the first term this intensive language learning programme occupied four hours of classes a day for six days a week. Courses on political economy, history, contemporary world problems, the theory and practice of the Russian Revolution, national and colonial questions and China's social development were compulsory: the detailed curriculum also included lectures on the history of the Chinese revolutionary movement, Chinese history, the history of social development, philosophy (dialectical materialism and historical materialism), political economy (based on *Das Kapital*), economic geography and Leninism. There were also regular lectures from senior officials of the CPSU (B) and the international communist movement to help the students relate their formal studies to the reality of world revolution as seen from Moscow. Recognising that the majority of its students, including Deng Xiaoping, would return to their home countries to fight in a revolutionary war, a further course on military studies was added.

This was not a broadly based education but a practical training for a revolutionary career to which the students were already committed. The distinctive teaching style at Sun Yat-sen University was designed to 'inspire students and enhance their mastery of theory and practice' rather than encourage deep reflection and comparative study. The instruction was formulaic, but there was less rote learning than in Deng's traditional Chinese primary school, and active participation in discussions was encouraged. The instructors lectured (in Russian, with Chinese interpretation), students asked questions at the end and the lecturer responded. Further discussion followed and at the end the lecturer summed up what they were supposed to know. When Deng arrived at the university in early 1926 there were over 300 Chinese students in 11 classes of between 30 and 40 students; by the following year the total number had grown to more than 500.

The educational level of the students varied considerably. Some were already established as leading lights of the Chinese communist movement and others had completed their secondary and university education in China; some 'worker–peasant cadres' had only an elementary education. Classes were organised on the basis of the students' knowledge and experience and preparatory classes provided remedial education. Students who attained a satisfactory standard in the Russian language were moved swiftly into a fast-track stream where they were trained as interpreters and translators. Deng Xiaoping was somewhere in the middle, but because of his experience of 'revolutionary struggle' in France he was placed in Class 7, the 'theoreticians' class' (*lilun jia ban*). The most politically active students from both communist and nationalist backgrounds were in Class 7: in addition to Deng, the communists in this class included Fu Chong and Li Zhuoran; the nationalists included Gu Zhenggang, Deng Wenyi and Qu Wu, the son-in-law of Wang Jingwei's secretary, Yu Zuoren. The brightest students from the two parties studied together and constantly discussed China's problems. Deng was in the same group as Jiang Jingguo, the son of Chiang Kai-shek and the future president of the Republic of China, or Taiwan. Neither was very tall, so they would often be shoulder to shoulder whenever the class lined up for formal photographs. Deng stood out as he was older and more experienced than many of his fellow students and he was always ready to laugh and joke. Outside class they explored Moscow and Deng often discussed his experiences in France. He and two others who had also been in France used to wear blue-and-white scarves: Deng maintained that in France they often had to clean up horse manure (quite well paid work, as manure was in demand for gardens) and French street cleaners wore these scarves. He was proud of the dirty jobs he had done.

Students at Sun Yat-sen University were exposed directly to the bitter ideological debates that ravaged the CPSU, and some of the prominent polemicists gave lectures on their political positions. Although Trotskyist and other oppositional groupings were eventually defeated in the CPSU as Stalin's authority prevailed, oppositionist ideas appealed to some of the Chinese students. Whatever political position they finally adopted, in the words of Jane Price, they 'returned to China with experience in the management of ideological debate and purge activities', techniques that would be useful in the future conflicts within the CCP. In addition to the internecine struggles in the Kremlin, the chaotic political situation in China led to constant debate and heated arguments. The divisions between the left and right wings of the Guomindang in China, and those between the Guomindang and the Communist Party, were mirrored in the Chinese student body in Moscow.[2]

Sun Yat-sen University had its own branch of the Chinese Communist Party (and the Guomindang). Fu Chong was the CCP branch secretary and Deng Xiaoping was the representative of Class 7. Party evaluation documents (*Dangyuan piping jihua an*) set out the responsibilities and activities of members in detail and included evaluations of how well they had performed. Deng was commended as an activist with a good understanding of the ideological position of the CPSU, quite an achievement at a time of such confusion. He had good relations with his fellow students and was praised for good attendance, appropriate relations with Guomindang students and tipped for a promising future in propaganda and organisational work.

In a formulaic and self-deprecating self-criticism that Deng wrote in Moscow, he admitted that during his time in France he had made mistakes because of his inexperience. He had wanted to study in Moscow to improve his theoretical grasp of Marxism and Leninism and 'test himself in the iron discipline of training as a Communist'. If this statement truly reflects his thinking at the time, he had already dedicated himself completely to the CCP and China's revolution and he was returning to China fortified by the confidence that his training at Sun Yat-sen University and his association with Soviet revolutionaries had given him. He was prepared to be a loyal footsoldier in the struggle to bring communism to China.[3]

TO THE CHINESE REVOLUTION

Deng's studies at Sun Yat-sen University ended after only one year of what should have been a two-year course and he left Moscow at the end of 1926. A political crisis was developing in China and the CCP had instructed him to return to work with the National Army (*Guominjun*) of Feng Yuxiang, one of the many warlords who had governed the provinces of China since the collapse of the Qing dynasty in 1911. Feng operated in the province of Zhili, around Beijing, and was sometimes known as the Christian General as he was, at least nominally, a convert to Protestant Christianity. Feng had become alienated from other Zhili warlords and came under the influence of Sun Yat-sen. His forces captured Beiping (now Beijing) on 23 October 1924 and he tried to persuade Sun to revive the republican government in the old capital: Sun was seriously ill and died on 12 March 1925. Feng became an important player in Chinese politics of the 1920s and he moved closer to the Soviet Union in his outlook. The United Front between the communists and nationalists, which had persisted during Chiang Kai-shek's Northern Expedition to unify China in 1926, was increasingly fragile. Feng's National Army had relieved the ancient capital of Xi'an in Shaanxi Province in 1926 from a siege by another warlord and Feng had allied himself with the nationalists during the Northern Expedition. The CCP was interested in exploiting Feng's interest in the USSR, which had been encouraged by Li Dazhao, one of the founding members of the CCP while Feng had been in Beiping. Li was instrumental in persuading Feng to visit Moscow in August 1926.

Deng Xiaoping and two colleagues arrived in Xi'an in February 1927 after a difficult journey which took them over a month by train eastwards from Moscow and then, using cars, camels and horses, through Mongolia and Gansu. They rode on camels for eight days and nights across the desert and were never able to wash or bathe properly during the whole journey. In Xi'an Deng met Liu Bojian, a fellow Sichuan man, whom he had known in France and who had studied in Moscow at the University of the Toilers of the East. Liu had accompanied Feng during his visit to the Soviet Union and through this high-level connection Deng was rapidly assigned to the Sun Yat-sen Military Academy as a political instructor and head of the political section. The academy was based at the Shaanxi Headquarters of the Guomindang's National Revolutionary Army (NRA) and the commandant, Yu Youren, was a supporter of the left wing of the Guomindang. Many of the most influential members of staff were members of the CCP, including the principal, Shi Kexuan, and his deputy, Li Lin, whom Deng had known in France.

When Deng arrived in Xi'an he took on the role of party secretary of the newly-emerging academy, which had been formed as part of the communist–nationalist United Front. Deng remembered it as a 'red school' with many Communist Party members among the students. Political education was second only in importance to military studies, and Marxism and revolution could be discussed openly. Deng was among friends and like-minded activists and he also became involved with other Xi'an colleges and in the wider community. He and some of the other CCP members were able to persuade their principal, who lived near the Drum Tower, to invite them to a meal once a week, so that they could eat *niurou paomo*, beef stew with flat bread broken into it. This is one of the culinary specialities of Xi'an, although many prefer lamb to beef. The principal, Shi Kexuan, died during the civil war that broke out in 1927 and his gravestone just outside Xi'an has an inscription proposed by Deng Xiaoping. In spite of the difficulties of the work in which he and his colleagues were engaged, Deng had the capacity for remembering the positive aspects of his time in Xi'an.[4]

TRAGEDY AND BETRAYAL IN SHANGHAI (1927)

On 12 April 1927 in Shanghai the Chinese political landscape changed dramatically. Troops and police controlled by the nationalist Guomindang, with the help of local underworld gangs, turned on communists and others suspected of being sympathisers. Hundreds were executed on the spot, many more were arrested and thousands fled for their lives. The CCP's organisation in Shanghai was destroyed and the alliance with the Guomindang, which had been under strain for months, was over. In May 1927 Feng Yuxiang's forces became the Second Group Army of the National Revolutionary Army and he marched east to join Wang Jingwei and his leftwing Guomindang government in Wuhan. Wang Jingwei had been working with the CCP, and leading communists hoped for another united front against Chiang Kai-shek, but he eventually turned against them. Liu Bojian, Deng's contact in Xi'an, travelled with Feng to continue his liaison work while Deng and other colleagues remained behind at the academy. Deng had worked with Feng's army for three or four months and took pride in having transformed it into an efficient force with a modern outlook, yet Feng was becoming increasingly anti-communist. In the summer of 1927 Feng ordered CCP supporters in his army to go to Kaifeng for a training session and promptly expelled them; he was, however, still regarded by the CCP as a progressive warlord who was a potential ally.[5]

After the departure of Feng Yuxiang's army, Deng also left for Wuhan where the CCP now had its headquarters: the Central Committee had rapidly moved there from Shanghai in early April after Chiang Kai-shek's putsch. Deng then went to Shanghai where he worked to rebuild an underground communist organisation, often at considerable personal peril, constantly in danger of discovery and on guard against possible reprisals by the nationalist authorities and their criminal henchmen. He had used various names in his writings, including Deng Xixian, by which he had previously been known since his school days. For added security in his underground operations he was now known as Deng Xiaoping.

The year 1927 had been catastrophic for the Chinese Communist Party, a year of tragedy and betrayal. Its Guomindang opponents believed that it had been wiped out and it could no longer function openly in the towns and cities. For the next 22 years it was the political arm of a military and guerrilla force in China's vast countryside: in the urban areas it could only operate underground.

During this traumatic period the leader of the CCP was Chen Duxiu, one of the founding fathers of the Party and its first general secretary. He was a doctrinaire Marxist who clung firmly to the analysis of the CPSU in Moscow that the Party had to rely on the urban working class but must also cooperate with bourgeois parties such as the Guomindang. After the Shanghai putsch of April 1927 it became obvious that, whatever the theoretical rationale, the CCP was physically unable to organise openly among factory workers in the cities. Although underground party work in the urban areas was still valued, an alternative political approach was gaining ground: the party should concentrate on a radical movement that was emerging among the peasantry. This was not a new argument as some CCP members had been working to create peasant associations and organise poorer farmers. In 1922–3, Peng Pai had organised the Hailufeng Soviet in Guangdong Province, but it was soon crushed and Peng, who fled to Shanghai, was imprisoned and executed. The moving spirit behind the strategic shift towards an agrarian revolution was Mao Zedong who in 1927 had been working with the peasant movement in his native Hunan.[6]

NEW RURAL STRATEGY AND MAO ZEDONG

Chen Duxiu was suspended as general secretary of the CCP on 12 July 1927 and, although the Central Committee was restructured, its organisation was in complete disarray. An attempt to carry out an armed insurrection in the Jiangxi provincial capital of Nanchang on 1 August failed miserably and the CCP and its military organisation were obliged to retreat to the countryside: *faute de mieux* the CCP was now effectively restricted to operations in the rural areas. The failure of the Nanchang uprising had brought home to its leaders the necessity of a strong military force and 1 August is still commemorated in the PRC as Army Day.

In the summer of 1927 Deng reported to the Military Commission of the CCP Central Committee at its headquarters in Wuhan, still under the control of Wang Jingwei's breakaway leftwing nationalist regime with which the CCP hoped to cooperate. Deng was employed in the CCP Secretariat under the then general secretary, Deng Zhongxia (a Hunanese who was not related to Deng Xiaoping), and worked mainly on the management of internal party documents and conmunications. He took minutes at meetings of the Central Committee and drafted confidential documents, although he was not allowed to handle the most politically sensitive papers. Zhou Enlai, who Deng knew well from their time in France, had also arrived in Wuhan at this time. Zhou was more senior in the party than Deng and had become a member of the Politburo and head of the CCP Military Affairs Department.

The Central Committee was still run by Chen Duxiu, one of the original founders of the CCP, until his suspension on 12 July 1927. Chen was not receptive to the new emphasis that was being placed by Mao Zedong on the role of the peasantry in the revolution. Deng recalled Chen as a dogmatic figure who tended to lay down the law at meetings and was given to *ex cathedra* pronouncements and arbitrary decisions. Chen preferred simple meetings that did not last long: he restricted discussion and would dissolve meetings abruptly if there was any opposition. Ironically, Deng was also criticised by Chen for drafting documents that were too concise. Chen came from a traditional intellectual background and insisted that the style of writing and presentation of documents and correspondence should be appropriately formal and rigorous.

In Wuhan, Deng Xiaoping found lodgings with Qu Qiubai, Qu's wife, and Li Weihan. Qu was a member of the Politburo Provisional Standing Committee and, after the purge of Chen Duxiu, was interim leader of the CCP. Li Weihan was secretary of the Central Committee. In his lodgings the 23-year-old Deng had direct access to some of the most important figures in the Party. He also made the acquaintance of Mao Zedong, who was his senior by 11 years and was actively promoting the idea that the Party should concentrate on a rural base and a peasant armed force. There is no evidence that Mao and Deng made much impression on each other but in time their political relationship was to prove of great consequence.[7]

RIFT WITH WANG JINGWEI

The historic August 7 Conference (*Ba qi huiyi*) was convened in great haste by the CCP in Hankou (one of the constituent towns of the Wuhan conurbation) on 7 August 1927 in response to Wang Jingwei's decision to cut the ties of his left wing Guomindang faction with the CCP. The possibility of cooperation with the 'progessive' wing of the Guomindang was no more, and Chen Duxiu, who had been closely associated with that policy, was severely criticised and excluded from the new provisional Politburo that was elected. Deng was heavily involved in the preparations for the meeting, which was attended by Vissarion Lominadze (1897–1935), the veteran Georgian Bolshevik who represented the Comintern and who personally supported the candidacy of Qu Qiubai as party leader. The Comintern still maintained that the CCP should find some section of the Guomindang with which it could cooperate but this was patently unrealistic and the meeting resolved to continue 'carrying out the agrarian revolution and armed resistance to the GMD reactionaries, and decided to make mobilisation of the peasants to stage autumn harvest uprisings the major task of the Party'.

Deng recalled that the meeting was held in great secrecy in a Western-style house that had been rented by Russians at 139 Poyang Street (formerly 41 Three Religions Street – *Sanjiao jie*) in the Jianghan commercial district of Hankou.

> There were twenty or so delegates who were brought to the meeting by underground party members in three groups over three days. The leading members of the Central Committee came in last and left first. The venue for the meeting was next door to a restaurant and the delegates came and went by the common back entrance.

As one of the organisers, Deng was in the first group to arrive, carrying a small suitcase because, although the meeting proper lasted only 'one day and one night', he would be there for a total of six days, sleeping at night on a bedroll on the floor. The atmosphere was tense: it was the hottest time of the year in Wuhan; for security reasons no doors or windows could be opened and delegates were not allowed to leave until the end of the meeting. The building later became a museum to commemorate the historic meeting and in 1980 Deng wrote the six characters *ba qi huiyi huizhi* (Site of the August 7 Meeting) to be copied for the sign.[8]

The meeting elected a provisional Politburo in which Qu Qiubai and Li Weihan were the leading members. Mao Zedong made a speech on the necessity of armed revolution and the need for the leadership to listen 'attentively to reports from lower levels', an instruction that he would honour more in the breach than the observance when he was leader of the CCP in the 1950s and 1960s. Mao became an alternate member of the provisional Politburo, as did Zhou Enlai. Northern and Southern Bureaux of the Central Committee were established to reflect the geographical spread of the CCP's activity. Deng was not a delegate and was not sufficiently senior to expect a Central Committee or Politburo appointment, but he had played a crucial part in the preparation of documents and the organisation.

The fact that both the Politburo and its Standing Committee, the most powerful organs of the Party, were acknowledged to be provisional is an indication of the instability of the CCP after the Shanghai putsch. The August 7 Conference was a turning point as it marked the end of the old-style leadership under Chen Duxiu, though Mao was not yet in a position to replace him. The first recorded meeting between Deng and Mao Zedong was at the conference, but Deng was somewhat in awe of Mao's reputation and there is no record of any conversation between the two.

In the immediate aftermath of the meeting, two insurrections took place, the Autumn Harvest Rising led by Mao on the border between the provinces of Hunan and Jiangxi on 7 September and the Guangzhou Rising under Zhang Tailei on 11 December. Although both insurrections failed, these rural uprisings embodied the determination of the CCP to abandon the cities and appeal to the peasantry for support.[9]

RETURN TO SHANGHAI WITH ZHOU ENLAI

In late September or early October 1927 the Central Committee moved its leading political and military organisations to Shanghai, judging that although it was far from secure it was less dangerous than Wuhan. Deng moved with them. The CCP could not operate openly in Shanghai and had established a network of secret organisations. Deng played an important role in these and was responsible for the party's documentation, telegrams and other communications, for the expenditure of the Central Committee and arrangements for meetings. By 1928 he had the title of secretary-general (*zhongyang mishuzhang*): this entailed administrative responsibility for the work of the Secretariat but not a political role as secretary to the Central Committee, which was Qu Qiubai's role. There is some confusion over the use of the terms 'secretary-general' and 'general secretary' which would continue into the 1950s. At the end of 1927, Deng was an able and trusted administrator and bureaucrat rather than a political leader but, even at the tender age of 24 and with only limited experience, he inspired confidence and was entrusted with risky and sensitive tasks.

It was far too dangerous to hold the CCP's Sixth National Congress in China so it took place in Moscow from 18 June to 11 July 1928 and the main reports were given by Qu Qiubai and Zhou Enlai. Deng stayed to support Li Weihan and Ren Bishi who had remained behind in Shanghai. The three met every morning at 9 am to deal with day-to-day party business and were in charge of the CCP's operation from the beginning of April until September when the new leadership that had been chosen with Moscow's approval returned to China.

Deng frequently accompanied Zhou Enlai to the party's underground headquarters in Shanghai and responded to requests for assistance from different sections of the party. Deng was the efficient organiser, the administrator who made things happen: he was never a charismatic leader or a theoretician. He was responsible for the agendas of the Politburo and its Standing Committee and for arranging the times of meetings, and was constantly in and out of the Politburo's main rendezvous. From November 1928 until April 1931, this was at 447 Sima Road (now Fuzhou Road) in the centre of bustling Shanghai and behind the Tianchan Theatre (which was rebuilt in the 1990s and today offers performances of Shanghai, Beijing and Shaoxing opera). He naturally took notes for the minutes of meetings but although he kept a low profile he was well enough regarded to be able to voice his own opinions; he did not speak often but when he did others listened. After the meetings he prepared and circulated the minutes and any other documents and had overall responsibility for the efficient functioning of the underground secretariat. He was discovering that the role of secretary was powerful and he had taken to it like a duck to water.

Deng dressed in the manner of most poor Shanghai men, sometimes wearing a traditional long robe and an old-fashioned hat. He ran a small general store on Wuma Road, selling cigarettes, soap, matches and other basic necessities. This was a useful cover for his political activities, as was an antique or curio shop that he also managed from time to time. He got to know the alleyways and back streets of Shanghai very well, especially in the area where the Party's clandestine organisations met. He was never arrested during the three years he worked in Shanghai: he had never had his photograph taken and had never even been to a cinema as he was concerned that appearing anywhere in public might have blown his cover. He came close to capture on two occasions, once when he was betrayed while meeting a contact and later when the police discovered where Zhou Enlai had been living. Underground work of this nature required courage, meticulous preparation and caution. Deng had the nerve, the aptitude and also the luck for this clandestine life and he is often described as sharp, alert and resourceful. These characteristics, and his unusual ability to sum up a situation swiftly and accurately, were finely honed during his three years working undercover in Shanghai and helped to keep him alive. However, those who knew Deng in Shanghai in the 1920s also recalled that, in spite of the pressure, he remained essentially the lively, unassuming and amiable joker that he had been in France and loved nothing better than to sit round a table chatting over bowls of the spicy food of his native Sichuan.[10]

GUANGXI INSURRECTIONS OF 1929–30

In early December 1929 Deng was instructed by the CCP leadership to intervene in a complex outbreak of unrest in Guangxi Province, a south-western frontier region, close to the border with Vietnam, now known as the Guangxi Zhuang Autonomous Region. The National Government of Chiang Kai-shek was beginning to establish itself in its chosen capital of Nanjing. Guangxi Province was controlled by a group of warlords – the New Guangxi Clique which had broken away from Chiang and was defeated militarily by his troops in 1929. The warlords sought allies against Chiang, including Chen Jitang, who became governor of neighbouring Guangdong in 1931. After the Japanese invasion of Manchuria on 18 September 1931, the Guangxi warlords pledged allegiance to China and the national resistance against Japan but in practice ruled their province independently.

It is not known for certain how Deng travelled from Shanghai to Guangxi, but because the overland route from Guangzhou was too dangerous he may have taken a boat to the Vietnamese port of Haiphong from where he was assisted by CCP contacts to travel north by train to the Chinese border. This was a route that had been used by young Vietnamese radicals of the Thanh Nien (Vietnamese Revolutionary Youth Association) to travel to and from their headquarters in exile in Guangzhou until it was wiped out during the suppression of the Canton Commune in 1927. There are even tantalising rumours that Deng met and consulted the legendary Vietnamese revolutionary Ho Chi Minh, who had developed close relations with some Vietnamese students in France, but these stories cannot be substantiated.

The Guangxi insurrections embroiled Deng in a complicated and bitter internal party struggle that left him politically damaged and personally isolated. The first outbreak of unrest began in Baise (sometimes called Bose) on 11 December 1929 when officers and men of the General Training Unit of the Guangxi Garrison 4th Brigade, already heavily infiltrated by members of the CCP, declared that they were now the 7th Chinese Workers' and Peasants' Red Army. The commanding officer of this new army was Zhang Yunyi, who had been one of the original representatives of the CCP in Guangxi; Deng Xiaoping was there to establish political control and became secretary of the Front Committee and a member of the army's Political Committee. The CCP politicised and armed local peasant farmers and implemented policies of land reform. It established its own government, the Right River (*Youjiang*) Soviet in Enlong County (now known as Tiandong). The chairman of this new Soviet Government was Lei Jingtian, another of the original CCP activists.

The preparatory work, carried out mostly by Deng, had been satisfactory and the insurgents had managed to win over a substantial number of Guomindang troops. In February 1930 the 5th Brigade of the nationalist Guangxi Garrison based in Longzhou, which is further south than Baise and close to the border with Vietnam, also mutinied and reconstituted itself as the CCP's 8th Red Army. Deng was also a member of the Political Committee of this army unit which went on to establish the Left River (*Zuojiang*) Revolutionary Commitee. The terms Right and Left River do not have any political significance as they are the names of the two watercourses that combine to form the Yong River at Nanning.

DENG XIAOPING'S ROLE IN THE BAISE AND LONGZHOU INSURRECTIONS

The insurrections were far more confusing and chaotic than this simplified narrative suggests. Deng Xiaoping's role is far from clear and he was not even in Guangxi for the duration as he was recalled to report to the Party centre in Shanghai. Deng had been sent by the Party to the Guangxi provincial capital, Nanning, to carry out a continuation of the CCP's 'united front work'. This sounds strange because the first united front of the CCP and the Guomindang had broken down in April 1927 after the Shanghai putsch. The CCP were not on friendly terms with the nationalists but neither were the Guangxi warlords. Deng's twofold mission was to liaise openly with the warlord government and assess the possibility of forming an alliance with them, while simultaneously and clandestinely mobilising support for the CCP.

In this essentially military enterprise, his role was primarily political and he acted as Party secretary and political commissar to the CCP 7th Red Army. This was probably for the best since by his own admission he had little experience of military matters. He liaised with the chairman of the Guangxi Provincial Government Yu Zuobai and Li Mingrui, the commander of the Provincial Pacification Force (the local garrison), and was responsible for deploying cadres who had been sent by the Central Committee to Guangxi. He used the name Deng Bin while in Nanning and had an official appointment as secretary to the Guangxi Provincial Government, which provided a cover for his clandestine Party work. He found accommodation in Nanning at the Guangchang gas lamp shop on Zhongshan Street and this became his base for liaising with Lei Jingtian and other underground communists. He planned the infiltration of communist supporters into military units and made oral reports to contacts in the Central Committee. As he was officially in Nanning at the invitation of the Guangxi government, Deng was not technically planning a military uprising, yet both his work to rebuild the CCP's local organisation and strengthen its publications and his work with the local government proved highly effective for the interests of the Party. Yu and Li agreed to release a large number of CCP members and sympathisers who had been placed under arrest before 1927.

Under the guise of improving the strength of the army by training junior officers, Deng suggested to Li, via a clandestine party member, that a Guangxi General Training Unit should be established. Over 100 CCP members were enrolled as students in this unit: they were formally assigned to the Guangxi Garrison but were in fact under the control of communist officers. Yu Zuobai also agreed to the appointment of Deng's nominees as county magistrates in the Right and Left River areas and he supported the establishment of peasant militias, which they armed, a useful basis for an insurrection.

When the warlords' direct resistance to Chiang Kai-shek's National Government troops failed, it was decided that an armed uprising, based on the units that were controlled by communists, was opportune. These units were withdrawn from Nanning and moved to two areas around Baise and Longzhou, in the Right and Left River regions respectively, with the intention of stimulating an insurrection of workers and peasants. A Soviet base area was declared in Baise in December 1929 and another in Longzhou in February 1930 (where the CCP troops were initially known as the 8th Red Army), but the CCP forces were then ordered to leave their base areas and march on the cities of Liuzhou, Guilin and Guangzhou to support anticipated urban insurrections. This was part of the heavily criticised Li Lisan strategy. Deng and the majority of the 7th Red Army obeyed these instructions and moved out, leaving the Soviet base guarded by a small garrison of troops whose officers did not want to participate in the insurrections. The under-manned base soon fell to nationalist forces.

In September 1930 the 7th Red Army was ordered to march east and Deng received a cryptic order from the Central Committee instructing him that 'developments in the Guangxi Soviet should only be in the direction of Hunan and the Beijiang River for direct liaison with the Central Soviet', (in Jiangxi). The Central Committee was shifting its focus to the Jiangxi Soviet, which was to become the main base for the CCP until the Long March of 1934–5. Deng called a meeting to explain to his officers that the 7th Red Army would now be moving towards the north of Guangdong Province and its border with Jiangxi.

Between 30 January and 5 February 1931, the communists suffered huge losses at the battle of Meihua, a village in northern Guangdong Province close to the border with Hunan. Deng claimed that there were greater casualties among the enemy forces but he lost a number of close comrades and friends at Meihua. He remained with the 7th Red Army for a series of battles with local militia and warlord troops that took place in northern Guangdong during the spring of 1931. In these battles the communists lost as much as two thirds of their strength and the attempt to storm the cities was abandoned.

RECALLED TO SHANGHAI

Deng was recalled to Shanghai in May 1931 and was finally able, together with his younger brother, to visit the grave of his wife, Zhang Xiyuan. They had met at Sun Yat-sen University in Moscow and married in Shanghai in 1928. While Deng had been in Guangxi she had died in hospital giving birth to their child, who also died a few days later.

Accounts of Deng's part in the Guangxi insurrections often associate him with the successes, including the initial uprising in Baise, and blame the failures on others, notably the reckless Li Lisan, who had been pressing for uprisings to seize China's major cities, he was not even in Guangxi for the Baise insurrection of 11 December 1929. Deng had been summoned to Shanghai to present a report on the insurrections to the Central Committee, which he did in January 1930. An article in *Military Dispatch* (*Junshi tongxun*), '*Dui Guangxi hongjun gongzuo buzhi de taolun*' ('Discussions on the arrangements for work in the Red Army in Guangxi'), reflected Deng's report and the discussions that followed it. Deng is not mentioned by name in the article, indeed he could be the author. This is a controversial episode in Deng's career as there were accusations that he had deserted his post, or was somehow responsible for the eventual defeat of the 7th Red Army; these allegations were to dog him well into the 1970s. On 2 March 1930 the Central Committee sent a message to the CCP's Guangxi Provincial Committee informing them that Deng was returning to Guangxi with instructions that included the formation of a new 7th Red Army Front Committee on which Deng would serve and act as secretary, in addition to his role as political commissar. It appears that the Central Committee in Shanghai had accepted his account of events in Guangxi and returned him in a more senior post with the 7th Red Army. He had stayed in Shanghai for about a month, arriving and leaving in some haste, and returned to Guangxi, to Longzhou, on 7 February.

He was back in Shanghai again in February 1931 to make a second report, this time primarily on the actions of the 7th Red Army. Deng did not find it easy to report in person, much preferring to submit a written version and his report, which was 17,000 characters in length, was completed on 29 April. For reasons that are not entirely clear the Central Committee did not schedule a meeting to hear this report and did not assign him to any work in Shanghai. He was able to draw monthly living expenses from his underground contact but was effectively out in the cold. What Deng had not anticipated was that between 9 March and 4 April another (unnamed) cadre from the 7th Red Army in Guangxi had also been brought to Shanghai and was busy producing a report which differed considerably from Deng's. Neither was Deng aware that, before his arrival in Shanghai, the Central Committee, acting on the suggestion of Pavel Mif, the representative of the Comintern, had secretly convened a Fourth Plenary Session of the 6th Central Committee on 7 January 1931. The meeting was engineered by Mif to attack the policies of Li Lisan who, with the support of CCP Secretary-General Xiang Zhongfa (elected as leader at the 1928 congress in Moscow), had conceived a grandiose plan for nationwide insurrections based on Wuhan. Mif planned to replace Li in the Politburo with his protégé Wang Ming (also known as Chen Shaoyu), one of a group known as the '28 Bolsheviks' that had formed around Mif at Sun Yat-sen University in Moscow. Li Lisan was purged from the Politburo. Xiang Zhongfa was betrayed and executed by the Guomindang. Wang Ming was elected to the Politburo but, after a series of arrests and executions of communist leaders by the Guomindang secret police, he sought refuge in Moscow from where he continued to try to control CCP policy. Bo Gu (Qin Bangxian), who was allied to the Comintern adviser Otto Braun and was an opponent of Mao Zedong, became secretary-general. He was not a friend of Deng Xiaoping.

Deng thus remained out in the cold. He kept in touch with a few of his old comrades but some were uncomfortable about associating with him in what was a precarious situation politically. On the one hand the Party leadership was so preoccupied with the sectarian internal strife that had been exacerbated by Mif and the 28 Bolsheviks, not to mention fear of infiltration by the Guomindang secret police, that there was no time to consider Deng or his report. More seriously the Guangxi insurrections with which he had been involved – on the orders of the Central Committee – were no longer in keeping with Party policy and they could be dismissed as having been part of the discredited 'Li Lisan line': this was made explicit in a directive issued by the Central Committee on 14 May 1931, entitled 'Message from the Chinese Communist Party Central Committee to the Front

Committee of the 7th Red Army'. The Central Committee made its lack of confidence in the leadership of the 7th Red Army clear and although Deng was not named he felt slighted. Deng had counselled against reckless political action in the period leading up to the Baise uprising, arguing that orders to create a Soviet government within ten days were premature. The central bodies of the CCP were in chaos and Deng was still a relatively junior party official who did not have authority over military tactics, yet he was politically damaged by his association with the failures.

Deng was ordered to go to Wuhu in Anhui to inspect the Party's work there, but the local organisation had been virtually destroyed and his contact failed to respond to pre-arranged secret signals, so Deng had to buy a boat ticket and return to Shanghai. No one was interested in listening to his report from Wuhu; his requests either to return to Guangxi or to work in the Central Soviet base that had been established in the south of Jiangxi Province were turned down, and once again he was twiddling his thumbs in Shanghai. Eventually his persistence paid off and in mid-July 1931 he was permitted to travel to Jiangxi. This entailed a sea voyage from Shanghai via Shantou in Guangdong Province and an overland trek through Guangdong and Fujian to the Central Soviet base in Ruijin, Jiangxi.

Deng's final months in Shanghai had been unhappy and frustrating but what was probably the most difficult phase of his early political life had come to an end. His time had not been entirely wasted as he would build on his political and military experiences in Shanghai and Guangxi over the next 18 years of his life in the Jiangxi Soviet, on the Long March, in the Taihang base area and finally during the civil war with the nationalists that brought the CCP to power. His encounter with factional and ideological disputes within the Party had been bruising and in the years that followed he found the relative simplicity and the comradeship of military life more to his taste. Wherever possible he avoided taking an ideological postion in factional squabbles, preferring to make judgements on a pragmatic basis.[11]

4

SOLDIER AND COMMUNIST: TRIUMPH OVER ADVERSITY IN JIANGXI (1931–4)

I am a military man. My true vocation is combat.

I spent so many years in the army without being wounded and worked underground without being arrested.[1]

Most members of the Chinese Communist Party leadership who rose through its hierarchy before 1949 had some military experience, even if only as a political commissar in an army unit. In the early days the Party and the Red Army that it created in 1927 were so closely interlinked that it was not always possible to distinguish clearly between military and political chains of command. As the influence of the communists increased and their organisation expanded, the roles of its leaders became more specialised. Some like Lin Biao and Peng Dehuai excelled at army life and forged careers that were almost entirely military: both became marshals of the PRC. Others were primarily political activists, notably Mao Zedong although even he originally intended to retain a military role, a role for which many of his colleagues felt he was utterly unsuited.

Deng Xiaoping's military experience began in the 1920s and continued throughout the 1930s, during the CCP's first experiment in government in the

Jiangxi Soviet. He liked to describe himself as a military man although he was originally an army politician; a political commissar, rather than a combat soldier. However, in the heat of battle he often found himself in command of combat units and was deeply involved in tactics and strategy. After 1949, he found his niche in the Communist Party and the government, returning to the type of administrative roles that he had tasted in France and Shanghai, but his experience of army life left a profound impression and his respect for the military and its ethos never left him. His highest military responsibility, which came after the foundation of the PRC, was as chairman of the Central Military Commission, formally in political control of the People's Liberation Army (PLA). This was the position that he retained until 1989, at the very end of his political career and 60 years after his first appointment as a political commissar in Guangxi. Although he regarded himself as a military man and liked to think of himself as an old soldier, he always refused to use a military rank. The marshals of the PLA, the most senior military men of the People's Republic, referred to him as the 'marshal without a rank' (*meiyou junxian de yuanshuai*) or the 'old commander' (*laoshuai de lingban*), an indication of the authority that he exercised and perhaps also the affection and esteem in which he was held by senior officers, in spite of the fact that he had not risen through the rank system of the mainstream military.[2]

IN THE JIANGXI SOVIET

In the summer of 1931 Deng arrived in the Central Soviet District (*Zhongyang Suqu*), which had been established around the city of Ruijin in southern Jiangxi and is usually referred to as the Jiangxi Soviet. It was the main base of the Chinese Communist Party in the period between its breach with the Guomindang in 1927 and the Long March of 1934–5 and was the first formal government established by the CCP. Deng travelled there on the instructions of the Central Committee, so it must be assumed that any doubts about his reliability following the failed uprisings in Guangxi had been resolved. His first wife, Zhang Xiyuan, had died in childbirth in Shanghai and he was accompanied on his journey to Ruijin by Jin Weiying, who was to become his second wife. Jin was the same age as Deng and came from Zhejiang Province in eastern China where she had been educated in a girls' school run by the local county government. She had joined the CCP in 1926, had been active in the labour movement and had already held positions of responsibility in the Party; from 1931 to 1939 she and Deng were political comrades as well as partners. Active communists were in danger of imprisonment and possible execution if discovered by the nationalist authorities, so they travelled to Jiangxi with the help of an underground Party network, taking a boat from Shanghai to Shantou (formerly Swatow) in Guangdong Province. From Shantou a guide led them to a train bound for Chaozhou in the east of the province, and a small steamer then conveyed them north to Chayang from where they travelled up river to Qingxi in Dabu County. This was on the border of the Soviet area, which they reached by a rugged mountain path, finally arriving in early August 1931 at the town of Changding where the provisional party committee of the Fujian, Guangdong and Jiangxi provinces was based. A further journey westward through equally inhospitable terrain took them to Ruijin County where the Red Army of Mao Zedong and Zhu De was actively defending their Soviet base.

CAMPAIGN AGAINST THE 'SOCIAL DEMOCRATIC PARTY'

When Deng and Jin arrived in Ruijin County it was early autumn, *lihuo* in the traditional agricultural calendar: the paddy rice had ripened but there were few peasants in the fields, there was no singing and none of the sound of laughter that might be expected at harvest time. The villagers were gathered under the trees arguing. Deng and Jin were led into the village by their guide who asked where they might find the Soviet government and the party committee, but no-one would tell them. They discovered that there had been chaos and indiscriminate executions following a campaign led by the local communist leader Li Tianfu to liquidate the 'Social Democratic Party', a group which, in spite of its reformist sounding name, was linked to the Anti-Bolshevik League, an anti-Communist group run by the Guomindang. In fact this deadly conflict did not involve the 'Social Democratic Party' but was a factional struggle between local communists and Mao Zedong's newly arrived forces. Some communists were executed in an internal witch-hunt and in 1956 Mao was to agree that people had been wrongly executed during this struggle. This conflict and confusion over who had authority over groups that claimed to be communist is an indication of the instability of the Jiangxi Soviet.

PARTY SECRETARY OF RUIJIN COUNTY: RIGHTING WRONGS DONE BY LI TIANFU

Deng and Jin urgently needed to find the headquarters of the 1st Front Red Army (*Hong yifangmianjun zongbu*) and its leaders Mao and Zhu De. After much wasted time and many blind alleys they finally made contact with the East Jiangxi Special Committee of the Chinese Communist Party in Ruijin where it had relocated on 7 August 1931 after coming under attack by military units of the Guomindang. The secretary of the East Jiangxi Special Committee was Xie Weijun, who had been with Mao Zedong since his forces had left the Party's temporary base at Jinggangshan. Deng and Jin did not know him or any other local communists, but they were warmly welcomed. Xie told Deng that Mao and Zhu, together with the main force and headquarters unit of the 1st Front Army, were in Xingguo, to the north-west of Ruijin, and were engaged in a desperate battle with the Guomindang's 26th Army, which was trying to breach the defences of the Soviet base. Communications between Xingguo and Ruijin had been cut off and there was no possibility of contacting Mao, Zhu or any of the senior officers for the foreseeable future. Deng was excited to hear detailed news about the Red Army but concerned about the perilous situation they were in. He took out a packet of cigarettes, offered one to Xie and as they smoked together asked him why there had been such problems in the Jiangxi Soviet. Xie and his colleagues described how Li Tianfu had dealt with the problem of the 'Social Democratic Party', believing that the Jiangxi Soviet was in danger of collapse. Deng and Jin listened to his analysis of the conflict as did two other new arrivals. Yu Zehong had worked in the underground Party organisation in Shanghai and been in charge of propaganda for the Party's Northern Bureau before being sent to Ruijin by the Party centre to strengthen the leadership of the Soviet, and his wife Wu Jingdao accompanied him.

It was agreed that Deng Xiaoping should act as CCP secretary for Ruijin County and his appointment is usually dated from August 1931. At first he operated under the auspices of the East Jiangxi Special Committee of which Xie, a confidant of Mao's, was secretary. For these active Party members, even while they were close to a combat zone, it was important to use the correct names for their organisation and positions, as important as if they had been Confucian officials under the Empire. On his arrival in Ruijin and in the absence of Mao Zedong, Zhu De or other members of the senior leadership, who were away battling with the Guomindang, Deng had taken charge and, by a combination of his personality and his political credentials, had established his authority. He was willing and able to grasp the responsibility involved in turning round what had been a desperate situation in Ruijin. In Guangxi and Shanghai he had already experienced fierce internal party disputes and was well aware of the risks that he would run if he tried to correct the mistakes that had been made. Deng heard that Xie Jingshan, the previous chairman of the Ruijin Soviet Government, had been opposed to the indiscriminate arrests and executions and, as a result, he had been accused of being a member of the Anti-Bolshvik League, arrested and beheaded. Deng came to the conclusion that it was his duty to put an end to the outrageous behaviour of Li Tianfu.

Deng and the new colleagues that he trusted steered well clear of Li, and taking care not to alert him to what they were doing, set out for Wuyang and Taoyang, the two districts that had been most seriously affected by the purge, and conducted their own investigations in great secrecy. Wuyang had been one of the earliest parts of the Ruijin area to support the communists and as early as April 1930, Yang Douwen and other CCP leaders there had set up a Soviet government in Wuyang based on a peasant militia and Red Guard troops. Supporters of the rising in Wuyang had played a key role in the formation of the Jiangxi Soviet but many had been condemned as supporters of the 'Social Democratic Party' and executed. The CCP's party and government organisations were paralysed as no-one was willing to accept any posts of responsibility. Surviving party officials who had been under attack 'shouldered their red flags' and headed for the mountains where they hid for their own protection. Taoyang district had also been quick to respond to the revolutionary upsurge and many of the district's communist officials had also fallen victim to the purge of 'Social Democratic Party' members.

Deng and his colleagues interviewed cadres and residents in these districts and discovered that they were still living in terror. They told him that the wide-ranging purge of the 'Social Democratic Party' had started in May 1931 when Li Tianfu had convened a mass meeting of active Communist Party and Communist Youth League members, which was attended by a range of Party cadres. After this meeting over 80 per cent of the members of the County Soviet Government and the County Trades Union Federation were arrested and within ten days they had been executed. Li Tianfu then announced the dissolution of these two organisations but within two weeks the majority of the members and officials of the new bodies set up to replace them had also been arrested by a Committee to Eliminate Counter-Revolutionaries (*Sufan weiyuan hui*). Before the purge the local Trades Union Federation had about 50 cadres and armed personnel but after the suppression of the 'Social Democratic Party' there was only one left, Qiu Weigui, who was described as a hunchback. From May to July, ten to 20 people were executed by firing squad almost every day; in one day alone 50 or 60 were killed. Little information was given about the reasons for the executions. Names, ages and places of birth were listed but no details were given of the crimes of which they had been accused. The conduct of the trials was brutal and oppressive and confessions were regularly obtained by force. Cadres were frightened to wear the red over-sleeves that identified them as Party officials as their names were written on the sleeves and they were anxious that someone might take revenge on them.

The information that Deng and his colleagues accumulated from their enquiries convinced them that Li Tianfu, who had been the chief instigator of the campaign to eliminate counter-revolutionaries, was not only not a genuine revolutionary but a dangerous individual who had to be dealt with accordingly. Deng concluded that the only way to stop this tide of executions from getting worse was to mobilise the local people in a campaign to demonstrate what Li was really like and then deal with him severely. As soon as he returned to Ruijin, Deng convened a meeting of activists from across the county in the name of the Eastern Jiangxi Special Committee. He did not chair the meeting in person but left that task to his wife Jin Weiyang, who had a reputation for effective propaganda and agitation work. She spoke on the significance of a campaign against counter-revolutionaries and the policies that should be adopted. Deng let them know his views on the campaign against the 'Social Democratic Party' and after he had finished there was complete silence; no-one dared speak for fear that they might be dragged off to be executed. Deng and Jin understood their misgivings and gradually persuaded people to express their doubts about the purge. The battle against the Guomindang encirclement campaign was the priority, Deng told them. Li Tianfu attended the meeting but Deng did not allow him to speak: he stopped ordering executions.

In September, after further investigations, Deng called another meeting of communist cadres from county, district and village level bodies. Deng and Jin, who chaired the half-day meeting, were sufficiently confident of their ground to launch a direct attack on the errors of the campaign against the 'Social Democratic Party' and blamed it on the local leadership for not having followed the correct Communist Party policy. Jin asked the assembled cadres whether there had really been any members of the 'Social Democratic Party' in Ruijin. They looked at each other, but none dared answer. Jin challenged them again and told them that there were, present at the meeting. Predictably there was stunned silence but she went on:

What sort of person is Li Tianfu? Is he a revolutionary or a counter-revolutionary? You should know that he has deliberately wrecked our work on suppressing counter-revolutionaries. Do not be afraid as there are senior cadres here who will stand behind you. He must be exposed for what he is.

There was an audible sigh of relief among the assembled cadres but the colour drained from the face of Li Tianfu, who was sitting on the podium.

Another meeting, the Third Congress of Ruijin County Workers, Peasants and Soldiers, representatives, was convened in the Guangdong Guildhall (*huiguan*) in Ruijin. Xie Zaiquan, the chairman of the Soviet Government, who had been in power when the most serious repression had taken place, was dismissed and replaced with Huang Zhengren. Deng Xiaoping, speaking on behalf of the CCP's East Jiangxi Special Committee, announced the arrest of Li Tianfu and his dismissal from the posts of county Party secretary and director of the Counter-revolutionary Suppression Committee. Li was then tried in public and sentenced to death.

Deng now acknowledged openly that he was Party secretary of Ruijin County and in that capacity he announced a number of key decisions: executions must stop immediately; no-one else who had been wrongly named as suspected 'Social Democratic Party' members should be arrested; all those who were classified as poor and middle peasants and had been imprisoned should be released and allowed to return to their original places of residence to 'continue to take part in the revolutionary struggle'. Landlords and rich peasants who could pay fines should be fined and then released and those who could not raise the fines could be released if someone stood bail for them. Over 300 people who had been imprisoned without trial and were in danger of being executed were released, to the general relief of the population of Ruijin. Some even spoke of him as a 'living Judge Bao' (*Bao gong zaishi*), referring to Bao Zheng (999–1062), a legendary official of the Song dynasty honoured in both history and fiction for his commitment to justice.

Even when allowance is made for the reverence that the authors of these recollections feel necessary to show for a senior leader's revolutionary past, Deng's actions appear decisive and positive. He swiftly assessed the problems in what was a complex and murky conflict, took soundings among people he trusted, and acted, at considerable personal risk, to bring an end to the unjust persecution of people who were wrongly accused of belonging to an anti-communist organisation. He used the CCP's bureaucratic structures and his own personal status in the Party to eliminate those who had been guilty of crimes, in both the political and legal senses, with of course the active participation of Jin Weiying. The justice that he administered, including the execution of Li Tianfu, was rough justice, but it proved popular in a community that had been terrorised for months. The leadership of the Jiangxi Soviet, primarily Mao Zedong and Zhu De, were well aware that the actions of people like Li Tianfu could make or break the Soviet, and the prevention of corruption and injustice became a high priority for the CCP. Deng began to acquire a reputation for insisting on the swift and fair administration of justice in his county, especially in cases of maladministration or corruption by communist officials including the allocation of confiscated agricultural land.[3]

RUIJIN: FIRST SOVIET CAPITAL

On 7 November 1931 a conference of CCP members met in the city of Ruijin and formally approved the establishment of the temporary Central Government of the Chinese Soviet Republic (the Jiangxi Soviet). Ruijin was chosen as the capital.

Although the Jiangxi Soviet is normally associated with Ruijin, in the early days of the Soviet, Ningdu had been the preferred location for the key organs of the Soviet, including the Central Bureau (*Zhonggong suqu zhongyangju*) and Central Revolutionary Committee (*Zhonghua suweiai zhongyang geming junshi weiyuan-hui*) and later the CCP's Jiangxi Provincial Committee and Provincial Soviet Government. Ningdu was, as its current local government insists, the cradle of the Jiangxi Soviet by virtue of a mutiny by officers of the Guomindang 26th Army based in Ningdu who transferred their allegiance to the Red Army in December 1931. The troops were incorporated into the Red Army as the 5th Corps and their actions were then immortalised as the Ningdu Uprising, the eightieth anniversary of which was celebrated with a variety show in Ningdu County on 13 December 2011.

As a staunch communist Deng was gratified that Ruijin, of which he was county Party secretary, had been selected as the headquarters of the new government, but as a pragmatic administrator he was concerned about the practical implications. Providing for the new political administration and furnishing supplies for the Red Army to defend it against the 'encirclement campaigns' of the Guomindang military would impose additional economic burdens on the city and its people. To achieve this, without risking the local population starving or freezing to death as winter deepened, Deng initiated a county-wide campaign to protect the harvest and develop the local economy.

Construction projects were launched in all the districts of Ruijin County: these included dams and irrigation canals which were essential for increasing agricultural production, but also small enterprises producing paper, wine and spirits, cigarettes, quilts, clothing, saltpetre for gunpowder and salt. To deal with the problems of distribution and labour the government organised consumer and grain cooperatives, mutual aid teams, women's ploughing teams and even 'fertiliser collection assault teams'. This military or quasi-military organisation not only provided the economic basis for the government of the Jiangxi Soviet and the Red Army but also kept the population busy and fed. Deng Xiaoping's practical economic work, an early intimation of his approach to reform in the 1980s, is barely mentioned in standard Western histories of the Jiangxi Soviet period.[4]

Although the Jiangxi Soviet had become the main physical base of the Chinese Communist Party by 1931, the Party's most powerful figures in the 'provisional central leadership' had remained in Shanghai, operating underground in territory controlled by the Guomindang, the 'white area' (*baiqu*). They were cut off from the military campaigns and rural administration of Mao Zedong, Zhu De and Deng Xiaoping and many of them still harboured dreams of an uprising that would lead to the capture of major cities. In March 1933 as a result of increased surveillance and arrests by the Guomindang police – the 'white terror' – and internal conflicts, the 'provisional Politburo' (*Zhonggong linshi zhongyang zhengzhiju*) recognised that their position in Shanghai was untenable and decided to move to the Jiangxi base. This was an acknowledgement of the political significance of the Jiangxi Soviet, but it resulted in serious conflict between the former Shanghai leadership and those who had constructed the Jiangxi Soviet. The outcome of this clash was a major political defeat for many CCP cadres in Jiangxi, including Deng Xiaoping. For Deng it was a serious setback in his revolutionary career, after the debacle of the Guangxi insurrections, although there were to be many more.

In the early 1930s the CCP was plagued by internal conflicts. Over-simplified accounts tend to reduce these to a dispute between the '28 Bolsheviks', led by Wang Ming and loyal to Moscow and the Comintern, and the group around Mao who were struggling to develop a distinctively Chinese strategy for revolution. In the confusion of the defeat of the CCP by the Guomindang in 1927, the withdrawal to the countryside and the bitter civil war that followed, it is not surprising that the reality was more complex than this. Some of the 28 Bolsheviks moved to Jiangxi. In the autumn of 1931 some retreated to Moscow from where they attempted to direct the Chinese revolution. Among this group was Wang Ming who was the *éminence grise* of the group, a devoted follower of Stalin and a severe critic of Mao Zedong.

Zhou Enlai also arrived in Jiangxi towards the end of December 1931 and he replaced Mao Zedong, who had been acting as secretary of the Central Bureau, depriving him of any involvement in military matters. At the Ningdu Conference, a meeting of the Central Bureau which probably took place in October 1932, there was deep disagreement on matters of military strategy and tactics, principally over whether an immediate national uprising was feasible or whether the top priority should be defence against the encirclement campaigns by the Guomindang forces. The circumstances of this conference remain obscure, largely because all the evidence points to Zhou Enlai being responsible for edging Mao out and, to soften the blow, suggesting that he be granted 'sick leave'. Since mainstream CCP history has painted Zhou as a constant supporter of Mao Zedong, this interpretation is somewhat inconvenient. Deng Xiaoping was broadly in favour of Mao's policies and with Mao's defeat lost a key supporter at the Party centre, but in the long term he gained a powerful patron.

DENG UNDER ATTACK

Members of the former Shanghai leadership refused to abandon their orthodox Marxism–Leninism as determined by the Moscow Comintern. Those who opposed them, many of whom were supporters of Mao Zedong, were frozen out. In February 1933 serious conflict broke out between the party leadership and a communist group led by Luo Ming who were over the border in Fujian in transit to Ruijin. Criticism of Luo Ming was similar to the criticisms later made of Mao, and both Luo and Mao argued strongly that the Party should take local conditions into account rather than follow a universal strategy for revolution.

This campaign against the 'Luo Ming line' in Fujian spilled over into Jiangxi in March 1933 where it was directed specifically at Deng Xiaoping, Mao Zetan (the younger of Mao Zedong's brothers), Xie Weijun (who had been an aide to Mao Zedong) and Gu Bai. On 12 March the Politburo in the Jiangxi Soviet wrote to Party members in the counties of Huichang, Xunwu and Anyuan, accusing the leadership there of making the same political errors as Luo Ming and in particular singling out Deng Xiaoping, who was then running the central county of Huichang, and censuring him for lack of courage in the face of the Guomindang encirclement campaigns. Towards the end of March the Central Soviet Politburo called a meeting of activists in the three counties and issued a resolution condemning Deng's approach as 'pessimistic and purely defensive'. The Politburo instructed Deng to write a self-criticism and demoted him to the post of head of propaganda for the Jiangxi Provincial Committee. Deng faced continuing criticism, demands for statements and self-criticisms, articles attacking him in the Party newspaper *Struggle* (*Douzheng*) and formal Party documents denouncing him. He defended himself as well as he could, setting out the military principles underlying the 'defensive line' that he had taken and argued strongly that it had been the correct approach. Nevertheless, he was mercilessly attacked as an opportunist and at a province-level Party meeting that lasted from 16 to 22 April 1933, his entire career came under scrutiny. At a meeting called by the Provisional Politburo of the CCP at the Workers' and Peasants' Red Army School on 4 May, Deng and his three colleagues were attacked as petty-bourgeois opponents of the Party's correct policies. They were removed from their posts, their revolvers were taken from them in public and they were ordered to re-educate themselves among the masses. Deng soon found himself carrying out a tour of inspection in the Nancun District of Le'an County in the centre of Jiangxi, well away from the centre of the Soviet's political activity in Ruijin.

This was a desperate setback to his position in the CCP after the progress he had made in Shanghai and Jiangxi, but it would not be the last and there are uncanny similarities between his experience in Ruijin and his later treatment during the Cultural Revolution, not least his rustication, which in 1969 was to take him once again to rural Jiangxi where he worked in a tractor factory. As the Cultural Revolution began to wane, Deng was allowed to travel to the areas that he had served in during the 1930s. He revisited Ruijin County and received a warm welcome as their 'old party secretary'.

In the longer term this serious reversal helped his political career. Although Deng may have been strictly accurate when he later argued that during the Jiangxi Soviet there was no such thing as a 'Mao faction', his opponents took the opinion that there was and he was criticised as being one of its leading lights and attacked for following the political line that Mao Zedong had espoused. When the CCP came to power after 1949, Mao recognised this loyalty and was one of Deng's patrons in his career in the new government.[5]

EXILE AND HUNGER IN NANCUN AND SEVEN LI VILLAGE

Nancun, where Deng had been effectively exiled after the April 1933 meeting, was on the borders of the area under the control of the Central Soviet and, as a front-line base, it was frequently under attack by Guomindang forces. Deng arrived there alone in June 1933 in the scorching heat of high summer. Under a blazing hot sun he carried his backpack to the offices of the Nancun District Committee where he was to live. When local officials came to see him they found him downcast but determined to fulfil his mission in spite of the humiliation that he had suffered. He was not disposed to brood and rapidly recovered his optimistic and positive approach, the ability to bounce back for which he was later to become renowned. He made no bones about the devastating criticism that he had faced for being a supporter of the 'Luo Ming line' but resolutely defended his position and refused to accept any kind words of consolation, reminding his new colleagues that revolution was never plain sailing.

He had been in Nancun less than two weeks when he was ordered by the Provisional Central Committee to return to Ningdu, where the Provincial Party Committee was then based (the government being in Ruijin), possibly because his supporters were concerned that there might be a mishap in such a dangerous border area. He was sent out to the poor and backward Seven Li Village (it was 7 *li* outside Ningdu) to work on a farm. This was in a bare and treeless mountain landscape where he spent long days clearing new land for cultivation. Although he was small in stature, he was tough and could manage the backbreaking work, but the long hours and insufficient food made life difficult. The area he had been sent to was a Hakka area, and the people and their culture were familiar to him from his upbringing in Sichuan.

FRIENDS AND COMRADES

These were difficult times for Deng, but he was sustained by his close and lasting friendship with Li Fuchun, Cai Chang (who had married Li in 1923) and Chen Yi. The four had all been in France and Deng had worked with Li and Cai in Paris. Li was now secretary of the Jiangxi Party Committee and political commissar for the Jiangxi Military District; Cai was head of both the women's and organisation departments; and Chen served as the officer commanding the Jiangxi Military District and head of the Jiangxi Party Committee's military department. All four had worked together in Jiangxi and the sympathy and support of this group of friends, all working in influential posts, meant that he was not as isolated as might have been expected after the campaign that was designed to exclude him from the centre of political decision making. Cai Chang was particularly concerned about

Deng's health and she sent a friend and colleague out to Seven Li Village, ostensibly to investigate the situation of women in the district but in fact to see how Deng was. Deng realised what was going on and sent a message back to say that he was not getting enough to eat for the heavy work that he had to do. When this report reached Cai Chang, she and Li Fuchun bought pork, garlic and hot peppers, cooked a meal and sent her colleague to bring him to her house in secret. This was the first proper meal that he had eaten for some time and Cai Chang was able to pass on a message that Li Fuchun had gone to Ruijin to make a routine report but was also going to repeat his request for a reconsideration of Deng's position. Li managed to secure support from Wang Jiaxiang, the director of the Red Army General Political Department (*Hongjun zong zhengzhibu*) and his colleagues, who were well aware of Deng's excellent track record in Moscow and Guangxi. They appreciated his military background, political judgement and organisational ability and agreed that in a time of war when there was a critical shortage of experienced cadres it made no sense at all to waste someone of Deng's calibre by making him do manual labour. Arms were twisted and strings pulled and, in the second half of 1933, Deng was transferred to the General Political Department.

On his way to take up this new post at Shazhouba in Ruijin, Deng called in at Ningdu where Li Fuchun, Cai Chang and Chen Yi again invited him for a meal and the four of them sat together reminiscing. They talked about Paris and the River Seine, Red Square in Moscow, the uprising in Guangxi and the prospects for his new job in Ruijin. Li Fuchun procured a horse from the Red Army Logistics Unit for Deng to travel the 100 kilometres to his new post and arranged for a journalist to guide him on his way. Personal relationships of this sort were the foundation for the comradeship of the communists during the revolutionary war. When they worked well they provided much needed support, but if they broke down it could spell disaster. In this case the bonds were particularly close and of long standing. A biography of Cai Chang (*Cai Chang zhuan*), cited in *Deng Xiaoping jishi*, refers to her wedding, or 'revolutionary partnership' (*geming banlü*), as the author prefers, to Li in 1923. When Li and Cai were tentatively embarking on a relationship, Deng was their invaluable 'chief of staff' and was chief witness at their 'wedding'. This consisted of the three of them sitting together, drinking a little wine and agreeing that this was a sufficient and appropriate marriage ceremony for revolutionaries. In this way the personal and the political were closely intertwined in the early history of the Chinese Communist Party and in the life of Deng Xiaoping.[6]

RED STAR

The news that he was to be transferred to the General Political Department of the Red Army as general secretary came as a blessed relief to the dejected and exhausted Deng Xiaoping, although to observers who did not know him he appeared as phlegmatic and unmoved as ever. When he discovered that this new post did not have many responsibilities he offered to edit *Red Star* (*Hongxing*), the official newspaper of the army's General Political Department, and this was accepted with alacrity by his chief, Wang Jiaxiang. *Red Star* had been published by the Red Army Political Department since 11 December 1931, the press being regarded as a vital instrument to inform and guide the troops, and when Deng took over as editor-in-chief he was able to draw on his experience in Paris with Li Fuchun of publishing *Youth* (*Shaonian*) and its successor. Before Deng's arrival, a newspaper usually of four sides, but sometimes only two (and occasionally as many as six) was run off every five days on an antique duplicator that had obviously seen better days. By issue 31, published on 3 March 1933, it had expanded to 32 pages and was mimeographed using the more advanced spirit duplicator or Roneo system.

As mentioned, Deng's skill with the duplicator in France had earned him the nickname of 'Doctor of Duplication' and when he took over *Red Star* he restored the original four-page format on the grounds that it could be revised more quickly and printed more frequently to reflect the changing military situation on the ground. Deng Xiaoping's handwriting was all over *Red Star*, metaphorically as he was responsible for many of the articles (although not always using his own name), but also literally because he often wrote headlines and other short pieces of text by hand on the stencils. The grand title of editor-in-chief concealed a low-level operation. While Deng was not a one-man-band, he had only a small staff to help him. He had to write many of the articles and edit the paper, and often took it to the printers himself. He was eventually provided with assistants, but more importantly created and cultivated a network of 'correspondents' in the Red Army and the Party who would write for him or at least provide notes that he could use as the basis for an article.

Few of Deng's articles written in these early years as a revolutionary have survived. Official collections of his writings have included little from before 1975 when he began to advocate the economic reforms for which he became celebrated. It is not possible to be definite about which pieces in *Red Star* were written by Deng: decades later when asked to identify his work for the paper he was unable or unwilling to do so. However, *Red Star* under his editorship does provide an insight into his priorities and his tactical thinking. It does not reveal much about his political philosophy, but philosophic reflection was never Deng's forte. Using a variety of journalistic formats and styles, including straightforward news reports (*xiaoxi baodao*) and regular columns such as 'Latest Dispatches' (*zuihou tongxun*), 'News of Victories' (*jiebao*), 'Dispatches from the Front' (*qianxian tongxun*) and 'Revolutionary War' (*geming zhandou*), he strove to convey to the troops, as quickly and efficiently as possible, information about the combat situation and the victories of the Red Army. In the issue of 4 November 1933, two full-length articles occupied most of the space available. They were 'Table of the Red Army's victorious campaigns in the Central Soviet District' (*Zhongyang suqu hongjun lici zhanyi shengli biao*) and 'Guerrila war in the Central Soviet District' (*Zhongyang suqu de youji zhanzheng*). Between them they presented a comprehensive analysis of the successes of the main force and local armed units of the Red Army from the spring until October 1933 and, if not written by Deng, they certainly reflected his political and military priorities.

Articles such as these were not intended to be objective news and analysis but rather wartime propaganda designed to boost morale and encourage further efforts by its readers. Because of the speed at which *Red Star* communicated with the troops, it became known as 'a great radio station' (*yijia da wuxian diantai*), which suggests that as far as his readers and superiors were concerned Deng was doing a good job.

The reporting of the Battle of Wenfang well illustrates why *Red Star* was compared to a radio station. The battle was led by the highly respected military and political leader Zhu De, who had also devised the strategy which involved close cooperation between the 1st and 19th Army groups (*juntuan*). The combined Red Army units claimed that they had wiped out over 4,000 Guomindang troops and captured at least 1,600 weapons while sustaining only light casualties in their own ranks. Since the start of the Guomindang's Fifth Encirclement Campaign the Red Army had been primarily engaged in passive positional warfare, sustaining heavy losses with each battle, and the change of tactics to an active drive to annihilate their opponents paid dividends. Immediately after the battle Deng persuaded nine of the key battlefield commanders to draft accounts of the fighting and crafted them into a vivid 'Dispatches from the Front' entitled 'Victory in the Battle of Wenfang' (*Wenfang zhandou de shengli*), which offered a provisional analysis of the battle and the lessons to be drawn from it. Deng used editorials and signed articles and created new regular columns such as 'Life of the Party' and 'Branch

Communiqué' to create, in *Red Star*, a forum where all aspects of the political, military, cultural and social life of the Red Army and the Jiangxi Soviet could be discussed. He saw the newspaper as a 'great mirror' to life in Jiangxi, but it was also a formidable guide to how people should behave and think. In specially created columns under the headings of 'Iron Hammer' and 'Self-Criticism', he attacked the bureaucratic approach, negativity, corruption, waste and self-preservation at all costs which were seen as the greatest dangers to the success of the Jiangxi Soviet. *Red Star* was unflinchingly loyal to the Party and the Red Army but Deng was not afraid to use it to deal with knotty problems and, where appropriate, to criticise cadres, however senior. The paper also functioned as the newsletter of the Red Army Club, acting as judge for competitions run by different units. Deng had come in from the cold and was now exactly where he wanted to be, right at the centre of military and political life in the Jiangxi Soviet.

Even Deng's finely honed propaganda skills, his undoubted devotion to the cause and his energy (provided that he was properly fed) could not alter the fact that in the long term the Jiangxi Soviet was unsustainable. It was faced with punishing assaults by the superior military forces at the disposal of the Guomindang, who were determined to encircle and put an end to what they considered to be the desperate last stand of their communist adversaries. Towards the end of September 1934 as Deng was working on issue 67 of *Red Star*, he received an order to cease publication immediately and pack his belongings. The General Political Department was withdrawing from Jiangxi and Deng and his *Red Star* office would be following. Some military and political cadres, including comrades and friends of Deng, remained behind in Jiangxi, but otherwise the whole of the Soviet apparatus was evacuating, taking with them everything that was possible to move, including the printing presses that belonged to the General Political Department. *Red Star* did not possess much equipment and Deng was able to pack his reference books, writing materials and unfinished drafts of articles without much difficulty. At dusk on 10 August 1934 Deng took part in the exodus from Jiangxi as the Communist Party and the Red Army broke through the encircled forces of the Guomindang and embarked on the Long March. The Jiangxi Soviet was no more and *Red Star* appeared to have perished with it.[7]

5

REVOLUTION AND RESISTANCE: THE LONG MARCH, YAN'AN AND THE TAIHANG MOUNTAINS (1934–45)

When I left Yudu on the Long March I grabbed a quilt weighing 4 *jin*. It accompanied me throughout the Long March and I still use it today.

There were several large liberated areas but the most concentrated was Shanxi-Hebei-Shandong-Henan (*Jin Ji Lu Yu*).[1]

The Long March was never conceived or planned as such. It began as a strategic withdrawal when the communist leadership in the Jiangxi Soviet finally concluded that they were no longer able to resist the Guomindang onslaught. The Guomindang saw this as a victory and a vindication of their determination to crush their erstwhile allies. As the Chinese Communist Party moved men, women and equipment out of Jiangxi with no clear idea of their ultimate fate, the future of their revolution hung in the balance. For Deng Xiaoping this retreat from the CCP's first attempt at establishing a government, which at first sight appeared a complete disaster, was to prove something of a blessing in disguise. In October

1934 he and his small *Red Star* team were evacuated from Jiangxi as part of the Red Badge column. In December, after a meeting of the Politburo held at Liping in Guizhou Province, he was readmitted to the inner circle of an influential section of the divided CCP leadership.

In spite of the difficult conditions, marching and fighting their way past the Guomindang troops, Deng and his small team still attempted to produce at least a version of *Red Star*. Zhao Fasheng, who worked with Deng to produce the stencils from which the paper was printed, recalled that they had two carrying poles on which they carried four metal boxes day and night as they marched behind the Central Military Committee. The boxes held all the equipment needed for printing *Red Star*, including a Bell Spirit mimeograph printer (although this was so heavy that by the time the column entered Hunan Province they had decided to get rid of it and buy a lighter hand-turned machine); boxes of duplicator ink; a supply of stencils and two steel boards to cut them on; steel-nib pens; and writing paper. When they stopped to establish a temporary base, the metal boxes became the office desks at which they worked, often while under attack by Guomindang bomber aircraft. During the first stage of the Long March the communists sustained heavy losses: some commentators later blamed a misguided strategy of escaping from the Guomindang blockade at all costs. Towards the end of November 1934, the Red Army succeeded in breaking through and crossed the Xiang River which divides Hunan Province, but they paid a terrible price. Of the original 80,000 people who had left Jiangxi only 30,000 remained and the Red Army was in a precarious situation.

THE ASCENDANCY OF MAO ZEDONG

On 12 December 1934, a meeting of prominent communist political and military leaders, including Qin Bangxian (Bo Gu), Zhou Enlai, Otto Braun (the Comintern's military adviser who was also known as Li De), Mao Zedong, Wang Jiaxiang and Zhang Wentian, was held at Tongdao, which lies in the southwest of Hunan close to the border with Guizhou Province. Qin and Braun, who were largely responsible for the strategy that had resulted in the disastrous losses, were in favour of continuing with the original plan to march north to link up with the CCP's 2nd and 6th Army Groups. Mao Zedong argued that, in the light of the relative strengths of the Red Army and the Guomindang forces, the march north should be abandoned and the remnants of the Red Army should move into

Guizhou where the nationalists were much weaker. Wang and Zhang supported Mao and so did Zhou Enlai: Zhou had originally agreed with Qin and Braun but was now aligning himself more with Mao whose influence had increased significantly. The majority agreed that the Red Army should attempt to take the town of Liping just over the border in Guizhou and this was achieved on 15 December.

Once the Red Army was established in Liping a meeting of the Politburo was convened on 17 December 1934, apparently at the suggestion of Zhou Enlai. Qin and Braun were still unwilling to abandon the original plan and wanted to move north and establish a new Soviet in western Hunan, but after an intense debate and, critically, Zhou Enlai's intervention on Mao's side, it was decided to establish the new base area on the Sichuan–Guizhou border: as the Liping Conference had been designated a meeting of the Politburo its resolution carried considerable force. Marshal Nie Rongzhen in his *Memoirs* (*Huiyi lu*), that are cited in *Deng Xiaoping jishi*, described this decision as a turning point in the strategy and the fortunes of the CCP. It was certainly a turning point for the leadership of the CCP or at least for this powerful section. Mao Zedong, who had been excluded from military decisions, had regained much of his political influence. Zhou Enlai, who had been to a large extent responsible for Mao's loss of power during the Jiangxi Soviet, was now firmly backing him. The stage was set for Deng Xiaoping, an old comrade of Zhou's from their time in France and a purged supporter of Mao during the Jiangxi Soviet, to make a political comeback.[2]

After the Liping Conference the Central Military Committee decided to reorganise its cadres and replenish its combat troops. Liu Bocheng, the legendary 'one-eyed dragon', who had been chief of staff of the 5th Army Group, was now elevated to the position of chief of the general staff, answerable directly to the Central Military Committee. Deng was transferred from *Red Star* (where he was replaced by Lu Dingyi) and became secretary-general (*mishu zhang*) of the Central Committee. The previous secretary-general had been Deng Yingchao, who was the wife of Zhou Enlai, and not related to Deng Xiaoping. She had contracted tuberculosis in August 1934 and asked to be relieved of the post as she was often seriously ill with a constant fever and was bringing up blood in her phlegm. There is no doubt about the seriousness of her illness, and she confirmed this in an article she wrote for the magazine *China Reconstructs* in 1984, although she did manage to continue on the Long March. Nevertheless, her resignation provided an opening for Mao and Zhou to bring Deng Xiaoping into the Central Committee. Deng's duties included recording the minutes of meetings, organising and archiving documentation, receiving and writing letters on behalf of the committee and 'drafting revolutionary orders'. The secretary-general was not considered a full political member of the Central Committee and these responsibilities were administrative rather than executive, insofar as it is possible to make a clear distinction between the two in such a small revolutionary organisation, but Deng had access to knowledge, power and influence.

ZUNYI CONFERENCE (JANUARY 1935)

The Central Committee decided to convene an enlarged meeting of the Politburo in the town of Zunyi, which lies in the north of Guizhou Province, from 15 to 17 January 1935. This meeting is far better known than those held at Tongdao and Liping and the political significance of changes in the leadership at the two earlier meetings has often been ignored. The Zunyi Conference was attended by Mao Zedong, Zhang Wentian, Zhou Enlai, Zhu De, Chen Yun, Qin Bangxian (Bo Gu) as full members and Wang Jiaxiang, Liu Shaoqi, Deng Fa and He Kequan as alternate members. Military representatives at this enlarged meeting included Liu Bocheng, Li Fuchun, Lin Biao, Nie Rongzhen, Peng Dehuai, Yang Shangkun and Li Zhuoran. Otto Braun the Comintern military adviser and his interpreter, Wu Xiuquan, also attended. Yang Shangkun (later president of the PRC) recalls Deng Xiaoping taking the minutes and Deng was also responsible for most of the preparatory work.

The Zunyi Conference had been called to make authoritative decisions about the future of the Long March and in particular its military strategy, and to analyse and criticise earlier mistakes. Zhang Wentian was given the task of drafting the resolution that would encapsulate the view of the Politburo: he based it on the majority view but especially on a long speech given by Mao Zedong. This became the official communiqué of the conference after it had reconvened in Zhaxi (now Weixin County) in Yunnan. The Zunyi resolution was a clear rejection of the serious mistakes made by Qin Bangxian and Otto Braun and an endorsement of the basic principles of Mao's position. The central leadership of the Party and army was reorganised and Mao was elected to the Politburo Standing Committee. The political authority of Qin Bangxian and Braun over the Red Army was rescinded, but Zhou Enlai and Zhu De remained in overall charge of military affairs. Zhang Wentian replaced Qin Bangxian in overall charge of the Party's Central Committee and Mao Zedong also became a member of the Political Committee of the Central Military Committee's Front Line Command which was headed by Zhu De. On 11

March 1935 a three-man committee consisting of Mao Zedong, Zhou Enlai and Wang Jiaxiang was established to coordinate the activities of the Red Army.

The Zunyi Conference of January 1935 is often depicted as the point at which Mao Zedong was elected as chairman of the Party. The evidence from Deng Xiaoping's perspective does not support this. Mao had become significantly more influential in military matters but he did not become 'chairman' at Zunyi. Indeed there was no party chairman and if it could be said that there was one overall leader, it would have been Zhang Wentian who was later referred to not as chairman but as general secretary (*zong shuji*) (he was not secretary-general [*mishuzhang*] which was Deng's position). Not only was there no position of 'chairman', but also it is not clear to what extent the terms 'Politburo' and 'Central Committee' were current in the early 1930s or whether they have been superimposed retrospectively on the meetings. Military organisation and strategy took priority over political considerations at that critical time. In practice Mao was able to exercise more authority, especially on matters of political principle, and, irrespective of his precise title, had indisputably begun to rise in the party hierarchy at the expense of the 28 Bolsheviks. Deng Xiaoping benefited from this political shift: after the Zunyi Conference, he regarded himself as part of the central leadership of the CCP with Mao at its centre, but that cannot be documented in terms of formal political appointments. Deng worked constantly with the political leaders – Mao, Zhou and Zhang Wentian – often waiting up with them till late at night for telegraph messages from various military units before decisions could be made on the Red Army's next move.

The section of the CCP in which Mao was beginning to emerge as leader was not the only communist group active after the collapse of the Jiangxi Soviet. In June 1935 Mao's group, now designated the 1st Front Army, met the 4th Front Army at Lianghekou in Sichuan's Yajiang County. The 4th Front Army was a rival communist force commanded by Zhang Guotao, which had marched into Sichuan. Zhang was in favour of consolidating the two armies to establish a new base in Sichuan but Mao wanted to use their combined forces to move northwards and create a base on the borders of the provinces of Sichuan, Shaanxi and Gansu.

Deng Xiaoping was transferred to the 1st Front Army as head of its propaganda department. This was in effect a continuation of his previous work on *Red Star* and it was part of the CCP's mission that he took extremely seriously. He was remembered as a tireless propagandist, insisting that his team prepare posters and slogans whenever the army paused for an overnight stop, even though his staff wanted to heat water to wash their tired feet and sleep after their evening meal. The

Long March took Deng and his comrades a whole year from October 1934 to October 1935 and they had to cross difficult and dangerous terrain. It was not until 19 October 1935 that the 1st Front Army reached its final objective, Wuqi in the north of Shaanxi Province, a town that was to become the industrial centre of the Red Army's new Shaanxi-Gansu-Ningxia (*Shaan-Gan-Ning*) base which eventually established its capital at Yan'an.

MARSHAL LUO RONGHUAN

Deng Xiaoping liked to emphasise his military background, and his attachment to the army was never in doubt. During the Jiangxi Soviet period and the Long March his closest friend and confidant was Luo Ronghuan. Luo had supported Mao Zedong's strategic position in Jiangxi and, like Deng, had been condemned for his views. Deng and Luo completed the 25,000 *li* Long March together and throughout the trek were able to support each other. They were great friends despite having very different personalities. Deng was a great talker and liked nothing better than to laugh and joke, whereas Luo was the strong, silent type; this difference did not stop them from talking about everything under the sun. Luo's wife, Lin Yueqin, related that during the Long March they would often amuse themselves by joking and bantering. Deng insisted that Sichuan hot peppers were the best food whereas Luo complained that they made him dribble; Deng argued that *huiguo rou*, 'twice-cooked pork', from Sichuan was the only one worth eating while Luo supported the *huiguo rou* from his native Hunan. They had very little if anything to eat during the Long March so these were just food fantasies. When they ran out of cigarettes they would pretend to smoke leaves. The jokes and repartee relieved the tedium, the tiredness and the hunger of the seemingly unending trek and cemented a lasting personal and political friendship.

Deng and Luo both served as political commissars during the 1946–9 civil war and after the establishment of the People's Republic of China they were both long-term residents of Beijing and senior figures in the new administration. While Deng became general secretary of the CCP, Luo was chief of staff of the PLA and a full member of the Politburo. They remained close friends and their families, including their children, were also very close. After 1949, when Deng came back to Beijing after his assignment in the south-west, he was allocated a rather superior house to live in: he turned it down and asked that it be offered instead to Luo, who was living in cramped quarters and was also in poor health. When Luo was promoted to the rank of marshal of the PLA in 1955, Deng and his wife Zhuo Lin were invited to the celebratory banquet and when Luo died in 1963 at the age of only 61, the whole Deng family attended his funeral.[3]

INTO THE TAIHANG MOUNTAINS

In tracing the account of Deng's rise through the communist military and political hierarchy in the late 1930s and the 1940s, it is impossible to avoid the grand and fluctuating titles that he acquired and the names of the party and army bodies in which he served. This is not made any easier by the fact that after the full-scale Japanese invasion of China in July 1937, even the designations of communist military formations were changed to demonstrate unity between communists and nationalists during the Second United Front. Most significantly, units of the Chinese Communist Party's Red Army were rebadged as either the Eighth Route Army, which operated in the north-west of China (and of which Deng Xiaoping was a member), or the New Fourth Army which was active to the south of the Yangzi River.

The communist forces retained control over Yan'an and their main Shaanxi-Gansu-Ningxia base area until they were obliged to withdraw in 1947 in the early phase of the civil war against the Guomindang. The other major base area in the north-west, the Shanxi-Chahar-Hebei (Jin-Cha-Ji) Border Region, was inaugurated in Hebei Province's Fuping County in January 1938; a military district of the same name had existed there since 7 November 1937.[4]

Japan's occupation of China Proper – it had already controlled Manchuria since 1931 and Taiwan from 1895 – is generally dated from the Marco Polo Bridge Incident (*Lugouqiao shijian*) of 7 July 1937. The communist base areas were in the front line of national defence and they had to be defended and expanded wherever possible. The relative contribution of the communists and nationalists to resistance and defence against the Japanese invaders has remained controversial; both sides claimed to have been the most patriotic. Chiang Kai-shek's views on the communists, at the time theoretically in an alliance with his Guomindang, were expressed forcefully in a speech that he made in 1941:

> You think it is important that I have kept the Japanese from expanding during these years [. . .] I tell you it is more important that I have kept the Communists from spreading. The Japanese are a disease of the skin; the Communists are a

disease of the heart. They say they wish to support me, but secretly all they want is to overthrow me.[5]

This striking analogy has frequently been resurrected to reinforce the argument that Generalissimo Chiang sat out the war in Chongqing, waiting for others to defeat the Japanese while he concentrated his resources on containing the communists. What is indisputable is that the communists organised the independent defence of their base areas and, using both positional and guerrilla tactics, were in many cases successful in resisting further Japanese military advances. More importantly in the long run, in the areas that they controlled, the CCP mobilised the population against the occupation, and the political credibility that they accrued from this mobilisation played a crucial role in their ability to win the 1946–9 civil war and establish the People's Republic of China.

In January 1937 Deng Xiaoping became director of the Political Department of the 1st Army Group in the Eighth Route Army. His new role was in some ways a continuation of his propaganda work, but he now focused on political training for the army and the Political Department ran courses on military and political training for cadres. Deng also gave lectures on politics and political economy and was noted for his simple and regular lifestyle and as a stickler for punctuality. He had a reputation for being exacting with his men and did not hesitate to enforce strict military discipline in the areas under his control, even approving sentences of death when he deemed it necessary, as in the case of a soldier found guilty of rape.

In July 1937 he was transferred to the headquarters of the Red Army (the name Eighth Route Army was not used until 25 August 1937), which had moved earlier that year from Bao'an to Yan'an, and became deputy director of the Political Department. Although he was not a full member of the delegation that went to Nanjing after the Japanese invasion to discuss cooperation with the Guomindang to resist the Japanese, he travelled with the CCP delegates, Zhou Enlai, Zhu De and Ye Jianying, providing administrative support. It was Deng who prepared the draft of the document on cooperation that led to the establishment of the Second United Front and, on paper at least, led to the incorporation of the communist forces into a single national army with the Guomindang military units. The names Eighth Route Army and New Fourth Army for the communist units were now in use both formally and informally.

Yan'an is always thought of as the headquarters of the CCP after the Long March, but many of the significant communist military units were based elsewhere.

A meeting between senior officers of the Eighth Route Army and representatives of the Central Committee's Northern Bureau took place in Taiyuan, the provincial capital of Shanxi, on 21 September 1937, to discuss the situation of the communists in northern China. Two days later, following decisions made in Taiyuan, Zhu De, the commander-in-chief of the Eighth Route Army established his general headquarters in Wutai County to the north-east of Taiyuan while Deng Xiaoping set up the Political Department in Dongru village, which now lies within the city boundaries of Taiyuan.

Shanxi Province was an obvious target for the Japanese military, primarily because of its extensive coal resources and also because the local warlord, Yan Xishan, had constructed a major arsenal that produced a wide range of weaponry from small arms to heavy artillery pieces. In September 1937 units of the Imperial Japanese Army stationed in Chahar (now incorporated into Inner Mongolia) were deployed to attack the Taiyuan region. The Taiyuan campaign which lasted from 1 September to 9 November is also remembered by the names of individual battles, notably those at Pingxingguan (Eighth Route Army, 25 September) and Xinkou (Guomindang National Revolutionary Army, September–November). The conflict in Shanxi, and in particular the battle of Xinkou, was marked by genuine cooperation between the forces of the CCP, the Guomindang and the local warlord Yan Xishan, but Chinese defences were inadequate against Japanese tanks. By early November the Taiyuan region had fallen and the Taiyuan Arsenal and Shanxi's coal were in the hands of the Japanese, although guerrilla units of the Eighth Route Army continually harried them.

One concrete example of Deng's work with the Eighth Route Army Political Department was a mission that he undertook in October 1937 to Xiaoyi County in western Shanxi. His instructions were to develop new communist bases, including some behind enemy lines, and to improve skills in guerrilla warfare against the Japanese. Deng spoke at village meetings, encouraged local people to join the Eighth Route Army and looked for ways of securing funding and food for the troops as well as strengthening the CCP's presence and authority in the district. One of his key objectives was to cement an alliance with the Shanxi League of Sacrifice for National Salvation (*Shanxi xisheng jiuguo tongmenghui*), an influential local group that was associated with the Guomindang. This task became even more urgent when news of a renewed Japanese push into Shanxi reached him.

POLITICAL COMMISSAR OF 129TH DIVISION, EIGHTH ROUTE ARMY (1938)

In January 1938, one year after Deng had moved to the Political Department, he was transferred again, this time to an appointment as political commissar of the 129th Division of the Eighth Route Army, which was based in the Taihang Mountains and was commanded by Liu Bocheng. The news was given to the two men on 2 January by Peng Dehuai, the CCP's most senior officer in the resistance to the Japanese advance into Shanxi. The official telegram confirming the appointment arrived on 5 January, and the following day Deng's new role was announced publicly. The arrangement suited both Deng and Liu well. Liu was also from Sichuan, although he was 12 years older than Deng and they had not known each other in their home province, but they established a close working relationship as the senior military and political officers of the division. This close relationship was to continue into the People's Republic and when Liu became one of ten Marshals of the PLA in 1955, he was an important link between Deng and the military elite.

Deng arrived at the 129th Divisional Headquarters on 18 January 1938 to take up his new post. Liu Bocheng, together with Zhu De and Peng Dehuai, had been attending a high-level meeting in Luoyang with Chiang Kai-shek and he returned to his command on 27 January. Deng lived in the headquarters building close to Liu's accommodation and it rapidly became clear that they operated as a team. If Liu were not available Deng could issue orders in his stead.

When Deng's appointment as political commissar had been formally announced, he and Peng Zhen, who represented the CCP Central Committee's Northern Bureau in the Shanxi-Chahar-Hebei (Jin-Cha-Ji) base area, went to Liu Shaoqi's quarters. Liu had been secretary of the Northern Bureau and was increasingly influential in the Central Commitee and Politburo. Deng and Peng wanted to discuss policy on the United Front that was imposing restrictions on the activities of the Eighth Route Army. They found a willing listener in Liu Shaoqi, but he was reluctant to re-ignite the vicious internal conflict with the 28 Bolsheviks in which he had been personally attacked by Wang Ming. Wang had recently returned to Yan'an after six years in Moscow and, although he was treated with respect as a representative of the Comintern, he was widely regarded as hopelessly out of touch. He insisted that the CCP should continue to support the Guomindang and lost any influence that he still had in the Party as Mao Zedong's star rose.

After hearing Liu's reluctance to air these issues publicly, Deng sought out Ren Bishi, a member of the Central Committee and director of the Political Department of the Eighth Route Army (as it became on 25 August), who backed him, and in the evening Liu and Peng went back to Deng's quarters to continue their discussions.

Peng Zhen sat cross-legged on the *kang* (the raised platform in northern Chinese houses under which is heated underneath and on which bedding is laid out at night) in Deng's quarters and argued that the CCP could not rely on the Guomindang. The nationalists had been forced to take a stand against the Japanese but had failed to alter their political approach and had even promoted some individuals who were sympathetic to Japan. Peng was particularly critical of the nationalist opposition to the idea of mass resistance against the Japanese which was one of the CCP's main strategies. Deng Xiaoping cited a speech that Mao Zedong had made to Party activists in Luochuan in which he insisted that the CCP had to maintain a Marxist position: they should not forget the differing interests and approaches of the different social classes and must ensure that the CCP was taking the lead and resisting the temptation of being sucked into the politics of the GMD. Deng stubbed out his cigarette, shook his right arm to emphasise his point and insisted that it was the responsibility of the CCP to take the lead and put pressure on the Guomindang to do the right thing. The Communist Party could not, he said, keep leaving the responsibility to others (*dang ren bu rang*) and he kept repeating this classical Chinese phrase from the Confucian *Analects*. If they did not take responsibility they would never be able to develop independent guerrilla warfare behind enemy lines and would never be able to create or consolidate their base areas. Peng Zhen repeated the literary allusion with great pleasure and agreed with Deng that they had to take the lead for the sake of the Chinese people and the Chinese state, the very existence of which was threatened by the Japanese occupation forces.

They had spoken to Liu Shaoqi, who did not disagree with them, and Ren Bishi, who was supportive. As far as Deng was concerned this was as near as possible to a consensus. If Chiang Kai-shek was making plans for going it alone after the eventual defeat of the Japanese, so were the communist political and military leadership in Shanxi.

The men with whom Deng was discussing such life-and-death matters in 1938 – Liu Shaoqi, Peng Dehuai, Peng Zhen, and Liu Bocheng – were all political and military leaders of the Chinese Communist Party in north-western China. Their immediate concerns at that time were resisting the Japanese invasion and the impossibility of cooperation with the Guomindang. Twenty years later they would all hold senior positions in the People's Republic of China and, moreover, they would all eventually find themselves on the same side as Deng Xiaoping in the ideological battles with Mao Zedong that dominated the late 1950s and the 1960s. All were purged during the Cultural Revolution, if not earlier. Their relationships in the turbulent waters of Chinese politics in the second half of the twentieth century were underpinned by powerful political and personal bonds that had been forged in what they regarded as a patriotic and revolutionary war, a war for the very existence of China.

The 129th Division rapidly expanded its guerrilla activities, reasoning that this did not contravene directives from the CCP Central Committee and the Eighth Route Army headquarters. Between 28 January and 17 February 1938 the division created a Guerrilla Brigade, a Guerrilla Detachment, a Forward Detachment and an Independent Guerrilla Brigade. These were formed mainly from existing units of the 129th Division, but all included cadres from the Divisional Instructor Regiment (*shi jiaodaotuan*) who were considered to be the core of each of the new guerrilla formations. The Instructor Regiment cadres were trained to be aware of the political and ideological reasons for the expansion of guerrilla warfare at that time and could be relied on to spread this consciousness among the rest of the troops. A series of meetings was also organised by Divisional Headquarters and the Provincial Communist Party Committee to motivate the troops as they fanned out to occupy positions in the Taihang Mountains that were easy to defend. Their mission was to extend the Eighth Route Army's remit in territory close to the Japanese bases and establish local governments that would back the communists, defending and extending the influence of the Shanxi-Hebei-Henan (Jin-Ji-Yu) Border Region administration.[6]

To drive home to the rank-and-file soldiers the necessity for urgency, five consecutive military administrative conferences were convened at the divisional level by Liu Bocheng, the commanding officer, and Deng Xiaoping, as political commissar. Deng's authority and experience were invaluable and he wrote a paper entitled 'Political work to motivate new military units and new troops' (*Dongyuan xin jun ji xin bing de zhengzhi gongzuo*). This document was used as the basis for talks that Deng gave at the meetings and was later published in *Frontline* (*Qianxian*), the journal of the General Political Department of the Eighth Route Army, in the issue of 2 December 1938. An extract reads:

> It is necessary to exert the greatest effort and use all possible means to motivate the broad masses of the people to join the army, to complement existing

formations, organise new units and build up and extend the armed strength of the nation to support a long hard struggle.

In the Taihang Mountains, Deng Xiaoping was putting his ideas into practice. He may not have been a soldier in the strictest sense of leading troops into combat, but he had considerable influence on the organisation and deployment of military units in consultation with his divisional commander-in-chief, Liu Bocheng.

When senior cadres of the 129th Division met on 4 and 5 February 1938, Deng passed on decisions taken by the CCP Politburo at their December meeting, and at meetings of the Northern Bureau. This illustrates the basis of Deng's authority in the 129th Division: he was the conduit for political decisions taken at the highest level in the CCP, and his detailed instructions on countering the Japanese advance and building communist bases had the authority of the Central Committee. Liu Bocheng spoke after Deng on organisational and tactical matters.

Peng Zhen and Li Xuefeng were also briefing communist-controlled local government organisations on the need for independent resistance against the Japanese. In the middle of March, Deng Xiaoping, together with Ni Zhiliang, the officer commanding communist forces in the region, supported Li Xuefeng's work in creating the Taihang base area, by bringing together officials from ten counties to discuss resistance and defence strategies. This included the creation of guerrilla units, whose members would be released from work in the fields and factories, and also a number of part-time self-defence units (*ziweidui*).

ON THE FRONT LINE IN XINGTAI COUNTY (1938–9)

Early in April 1938 the Imperial Japanese Army laid siege to the Taihang base area and the 129th Division was deployed as part of a joint defence force. In May and June Deng spent 49 days in the mountain village of Daogoucun in Xingtai County, to the east of the Taihang range, where the 129th Division had taken up its position. In a tiny building with hardly enough room to swing a cat, the villagers of Daogoucun have preserved a wooden table and bench where Deng sat when he arrived with the 129th Division on 5 May 1938 in the room that was to be his home and his office for over seven weeks until 23 June; it was here that he studied documents on the situation in Daogoucun and compiled his own reports. The following day, the head of the local Anti-Japanese County Government, Hu Zhen, and several of his colleagues hurried from the government headquarters to greet them, looking tired and travel-worn. Hu Zhen was a local man who had joined the CCP in 1927 and had been a student at the Sun Yat-sen Military Academy in Xi'an. Deng was then in charge of the academy's political department so they knew each other well. Hu had returned to his home village after the defeat of an uprising in Weihua in Shaanxi Province in March 1928. Later he had organised guerrilla bands in the mountains, and the Anti-Japanese County Government that he now headed had emerged from these irregular forces. Hu was delighted to see his old officer and to hear his thick Sichuan accent, especially when he greeted his former student, saying, 'You worried us, Hu Zhen. We had no idea what had happened to you after the insurrection. I thought you had had it and all the time you were back in your own village with your parents.' Hu told Deng that his Anti-Japanese County Government had only been in place for less than six months; things were not going too well and they had not really made the necessary breakthrough. Deng responded that this was precisely why the Party centre had sent him and they would work together to establish an effective base in Xingtai County.

The important market town of Xingtai on the edge of the Taihang Mountains was close to the Beiping-Hankou (Ping-Han) Railway. It was on the front line in the CCP's resistance to the Japanese military, which had occupied the town in October 1937 and then used it as a base for mopping-up operations (*saodang*), striking westwards into the mountains and endangering the local population. The Anti-Japanese County Government had made some progress, but local Chinese forces hostile to the communists were making life difficult. Deng and Liu Bocheng worked to root out these local groups that they considered no better than bandits or renegades. By 13 May they were in a position to push back the Japanese from the railway; this also extended the influence of the base area and resulted in the recruitment of over 200 local people.

Deng and Liu were also developing a cadre of supporters to build the Xingtai County Committee (also known as the Eighth Route Army Work Corps [*Balujun gongzuotuan*], a revealing indication of the overlap of military and political organisation and authority). A key role was played by a training course for anti-Japanese activists at their headquarters in Daogoucun. Deng gave political lectures, marrying his understanding of local conditions with instructions from the Party centre, of which he was the custodian and transmitter. The participants would act as the Party's shock troops in the region and Deng, who had spent his evenings getting to know the villagers, ensured that he was not seen as an aloof military commander. The officers and men of the Eighth Route Army constantly had to demonstrate that they did not behave like the troops of the Japanese or even the

Guomindang. Decades later, local people in the Taihang Mountains would come forward with anecdotes about Deng Xiaoping: carrying firewood just like the peasants; preventing his bodyguards from pushing aside children who were blocking his progress; or insisting on sending a sick boy to hospital. If this was a public relations exercise it was an effective one.

Although the Japanese had withdrawn in May 1938, their 'mopping-up operations' continued to harry the communist forces, and the Eighth Route Army units frequently moved their headquarters, sometimes even several times a day, to evade the Japanese or local 'bandits'. By the spring of 1939 there was a stalemate and Deng was with a company of the 17th Regiment preparing to go behind enemy lines. He took overall responsibility for liaison, discipline and morale, and especially for relations with the local people. As political commissar he naturally directed the political work to ensure that the people of Xingtai were not swayed by anti-communist propaganda put out by the Japanese or collaborators. Stories spread by anti-communist elements had frightened many of the local people so much that many had fled to the hills.[7]

As the new year of 1939 dawned, the headquarters of the 129th Division, necessarily mobile to avoid the Japanese, was in Zhangjiazhuang in the south of Hebei Province. Liu Bocheng and Deng Xiaoping were defending their base against relentless Japanese attacks while negotiating on strategy and tactics for the resistance with representatives of their unenthusiastic Guomindang coalition partners. The scale of these operations, which continued until July, demanded a response from Liu and Deng and they decided to reorganise their forces again. A concentrated main force would be supported by small mobile units for 'dispersed and protracted guerrilla warfare' with the aim of tiring out the enemy and reducing their capacity for attack. Although Deng was officially the political commissar of the 129th Division, he also 'either commanded troops in operations or marched. He was busy with military affairs.' Accounts of the 129th Division during this phase of the resistance to Japanese occupation usually refer to decisions as having been made jointly by Liu Bocheng and Deng Xiaoping, usually after discussions between the two. Under fire it was difficult to separate military and political authority and this experience proved invaluable to Deng and provided him with additional credibility in his subsequent political career.

Towards the end of August 1939, Deng was summoned to Yan'an to attend an enlarged meeting of the Politburo. He had been to Yan'an twice during the Anti-Japanese War, first in December 1937 and then for the Politburo meeting in September 1938 that put an end to the Wang Ming line and enhanced Mao

Zedong's position. He later visited in June 1945 to attend the first Plenary Session of the Seventh Central Committee. These four visits to Yan'an enhanced his career in the CCP. He acknowledged Mao's political and ideological leadership, still by no means universally accepted, and undertook new responsibilities within the Party. While in Yan'an in August 1939, he stayed with Deng Fa, an old friend who lived in one of the cave dwellings used by the CCP leadership; this friendship led to an important change in his personal circumstances.[8]

ZHUO LIN

As with all the revolutionaries of twentieth-century China it is impossible to disentangle Deng's personal and political life. He had been married twice and had met his first wife, Zhang Xiyuan, at Sun Yat-sen University in Moscow. The wedding reception at a Sichuan restaurant on Guangxi Road in Shanghai had been attended by over 30 people including Zhou Enlai and his wife Deng Yingchao and the couple lived with the Zhous for six months after the wedding; Deng Yingchao recalled constant talking and laughter. The young and pretty Zhang Xiyuan died in January 1930. Deng had been ordered to organise the Guangxi uprising and was not even present at the funeral. Her remains were eventually interred in the Martyrs Memorial Cemetery (now the Longhua Revolutionary Cemetery) in Shanghai in 1969.

Jin Weiying, who became his second wife in the Jiangxi Soviet, divorced him after his political disgrace. She became ill on the Long March and died in Moscow in 1938. Deng blamed the political conflicts for their separation and retained some affection for her memory. When he visited the former Shanxi bases in December 1972, he reminded local people that Jin had been their County Party secretary. Deng was not a sentimental man, but he did not forget his first two wives or treat their existence as a political inconvenience and always ensured that their graves were cared for.

While Deng was in Yan'an in the autumn of 1939, he was introduced by Deng Fa and others to Zhuo Lin and she became his third wife. They remained married until the end of Deng's life and she was the mother of his five children. Zhuo Lin survived her husband and died in Beijing on 29 July 2009 at the age of 93. She was born Pu Qiongying in April 1916 in Xuanwei County in the south-western province of Yunnan. The area is well known as the home of Xuanwei ham and her father, Pu Zaiting, was a leading businessman, famed as the local 'ham king'. Her family supported her educational aspirations and in 1932 she passed the examination for the Beiping No. 1 Girls' Middle School. In common with many educated young Chinese she joined patriotic associations and demonstrated against Japanese incursions. In 1937, after the Japanese invasion of China Proper, she made her way to Yan'an. She studied at the North Shaanxi College and after graduation worked in the college library. She joined the Chinese Communist Party in 1938 and was trained for undercover work behind enemy lines. For security reasons she took the name Zhuo Lin.

Deng had travelled to Yan'an from the Taihang Mountains to take part in the CCP's Seventh National Congress. The congress was postponed (eventually convening in April 1945) and Deng decided that he was needed back at the front. He was unmarried and Party colleagues, including Deng Fa, who was head of the Party School, decided that he needed help. There was no shortage of suitable young women in Yan'an: the patriotic reputation of the communist headquarters was attracting bright and concerned young students from all over China and many enrolled in North Shaanxi College and the Women's College. Zhuo Lin was young but considered acceptable and she had already graduated from North Shaanxi College. She didn't know Deng at all but she was aware of his reputation as a Red Army veteran and a leading front-line cadre, although she did not know what his responsibilities really were. What brought them together was a shared commitment to China's revolution.

Late one afternoon in early September 1939 tables were set out in front of the cave house in Yan'an in which Mao Zedong lived, and the Central Committee organised a simple wedding ceremony for two couples, Deng Xiaoping and Zhuo Lin and Kong Yuan and Xu Ming. Many senior party leaders were present, including Mao and his wife Jiang Qing, Zhang Wentian and his wife Liu Ying, Bo Gu, Liu Shaoqi, Li Fuchun and his wife Cai Chang and the Central Committee Secretary-General Wang Shoudao. Zhou Enlai, Deng Xiaoping's honorary 'elder brother', was in the Soviet Union to be treated for injuries sustained when he had fallen from a horse. There was no expensive banquet but the celebrations were noisy and cheerful and the guests tucked into rice and peppers, with the addition of a little chicken. Kong Yuan drank too much and was seriously scolded by his wife for being drunk. Deng drank glass after glass when the toasts were being made with no apparent effect. Liu Ying who knew him well could not understand this but her husband, Zhang Wentian, explained that Deng was drinking plain boiled water that his comrades had substituted, knowing full well that he had no head for alcohol. Deng Xiaoping may have been a mere divisional political commissar, but it was an exalted company of CCP leaders that attended the wedding, even though all were dressed in patched Eighth Route Army uniforms made of homespun cloth.

The celebrations were soon over and within a few days the 23-year-old Zhuo Lin accompanied her new husband, who was 12 years her senior, to the front line in the Taihang Mountains. He immediately threw himself into his work. Zhuo Lin's role was office-based, but she also went with him during marches and emergency manoeuvres that were necessary to avoid the Japanese mopping-up operations. The Taihang region came under sustained attack by the Japanese from December 1939 and Zhuo Lin was by Deng's side as she had been reassigned to the secretarial section of the 129th Division. They spent five difficult years together in the Taihang Mountains. They had three children, but it was impossible to bring them up safely in the mountains so she reluctantly agreed to send them to her family home in Yunnan. Zhuo Lin did not see her children again until 1945 when Deng's unit was moved to Wu'an County in the south-west of Hebei and she then made up for lost time by devoting herself to looking after them and creating a family home. Deng was busier than ever with weighty military and political matters and as the war against Japan turned inexorably into another civil war with the Guomindang, the army moved and the family went with it. From Wu'an they went to Handan, the nearby prefectural city, then to Luoyang, Shanghai and finally to Chongqing in Deng's home province of Sichuan. In Chongqing the family increased by three – a daughter, a son and Deng Xiaoping's stepmother. Zhuo Lin continued to concentrate on educating the children and running the home as Deng's responsibilities increased. Zhuo Lin and the family eventually followed him to Beijing when he joined the central government in 1952 and for many years they enjoyed a settled and comfortable life. Deng Xiaoping rarely spoke of his family life and did not approve of it being described in print, even in well-intentioned articles that portrayed the couple's union as a model marriage. It was extremely important to him.[9]

'LETTING THE MONKEY SEE YOU KILL THE CHICKEN': 'FRICTION' WITH THE GUOMINDANG (1939)

The Japanese may have been the main enemy during the war of resistance against Japan (*Kang Ri zhanzheng*) but the CCP was also preoccupied with plots, real or imaginary, by diehard anti-communist military commanders, some of whom were accused of collaborating with the Japanese. This was 'fighting the tiger at the front door and resisting the wolf at the back' (*qianmen da hu, hou men ju lang*). A crucial element of the CCP's strategy was to win over military units loyal to the Guomindang as well as unaligned militias. If they changed sides they were welcomed with open arms; if they refused they could be dealt with ruthlessly.

In 1938 Chiang Kai-shek had called for the CCP to recover territory it had lost, but he had also issued instructions to some of his anti-communist generals, including Zhu Huaibing and Lu Zhonglin, to prepare for attacks on the communist bases. The CCP Central Committee had addressed this tricky issue in a document entitled 'Directive on Problems of Friction in Huabei' issued on 10 February 1939. The understated 'friction' was conflict, often costly in lives, between communist and nationalist military units, which were in theory allies. During a campaign for ideological education and rectification within the Eighth Route Army, Deng spelled out the main differences between the two sides, reminding the cadres and troops that they were engaged in a class war, not just a national patriotic struggle. Wealthy landlords, he argued, could hardly be expected to respond to the Japanese in the same way as the poorer farmers. It was the task of the Eighth Route Army to prevent the landlords from capitulating to the enemy.

By March 1939 Yan Xishan, the warlord of Shanxi Province, who was aligned with but not controlled by the Guomindang, was becoming alarmed by the CCP mass organisations. Mass mobilisation was a fundamental part of the long-term strategy of the CCP but it was anathema to the nationalists. Activity against the communist base areas was intensified and in June 1939 units of Guomindang troops under Zhang Yinwu attacked the Eighth Route Army in central Hebei, killing over 400 officers and soldiers. Zhang's troops were wiped out by communist units, a tactic that was described as 'shooting the bird that sticks its neck out' and 'letting the monkey see you kill the chicken' (*qiangda chutou niao, shaji gei hou kan*). Dealing with the enemy ruthlessly would deter others. If this tactic was not initiated by Deng Xiaoping it reflected his approach.

In March 1940 two undoubtedly 'diehard' divisions of nationalist troops attacked the communist bases. Deng took personal command and once again acted as a military commander rather than just as a political commissar. Orders issued in Deng's name between 5 and 9 March 1940 give precise instructions on the deployment of military units and location of attacks. These were purely military in nature, but his political sensitivity and intelligence and his ability to use known conflicts to attack the most 'diehard' units, while giving others the opportunity to surrender, contributed significantly to victory in this campaign.[10]

THE HUNDRED REGIMENTS CAMPAIGN: A TURNING POINT IN THE WAR WITH JAPAN (1940)

In the spring of 1940 a military team led by Nie Rongzhen, the political commissar of the 115th Division, arrived at the Eighth Route Army's headquarters in Wutongzhen in Shanxi's Liao County to exchange ideas and discuss tactics with the 129th Division. The tiny hamlet of Wutongzhen is at the foot of a high mountain range and while soldiers of the guard tended the horses on a small area of level ground, the officers posed for an official photograph against the backdrop of the mountains. Nie Rongzhen stands on the left and next to him are Zhu De, Liu Bocheng and Deng Xiaoping, all wearing padded jackets and greatcoats and with their arms folded or hands behind their backs. Their deliberations on the timing of a major combined offensive against the Japanese led to the highly successful Hundred Regiments campaign.

After a counter-attack against the Japanese forces in March 1940 the 129th Division was able to join forces with other units and in the middle of July Zuo Quan, deputy chief of staff of the Eighth Route Army came to the 129th headquarters to pass on in person Peng Dehuai's plans for sabotaging the Japanese lines of communication in north China. Deng and Liu were enthusiastic and on 22 July the Eighth Route Army General Headquarters issued preparatory battle orders. At a meeting to discuss tactics Liu outlined the dispositions and missions of each unit and Deng gave his political commissar's pep talk.

The Hundred Regiments campaign was officially launched at 20.00 hours on 20 August and continued until 10 September. It was fought by 105 regiments of the expanded and increasingly confident Eighth Route Army, commanded by Peng Dehuai, and included 47 regiments of the 129th Division. For the 129th, combat began at 04.00 hours before dawn on 30 August and ferocious fighting ensued until midday. They suffered heavy casualties and unit commanders called headquarters on the field telephone to request that the attack be halted. Liu Bocheng ordered them to continue and Deng took the handset and urged them on, insisting that they should consider the 'overall situation' (*quanju*) not just the safety of their own regiment or platoon. At the height of the battle Liu ordered an attack with hand grenades and lime mortars on caves and foxholes to 'choke to death' Japanese troops using them; Deng called for brush fires to suffocate them or smoke them out. Deng took second place to the commanding officer, Liu Bocheng, but only just. He was committed to the strategy laid down by the General Headquarters but he also understood the necessity of accepting casualties, an unpleasant but essential consideration for any field commander. Nothing that he was to encounter in domestic politics after 1949 was as traumatic as the need to sacrifice thousands on the battlefield and this contributed to the toughness that he exhibited in later life.

If there was a single turning point in the CCP's resistance to the Japanese occupation, it was the Hundred Regiments campaign which dominated the second half of 1940 and represented the greatest single military campaign victory by the armed forces of the CCP. The Eighth Route Army gained territory, destroyed Japanese-controlled infrastructure and denied the invaders access to rail links and essential sources of coal. A high price was paid for this success: Eighth Route Army losses are calculated as 17,000 killed and wounded, though this was set against a much higher Japanese figure of 25,800.

Deng's view of the significance of the campaign was summed up in an article that he wrote on 28 April 1941 for *Party Life* (*Dang de shenghuo*), the organ of the CCP's Northern Bureau:

> The Hundred Regiments Campaign was a test for the Shanxi-Chahar-Hebei Border Region and the 129th Division [of the Eighth Route Army] in all aspects of their work. [The campaign] demonstrated that, whether in military affairs, politics, or the work of the party and the masses, it was possible to strike terror into the enemy and their collaborators and to inspire our military and civilians with the full confidence to go forward on the road to victory in the war of resistance against Japan.

The success of the Hundred Regiments campaign did wonders for the confidence and prestige of the Eighth Route Army and scotched rumours that were circulating among Guomindang politicians and officers that the CCP's mobile warfare was an excuse for not attacking the enemy. Mao Zedong telegraphed Peng Dehuai to say how excited he had been at news from the campaign and asking him if it could be repeated. On 11 September even Chiang Kai-shek telegraphed Zhu De and Peng Dehuai to congratulate them on the successful action. To be associated with such a clear and public victory was a boost to Deng Xiaoping's status.[11]

Between 1940 and 1945 Deng Xiaoping's name does not appear in accounts of central Party meetings and he was not involved in policy decisions at the highest level. He was on the periphery, perhaps inevitably in view of the geographical isolation of his 129th Division in the Taihang Mountains. However, slowly but surely, in addition to his acknowledged position in the military, he was establishing himself in the middle ranks of the Party.

TAIHANG BASE AREA (1940–5)

Building up the base areas was a vital part of resistance to the Japanese but the CCP was also determined to create a national government, with or without the cooperation of the Guomindang. In March 1940, in line with the Central Committee 'Directive on questions of state power in the border regions', Deng had taken the lead in implementing what became known as the 'three thirds' system in the Taihang Mountains. This was a formula for appointing government officials in accordance with the spirit of the United Front. The jobs of cadres were to be distributed in three roughly equal groups: members of the CCP; 'leftist or progressive elements' who were broadly supportive of the Party; and 'intermediate and other elements' who were at least not overt opponents. The intention was to create an administration that included as many non-Party cadres as possible without risking loss of control by the CCP. On 1 August a Liaison Office (*Ji Tihang ban*) was established to administer the base areas of southern Hebei, Taihang and Taiyue. This became the main political and legislative body of the Shanxi-Hebei-Henan (*Jin-Ji-Yu*) base area and its slogan was 'democratic politics and clean government'. Deng faithfully implemented central policy and when an administrative conference of the Liaison Office was convened on 16 March 1941 he was instructed by the Northern Bureau to create a Provisional Assembly on the basis of the 'three thirds' system.

Deng was the good soldier, putting into practice at the local level the policies and broad-brush plans laid down by the Central Committee. He elaborated in some detail his experience on how this had worked in an article dated 15 April 1941 that he wrote for *Party Life* (*Dang de shenghuo*). Deng took the view that his task in Taihang was to establish democratic political power. Although the leadership role of the CCP had to be maintained at all costs, it was necessary to maintain a 'democratic spirit' in the Taihang Mountains. He spoke out against opponents of the 'three thirds' system within the CCP who he said were wedded to the idea of 'the party controlling the state' (*yi dang zhi guo*) and argued that their position was an 'evil legacy' of the influence of the Guomindang which had infected parts of the CCP. This pernicious anti-democratic viewpoint was, in his opinion, 'paralysing, corrupting and damaging' the Party by isolating it from the local population. It was essential for their success that they establish the correct relationship between the Party and the administration. The Party had the responsibility for leading the administration and ensuring the implementation of its policy but in the spirit of the United Front, the Party's role should be supervisory and it should not 'monopolise the whole show' or interfere at every possible opportunity. The authority of the Party could not automatically be regarded as higher than everything else. Photographs from 1941 demonstrate the creation of the 'three thirds' system in the form of assemblages of CCP and military officials and 'democratic personages' who had been persuaded to throw in their lot with the communist administrations. This may seem a recondite discussion and relevant only to the Second United Front period of 1937–45, but Deng's attitude to the authority of the Party and its relationship with the government and non-communist organisations had profound implications for his later role in government.

Between 7 July and 15 August 1941, 133 delegates attended the Provisional Assembly of the Shanxi-Hebei-Henan (Jin Ji Yu) Border Region, which opened with great pomp and ceremony in the town of Tongyuzhen in Liao County (now Zuoquan), Shanxi Province. On the instructions of the Northern Bureau, 33 counties of western Shandong were transferred to this administration, which accordingly changed its name to the Shanxi-Hebei-Shandong-Henan (Jin Ji Lu Yu) Border Region. Deng became a member of the Provisional Assembly; its chairman was Yang Xiufeng, and his deputy was Bo Yibo. Bo was one of the legendary 'Eight Immortals' who were Deng's closest advisers in the 1980s – he was also the father of Bo Xilai, the Party secretary of Chongqing who fell from power in 2012.

At the time of the conference, the CCP newspaper *Liberation Daily* (*Jiefang ribao*) carried an article, entitled 'Great contributions on democratic politics behind enemy lines', which praised the expansion of the base area and the embryonic 'new democratic' (*xin minzhu zhuyi*) forms of government. Deng was at the centre of a political movement in a strategically important base area and had guided the region along the lines prescribed by the Central Committee.

'BETTER TROOPS AND STREAMLINED ADMINISTRATION'

Although the Taihang Mountains were isolated from the central leadership in Yan'an, the base area was not entirely a backwater as it was home to a concentration of different 'leading organs' (*lingdao jiguan*) of the Party, army and government. The Taihang branch of the Northern Bureau was based there, as was the border region government and its provisional assembly. There was also the 129th Division of the Eighth Route Army, Peng Zhen's Northern Bureau, which was in overall charge of the war effort in north China, and the Eighth Route Army's

Front Headquarters (*qianfang zongbu*). The burden for supplying all of these organisations naturally fell on the population of Taihang. After 1941 the Japanese mounted an economic blockade on the communist areas in addition to the regular military assaults. The area controlled by the communists began to shrink, the burden on the local people increased and the position of the base area, like 'a large fish in shallow water' (*yu da shui shao*), was increasingly difficult to sustain.

The CCP's response to a crisis of this nature was in one respect to press for an increase in production, but they also turned to the tried-and-trusted method of a political campaign, in this case a campaign to ensure 'better troops and streamlined administration' (*jingbing jianzheng*), to boost morale and foster unity under fire. This was an old slogan, but it was relaunched in January 1942 and the 129th Division played a leading role. At a meeting on 7 January, the divisional military-political double act of Liu Bocheng and Deng Xiaoping issued instructions for the conduct of the campaign at company level. Deng spoke of the need to reduce the burden on the local people so as not to lose their support and reminded his officers that, although things were difficult for them, they were much worse in the areas under Japanese occupation. Orders to implement the 'better troops and streamlined administration' campaign were issued on 15 January, with a particular emphasis on the need for educating and training senior cadres. Suitably experienced and qualified soldiers were to be sent to the Chinese People's Resisting Japan Military and Political University (*Zhongguo renmin kangri junshi zhengzhi daxue*), usually known as *Kangda*, in Yan'an or, if their standards were too low, a military middle school. Cadres not sent away to study took part in training programmes within their regiments and Deng personally lectured many of the troops. This was an ideological and a psychological response to a serious military and economic crisis and it was regarded by the Party hierarchy as a success in boosting morale. It received the imprimatur of Mao Zedong, which was important not only for the policy but also for Deng's career.

MAO ZEDONG AND THE RECTIFICATION CAMPAIGN (1942)

In Yan'an, Mao Zedong's priority was his Rectification Campaign (*Zhengfeng*), which was designed to integrate the diverse collection of radicals and rebels who had migrated to the communist capital in response to the Japanese invasion, in particular young students and intellectuals who were full of patriotic fervour and zeal for social reforming but who could not be relied on to follow the kind of

Marxist line that Mao was formulating. Mao made two speeches, on 1 February and 8 February 1942, criticising factionalism, dogmatism and other faults that threatened the long-term success of the CCP. Mao was demanding unity of action and unity of thought, with no room for individual or factional differences, or alternative policies. This authoritarian and totalitarian worldview would afflict the Party until the end of Mao's life in 1976. It was at the conclusion of this 1942 campaign that Mao emerged as the single, almost unchallenged, leader of the Party. The Rectification Campaign spread from Yan'an through the communist resistance bases and among communist organisations in Guomindang-controlled areas, and as it became clear that Mao was the leader, senior party figures in the base areas lined up to show their support for him.

The extension of the Yan'an Rectification Campaign to the Shanxi-Hebei-Shandong-Henan (Jin Ji Lu Yu) Border Region began in May 1942, eclipsing the push for 'better troops and streamlined administration', which would have been of more practical use in the military. Deng Xiaoping chaired all the key committees that ran the campaign in the Border Area. In September 1942, in addition to his post as political commissar of the 129th Division, Deng had been appointed secretary of the Taihang Sub-Bureau of the Central Committee, which enhanced his political status in the Party centre. In January 1943 he spoke at a meeting of senior cadres of this committee, in support of Mao's Rectification Campaign. Committees and training and study groups were established to carry out this campaign in all the counties under the control of the CCP, and in one form or another they operated from 1943 to 1946. By 5 June Deng could feel confident that he had successfully carried out the instruction of Mao and the Central Committee. The Border Region could be under no doubt about the new working style and new direction under Mao Zedong which would remain in place throughout the civil war from 1946 to 1949. Deng's feelings about the eclipse of the 'better troops and streamlined administration' are not known, but this was a foretaste of the struggles between Mao's political rhetoric and the pragmatic policies of Deng and Liu Shaoqi that were to dominate the PRC in the 1950s.

MAO'S MAN IN TAIHANG

During the Rectification Campaign, Deng identified himself clearly and unequivocally as a supporter of Mao Zedong and praised Mao's 'sinification of Marxism' and the significance of Mao Zedong Thought (*Mao Zedong sixiang*) for the Chinese revolution. Mao Zedong Thought had been popularised during the Rectification Campaign and the term probably appeared in print for the first time in an article written by Wang Jiaxiang for *Liberation Daily* on 8 July 1943, when he hailed it as 'China's Marxism, Bolshevism and Communism'. Deng was one of the first CCP leaders to follow Wang Jiaxiang's use of this term. Although Deng had seen the way the wind was blowing and was inclined to align himself with the newly assertive leadership of Mao, he had been an ally of Mao during the Jiangxi Soviet and had been purged when Mao's star waned, so it was not simply an opportunistic move. By his own speeches during the campaign he had become identified as Mao's man in the Taihang Mountains.

In October 1943 Deng replaced Peng Dehuai as acting secretary of the Central Committee's Northern Bureau, thus acquiring even greater influence over the political direction of the General Headquarters of the Eighth Route Army. These incremental rises in position and status were vital for building Deng's political authority. As his area of responsibility broadened his horizons expanded, and once again, as in the early years of the Jiangxi Soviet, he had to embrace both the political and the practical. This is reflected in two of the few articles written by Deng before 1975 that remain in print in China, 'The Establishment of Base Areas and the Mass Movement' and 'Economic Development in the Taihang Area' which were originally published in the Yan'an newspaper *Liberation Daily* on 20 February and 2 July 1943. While Mao and other CCP leaders were addressing themselves to theory and grand strategy, Deng was concerned with the bread-and-butter issues of running the base area, particularly the need to develop an economic structure that could support the CCP without antagonising the local populace. This included policies on banking, currency supply, taxation and trade and other aspects of economic organisation, in addition to the familiar CCP policies of rent and interest rate reduction which directly and immediately lessened the burden on the poorest farmers who were the core of the CCP's political support. Crucially, as he told liaison staff of the 129th Division on 21 September, the military would have to assist in food production: it was no good having rifles if they had no food, and they could not rely on the farmers to provide food without risking losing their support. He instituted a system of awards, not only honouring troops with titles such as 'hero of labour' but also offering rewards of several hundred *yuan* to those who excelled in supporting food production. With the agreement of senior colleagues, 2 *mu* of rice paddy was requisitioned for the use of each unit in partnership with the local village administration, with the promise that rent would be paid the following year if the situation permitted. Experienced older farmers were brought in to give technical advice to the soldiers who were deployed to work the land. This developed into a 'high tide of land reclamation' as units were set to vie with each other to clear 2 *mu* each and prepare the land for autumn ploughing. On 1 April 1944 orders from the Eighth Route Army General Headquarters formalised the economic activities of these soldiers. Deng Xiaoping's 129th Division was one of the units leading this campaign for production and self-sufficiency, which generated not only food but essential weaponry, including rifles, ammunition, hand grenades and mortars. Mao Zedong had received a report on the success of the spring 1945 production campaign in the Taiyue military district and on 12 April sent a telegram, endorsing the policy that Deng had been promoting.[12]

6

CIVIL WAR AND NEW CHINA (1945–9)

Everybody says I was a member of Mao's faction.
Of course there was no such thing. There was no Mao faction.[1]

The Chinese Communist Party's War of Resistance against Japan (*Kangri zhanzheng*) came to an end on 15 August 1945 with the Japanese unconditional surrender that brought to a close World War II in the Pacific. For the Communist Party this was the culmination of eight years of resistance and a vindication of their patriotic stance even though it was Allied atom bombs dropped on Hiroshima on 6 August and Nagasaki on 9 August that forced the Japanese surrender. Even the CCP leadership could not pretend that they were primarily responsible for defeating Japan, but they continued to claim credit for holding back their military advance in China and criticised the Guomindang for withdrawing to Chongqing and waiting for the Americans to win the war. The nationalists have always downplayed the communist resistance, but it undoubtedly preoccupied significant numbers of Japanese troops in the north-west and the CCP emerged from the war with far more authority, prestige and support than they had in 1937. This support was stronger in the rural areas and less so in the cities, and the CCP was determined to capitalise on this and defeat the Guomindang.

In conventional accounts of contemporary China, the final civil war between the nationalists and the communists began in earnest in May 1946 and ended in 1949 when Mao Zedong appeared on the balcony of the Forbidden City's Tian'anmen Gate to proclaim the establishment of the People's Republic of China. In reality the war, and certainly the military culture that grew out of it, persisted for many years after 1949. Anti-communist resistance continued, especially in the border regions, and, even if the disputed territories of Tibet and Xinjiang are excluded, many areas did not come under the effective control of Beijing until at least 1953. Military and security concerns dominated national politics as the new government strove to eliminate any remaining opposition. The Korean War, which broke out in June 1950, intensified the influence of military culture on politics and the patriotic fervour that it engendered helped to enhance the prestige and authority of the People's Liberation Army as well as the Chinese Communist Party. The CCP was battling internal and external enemies but was simultaneously attempting to create a constitutional framework for its political control: one of the key features of the politics of the early 1950s was the struggle between the Communist Party's soldiers who were intent on preserving the spirit of the revolutionary war and the constitutional politicians seeking broader support for their rule in what they termed a New Democracy. The China that emerged from World War II did not have a democratic tradition on which it could draw, and the influence and status of the military remained high as a result of the army's central role in the creation of the new state. In these circumstances it is not surprising that many successful and politically well-connected high-ranking officers of the People's Liberation Army metamorphosed into senior Party and government cadres. As an experienced military politician with close connections to Mao Zedong and the central Party leadership, Deng Xiaoping was particularly well placed to advance in this new hierarchy.

SEVENTH PARTY CONGRESS (APRIL–JUNE 1945)

On 23 April 1945 the CCP convened its Seventh National Congress in Yan'an, the last before the Party took power and the first with Mao Zedong as Party leader. The 755 delegates who attended represented a party that claimed a total membership of 1,210,000. Mao dominated the congress and presented his long political report, 'On Coalition Government' even though there was little enthusiasm for the existing relationship with the Guomindang and an all-out civil war appeared more likely. The CCP leadership judged that the Party was in such a strong position that it should only make alliances on its own terms. Other key speakers included Zhu De on the military situation, Liu Shaoqi introducing a revised Party constitution which the congress adopted, and Zhou Enlai spoke on the sensitive issue of the United Front. Deng had arrived late, in response to an urgent telegram from Mao Zedong requesting his attendance. He was not sufficiently senior to make a speech, but he was elected a member of the new Central Committee. Although he was not a member of the powerful Politburo or the Secretariat, this was a significant step for Deng, the first time that he had been a member of the Central Committee, and it marked his entrée into high CCP politics. The determining factor in his election was the patronage of Mao, who recognised his loyalty as well as his all-round competence.

FIGHTING THE GUOMINDANG

The CCP celebrated the defeat of Japan, but were well aware that this did not spell peace for China. Between 28 August and 11 October 1945, representatives of the communists and nationalists met in Chongqing, the Guomindang's temporary capital since 1937, to negotiate an acceptable postwar settlement. The military conflict between their armed forces had never completely ceased during the Japanese occupation, and it now broke out again. On 16 August 1945, the armies of the former Shanxi warlord Yan Xishan, acting on what were said to have been secret orders relayed from Chiang Kai-shek, attacked the strategic communications centre of Shangdang in the communists' Shanxi-Hebei-Shandong-Henan (Jin Ji Lu Yu) base area. Chiang Kai-shek's power base was in Chongqing in the south-west and, if he were to have any chance of restoring a national Guomindang government, he would have to retake the north-west from the communists – who regarded it as theirs by right since they had wrested it from the Japanese. The battle for Shangdang, the gateway to north China, took place between 10 September and 12 October, while Mao Zedong and other leaders of the CCP were in Chongqing negotiating with Chiang Kai-shek.

If the nationalists needed to take Shangdang, it was no less essential for the communists to defend it. On 20 August 1945 the CCP Central Committee established a new central Shanxi-Hebei-Shandong-Henan (Jin Ji Lu Yu) Bureau with Deng Xiaoping as director and Bo Yibo as his deputy. Liu Bocheng was appointed as commanding officer of a new combined Shanxi-Hebei-Shandong-

Henan (Jin Ji Lu Yu) Military District of which Deng and Bo were respectively political commissar and deputy political commissar. Deng was the right man for such a critical battle.

On 25 August a group of CCP delegates including Deng, Bo and Liu climbed aboard an aircraft in Yan'an to fly back to the Taihang Mountains. The aircraft was probably the Douglas C-47 Skytrain (a *Dakota* to the Royal Air Force) that belonged to the United States Army Observer Group – the 'Dixie Mission' that was in Yan'an from 22 July 1944 until 11 March 1947 – and was used for liaison flights between Yan'an and Xi'an. Deng and his colleagues had persuaded the Americans to allow them on board and it is not clear whether the Americans, who were negotiating with the communists but backing the nationalists, knew the true identity of their passengers or their mission in Taihang. After a four-hour flight the C-47 landed at a makeshift airfield deep in the Taihang Mountains and the communist hitchhikers made their way to their military posts at the front where fighting had already become intense. Wang Shuzeng, the author of a major study of the 1945–9 civil war, savoured the irony of the US military helping 21 of the most senior communist leaders to reach their posts on the Taihang front so that they could organise the war against America's allies, the Guomindang.

On 26 August 1945 the CCP Central Military Commission ordered Taihang troops to retake Shangdang from Yan Xishan. On 29 August Liu Bocheng and Deng Xiaoping sent a telegram to the Central Military Commission with detailed proposals for committing a total of 28,000 men against an estimated 16,000 under Yan. The Central Military Commission approved, troops were deployed, and preparations were also made for a separate operation on the Beiping–Hankou railway line. The communist military units were small, ill-equipped and frequently running out of ammunition. The troops wore a motley collection of uniform and civilian outfits, many sporting the traditional white cloth head-dress of the Shanxi sheep herder rather than military caps. The battle for Shangdang was fought using conventional techniques rather than those of guerrilla war, lasted for over a month and involved rapid and decisive changes in tactics which were decided on by Liu Bocheng and Deng Xiaoping working in concert. The nationalist forces were wiped out in fierce fighting, but the communists sustained relatively light casualties. They regained their lost territory and captured significant quantities of weapons and ammunition.

This military victory strengthened the negotiating position of Mao Zedong and Zhou Enlai in their discussions with Chiang Kai-shek in Chongqing, which continued in spite of the fighting. Mao had heard that officers in Shangdang were

concerned about his safety while he was staying in Hongyan (Red Crag) village –
which is now part of the Shapingba district of Chongqing but in 1945 was the site
of a massacre of communists by the Guomindang – and sent a message to reassure
them that the best way of ensuring his safety was to fight the nationalists and win.
The negotiations ended with the signing of a 12-point Double Tenth Accord
(*shuangshi xieding*), concluded on 10 October 1945, the tenth day of the tenth
month, the anniversary of the 1911 Revolution from which both nationalists and
communists drew political legitimacy. The Double Tenth Accord provided for the
establishment of a Political Consultative Conference and cooperation in the
peaceful reconstruction (*heping jianguo*) of China, but the differences between the
nationalists and the communists were irreconcilable and neither side was willing to
share power. The future of China would be decided not at the conference table in
Chongqing but on the battlefield.

On 17 October 1945 Mao sent a telegram to Deng Xiaoping, congratulating
him on his role in the victory of Shangdang and encouraging him to further
successes in the fighting along the Beiping–Hankou railway line, which did
eventually result in a comprehensive victory for the CCP. Deng was accumulating
credit for these victories, although the strategy had been worked out jointly with
Liu Bocheng. In most Chinese accounts, decisions are attributed jointly to Liu and
Deng, and their forces are referred to as the Liu and Deng Army (*Liu Deng dajun*)
– almost as in the early days of the Red Army when Zhu (De) and Mao (Zedong)
appeared inseparable and were sometimes believed to be one person, Zhu Mao.

In late 1946, attempts to broker a peace agreement were made by Chinese
politicians and international players, notably General George C. Marshall, the
special representative in China of the United States President, Harry S. Truman.
After the failure of the Marshall mission, the communist armies returned to the
offensive. The next major battles for Deng and Liu were in January 1947 when a
telegram from Mao ordered them to attack to the north and south of the
strategically important Long-Hai railway line. In March 1947 the nationalists
captured Yan'an, which had been the communist capital since soon after the Long
March, and this was hailed as a major victory for the Guomindang.

INTO THE DABIE MOUNTAINS (1947)

Liu and Deng's troops, now designated the Shanxi-Hebei-Shandong-Henan Field
Army, attacked the nationalist defensive lines along the Yellow River and were

ordered to push further south to establish a new base on the south bank of the river in the Dabie Mountains, a risky strategy but one that would not only extend the influence of the CCP but also take the pressure off its military units in the north-west. The stretch of the Yellow River between Dong'a in Shandong and Kaifeng in Henan was the sector they had to hold in preparation for crossing the great river that would take them into central China. They were faced with formidable nationalist forces on the other bank and, as they prepared to cross, the weather changed and prolonged heavy rainstorms created mud, which favoured the nationalist defensive forces. They decided to cross at night on 30 June: the sky was pitch black with not even a glimmer of moonlight and the troops 'could not even see their hands in front of their faces' as they rowed across. An advance party of troops swam across, making so little noise above the sound of the rain and the waves made by the wind on the river that the nationalist guards did not hear them until it was too late. The swimmers met with a hail of small-arms fire but were able to capture the position in preparation for the main body of troops who followed in wooden boats that had been hidden in the reeds.[2]

In total some 120,000 communist troops crossed and eventually received orders to establish a base in the Dabie Mountains, a strategic location on the borders of the provinces of Hubei, Henan and Anhui. This manoeuvre involved recrossing the Yellow River to the north bank but contemporary photographs indicate that on this occasion bridges were available although some of the troops had to resort to barges or wading across narrow waters. The base in the Dabie Mountains was established but with considerable losses. In early November 1947 the headquarters and other units moved into a more fertile area in flat plains among the uplands. In the course of this manoeuvre Deng discovered that communist-controlled towns and villages were still secure and that a land reform programme was underway. In a report that Deng Xiaoping presented to his colleagues after they had established a base camp in Taihu County on 11 and 12 November, he wrote that the central tasks they faced were land reform and combat (in that order), building up their armed forces, learning lessons and improving their style of work. Deng personally met with poorer peasants, both to explain communist policies on land reform and to improve his understanding of their living conditions. The troops did not stay long in this part of the Dabie Mountains but Deng continued to investigate and take notes as they passed through, specifically noting the state of communist administration and military establish-ments. These brief accounts would later be incorporated into formal reports that he made to Mao Zedong. They encountered nationalist troops as they were trying to cross the Yellow River at one point and as Liu Bocheng was suffering from a painful eye condition the responsibility for getting the troops across the river fell entirely on Deng's shoulders. He managed to find a weak point in the enemy's defences and guided the men across a bridge.

After two months of continuous fighting, Liu and Deng's troops, later designated the Second Field Army, arrived at Qiliping in Huangan County, Hubei, where they joined forces with other communist units under Li Xiannian and Wang Hongkun. They set up a combined headquarters where they were able to receive radio broadcasts from the communist New China News Agency. These were beamed from a new transmitter in the Taihang Mountains that had been installed to ensure that cadres in the more remote regions were aware of central Party communiqués and decisions. The latest of these was Mao Zedong's speech, 'The present situation and our tasks' (*Muqian de xingshi he women de renwu*).

Local cadres who did not know Deng were initially reserved when talking to him, but he insisted on frank and open discussions about practical problems. One serious issue was the shortage of food, especially in the winter when the mountains were covered with snow. Deng drafted an order for the requisition of grain: it could be taken on the basis of a promissory note when there was insufficient cash available to pay the farmers and even removed where the owner was absent, but the intention was to replace it later. This order did not comply with regulations and was not the way communist troops were supposed to behave, but times were desperate, the soldiers were hungry and nationalist armies were besieging the Dabie Mountains. Deng the pragmatist just found a solution to the problem. Looking back on the Dabie Mountains campaign 40 years later, Deng acknowledged that they had not inflicted as much damage on the enemy as they should have, but as conditions in the mountains were so difficult his troops had done well to hold their ground.[3]

ADMONISHING THE 10TH BRIGADE (1948)

On New Year's Eve 1947, Deng Xiaoping and his comrades sat round an open fire in their mountain fastness, warming themselves and eating roasted wheat cakes and red dates. 'Not bad for a New Year feast', declared Deng. The new year of 1948 was going to be a decisive year for Deng and for the Chinese Communist Party. Military considerations obliged Liu and Deng to go their separate ways. Liu took command of the main force that was moving on to combine with the East China

Field Army. Deng remained in the Dabie Mountains with part of the Shanxi-Hebei-Shandong-Henan Field Army to defend the base.

Deng was already something of a legend among the troops as one of the outstanding early revolutionaries and in April 1948 there was a buzz of excitement when it was announced that he was coming down from Field Army Headquarters to speak to the 10th Brigade (also 10th Column – *shi zong*). The 10th Brigade was part of the Western Front Corps of the East China Field Army and on 30 June 1947 it had been deployed to provide cover for the advance of Liu and Deng's forces into the Dabie Mountains and had later been transferred to their command. The 10th Brigade were attempting to establish a new communist base in a poverty-stricken area known to be full of Guomindang agents and still controlled by the remnants of the old nationalist administration. When they arrived the troops had little more to eat than the locals but they requisitioned and confiscated supplies and forced local people to work for them. This was completely contrary to the regulations and spirit of the Eighth Route Army and was characterised as a 'leftist' style of operating.

Deng visited the 10th Brigade on 4 April 1948 and spent some time working with the troops to study the nature of the problem. At a meeting of the brigade the commanding officer, Song Shilun, introduced him: 'This is Political Commissar Deng Xiaoping of the Shanxi-Hebei-Shandong-Henan Field Army. He has been with the brigade for some days and today wants to meet the whole unit.' The men applauded. Deng welcomed them to the struggle in the Central Plains on behalf of Liu Bocheng and the troops were pleased to hear his Sichuan accent, which reminded them of their previous commander Chen Yi of the Eastern China Field Army. 'In the last nine months', Deng went on, 'we have achieved great gains and made progress in the struggle for the Dabie Mountains.' He acknowledged that they were drawing the fire of over half of the military strength that Chiang Kai-shek could muster on his southern front, thereby assisting communist victories in other areas. He asked them not to consider only their own difficulties but to be aware of the sufferings of others, as true heroes would. There had been progress in land reform in some areas under the 10th Brigade's control, but on the whole the masses had not been mobilised and did not understand what the CCP stood for. It was not correct to use methods that might have been appropriate in a more established base. Deng's tone of voice was mild and gentle, and he spoke effectively in straightforward language. When he finally got to the point of his talk – the forced requisitions – he had the full attention of his audience and, although he did not criticise them directly, he made it clear that they should not have been requisitioning supplies and raising funds. They risked alienating the moderately wealthy peasants and businessmen, who could use any failings of the CCP and its troops to foment opposition. Military needs were important and naturally food, clothing and other supplies had to be procured, but the needs of local merchants and manufacturers also must be taken into account. Senior officers were impressed by the way he made his point without haranguing them, and discussed how they should follow his instructions.

Deng set out his views on the problems in the new base area in two articles. In 'The situation following our triumphal advance to the Central Plains and our future policies and strategy', a report to joint military committees, larded with the now obligatory praise for Mao Zedong's leadership, Deng argued that although many of the problems could be attributed to the war in general, the wrongheaded actions of PLA commanders in defiance of Party policy was sometimes to blame. He reiterated the points that he had made to the troops about dealing fairly and properly with the better-off farmers and businessmen. Private industry and commerce, he argued, were 'an integral part of the new-democratic economy' and the CCP should assist their development. A second article, 'Some suggestions concerning our entry into new areas in the future', was submitted as part of a system of reports requested by the Central Committee with copies sent to Mao Zedong. After considering the need for adequate preparation before moving into a new area, he turned to the economic issues. Supplying the troops, he argued, was 'the first, the biggest, and the most important question of policy we come in contact with in the new areas'. Methods of requisitioning supplies had been chaotic and he proposed a new approach which involved carrying silver dollars and giving 'each of our men two dollars every month for half a year to cover the cost of non-staple foods, tobacco and straw sandals'; issuing 'paper money for troops to use and exchange', although recognising that exchange rates and acceptability would be problematic; levying taxes in towns where CCP troops were stationed; borrowing grain using the traditional *baojia* system; and contributing captured grain and money from enemy forces for general usage. This complex semi-official economy was to be managed by field administrative committees.

Deng Xiaoping, the political commissar who had deputised for the divisional military commander when necessary, and was in any case involved in all key military decisions, was here concerning himself with the day-to-day issues of feeding his troops without alienating the local population. His assessment of the economic problems, and what needed to be done to resolve them, was based on practical possibilities rather than strict ideological principles, although he naturally took care to couch his reports in the language of 1940s Chinese Marxism. It is not surprising that 30 years later, after the death of Mao Zedong, it was Deng who was able to grasp the nettle and encourage the development of a thriving market economy.[4]

SEPTEMBER CONFERENCE OF POLITBURO IN XIBAIPO (1948)

The civil war was in its third year; Guomindang military losses were assessed by the communists at 2,641,400 and its front-line forces were weakening; and in political and economic terms China was facing a catastrophe. In August 1948 Chiang Kai-shek had convened a crisis meeting in Nanjing to try to find a solution. The CCP convened its own meeting, an enlarged meeting of the CCP Politburo, the September Conference, which lasted from 8 to 13 September in its temporary capital of Xibaipo. The Politburo reviewed military plans that had been drawn up in July 1947 and agreed to tighten control over all the military units and insist that they request instructions before acting and submit reports afterwards. This had the additional effect of concentrating all political power in the hands of the Central Committee and the Politburo and strengthening Mao Zedong's control over the Party and the military. Mao had brought together the members of the Central Committee Secretariat, which met from 28 August to 7 September, to prepare the agenda and the documentation for the enlarged Politburo meeting.

Deng Xiaoping had been with his unit in a small village in Henan Province's Baofeng County when orders came to travel to the CCP's temporary headquarters. He had a long discussion with Liu Bocheng before dawn on 25 July 1948 and set out for Xibaipo in an American military jeep that had been captured from Guomindang troops. He was accompanied, in another army vehicle, by others who also needed to make the journey. To travel from Baofeng to Xibaipo in Hebei Province was a difficult journey of several thousand *li* over poor roads, and the convoy was in constant danger of attack by enemy aircraft. Deng used every opportunity on the journey to contact CCP cadres and army officers and familiarise himself with the situation on the ground. He did not have a secretary or a staff officer with him so asked Zhang Younian, one of his fellow travellers, to assist him in taking notes. The poor roads had been made worse by damage during the war with Japan and it was often necessary to travel at night to avoid air attacks. Deng was concerned that he might not arrive in time and urged the driver of his jeep to forge ahead, leaving the others to follow.

Since Mao Zedong had arrived in Xibaipo the CCP's Central Committee and

Central Work Committee had been amalgamated and the CCP was run by the Secretariat, composed of the five 'Grand Secretaries' (*wu da shuji*) sometimes known as the 'Big Five', Mao, Liu Shaoqi, Zhu De, Zhou Enlai and Ren Bishi, who had been reunited after being separated for over a year by the exigencies of the civil war. The Secretariat would remain the most powerful body in the CCP until the creation of the Standing Committee of the Politburo by the Eighth National Congress of the CCP in 1956. With the exception of Ren, who became seriously ill and died in 1950 at the age of 46, this group remained at the centre of power throughout the early years of the PRC. Xibaipo was the CCP's temporary capital and the 'final rural command post' of its Central Military Commission before the entry into Beiping (now Beijing) at the end of the civil war.

When Deng arrived in Xibaipo to attend the September Conference in his role as secretary of the Central Plains Bureau, he was warmly welcomed, as many of his comrades had not seen him since he had left Yan'an in 1945. Mao 'grasped his hand tightly asking him again and again how he was, and, noting how thin his face had become, said that he had changed into Little Monkey Deng'.[5] In a political sense Deng had come home; he met the 'Grand Secretaries' but also senior military officers including Xu Xiangqian, Nie Rongzhen and Bo Yibo, and as there was very little accommodation available in Xibaipo he stayed with Ye Jianying and his family. Before the September Conference formally convened Deng talked to Mao and reported on the situation in the 'liberated areas' of the Central Plains. Mao wanted more detail and Deng repaired to a quiet corner to prepare a formal written report, summarising his experiences. Zhou Enlai called a preparatory meeting on 5 September 1948 to discuss military affairs, at which Deng spoke. Deng was not one of the seven full members of the Politburo – those were Mao Zedong, Liu Shaoqi, Zhu De, Zhou Enlai, Ren Bishi, Dong Biwu and Peng Zhen – but he was listed as one of 14 alternate members. Deng felt the need to maintain regular contact with his unit by telegraph, passing on news and instructions from the Politburo meeting, with the now obligatory references to Mao's speeches and thought.[6]

HUAI-HAI CAMPAIGN (1948–9)

The Huai-Hai campaign was one of the three military campaigns (the other two being Liaoxi-Shenyang and Beiping-Tianjin) in which units of the greatly expanded and newly confident People's Liberation Army were victorious, ensuring the final triumph of the CCP in the civil war. A General Front Committee had been formed on the instructions of the Central Committee to coordinate the campaign, which was launched on 9 November 1948, officially ended after 66 days in January 1949 and had been designed to wrest control of central China from the nationalist forces. During the Huai-Hai Campaign, Deng Xiaoping and Liu Bocheng worked together again as members of the standing committee of the General Front Committee in which they were joined by another veteran officer, Chen Yi, who had commanded the Eastern China Field Army. Deng Xiaoping had not only been appointed to the committee and its standing committee, which had day-to-day oversight of the battles, but he was also the committee's secretary, which meant that he was personally responsible for liaising with the Central Committee. In addition, he led one of the two units of the Central Plains Field Army which was deployed to cut off railway communications between Xuzhou and Bengbu, this time with Chen Yi as military commander, although, as before, Deng appears to have issued some of the military orders. His old comrade-in-arms Liu Bocheng commanded the other unit, which had the task of holding back any nationalist attack from the south-west. After successful actions in December 1948 in which the armies of the nationalist commander Huang Wei were routed, the Central Committee ordered a meeting of the General Front Committee to meet to discuss the next phase of the civil war, the southward advance of the communist armies and the highly symbolic crossing of the Yangzi River. On 31 January 1949 the PLA entered Beijing and the Huai-Hai campaign, in which Deng had played such an important part, had come to an end.[7]

CENTRAL COMMITTEE MEETING AT XIBAIPO, MARCH 1949

In March 1947 the CCP had been obliged to withdraw from its capital, Yan'an, after a sustained attack by forces commanded by the nationalist general, Hu Zongnan. The PLA entered Beiping (as Beijing was known during the nationalist period) at the end of January 1949, but the Central Committee did not relocate until 25 March. During the ebb and flow of the civil war the CCP leadership was peripatetic until, in the summer of 1947, it established a temporary headquarters in the village of Xibaipo, close to the city of Shijiazhuang and to the south-west of Beiping. Deng Xiaoping, who had been elected to the Central Committee in 1945, attended its 2nd Plenary Session in Xibaipo which lasted from 5 to 13 March 1949. This was an eve of victory meeting for the Central Committee and it was recognised that the Party had to switch its focus from the countryside to controlling the cities. Once the formal business of the committee had been concluded a special meeting was arranged to discuss personnel issues, specifically the names of people to be assigned to run the new administrative regions that the CCP was creating. Deng introduced a list of names of possible appointees for the eastern region. This was to be under the jurisdiction of a new East China Bureau which would have 17 members including Liu Bocheng, Chen Yi and Deng himself, who would be its first secretary. The East China Bureau was a powerful body as it had authority over many major cities including Shanghai and Nanjing.

The existing Field Armies were re-designated with numbers, and the Liu-Deng Central Plains army now became the 2nd Field Army. The General Front Committee that had run the Huai-Hai Campaign was re-dedicated to the Yangzi crossing and control over southern China, and Deng remained its secretary. Mao had asked Deng personally to lead this campaign, and it began on 20 April 1949. The Yangzi River is an impressive natural barrier and was effectively Chiang Kai-shek's last line of defence. It was breached by Deng's 2nd Field Army, joined for this campaign by the 3rd (East China) Field Army, with the aid of thousands of wooden boats for the river crossing. Chiang Kai-shek's pre-war capital of Nanjing fell on 23 April and Deng told his daughter that he and Chen Yi had walked into Chiang's presidential palace and 'sat on his throne'. Shanghai was taken on 27 May and for a time Deng and his family lived in this great treaty port city, the very symbol of the dominance of Western commercial and political interests in China.

After the fall of Shanghai, Mao instructed Deng Xiaoping, as secretary of the East China Bureau and Chen Yi, Mayor of Shanghai, to pay their respects to Song Qingling, who lived in Shanghai. Song Qingling, the widow of Sun Yat-sen, was not a member of the CCP but she had broken off relations with Chiang Kai-shek and those family members who still supported him and was regarded by the communists as a genuine revolutionary and a sympathiser. More importantly, she represented the link with Sun, on whose legacy the CCP continued to draw – making contact with her was part of the task of political reconstruction that was underway even while the civil war was still raging. At this stage the CCP aimed to construct a New Democracy, a broadly based administration that would also include non-communist parties and individuals. Mao Zedong and Zhou Enlai had sent Song a telegram on 19 January 1949, inviting her to take part in talks on plans for the new government; she had replied that she was unable to attend for health reasons but sent a message of support to the CCP leadership. Deng and Chen went to visit her and Mao also deployed a guard unit, although it is not possible to say whether this was to ensure her safety or to guarantee that she continued to support the CCP. Deng and Chen made contact with Song through a local woman considered to be a 'patriot' and went to visit her, accompanied by several CCP members who had been working underground in Shanghai for some years. Discovering that she was in considerable financial difficulty, they arranged for her to receive a sum of 1 million *yuan* in *renmin piao* ('people's notes'). The currency was not formally known as renminbi until June 1949 and the large amount given to Song Qingling is a reflection of the hyperinflation that China suffered until the revaluation of 1955. The Central Committee issued instructions that Sun Yat-sen's old residence was to be preserved as a memorial and that Song Qingling's needs were to be provided for. Mao and Zhou Enlai arranged for Deng Yingchao (Zhou's wife but also an alternate member of the Central Committee in her own right) to visit Song and take handwritten letters from Mao and Zhou asking her to take part in the multi-party talks on political reconstruction that were taking place in Beiping. Deng Yingchao arrived in Shanghai with the letters on 25 June 1949 and Song Qingling agreed to cooperate. Mao Zedong was delighted and praised Deng Yingchao, Chen Yi and Deng Xiaoping for the success of this sensitive and politically vital mission.

Deng had formed a close relationship with his fellow Sichuanese, Chen Yi, who had also shared the experience of studying in France with him. The Deng and Chen families were also close and had managed to enjoy some domestic life in spite of the exigencies of war and revolution: a group photograph shows the two men relaxing with their wives and children in Shanghai shortly after it had fallen to the communist forces.

In September 1949 Deng arrived in Beijing, with his wife Zhuo Lin; it was their first visit to what was once again the capital of China. Deng was recuperating from an illness, which was unusual for a man who generally seemed to remain fit and well in the most difficult circumstances. He was able to attend the Chinese People's Political Consultative Conference, which opened on 21 September in the Huairen Hall (Hall of Cherishing Benevolence) in Zhongnanhai. This was the former imperial garden and palace complex that had been home to some members of the Qing imperial family, including the Empress Dowager Cixi, and also of the first president of the Chinese Republic (and subsequently imperial usurper), Yuan Shikai. Zhongnanhai lies to the west of the Imperial Palace, and is also known as the Forbidden City (*Gugong*). It became the headquarters of the Chinese Communist Party and its government, the place where Deng Xiaoping would eventually work and live. Deng remained in Beijing until 1 October 1949, when

Mao Zedong, standing on the rostrum over the Tian'anmen Gate (the Gate of Heavenly Peace) on the southern wall of the Imperial Palace, proclaimed the establishment of the People's Republic of China. Mao and Deng's goal had finally been achieved.[8]

7

LIBERATING SICHUAN AND RULING FROM CHONGQING (1949–52)

When the army entered the south-west, we resolved from the start to rebuild the region, beginning with the problem of communications.[1]

In the south-west I had to mobilise the mass of the population and improve the quality of our 600,000 cadres and troops.[2]

There was no rest for Deng Xiaoping, either in Beijing or in whatever remained of the fleshpots of Shanghai; there was work still to be done in bringing China completely under the control of the CCP. The Field Armies were assigned to different campaigns. The 2nd Field Army, once again under the command of Liu Bocheng, and with Deng as political commissar, was destined for the south-west, to Guizhou and also to Sichuan, Deng and Liu's home province. Chen Yi now left them and led his 3rd Field Army to take control of Fujian and other coastal regions. Instead of running the East China Bureau, Deng was appointed first secretary of the new South-Western Bureau, with Liu Bocheng and He Long assisting him. Deng Xiaoping had (almost) come home, but the task that faced him was not an easy one. Not only did he have to bring the region under the control of the CCP, he also had to oversee the reconstruction of the local economy and the restoration of communications.

On 23 May 1949 the Central Committee and Central Military Commission had decided to deploy the 3rd, 4th and 5th Corps of Liu and Deng's 2nd Field Army together with the 18th Corps of the 1st Field Army to south-western China. A telegraphed order from the commission on 2 June read simply 'Xiaoping – prepare to enter Sichuan' (*Xiaoping – zhunbei ru Chuan*) and Deng did what he always did – went to talk to Liu Bocheng. Detailed orders from the Central Military Commission followed on 16 July and these were conveyed to the troops two days later, but it was several months before they moved into the south-west.

Deng was concerned that he would not have enough cadres to do the job. Staffing had been a constant concern as the CCP expanded into new 'liberated areas' during the civil war. On 11 June 1949 the CCP Central Organisation Department decided that 30,800 cadres would have to be deployed from the North China Bureau, Central China Bureau, North-West Bureau and the Shandong Bureau. Cadres originally allocated to the 2nd Field Army were redeployed to the south-west, but Deng's army was still short of 10,000 cadres. Deng was concerned about quality as well as quantity: even in areas securely under CCP control, far too many of the cadres were uneducated, illiterate or otherwise unsuitable.

SOUTH-WEST SERVICE CORPS

Deng found a bold and imaginative solution to this problem by creating the South-West Service Corps (*Xinan fuwutuan*). At a meeting of the 2nd Field Army Front Committee in Nanjing he proposed that they recruit 'progressive and talented' students from universities and secondary schools and other technically qualified people. He reasoned that there would be sufficient talent in the areas that they currently controlled as this included Nanjing, Shanghai, Suzhou, Wuxi and Hangzhou, all highly developed and cultured cities. If the new recruits were joined by experienced cadres from the old 'liberated areas' there should be sufficient manpower to take control of the south-west. He entrusted the task of creating this South-West Service Corps to Song Renqiong who had been his deputy political commissar in the 129th Division and who was then director of the Nanjing Military Control Commission (*junguan hui*). A trawl of the local schools and colleges produced the names of thousands of students, educated youngsters, teachers, engineers and other specialists who agreed to volunteer and this was whittled down to a list of over 10,000 who were considered sufficiently able and politically reliable. Deng also persuaded the Central Committee to let him have an extra 6,000 senior cadres from the established 'liberated areas', including specialists in policing, news and broadcasting, post and telecommunications and finance to join his South-West Service Corps. Deng had the confidence of the leadership and sufficient influence to secure the resources that he needed. After a period of frenetic activity the first batch of the South-West Service Corps was assembled in Shanghai on 12 June 1949; the second in Nanjing on 25 June; and a third in Wuxi on 12 July.

Deng was concerned about the practicalities of assembling his new and untested organisation but also about the need to prepare them ideologically for their task. In August and September he compiled documents clarifying their role and the party's expectations of them. Preparation and training took weeks but this was not the only reason for the delay in despatching the corps to the south-west. The Central Committee was concerned that the United States, still backing Chiang Kai-shek, might intervene to stop the CCP taking over China: they were weighing up the need to secure the south-west against the danger of having insufficient forces to defend the east coast. Eventually, after their 'little Long March', units of the South-West Service Corps arrived in Guiyang, Chongqing, Kunming and other cities of the south-west between 20 November 1949 and 20 February 1950.

It was not until 20 October 1949 that the 2nd Field Army left Nanjing en route for the south-western provinces to confront the remnants of the Guomindang Army under General Hu Zongnan. On 26 November they moved towards Chongqing, the largest city in the region and Chiang Kai-shek's temporary capital during the Japanese occupation. Mao Zedong had instructed Deng to delay taking over the city until Chiang Kai-shek left on 29 November: it was liberated the following day by Chen Xilian's 3rd Regiment and on 3 December the 2nd Field Army established its headquarters in Chongqing. The South-Western Bureau of the Chinese Communist Party began work on 8 December. Although Mao had proclaimed the inauguration of the People's Republic in Beijing, Deng Xiaoping could claim the credit for physically seeing off the remnants of the Chiang regime.

By the end of December 1949, all nationalist forces in Sichuan had been either wiped out or neutralised. The 2nd Field Army had triumphed in the South-Western Campaign (*Xinan zhanyi*), the 'final battle for the mainland'. Deng may have risen to the highest ranks of the Communist Party, but he had an important military role until the very end of the civil war. Deng and Liu issued a four-point 'admonition' (*zhonggao*), to the defeated Guomindang, advising former nationalist political and military officials that it would be in their best interests to cooperate in the peaceful reconstruction of Chongqing. By the end of December 1949 the remaining Nationalist units in the south-west had either surrendered or defected to the PLA: Chongqing and its region were firmly under Deng's control.[3]

SUPPRESSING 'BANDITS' AND COLLECTING GRAIN

Deng's immediate priorities as first secretary (*diyi shuji*) of the South-Western Bureau were campaigns to 'suppress bandits' (*jiaofei*) and collect tax grain (*zhengliang*). This populous, sprawling and mountainous region was a byword for poverty, poor communications and complex relations between ethnic groups, and the CCP had to work with officials, teachers and other public servants (*gongjiao renyuan*) who had been in post under the Guomindang. Providing food for a total of 2 million individuals (600,000 communists, 900,000 Guomindang supporters who had come over to the communists and 500,000 administrators and managers of the former regime) was a major problem. Deng's solution was to combine the collection of tax grain with a strict campaign to suppress 'bandits'. The combat troops of the 2nd Field Army had to be transformed swiftly into work teams to implement this policy. From experience Deng knew that military control was not enough: the army had to be able to produce its own food.

The 'bandit suppression' campaign was necessary because former Guomindang troops who had not surrendered and local brigands frequently attacked the CCP work teams when they were collecting grain – outlaws also needed food. It was estimated that in southern Sichuan only one tenth of the essential tax grain had been collected by the end of February 1950.

Throughout February and March 1950 Deng personally chaired working conferences (*gongzuo huiyi*) of staff responsible for grain collection in the provinces of Yunnan, Guizhou, Sichuan and Xikang (part of the Kham region of Tibet which was later incorporated into Sichuan). Two officials based in southern Sichuan argued that CCP policies on grain collection in areas where there was a shortage or a surplus of grain were unclear and too strict. Deng was unsympathetic to their special pleading and criticised them in what were for him unusually sharp tones. That evening he invited them to dinner, apologised for having criticised them severely, and acknowledged that many others took the same view. However, he insisted that, in the crisis that they faced, the impact of a more moderate policy might mean that they could not feed people at all. Deng had rejected a reasoned argument which had considerable merit but he had also demonstrated a sure political touch and did not alienate his staff. He deployed the 15th Army to reinforce existing units, effectively supporting the views of his critics but also removing any excuse for not collecting suffient tax grain. By the end of August the grain collection campaign was on target.

Over 850,000 'bandits' were reported to have been 'wiped out' in 1950. As with similar figures presented to indicate the CCP's success in eliminating opposition in the early years of the PRC, it is not possible to be certain whether this figure reflects the number of people executed or simply the size of opposition groups rendered ineffective. In either case the implication was clear: problems in collecting tax grain had not been the result of local economic conditions, but a show of resistance by landlords and officials to the authority of the new government. Deng demonstrated that he had seen through their subterfuge and, by conveying his firmness (or ruthlessness) to his subordinates, had ensured the success of the policy. On 28 January 1951 Mao Zedong personally endorsed Deng's approach in the south-west and declared that his methods should be studied throughout China.[4]

'WEAPONS MUST CHANGE SHOULDERS'

The campaign against the 'bandits' was essential to the survival of the new regime. The capture of Chongqing was swift, but it was not bloodless, and armed resistance to the communists continued for some years. Just as the communist guerrillas had been described as 'bandits' by the nationalists during their decade of rule from Nanjing, now that the Communist Party was in power, armed opponents, whether they were the remnants of nationalist forces or just local bands of brigands of the type that had roamed the mountainous frontiers between provinces since time immemorial, were all branded as 'bandits' and ruthlessly eliminated. The boot was now on the other foot or, in the words of Deng Xiaoping at a meeting of senior cadres, 'the weapons must change shoulders' (qiang huan jian). The armed force that had been ranged against the communists must be turned against their opponents. In western Sichuan there were an estimated 500,000 weapons in the hands of local families (100,000 alone in the county of Qionglai, which is close to the provincial capital of Chengdu) and they had to be confiscated and placed on reliable shoulders. The South-Western Military District issued a joint directive, 'On the Establishment of People's Armed Force', to ensure that the weapons were on the correct shoulders – those of the peasant militias and rural self-defence squads.

GUIZHOU PEASANT MILITIA

New militias sprang up 'like bamboo shoots after the spring rain' throughout the south-west but they were particularly important in Guizhou, the province to the south of Sichuan which had long been a byword for desperate poverty and hardship. Guizhou had been neglected by successive regimes and only limited military resources had been deployed there. Banditry of the traditional variety was endemic and peasants leapt at the chance of acquiring weapons to protect themselves against marauding bands of outlaws. On 8 March 1950 over 100 ethnic Miao brigands attacked the CCP offices in a village in Pingba County, killing the district party secretary and at least 20 staff and students collecting tax grain. Many Miao villagers feared these brigands and were delighted to be issued with arms through Deng's 'weapons must change shoulders' policy. A poor Miao farmer, presumably chosen by the CCP, became head of the Pingba self-defence squad, one of many grass-roots organisations that were indebted to the new regime.

In another small Guizhou village, in the wooded hillsides on the banks of the Beipan River, families lived behind wooden stockades making earthenware pottery and other artifacts. A group of former Guomindang soldiers, the 'Anti-Communist Anti-Russian United Army', attacked and killed 43 grain tax collectors and joined local landowners in resisting the CCP's land reform movement. A peasant self-defence squad backed by the CCP was created to counter this and by October 1950 the South-Western Military District was able to report to Mao Zedong that over 600,000 people were enrolled in similar groups, eliminating 'bandit gangs' throughout Guizhou. By 1951 the number was over 800,000 and most had been trained and transformed into official People's Militias. Even if these figures were exaggerated by local officials, self-defence squads became an essential tool in the national campaign against counter-revolutionaries and in support of the land reform movement.

LAND REFORM AND MINORITY PROBLEMS

At the fifth full meeting of the South-Western Military Political Committee on 30 July 1950, Deng Xiaoping made a speech, 'On strengthening unity, rent reduction, returning deposits, ethnic minorities and opposing bureaucracy' to pass on a policy decision from Beijing. In common with much of China, rural society in the south-west was bedevilled by high rents and interest rates, but a particular burden for farmers in the region was a traditional system of deposits paid by peasants to their landlords. Organising opposition to this complex and oppressive system of taxation, which garnered support for the CCP and undermined the old order in the countryside, was such a high priority for Deng that he sometimes called it the 'Huai-Hai campaign of the south-west'. It was inseparable from the battle against 'bandits' and the arming of peasant militia and it relied primarily on cadres being able to organise hundreds of thousands of peasant farmers into peasant associations, the rural power base of the CCP. The success of this campaign depended on developing political consciousness and confidence in these associations and this was complicated by the proximity of the national border of China and inter-ethnic relations.

Deng focused on ethnic issues at another conference of the South-Western Bureau in Chongqing on 7 November 1950. The issue at stake was to what extent it was possible to carry out land reform in non-Han areas. Deng's conclusion, based on the reports from outlying regions, was that it was impossible among the 'tribes' (*buluo*) on the frontiers of Vietnam, Burma and India, in the Yi communities of the Greater and Lesser Liangshan Mountains or in the Kham Tibetan areas on the borders of Sichuan. In areas where Miao and Yi peoples lived close to the Han, similar social and economic patterns had evolved and standard land reform policies could be implemented. In the case of Han landlords with Miao or Yi tenants it would be more difficult.

The ethnographic analysis presented at the conference was unsophisticated, but it was a realistic assessment of the practical limitations of differences in customs and social organisation and the ability of the CCP to exert its authority. Deng restrained over-enthusiastic activists who favoured ignoring minority customs and as usual his report to Mao met with the chairman's approval and was widely cited as a model for the whole of China. Deng reinforced these decisions in 'The tasks for 1951', his speech to a plenary session of the South-Western Military Political Committee on 25 January 1951 and, on 9 May 1951, he reported to the Central Committee that the 'Huai-Hai campaign of the south-west' had been successful.

CONSULTING FEI XIAOTONG

Fei Xiaotong was China's most celebrated sociologist and anthropologist and an international authority on rural and minority issues who studied at Tsinghua

University in Beiping (later Beijing) and trained at the London School of Economics under the anthropologist, Bronislaw Malinowski. Fei was the author of *Peasant Life in China*, based on his doctoral thesis, and the co-author (with Chih-yi Chang, a lecturer at National Yunnan University) of *Earthbound China: A Study of Rural Economy in Yunnan*, which drew on fieldwork carried out during the war with Japan. Although he had been a member of the Democratic League, rather than the CCP, in July 1950 Fei was appointed leader of a delegation of ethnic minority specialists advising the Central Committee on policies towards minorities in Sichuan, Guizhou and Yunnan.

At the beginning of this visit, which lasted for over six months, Deng had a long meeting in his office with Fei and asked him directly what the main problems were. Fei realised that Deng was not an ideologue and was amenable to facts and he gave an equally frank response: the relationship between the minorities and the Han was the key issue. Although peasants were often exploited by landlords of their own ethnic group, exploitation by the Han ruling elite was at the root of minorities' hatred of the Han. Fei acknowledged diplomatically that there had been many improvements since the CCP took control but insisted that much work was needed to assist minorities in understanding communist policies. Deng blamed the historical legacy of 'Great Han chauvinism' (*da hanzu zhuyi*) and argued that the behaviour of cadres would demonstrate that there was a new type of Han (*xin hanzu ren*) who would live and work with the ethnic minorities in their own areas and befriend them. Deng conceded that, although the CCP had learned from the minorities during the Long March, mistakes had still been made and there were 'breaches of discipline' which had imposed serious burdens on minority communities – primarily due to the requisition of grain and other foodstuffs. This was due to the exigencies of a revolutionary period but the Party should apologise where necessary. For Deng, the main target was the eradication of the 'chauvinism' of the majority ethnic group, the Han, but the 'narrow nationalism' of ethnic minorities must not be allowed to replace it. Both 'isms' should be thrown out so that ethnic unity (*tuanjie*) could emerge. This reflected Lenin and Stalin's arguments about nationality in the Soviet Union and was also a forerunner of a debate that would emerge in China towards the end of the 1950s. The meeting began soon after 9 o'clock in the morning and lasted for over two hours. Deng pressed Fei to stay for lunch and they continued their discussions while eating. Deng described himself as a mere primary schoolchild in ethnic minority matters and asked Fei to be his 'teacher' and advise him on a regular basis. Fei appreciated Deng's candour and formed a positive impression of him.

This conversation is consistent with the inclusive and broadly based political culture of the early 1950s when drawing in talented and patriotic individuals from outside the Party was seen as both practical and a way of legitimising the authority of the CCP. Deng was willing to seek advice from a range of prominent intellectuals and this political culture of New Democracy lasted for six or seven years. It collapsed between 1956 and 1958 and was replaced by a dogmatic approach that excluded non-Party people and was more in tune with the character and ideas of Mao Zedong.[5]

RULING CHONGQING

Since 1949, most members of China's political elite, with the exception of the original core leadership including Mao Zedong, Zhou Enlai and Liu Shaoqi, served a period of time running a province or a region before moving to central government. For Deng Xiaoping, the city of Chongqing, the province of Sichuan and the south-western region were his introduction to government. Deng had administered remote rural areas conquered by the CCP armies but to run a city the size of Chongqing, with its powerful commercial and industrial elite, presented a challenge of a different order. Chongqing had been Chiang Kai-shek's temporary capital during the Japanese occupation and anyone associated with that administration was automatically suspect. Deng ran Chongqing for two years and eight months and much of his time was spent establishing control and setting up new joint military-political bodies. The way he managed political, military, economic and minority affairs in the south-west won the approval of the Party centre.

Like the rest of China, the people of Chongqing had suffered eight years of an often brutal Japanese occupation and another four years of a devastating civil war. Chinese citizens had not experienced prolonged periods of peace for decades. Chongqing was the base for one of the intelligence training schools of the Sino–American Cooperation Organisation (SACO) and was the scene of vicious retribution against the communists as the Guomindang prepared their final retreat in 1949. This episode was immortalised in the 1961 novel *Red Crag* (*Hongyan*) and is still part of Chongqing's collective memory, reinforced by gruesome photographs and displays in the Revolutionary Martyrs Museum, which is built on the site of nationalist concentration camps at Geleshan in which as many as 300 communist prisoners were massacred. This is a controversial period of China's modern history, not least because of allegations – strenuously denied – that

American intelligence operatives of SACO were implicated in the torture and deaths of communists in the camps.

After years of marching, fighting and revolutionary propaganda, some cadres took the view that, since Chongqing had fallen, the revolution was over; they turned to setting up businesses and acquiring houses or cars. Chongqing with its steep roads and narrow streets was too difficult for some to get around on foot and Deng referred to them contemptuously as 'five *li* legs' (*wuli tui*), who were not capable of walking more than 5 *li* (just over 2 kilometres).

This was becoming a national phenomenon; a minority of army officers and Party cadres were seduced by the soft city life, and were spoiled and potentially or actually corrupt. Deng tackled this issue by convening a meeting of county-level and above cadres in the assembly hall of the South-Western Bureau. It was an early spring morning and Deng, his hair closely cropped, was wearing a military-issue white shirt, his arms on the table as usual and in front of him an enamel cup. He was glowing with health, but his demeanour was serious, every inch the tough, spartan political commissar about to deliver an important but unwelcome message. In a polite but forceful manner he told the assembled cadres that the defeated Guomindang had left them with a gaping wound that had to be healed. Unemployment and poverty required the complete rebuilding of the local economy. He then turned to the 'five *li* legs', who had managed perfectly well when they were on the move with the army but within a few days of arriving in Chongqing discovered that they needed cars, not to mention fine houses. He announced that the South-Western Bureau had established an office to allocate houses and cars and that he would take personal responsibility to ensure that any seized without authorisation would be returned to their original owners. The rash of illegal confiscations ceased, but he reiterated these points at a meeting of the Chongqing Party Committee on 6 June 1950, linking them to a Central Committee document on rectifying the Party's style of work that had been issued in May. He also instructed senior staff of *Xinhua Daily* (the official newspaper of the South-Western Bureau) to publish a statement on his campaign, emphasising that the rules applied to everyone, no matter how distinguished their revolutionary past. Deng's actions in Chongqing contributed to the launch in 1951 of the nationwide Three-Anti (*sanfan*) campaign against the growth of corruption, waste and bureaucracy among new urban cadres. Dealing with industry and commerce in Chongqing involved a delicate balancing act. The CCP did not wish to alienate local businesses: their cooperation was essential to ensure that production and communications were restored, especially after the outbreak of the Korean War in

June 1950, in which Chinese military units played a major role. However, it was also essential that cadres who worked with and regulated businesses did not get too close to management and absorb their values. The 'socialisation' of industries, bringing them under state control, which was in part a response to this problem, did not become a national policy until the implementation of the first Five-Year Plan in 1953–7.

Deng Xiaoping had emerged from the civil war in a powerful political position but, in common with the rest of the Communist Party leadership, he had to make the difficult transition from military command to civilian administration. Deng did not move easily from a military to civilian style of management. Much military work still had to be done, including the relocation and absorption of former nationalist troops, and providing support for operations in Tibet for which Sichuan is a natural staging post. Friends and colleagues of Deng insist that he was always willing to listen to the opinions of others but he did not like long meetings: the first full session of the South-Western Military Administrative Council, which governed Sichuan until a provincial administration was established in 1954, lasted for only nine minutes, which cannot have allowed time for a great deal of listening or consultation.[6]

DEMOCRACY AND CHONGQING'S SCHOOLS

On 6 July 1951 a letter published in *Xinhua Daily* caught Deng Xiaoping's attention. It was written, using the name of Xu Xiuying, by a teacher at the Shapingba middle school, which was in what was then Chongqing No. 3 District but is now simply known as Shapingba. A number of universities and other educational establishments are based in Shapingba, many of them having been relocated there in the late 1930s during the war against Japan, and it was a centre of intellectual activity during Deng's tenure as Chongqing Party secretary.

Xu Xiuying complained about the inefficient way that teachers were being used in schools by the local cultural and educational management authorities, in particular that they were being required to take part in anti-illiteracy campaigns and forced to attend propaganda meetings that had nothing to do with education. Teachers did not have sufficient time to prepare lessons or take proper breaks, and the quality of teaching and the running of the schools were being adversely affected. She explained that she was writing under an assumed name for fear of reprisals and asked the paper to respect her anonymity. This letter, published so soon after the liberation of Chongqing, produced a strong reaction, including letters in a similar vein from other teachers at the same school. The editors decided that her criticisms should be taken seriously because of the mounting dissatisfaction at the way teachers and students were being used. Deng Xiaoping called for a report and personally put the finishing touches to a *Xinhua Daily* editorial entitled 'It is time to end the chaos in the educational work in our schools and colleges': he issued instructions that copies of the editorial should be displayed prominently in work units that had been guilty of moving staff around carelessly (*luanchou luandiao*).

There was a joint response to this reader's letter from 'the teaching and ancillary staff at the Shapingba Primary School' with the head teacher's name heading the list, described as a 'letter stating our position' (*shenming xin*). It criticised Xu Xiuying for making unwarranted criticisms, falsifying the truth and bringing the school's name into disrepute, and demanded that the paper print a rebuttal. A few days later the paper received from the District No. 3 People's Government another letter which claimed not only that Xu Xiuying's complaints were untrue, but that there was no-one by that name in the school; this was of course true since she had written using a *nom de plume*. Another letter from teachers at the school (also anonymous) revealed that the 'joint response' had been written by the principal who had forced all the teachers to sign. This letter added that they all felt that Xu's criticisms were justified and invited the paper to send a reporter to the school to investigate. Things were worse than Xiu had reported. The principal, who had bullied the staff into signing the letter, finally revealed that he had been forced to write the 'joint' letter by the head of the local Department of Culture and Education of the local People's Government. *Xinhua Daily* published the set of letters as classic examples of bureaucracy stifling democracy, put the blame firmly on the local People's Government and resolutely condemned this practice.

The head of Culture and Education continued to conceal what he had done for fear of being criticised, and assumed that no-one would take any notice of an unimportant primary school teacher. He refused to make a self-criticism and tried to find out who Xu Xiuying really was; he sent officials to the school and demanded that *Xinhua Daily* reveal her real name. When this was firmly rejected he flew into a rage at members of the editorial board.

Deng Xiaoping followed the story in *Xinhua Daily* and eventually issued written instructions to the Party secretary and the mayor of Chongqing, saying bluntly, 'Sort this out!' The matter was put in the hands of the Party's disciplinary body in District No. 3 and all of those involved in concocting the joint letter and attempting to intimidate the staff of *Xinhua Daily* were disciplined. On 29 November *Xinhua Daily* published a 'written self-criticism' by officials of District No. 3 and reported on the action taken against the staff in his department. Concern about the muddled way teachers were being deployed led to a reversal of the policy and teachers felt that education was being treated more seriously.

In 1951, less than two years into the new regime, the political climate was still fluid. Criticism of Party and government officials could result in accusations of lack of patriotism or even of being counter-revolutionaries at a time when the Chinese People's Volunteers had so recently been involved in the Spring Offensive in the Korean War. There was, however, still a sense that criticism and self-criticism, and a degree of democracy, were vital for a healthy political system and to gain the support of non-communists. Deng Xiaoping emerges from this controversy with considerable credit.[7]

8

BEIJING AND ZHONGNANHAI (1952–6)

After liberation, I was happy with our successes but I was also responsible for some of the mistakes. I was a leading cadre, not a junior one, and from 1956 I was General Secretary. At that time seven photographs were on display in China and mine was one of them.[1]

After less than three years in Chongqing, Deng was summoned to the capital to serve in the central government, initially as both a deputy minister of finance and vice-premier under Zhou Enlai. Deng and his family left Chongqing on a bright sunny morning at the beginning of August 1952 and, bidding farewell to friends and colleagues who had accompanied him to the airport, he took leave of the noisy city and his home province to which he had become even more attached during his time as Party secretary. A two-hour flight in an Ilyushin aircraft took him to an airport in the western suburbs of Beijing where he was received by staff from the central offices of the Communist Party. They escorted him along Xizhimen Avenue to the accommodation that had been allocated to him and his family. It was a traditional Beijing courtyard house (*siheyuan*) behind the Imperial Palace (*Gugong*) and close to Coal Hill (*Jingshan*). It adjoined the house in which Nie Rongzhen and his family lived. Nie, like Deng, was a native of Sichuan and was a successful Eighth Route Army commander who would be promoted to the rank of

Marshal of the PLA in 1955: the Nie and Deng families got on well. Deng was now firmly installed as part of the new political elite with whom he would mix socially as well as professionally.

Before long the Deng family moved even closer to the centre of power – into Zhongnanhai, the walled estate to the west of the old Imperial Palace where the most senior leaders lived and worked. The new house was an old-fashioned courtyard house in Courtyard 3 on the western side of Huairentang (the Hall of Cherished Compassion), a building that is now used for major Party meetings. There were four typical imperial courtyard buildings in Huairentang, surrounded by bright red walls with blue and grey tiled overhanging roofs. Deng's immediate neighbours in these sumptuous surroundings redolent of imperial splendour were Li Fuchun, Tan Zhenlin and Chen Yi, founding fathers of the new state. In two courtyards to the east of the Huairentang lived Dong Biwu, Politburo member and sometime president of the Supreme People's Court, and the diplomat and early CCP member Wang Jiaxiang. Behind the hall lived only one family, that of Liu Shaoqi. The residents of Huairentang were members of a 'great revolutionary family', but as conflicts developed over Mao's policies in the latter part of the 1950s it was by no means a happy family and Zhongnanhai became a hothouse of political intrigue and conflict.[2]

The new People's Republic urgently needed experienced individuals to spearhead the drive for postwar economic reconstruction. It was not easy to find the right people: the existing financial and industrial elite had been largely loyal to the defeated Guomindang regime so Mao and his advisers looked for politically reliable leaders within the Party and the army. With his high-profile military career, his proven administrative ability and his successful track record in economic organisation in the base areas, Deng was a natural candidate. The relationship between Mao and Deng went back to the Central Soviet government in Jiangxi in the early 1930s and although Deng always claimed that he had never been part of a 'Mao faction', by 1949 Mao regarded Deng as his protégé and had followed his career with great interest. There were no discernible ideological differences between Mao and Deng (largely because Deng was never overly concerned with theory or ideology), but his political and personal style of work and his approach to government were very different from that of Mao, and Deng would eventually become part of the opposition to the chairman.[3]

Only days after his arrival in the capital, at a meeting of the Government Administration Council (*Zhengwuyuan*, the forerunner of the State Council) on 7 August, Deng took up his appointment as vice-premier of the Government

Administration Council and deputy head of the CCP Finance Committee – his aptitude for financial affairs in the Taihang Mountains had been noted. He was minister of finance from 18 September 1953 until September 1954. These were powerful roles in government and Party bodies, two of the key elements in the new political structure created as the CCP moved from its revolutionary and wartime mode into a quasi-constitutional form of rule. The military was the third element and Deng already had an established position in the army. His immediate superior was Zhou Enlai, his old comrade in France and Shanghai, and they formed a new political partnership in Zhongnanhai.[4]

NATIONAL BUDGET (1954)

Recollections by former subordinates and colleagues shed light on Deng's approach to his work. Rong Zihe, a deputy minister of finance who had served for eight years in the army under Deng, recalled that his chief respected Mao Zedong and was adept at marrying Mao's vague political instructions with practical tasks. In December 1953 when the Ministry of Finance was working on the draft national budget for 1954, Rong was called in by Deng and asked about Mao's key instructions on the budget. He told Deng that there had been many instructions and that the ministry had compiled and printed a booklet of them, but in broad outline they could be summarised under three headings: 'adequate revenue' (*shouru dazu*), 'tighten up on expenditure' (*zhichu dajin*) and 'allow leeway for unforeseen circumstances' (*liuyou yudi*). These sound more like the principles of a cautious accountant than a revolutionary romantic like Mao. Deng approved and included them in a report in June 1954 which argued for a reliable and stable financial basis for the national budget and linked this with Mao's directives on increasing production. The actual income for 1954 was more than had been estimated and expenditure slightly less, so the People's Bank was able to use this surplus to make loans to industrial and commercial enterprises, relieving a shortage of capital that had existed in 1953. Deng's contribution was his political astuteness and authority rather than any financial expertise but he respected the knowledge of his specialists and was able to frame authoritative political statements in a way that allowed their views to be given sufficient weight.

Deng met Rong and other senior Party figures in the ministry when necessary and received oral reports from the deputy ministers on a weekly basis. Deng was conscious of the fact that the majority of cadres in the ministry were fiscally cautious and after the summer finance meeting of 1953 he uttered a homily for which he was to became famous: 'Don't allow one snake bite to make you so afraid that you won't touch the well rope for ten years.' If their work took into account current conditions and his decisions were wrong then the responsibility would be his. However, if their work was not based on the economic reality they would be to blame.

In his Ministry of Finance, there was a clear demarcation of rights and responsibilities which allowed his subordinates to work effectively and boldly. He insisted on clarity, precision and clear statistics and would not tolerate ambiguity or vagueness. Deng was respected and his deputies felt able to report to him accurately; this was not the case with Mao, whose subordinates often told him what they thought he wanted to hear.

Deng took the CCP's culture of criticism and self-criticism very seriously. He taught his staff that the Ministry should expect criticism from others; if the criticism was justified they should accept it, if not they should be prepared to argue the problem through as quickly as possible. They should not allow complaints and criticisms to build up because the time would come when it was not possible to clear things up. Staff who came into the office on business were not afraid to joke and even be ironic or critical. If Deng heard about criticism he would make enquiries, but if he was reassured that it was just banter he would let the matter rest. Deng was supportive of junior staff, even when they had been severely criticised, and was willing to address concerns even about his most cherished policies.[5]

PURGE OF GAO GANG AND RAO SHUSHI

A serious challenge by Gao Gang and Rao Shushi to Mao's leadership emerged in the second half of 1953 and dominated party meetings until the National Party Conference (*Quanguo daibiao huiyi*) – not a congress (*dahui*) – of March 1955 at which Gao and Rao were formally expelled.

Shortly after Deng's arrival in Beijing the leadership had initiated a process of restructuring in which powerful regional leaders including Gao Gang, Rao Shushi, Deng Zihui and Xi Zhongxun (the father of President Xi Jinping) were transferred from their regional power bases and moved to posts in the capital. Rao arrived in Beijing from Shanghai in February 1953 and Gao moved from the north-east the following November. Both had been highly regarded by Mao, especially Gao, and they resented the fact that in the party hierarchy they were subordinate to Zhou Enlai and Liu Shaoqi.

A draft document prepared on 10 March 1953 by Zhou at Mao's instigation proposed a further restructuring of economic responsibilities. This was approved by the Central People's Government on 28 April and Deng was given the important but unglamorous portfolios of supervision, ethnic minorities (because of his experience in the south-west) and personnel. Gao Gang had lost much of his authority but also concluded that Mao had lost confidence in Zhou Enlai and Liu Shaoqi. Early in autumn 1953, Gao and Rao began to oppose the restructuring openly 'by launching an unbridled attack on Liu Shaoqi and slandering him'.[6] To their critics, including Deng Xiaoping, they were simply trying to improve their own standing at the risk of splitting the party. The enmity between Gao and Liu went back a long way and Gao was taking the opportunity of settling old scores.

The conflict unfolded over the course of two critical meetings. Mao brought Chen Yun and Deng Xiaoping in to support him at a meeting to discuss financial matters between 6 and 11 August 1953. At the second National Organisational Work Conference that took place in September 1953, Liu Shaoqi had to defend the work of his Central Organisation Department against Gao and Rao. Gao and Rao also schemed behind the scenes and tried to win over Deng Xiaoping, arguing that Liu should be removed. Deng backed Liu and, with Chen Yun's support, reported the matter to Mao, alerting him to the seriousness of the threat posed by Gao and Rao.

In December 1953, Mao proposed that Liu Shaoqi should deputise for him while he was away from Beijing on holiday. Gao Gang vehemently argued that he should be the one to take over. On 24 December, at a meeting of the Politburo, Mao complained about the existence of two separate 'headquarters' in Beijing, his own and a shadow one run by Gao Gang. He demanded party unity and an end to the plotting. Gao and Rao were openly criticised at the Seventh Plenary Meeting of the Central Committee in February 1954 and were expelled from the CCP in March 1955, Gao posthumously, as he had committed suicide in August 1954.[7]

PREPARATIONS FOR EIGHTH CCP CONGRESS

Deng's role in the Eighth National Congress of the CCP, held in Beijing from 15 to 27 September 1956, was a clear indication of his elevation to what is now referred to as the 'first generation central leadership with Mao Zedong as the core'. There was no indication that he was anything other than a staunch and loyal supporter of Mao. The Eighth Congress was the first since 1945 and therefore the first since the Party had taken power. There were many reasons for the delay. It could be blamed partly on the civil war and military action to consolidate CCP rule. It could also be blamed on the Korean War, which diverted the CCP leadership from plans for control and reconstruction. However, the most important reason was the purge of Gao Gang and Rao Shushi.

This unpleasant and unseemly feud benefited the next phase of Deng's career. He was appointed secretary-general of the Central Committee (*Zhongyang mishuzhang*) in April 1954 and also replaced Rao Shushi as head of the Party's powerful Central Organisation Department. He presented the report on the Gao Gang and Rao Shushi affair to the National Party Conference of 21–31 March 1955 on behalf of the Party centre. He never repudiated the actions of the Party leadership and as late as 1980 would maintain that Gao Gang was a deceitful plotter and that exposing him and Rao Shushi was essential to avoid harm to many cadres. At the conclusion of the affair he was firmly on the side of Mao but also allied with Liu Shaoqi and Zhou Enlai. This served him well for 12 or 13 years, but would eventually bring him down in the Cultural Revolution when Mao turned against Liu.[8]

The Eighth Congress of the CCP, held in Beijing from 15 to 27 September 1956, was significant because it legitimised the Party leadership that controlled China during the late 1950s and early 1960s. That leadership fell apart in the Cultural Revolution and the Ninth Congress would not be held for another 13 years. The Eighth Congress, in the words of the Party History Research Centre, 'was held at a time when socialist transformation in China had been in the main accomplished and the Party was faced with a new situation and new tasks'. The key tasks were economic development, especially industrialisation, the strengthening of the authority of the CCP) but also 'to gradually and systematically work out a complete set of laws and improve the socialist legal system, and further broaden socialist democracy and vigorously combat bureaucracy'. 'Due to the fact that the Party at that time lacked sufficient mental preparation for building socialism in all spheres [...] many correct ideas advanced at the congress were not put into effect.'[9] In other words, serious conflicts were emerging within the Party leadership as Mao Zedong began advancing his own radical interpretation of Marxism–Leninism and the cautious advocates of economic and legal development were marginalised.[10]

On 31 March 1955, following an instruction from Mao, Deng produced a document proposing that the congress should take place in the second half of 1956.

He submitted it to Mao, who returned it with a note that read: 'Comrade (Zhou) Enlai to review and return to Xiaoping for implementation. In my view we can explain it in this way, only a few words need altering.' Although Mao had overall responsibility, it was Deng who originated key documents and piloted them through the highest echelons of the CCP leadership. Although the bureaucratic procedures of the CCP are not intrinsically fascinating, it is worth examining in detail how Deng used them to build up his authority.

In early October 1955, at the Sixth Plenum of the Seventh Central Committee, Deng tabled the revised document. With the thoroughness and precision for which he was becoming well known he outlined the background, the key elements of the agenda, the election of delegates and other matters. He was deeply involved in all the minutiae of congress arrangements, including the scheduling of the speeches, the checking and approval of drafts, the selection of delegates and the preparation of congress bulletins. On 21 April 1955 Deng submitted to Mao his list of names for membership of the committee to draft the report on the new Party Constitution and the Constitution itself. This was approved by the Politburo on 12 May. The members of the drafting committee for the political report were to be Liu Shaoqi, Chen Yun, Deng Xiaoping, Wang Jiaxiang, Hu Qiaomu, Chen Boda and Lu Dingyi. Members of the committee drafting the Party Constitution and the Report on the Party Constitution were Deng Xiaoping, Yang Shangkun, An Ziwen, Liu Lantao, Song Renqiong, Li Xuefeng, Hu Qiaomu, Ma Mingfang and Tan Zhenlin. Only Deng and Hu Qiaomu were members of both of these drafting committees and Deng's control over the documentation was crucial.

Li Xuefeng was secretary of the Secretariat and one of Deng's closest colleagues and, as a member of the Central Committee and the Chinese People's Political Consultative Conference (CPPCC) Standing Committee, attended most of the drafting meetings. He recalled Deng's evident enthusiasm for, and competence in, the work on the Constitution. Deng even convened a meeting on the eve of his visit to Moscow to attend the historic Twentieth Congress of the Communist Party of the Soviet Union in February 1956. On his return on 23 March 1956, Deng Xiaoping met senior staff of the Secretariat to discuss elections to the Eighth Congress.

The main work on the revision took place in April and May 1956. On 2 April Deng entered the meeting room at 9 am and announced that they were going to discuss a first draft; although he only had a small audience he spoke with great enthusiasm. He chose his words with care but did not hesitate to speak his mind and continued talking until 12.15 when they took a break. Within eight days they had completed a first draft and also a second one which incorporated revisions by members of the drafting committee and the Politburo.

Further meetings discussed the list of delegates to attend the Congress, a list that took five months to finalise. On the afternoon of 12 April he called another meeting, this time of key staff in central government organisations (*zhongyang jiguan*) to explain the process. It was then discussed at a meeting of the Politburo chaired by Liu Shaoqi on 19 April. Deng's authority was being developed by persistent and detailed hard work in the bureaucracy.

One of the most delicate political issues was the attendance of Wang Ming at the Congress, and Deng worked tirelessly to resolve this. Wang had been Mao's principal opponent in the 1930s and had lived in Moscow until 1949 apart from a brief period in the early 1940s. He was an outsider, but his status as a Comintern official had to be considered. On 31 July Deng drafted a letter on behalf of the Central Committee, at its summer retreat in Beidaihe, to send to the ailing Wang Ming. The letter informed Wang that the Eighth Congress would begin on 15 September and that he had been selected as a delegate for the city of Beijing. The Central Committee hoped that he would attend if his health permitted. Wang Ming did not respond, so on 6 August Deng drafted a telegram to Li Fuchun who was visiting the Soviet Union, asking him to call on Wang and inform him of the dates of the Congress. If Wang were not able to attend on health grounds, Deng asked whether he would submit his thoughts in writing. Wang Ming had no alternative but to make his position clear and on 8 September his belated response was rapidly handed over to Deng. Wang asked for his profound regrets to be conveyed to the Central Committee and the delegates and requested that they grant him leave of absence on the grounds of ill health. Mao agreed and authorised Deng to circulate this to delegates.

Wang Ming was elected as a member of the Eighth Central Committee, as he had been of the Seventh. Looking back at the Eighth Congress 40 years later, Li Xuefeng interpreted this as an expression of collective leadership in contrast with the move towards one-man rule by Mao that soon became apparent. The regulations for selecting candidates for membership of the Central Committee were changed. Previously, names for consideration had been drawn from the leadership of the military and the six Great Administrative Regions [*liu ge daqu*] into which China had been divided between 1949 and 1954. This system had enabled Gao Gang and Rao Shushi to accumulate power, but, after the work put in by Deng and his colleagues, anyone was permitted to propose names and over 400 were put forward, yielding a much wider range of candidates.[11]

As the date of the Congress approached Deng ran more meetings on the revision of the Constitution to resolve detailed issues that had arisen. This was difficult and time-consuming, but those involved were able to make suggestions without fear of being intimidated and felt that they were working to enhance democracy and collective leadership in the Party. One issue was Deng's wish to devolve military and State Council matters to another body, but Mao insisted that the Secretariat should handle everything. As a result the power of the Secretariat and of Deng extended into these areas as well.

Documents drafted by Deng Xiaoping were always succinct and clear, influenced by his experience in issuing orders on the battlefield. On 15 August 1956 he drafted the following communication for the Central Committee at Beidaihe:

> (1) The Eighth Congress will convene on 15 September. (2) It has now been decided to hold preparatory meetings for the Eighth Congress from 1 to 14 September. (3) Please inform all delegates that they must be sure to arrive in Beijing by 31 August and report to the Central Committee General Office. (4) The Central Committee has determined that alternate delegates elected by all districts and work units shall all without exception attend the Eighth Congress. Please instruct them to arrive in Beijing at the same time.

On 22 August 1956, the Seventh Plenary Session of the Seventh Central Committee was introduced to the underlying principles of the constitutional revision by Mao, who underlined the number of different versions that had come and gone and argued that this was a triumph for inner-Party democracy. Mao had emphasised the need to set out the general approach and principles underlying the Constitution before going into detail but Deng said that this was not always possible and that a document like the Constitution needed to be argued over character by character. Mao nodded his approval: he was notorious for being impatient with details, whereas Deng was in his element drafting and redrafting documents. Even at a meeting of this level Deng was prepared to correct Mao and Mao was prepared to accept his comments.

After the full meeting of the Central Committee Deng sat at his desk to ponder the circular that he had been instructed to draft and send to regional Party committees. There were still important details to be ironed out, including the number of vice-chairmen; whether there should be a system of permanent representatives in the Party leadership as there was in the National People's

Congress; the nature and authority of the Secretariat and how often the Party congress should meet, but he had been given the authority to proceed, as long as, in Mao's words, the Party Constitution 'fully embodied legality and the mass line'. Deng used the circular to highlight these outstanding issues and solicit comments. When responses had been synthesised, Mao arranged to meet Deng one evening to discuss them and within a few days Deng was in a position to report to Mao, Liu Shaoqi, Zhou Enlai and Zhu De with a revised draft of Clause 37 that dealt with the structure of the central organisation of the Party. By 10.00 pm on 10 September, with the Congress only five days away, Mao was still deliberating, but eventually responded to say that only Clause 3 needed further attention – the addition of three characters. Mao looked critically at Deng's revisions, but his alterations were usually on points of style rather than content.

Three days before the Eighth Congress convened, Deng had personally checked and approved the procedure to be adopted. The conference would open each day at 2.00 in the afternoon and close at 7.00 in the evening; speakers must all report their names to the platform and speak for no longer than 20 minutes unless the presiding chairman agreed otherwise; voting on congress decisions would be by two shows of hands, for and against; and the election of the Central Committee would be by secret ballot. This attention to detail and meticulous, even pernickety, approach to the mundane but essential groundwork for meetings assured him a measure of control that he would not otherwise have been able to achieve.[12]

DENG AT THE EIGHTH PARTY CONGRESS

On 16 September 1956, there was a solemn and expectant hush in the main conference hall of the Chinese People's Political Consultative Conference building as the presiding chairman announced that Deng Xiaoping was about to present his report on the revision of the Party Constitution to the Second Session of the Eighth Congress. It was followed by enthusiastic applause as Deng strode to the speaker's podium, wearing a grey *zhongshan* jacket: he positioned himself in front of a bank of six microphones, put on his spectacles and began to read his report. The Xinhua News Agency reported that 'Deng Xiaoping's report was 29,000 characters long; it took two hours and fifteen minutes to read and he was interrupted continuously by enthusiastic applause'.[13] There were 1,011 delegates assembled in the hall (15 had tendered their apologies). Mao Zedong, Zhou Enlai and Zhu De were sitting in a row, apparently concentrating on the text while Deng spoke.

The report emphasised the Party's policy on the 'mass line', democratic centralism and opposition to 'idolatory' (*chongbai*) of individuals and warned against complacency and bureaucracy. Deng had drawn lessons from observing the Congress of the Communist Party of the Soviet Union, held in Moscow from 14 to 25 February and renowned for Khrushchev's 'secret speech' denouncing Stalin's brutal despotism and the 'cult of the personality'. The Moscow conference, Deng argued, demonstrated clearly the dangers of deifying individuals, and he pointed approvingly to Mao Zedong's strictures against singing the praises of individual leaders and to the need for strengthening the collective leadership of the Party. There was much applause at this point, but Deng went on to say that the deification of powerful individuals was a long-standing social phenomenon in China and it would be surprising if it did not exist within the Chinese Communist Party.

Deng was following the general line of the international communist movement and attacking Stalin's dictatorship, but he was also criticising the tendency, already apparent within the CCP since the early 1940s, to treat Mao as a local version of Stalin. In the autumn of 1956 Deng could use Mao's own words to attack the Mao cult, which did not reach its height until a decade later in the Cultural Revolution.

Speaking in 1997, the last year of his life, Deng reviewed the evolution of leadership of the CCP since 1935:

> Our Party's leadership collective (*lingdao jiti*) was formed step by step after the Zunyi Conference (1935) and it was comrades Mao, Lu, Zhou, Zhu, and Ren Bishi. After comrade Bishi's death comrade Chen Yun was added. By the Eighth Party Congress, a Standing Committee of six had been established – Mao, Liu, Zhou, Zhu, Chen, Deng – and later Lin Biao was added. This collective leadership lasted until the Cultural Revolution.[14]

On the surface the Eighth Congress had succeeded in creating a unified leadership suitable for a ruling party (*zhizheng dang*), rather than a contender in a revolutionary war. The leadership had recovered from the debilitating conflict with Gao Gang and Rao Shushi and the Congress set out rational and achievable policies for development following the success, by common consent, of the first Five-Year Plan. This was the story for public consumption, but the underlying reality was serious conflict within the leadership. Mao was deeply dissatisfied with the direction in which the Party and government were heading and there was a concerted attempt by some of his most senior colleagues to reduce his authority. He was also growing increasingly disenchanted with the CCP's notional allies in the Communist Party of the Soviet Union, which provided the models for the political and economic institutions of the People's Republic, and was turning his attention to forging a distinctive Chinese form of development.

In spite of the prominence that had been given by the Politburo to Mao's April 1956 policy paper, 'On the Ten Major Relationships', at the Eighth Party Congress, in the words of the trenchant anti-Communist Jesuit analyst Laszlo Ladany, Mao's 'wings had been clipped' and the Congress was 'dominated largely by the men of the Party machine' around Liu Shaoqi and Deng Xiaoping. In the new Constitution, largely the responsibility of Deng Xiaoping, which was presented to the Congress, Mao's status as party chairman would be significantly reduced. All references to the 'thought of Mao Zedong', which had appeared in the preamble to the 1945 Constitution, were excised and, as Jürgen Domes argues, the new Constitution 'provided for institutional safeguards for a more open process of internal Party decision-making'. Former political adversaries of Mao were given greater prominence and, although Mao remained a member of the powerful Secretariat, he was to be one member among five in the Politburo Standing Committee, rather than its chairman as he intended. Deng Xiaoping may have begun the Eighth Congress as a protégé of Mao but by the end he had demonstrated a degree of independence and was more closely allied with Liu Shaoqi as part of the group arguing for a broader political base in the party.[15]

SECRETARY-GENERAL AND GENERAL SECRETARY

At the Seventh Plenum held two days before the Eighth Congress, Mao raised the question of appointing a deputy chairman and general secretary for the CCP and proposed Chen Yun and Deng Xiaoping for the two posts. The Central Committee had agreed informally that there should be four deputy chairmen – Liu Shaoqi, Zhou Enlai, Zhu De and Chen Yun; there was also general agreement on the need for a general secretary, and Deng Xiaoping was the obvious candidate. These appointments would provide a counterbalance to Mao within the Central Committee.

Smoking as he spoke, Mao acknowledged that these appointments were necessary for long-term stability: he was politically astute enough to recognise that they would restrict his power and he was not enthusiastic about devolving authority. He suggested that he, Zhu De and, to some extent, Liu Shaoqi were 'bit part players' who were not qualified to be 'leading actors', but should play supporting roles and assist where necessary. Zhou Enlai, Chen Yun and Deng Xiaoping were not considered to be 'bit part players'.

Deng, sitting bolt upright, made his response to Mao's proposals crystal clear. The position that Mao had set out had many positive aspects: (1) the security of the Party and the state – 'wind breaks' would be useful if anything unexpected happened; (2) the appointments would prevent problems of succession such as those that had followed the death of Stalin; (3) considerations of age, health and energy might mean that certain individuals would not always be able to continue to play central roles. Mao was not mentioned directly in this discussion but everyone in the room, including Mao, knew that the discussion was about him. He was 63 years old and his health was poor, although it had recently improved. In the draft of the revised Party Constitution that Deng had submitted to Mao on 5 August, Clause 37 that dealt with these new appointments simply read 'Deputy Chairmen – various' and Mao had added 'plus one General Secretary'. Mao still regarded Deng as a potential ally or at least as a useful counterweight in the power struggle that was developing within the Central Committee.

On Mao's insistence, Deng was appointed general secretary (*zong shuji*) of the Party's Central Committee, whereas previously his title had been secretary-general (*mishu zhang*). There is virtually no difference in the English titles but the *zong* ('general') in the Chinese title of the new post indicates higher status and greater authority. Deng, with modesty which may have been genuine or merely conventional, wondered aloud whether he was suitable for the honour of being general secretary and said he was 'fearful and in awe' (*chenghuang chengkong*) of the challenge but that he would accept it if 'the work of the revolution required it'. Mao countered that 'general secretary' was more in line with foreign conceptions of the work that Deng was already doing and that if everyone thought he was suitable then he was suitable. He proceeded to give his reasons why Deng should accept the appointment, his 'propaganda' as he called it.

> In my opinion Deng Xiaoping is a fair and reasonable man: like me, he is not without his faults but he is reasonable. He is able and capable at his job. Can we say that he is good at everything! Hardly! Like me there are many things that he has done wrongly and many things that he has said that he should not have. But comparatively speaking he is pretty good at his job. He is quite thoughtful and quite reasonable, a kind and honest man who does not frighten people. He says he is not good enough for the job but I think he is and, as for his suitability, that will have to depend on public opinion but from what I have observed he is quite

suitable. There will be those who are not satisfied with him, just as there are those who are not satisfied with me. I cannot believe that Deng Xiaoping has never offended anyone but generally speaking he takes the overall situation into account and is kind, reasonable and impartial when dealing with problems. He is very hard on himself when he has made mistakes and says that he feels 'fearful and in awe'; well, he has been through internal party struggles.[16]

Although sometimes presented as a supportive speech, this is hardly a ringing endorsement of Deng. At best Mao is damning Deng with faint praise and, when describing Deng's good points, he uses the word *bijiao* which means 'fairly'. He compares Deng's faults with his own but also emphasises Deng's fairness and kindness, which are not words that many in the Party would apply to Mao. Mao thought of Deng as a youngster (he was 52) and a member of the 'young and vigorous faction', and if he was not completely Mao's man, he probably hoped that this promotion would ensure that he became so.

Deng was appointed general secretary and also elevated to full membership of the Central Committee. At the first plenary meeting of the new Eighth Central Committee on 28 September 1956, he was elected to the Politburo and its Standing Committee as well as to the post of general secretary. The Standing Committee of the Politburo had six members – Mao Zedong, Liu Shaoqi, Zhou Enlai, Zhu De, Chen Yun and Deng Xiaoping. At the age of 52 Deng had become a member of the most powerful political body in China. As general secretary he directed the work of the Secretariat for ten years, a period that he regarded as the busiest of his life.

There were still disagreements about Deng's precise role as general secretary. Li Xuefeng, who was also elected to the Central Committee in 1956 but later supported Mao during the Cultural Revolution, suggested to Mao that the Secretariat over which Deng would preside worked for the Politburo and should only have responsibility for the distribution of military and State Council documents. Sensing an attempt to undermine the position of the man on whom he was now depending for support, Mao insisted that the Secretariat was an organ of the Central Committee and that any type of work dealt with by the Central Committee could be handled by the Secretariat and therefore by Deng, especially issuing any documents in the name of the Central Committee. Deng's remit was very broad and would later be extended even though he indicated his willingness to devolve some of his duties – he was never a voracious bureaucratic empire-builder. Mao sanctioned this expansion of role of the Secretariat, and the consequent concentration of power in Deng's hands, and in return he required support.

Although he rarely criticised Mao publicly, Deng was not an unquestioning acolyte, and the chairman desperately needed a henchman. This quality of loyalty rather than any ideological alliance with Mao Zedong had propelled Deng to high office. It is difficult to pin down Deng's philosophy during this period (or indeed at any time). He was a loyal servant of the Party, which was ruling in the orthodox manner based on the experience of the Soviet Union. Although he had been involved in internal disputes, notably the purge of Gao and Rao, there is no suggestion that he had any ideological differences with them: it was just a question of loyalty to the Party and the leader.[17]

9

CAMPAIGN AGAINST RIGHTISTS AND INTELLECTUALS (1956–7)

We do not advocate greater democracy, for it is not a good thing. Hungary tried it, and it will take several years for it to recover. It is the people who have suffered. The same thing happened in Poland, and it will also take quite a long time for that country to recover.[1]

The mistake was broadening the scope (of the Anti-Rightist campaign).[2]

In the middle years of the 1950s, conflict and crisis unsettled the CCP and all communist parties as a series of political upheavals shook the postwar Stalinist system in the Soviet Union and, particularly, in Eastern Europe. In China, serious disputes arose between the Party leadership and the educated elite, many of whom had been attracted by the idea of a 'New China' and were not necessarily fundamentally opposed to the CCP's rule but wished to retain their professional and intellectual independence. The Party's response to their concerns was the Hundred Flowers campaign which encouraged constructive criticism, but the level of criticism of the way the CCP was governing was far deeper and broader than the leadership had anticipated.

Externally, the world communist movement had been shaken by the trenchant attacks on Stalin's legacy launched by Khrushchev at the Twentieth Congress of the

CPSU in February 1956. Violent disturbances in Poland in June were suppressed, but there was a political thaw and the better-known Hungarian uprising began in October of the same year. The de-Stalinisation movement in the Soviet Union was a boon to senior CCP leaders desperate to curb the personal power of Mao Zedong, but the strength of opposition to Moscow's control of the international communist movement came as a shock and provoked different responses from Mao and his political adversaries.

'RIGHTISTS' TARGETED

The Hundred Flowers movement was followed by the introduction on 27 April 1957 of a Rectification Campaign which was directed at 'bureaucracy, sectarianism and subjectivism' in the leadership, intended to address some of the concerns raised during the Hundred Flowers. This was followed closely by the launch of another political campaign, against 'rightists' (*youpai*), a broad and ill-defined term that made it possible to attack a wide range of teachers, writers, scientists and other professionals who had been persuaded to make public criticisms of the system during the Hundred Flowers movement. This Anti-Rightist Campaign (*fan youpai yundong*) is generally blamed on Mao Zedong, and its evolution is illustrated by two different versions of his obscure and virtually incomprehensible philosophical essay, 'On the Correct Handling of Contradictions among the People', that appeared in February and June 1957. The Hundred Flowers movement is remembered because of the literary quotation with which it was launched, 'let a hundred flowers bloom and a hundred schools of thought contend' (*baihua qifang baijia zhengming*), and its optimistic expectation of an open exchange of views. The Anti-Rightist Campaign is remembered for the vicious denunciations of friends and colleagues that ended careers and ruined thousands of lives.

Deng's primary focus in 1957 was the Rectification Campaign, which addressed some of the criticisms that were raised during the Hundred Flowers and has been almost forgotten. He contributed a report 'On the Rectification Campaign' to the Third Plenum of the Eighth Central Committee that met between 20 September and 9 October 1957 – it was published in *People's Daily* on 19 October 1957. Deng divided the movement into four phases: (1) 'blooming and contending' which had ended in early June; (2) the Anti-Rightist Movement, which, he argued, was by that time drawing to a close; (3) renewed 'blooming and contending' to assist the Party in identifying its problems; and finally (4) a long-term re-examination of the process by all concerned. Deng argued that the principles of the Hundred Flowers movement were intended to encourage the participation of workers and peasants in intellectual discussion and that the Party reserved the right to deal 'decisive blows' against any opposition. His views on the intellectuals who were the most critical of abuses by the CCP and its government, as expressed in this speech, were entirely negative.

> Most of the intellectuals come from families of the bourgeois or petty bourgeois classes and they have had a bourgeois education; they belong therefore to the bourgeois class. Rightist elements have been found, mostly among intellectuals, in schools of higher education, in government offices, in newspapers, in publishing houses, in literature and art, among politico-legal workers, among scientists, engineers, doctors and pharmacists. Among the rightists, those of the democratic parties had a privileged position from which to recruit people [...] Some of them did become leftist in earlier periods but the majority have never abandoned their bourgeois class stance. The rightists said that 'amateurs should not lead experts' [...] they wanted independence and freedom, freedom of the press, freedom of publication, and freedom of literature and art. The Party has decided now to train intellectuals from among the working class. These will be both 'red and expert'. We must raise up cadres from among able workers and peasants. We must also get them from among able intellectuals, but these will have to go through the experience of production and struggle.

This could have come directly from the pen of Mao Zedong. The most charitable construction that can be placed on this is that Deng was following Mao's lead in public statements (in the tradition of democratic centralism) while pursuing the Rectification Campaign as a bureaucratic means of responding to some of the criticism of the Hundred Flowers period. It is a salutary reminder that, although the great economic reformer of the 1980s and 1990s was far more open and tolerant in dealing with colleagues than Mao, he was not a liberal, was no admirer of independent thinkers and was opposed to greater political democracy. Whether this was from deep conviction or from political sensitivity in the knowledge that he had to concede much to Mao and his supporters in order to push through what he really considered to be essential can only be surmised. When he came to power in the 1970s it was these independent-minded experts that he turned to in support of his reforms.

While Deng's speeches and writings from 1975 onwards have been widely publicised, this 1957 speech is not readily available in China and does not appear in his *Selected Works* that was published in English in 1992. Neither is it included in *Jianguo yilai*, an important multi-volume collection of key political documents. The 'democratic parties', non-Communist parties willing to work with the CCP in the 1950s, were early casualties of the Anti-Rightist Campaign and any possibility of their exerting independent influence on state policy was extinguished in 1957.

The Anti-Rightist Campaign is now viewed in China as the beginning of an erroneous and embarrassing lurch to the left, blamed entirely on Mao, and a veil has been drawn over whether Deng Xiaoping lent tacit support to Mao in the suppression of political criticism during the late 1950s. The campaign ended in victory for Mao over his internal critics and paved the way for the Great Leap Forward and the Cultural Revolution. Although much of the blame for the campaign and subsequent excesses can be laid at Mao's door, in the words of Jürgen Domes, 'Mao's policy could hardly have prevailed at the time had it not gained the approval of the leading men in the civil Party apparatus around [Liu Shaoqi] and [Deng Xiaoping]'. Deng and Liu were concerned about the direction in which Mao was leading the Party and the country but they either would not, or could not, prevent it. Deng had enjoyed a meteoric rise that was quite unusual in the leadership at the time. On the 1945 Central Committee he had only occupied the twenty-fifth position, but he had then been elected to the Politburo in 1955 and became general secretary in 1956. Even if he did not accept that he was a member of Mao's faction, he had been Mao's protégé and he knew that he owed his position to Mao. His strategy during the Anti-Rightist Campaign, and again at the Seven Thousand Cadres Conference in 1962, was to acquiesce in Mao's rhetoric while trying to put in place practical policies and procedures that mitigated its effects. He also tried to bridge the gap between Mao and Liu Shaoqi – a thankless task. He can be criticised for inaction or failing to oppose Mao actively, but he was not an enthusiastic supporter of the chairman's policies.[3]

MISSION TO THE NORTH-WEST (MARCH–APRIL 1957)

The entire senior leadership had to implement the 'spirit' of both the Eighth Party Congress and Mao Zedong's 'contradictions' speech and convey it to Party and state organisations in the regions. Deng was assigned to the north-west, specifically the provinces of Shanxi, Gansu and Shaanxi, with which he was familiar as they included his old stamping grounds at the time of the Long March and the Dabie Mountains campaign. Deng left Beijing towards the end of March 1957 on his first inspection tour after assuming the post of Party general secretary and his first port of call was Taiyuan in Shanxi. He was received by Tao Lujia (1917–2011), the Shanxi Party Secretary, who had made a speech at the Eighth Party Congress arguing for more local autonomy in the development of relations between agriculture and industry, one of the most hotly debated issues at the time. Deng listened to a report from Tao, assiduously read documentation on local developments, and responded in terms of 'resolving contradictions between the masses of the people and the leadership', echoing Mao's speech.

He spoke to students and teachers and gave his analysis of the international situation, including the developments in Poland and Hungary that had shaken the communist world. In his speech, reported in a local newspaper, he emphasised China's obligation to take either the capitalist or socialist road and told his audience that they really had no alternative to socialism. However, he added that they should 'study everything that is good in the world, including good things in the USA', noting, however, that the 'key things could not be learned from America'.

Turning to domestic conflict, 'contradictions', in Mao's terms, he blamed mistakes on inexperience, over-enthusiasm and trying to do everything too quickly, but argued that these were mistakes made during the course of forging ahead (*qianjin zhong de cuowu*). 'Success is important, shortcomings are secondary and some mistakes are inevitable,' he said, 'but the most important thing of all is to draw lessons from the mistakes'. He outlined the Central Committee's policy on key issues such as the suppression of counter-revolutionaries, democracy and centralisation, prospects for young people and leadership by the Party. He told his audience that 'strengthening the democratic life' (*jiaqiang minzhu shenghuo*) was essential and that there must always be opportunities for people to put forward their ideas. In the case of mass disturbances he argued that 'we should stand among the people to be able to deal with problems among the people' (*renmin neibu de wenti*), using the more neutral 'problems' (*wenti*) rather than the politically loaded 'contradictions' (*maodun*). In the end, he told them, those who were not prepared to be reasonable must be isolated: political and ideological work 'had been relaxed recently', but it had not been possible to resolve all problems and they should never 'slacken or waver' in this work.

This equivocal speech is an indication of the political tension in Beijing and Deng's growing unease about Mao's style of leadership. The response of the

Central Committee to the Hundred Flowers campaign was to impose greater restrictions on the publication of negative criticisms. Deng was walking a tightrope: his mission was to present the policies of the Central Committee, but that committee was far from unanimous.

On 30 March, Deng returned to the same issues when he spoke to representatives of industrial enterprises in Taiyuan and emphasised the four main themes that he considered necessary for officials to understand. These were leadership by the Party (*dang de lingdao*); mass disturbances (*qunzhong naoshi*); democratic centralism (*minzhu jizhong zhi*) in the management of factories; and the relationship between the CCP and the 'democratic parties' (*minzhu dangpai*). He did not give a dull and lifeless sermon using bureaucratic Stalinist jargon, but attempted to explain in clear language what these policies meant in practical terms, achieving a rapport with his audience. Deng then travelled by train with Tao Lujia to Taigu County to inspect industry and agriculture in this rural area. He attended a 'meeting of 3,000' (*sanqian hui*), attended by provincial, district and county cadres in Hongtong County, and listened intently to a report on plans for 1956–67. Unlike other senior leaders he reserved his comments until the end of the report, which was taken as an indication of genuine interest in what his subordinates said.

From Hongtong, Deng travelled to Linfen, still in southern Shanxi, where he was impressed by the use of spring water in the cultivation of vegetables at the Dragon Temple and arrived in Gansu Province on 4 April. The following day he outlined the current situation to cadres assembled in the auditorium of the North-West Nationalities Institute (*Xibei minzu xueyuan*) in Lanzhou, the provincial capital, emphasising the need for economic development and the balance between democracy and Party leadership. He was still using the 1956 slogan of 'letting a hundred flowers bloom and a hundred schools of thought contend' even though central policy was by this time rapidly moving towards rigid controls and the 'Anti-Rightist' movement. He made the obligatory inspection tours of the latest industrial developments and found time to visit an old friend, but his visit to Gansu, one of China's poorest provinces, was brief.

On 6 April he left for Xi'an, where, in addition to his primary mission of communicating the 'spirit of the Eighth Party Congress and Mao's speeches', he was particularly interested in finding out how well the targets of the first Five-Year Plan (1953–7) had been achieved. Under this plan, carried out with Soviet assistance, 24 major projects had been implemented in Shaanxi (17 military and the remainder civilian), including projects related to aviation, space exploration, weaponry, electrical, electrical power, electronics and optics. Deng did not allow this visit to be publicised, as so many of the projects were military in nature. At a tightly packed meeting in the large meeting room of the Zhiyuan Hotel's southern building, Deng sat in an upholstered chair, flanked by provincial and city officials including Zhang Desheng (Shaanxi Province Party Secretary) and Feng Zhi (Xi'an City Party secretary), who expressed his gratitude for the Party's assistance during the first Five-Year Plan. The Guomindang regime had left Xi'an in a complete shambles without even running water and now they had a flourishing electrical engineering sector in the western suburbs, textiles in the east and a cultural district in the south. Feng invited Deng to speak, but Deng insisted on hearing others first. The audience were initially reticent but gradually began to comment. Deng encouraged them not to hold back. The atmosphere grew livelier and the particiants commented on a range of topics including the use of prefabricated materials, reimbursement of work units and the relationship with projects outside the plan. These were detailed issues of immediate and practical concern to cadres in Xi'an, rather than the ideological and theoretical issues that had emerged from Mao's speeches and the Eighth Party Congress, and Deng was at ease in handling their comments and questions. He noted that 70–80 per cent of construction materials in the United States were prefabricated whereas in the USSR it was only 20 per cent, and that Khrushchev had dealt with this problem in his speech to the 1956 CPSU Congress. China had to do the calculations and decide which was best. He discussed contracts for labour and material; the lack of competition in the state construction sector and its impact on costs to the state; and also touched on the complex and ridiculous bureaucracy needed to get permission for expenditure from Beijing by telephone and telegram. This elicited a round of applause. On 7 April he visited other projects and was taken up in an aircraft for a bird's-eye view of Xi'an's development.

The following day, in a packed auditorium at the People's Palace (*Renmin Daxia*) hotel, built in the Soviet monumental style and then still brand new, Deng mounted the podium to another immediate and enthusiastic round of applause. In the modest and self-deprecating style that has become *de rigeur* among Chinese communist politicians, but in Deng's case often appears to be genuine, he explained that his trip had been brief and that his observations necessarily rather superficial but that he wanted to talk to them about problems in reconstruction generally. The construction of socialism, he warned, was likely to take longer and be more difficult even than the revolution that had brought them to power. He praised the progress made in Xi'an since his last visit in 1952 but cautioned against complacency and exaggerating their successes.

The content of this address was more overtly political than his previous, less publicised, talk and Deng referred more frequently to Mao's speeches. Deng emphasised the problems inherent in developing a poor and backward country and the specific conditions of Shaanxi and Xi'an, encouraging cadres to go to Shanghai and learn from the example of businesses run by its 'national capitalists' (*minzu zibenjia*). He was conscious of the problems in finding talented and qualified people, especially in the scientific and technical field, and urged cadres to use the experience not only of the Soviet Union but also of the rest of the world, including the United States. This hardly indicates wholehearted support for the campaign against 'rightists'. The seven years' experience that the PRC already had of construction should not be underestimated because it was experience of China's particular path towards development. Although Deng uttered the obligatory platitudes about the leadership role of the Party and the need for cadres to ensure that they were not cut off from the masses, what interested him most were practical issues such as the availability of shops, cinemas and theatres, and problems caused by inflexible zoning in the city plan.[4]

ZUNYI CONFERENCE CONTROVERSY

A meeting of communist leaders in the city of Zunyi in the early stages of the Long March, between 15 and 17 January 1935, is usually described as an enlarged meeting of the CCP Politburo. It has been discussed in Chapter 5 and it is important in the history of the Chinese Communist Party. For decades it has been presented as the point at which Mao and his colleagues took control, saved the Revolution and set the Party on course for victory. It is controversial because, since the death of Mao in 1976, considerable doubts have been raised as to whether he really did become the 'leader' of the CCP at this meeting, or whether Zhang Wentian (Luo Fu) was elected secretary-general at Zunyi. It also raises the question of whether this meeting of a section of the Party leadership on the Long March was a legitimate Politburo meeting of the whole Party.

By 1955 Mao was firmly in position as leader of both Party and state: the deep divisions that were to beset China for 20 years had not yet emerged openly. In that year a memorial hall was built at 80 Hongqi Road in Zunyi, the site of the conference. There has always been some doubt as to whether Deng Xiaoping was present at the Zunyi Conference, partly because of problems unearthing the relevant documents from Party archives and partly because of political chaos during the Cultural Revolution years and the sensitivity of any discussions that might have affected the legitimacy of Mao's position. When the museum was established, Deng's name was not included in the list of participants that was displayed in the exhibition room, whereas Dong Biwu and Lin Boqu – who did not attend – were listed. Dong and Lin were eventually removed from the list after written confirmation from the CCP General Office. On 18 November 1958 Deng Xiaoping visited the memorial hall with Yang Shangkun, then the director of the Central Committee's General Office (*bangongting*). Deng walked into the exhibition room and climbed the steps into the room where the conference had been held. It was set out exactly as it had been 23 years previously, and he immediately saw in his mind's eye the 1935 meeting and said firmly, 'The meeting was held in here' and, indicating a corner, he added, 'I sat there'.

In 1959, the staff of the memorial hall wrote a formal letter to the Central Committee General Office seeking clarification, based on archival material, of who had really attended the 1935 conference. In a reply dated 28 May 1959, the Central Committee Archive Office told the museum that they were unable to find any official, reliable documentation (*zhengshi kekao de wenjian*) but revealed that in the archives there was one unsigned document on which was written:

> Apart from full and alternate members of the Politburo, the following comrades attended the conference: the commanders and political commissars of the 1st and 3rd Army Group – Lin and Nie, Peng and Yang – and the political commissar of the 5th Army Group, Li Zhuoran. Director Li of the General Political Department (*zong zheng*) and Chief of Staff Liu both attended.

The Archive Office offered this to the museum for information only. Deng insisted that he had been at the conference: the document had no clear provenance; it did not in any case claim that the list was comprehensive; so it only added to the uncertainty. In 1965 the management added Deng's name to the list of participants on the strength of his recollections during his visit. It would have been unwise to suggest that they did not believe the General Secretary of the CCP. They also displayed, on the wall of the exhibition room, photographs of seven members of the current leadership who had attended the Zunyi Conference: Mao Zedong, Zhou Enlai, Zhu De, Chen Yun, Lin Biao and Deng Xiaoping, arranged in order of their ranking in the Politburo Standing Committee.

In 1966, China was engulfed by the tidal wave of demonstrations, political purges and collective violence that followed the launch of Mao Zedong's Cultural

Revolution. A nationwide 'great liaison' of Red Guards had been encouraged by Mao, and a Zunyi Red Guard group met students who had come to the city to 'rebel against the Liu [Shaoqi] and Deng [Xiaoping] line'. When they reached the memorial hall, they seized the letter from the Central Archives in 1959 and vilified Deng for 'distorting history and obstinately squeezing himself into the Zunyi Conference to seek political advantage' (*cuangai lishi, ying jiang ziji saijin Zunyi huiyi, laoqu zhengzhi ziben*). This was part of a campaign to settle accounts (*qingsuan*) with all of Deng's 'anti-party and anti-socialist crimes' and his misrepresentation was, in the eyes of his enemies, one of the most serious charges against him. A large black cross was painted over Deng's name on the list of participants and his photograph was removed from the exhibition room.

Chen Yun (1905–95) was an almost exact contemporary of Deng and later became one of his most important economic aides. He was also on the Zunyi Conference list, but in his document 'Outline of the enlarged meeting of the Politburo at Zunyi', a summary of decisions made by the conference 'for circulation to Red Army units', he did not mention Deng. Various reasons have been suggested for this: the paper was never intended to cover every aspect of the conference; not only was Deng not mentioned, neither was Li De (Otto Braun), the Comintern military adviser, or his interpreter, Wu Xiuquan. In the 1970s when Deng was out of office and twiddling his thumbs at home, he was visited by the child of an old cadre and during a casual conversation the question of the Zunyi Conference arose. Deng seemed irritated and asked whether his entire career really depended on whether or not he had been at that meeting.

In October 1976, after the death of Mao and the arrest of his closest Cultural Revolution allies the 'Gang of Four', the history that had been turned on its head during the 1960s and 1970s could be rewritten. In 1980 the Museum of the Chinese Revolution (the main national museum on the eastern side of Tian'anmen Square), the Zunyi memorial hall and books and articles on Party history all reinstated the name of Deng Xiaoping in the list of participants.

Various different theories have been propounded to explain the confusion, the principal ones being that: he was secretary of the Central Committee team (*zhongyang dui*) not the Central Committee; as editor-in-chief of *Red Flag* (*Hongqi*) he attended the conference as a non-voting delegate but during the course of the meeting he was elected as secretary–general (*mishuzhang*) of the Central Committee, which formally made him a full delegate. It was not until September 1984 when the CCP Central Committee Party History Materials Collection Committee (*Zhonggong zhongyang dangshi ziliao zhengji weiyuanhui*) published 'Investigations into aspects of the enlarged meeting of the politburo in Zunyi' that Deng's status at the meeting was formally clarified and it was acknowledged that he had been elected as secretary-general of the Central Committee at the Zunyi meeting.

The fact that an *ex post facto* decision had been made by an official body does not mean that this was the precise historical truth and Deng's supporters continue to adduce evidence to support his case. They argue that Deng always used this term on his *curriculum vitae* and on other documents that he has written. Deng Yingchao, a long-term member of the CCP and the wife of Zhou Enlai, confirmed that Deng was secretary-general at Zunyi, although she was also reported to have held that position. In material provided for an entry for the *Encyclopaedia Britannica* in 1984, the fact that Deng described himself as having become secretary-general of the Party at the end of 1934 was included without comment. On 26 October 1984, Yang Shangkun, a general who had joined the Politburo two years previously with Deng's support, and who would become President of the PRC in 1988, was asked by Harrison Salisbury whether Deng had been at the Zunyi Conference. Yang said that he had been asked this when he had been in Zunyi in the late 1950s or early 1960s and could not remember, but when he returned to Beijing and asked Premier Zhou Enlai, Zhou said that Deng had been there and that the records of the conference show that he was secretary-general and was responsible for the minutes of the meeting. In 1984, Salisbury asked Liu Ying, the wife of Zhang Wentian (who was also said to have been secretary-general) and she told him that soon after the Zunyi Conference Deng Xiaoping was sent to a combat unit and that she took over the work of the Central Committee secretary-general.

On the basis of this evidence some modern Chinese writers accept that Deng Xiaoping was present at Zunyi but agree that there is still confusion about whether the posts of secretary-general of the Central Committee team and secretary-general of the Central Committee were one and the same. The term Central Group, or team (*zhongyangdui*) was sometimes used to refer to the powerful triumvirate of Mao Zedong, Zhang Wentian and Wang Jiaxiang.

In discussions with Yang Shangkun and other senior leaders in the critical month of June 1989 when troops had been sent into Tian'anmen Square to suppress the Democracy Movement, Deng observed that the CCP leadership in 1935 had been unstable and immature after the internal factional struggles involving Li Lisan, Wang Ming and others and that only after Zunyi did a stable leadership under Mao emerge. Given the emergency of the time, Deng was clearly commenting on his own position and the post-Mao leadership, but nothing that he said conclusively settles the question of whether he was at Zunyi and, if so, in what capacity. The celebrated interview with Deng by the Italian journalist and author Oriana Fallaci in 1980 does not help to clarify matters.

> I was accused of agitating against the Mao Zedong group and was thrown out of office and had to wait for three years before being rehabilitated. That happened in 1935 at Zunyi during the Long March because at Zunyi extreme leftist opportunists were defeated, Wang Ming was pushed to one side and Mao Zedong took back control of the party and made me secretary-general.

At first this appears to be a clear statement by Deng that he was secretary-general but there are various problems with the text. Firstly he would not have been accused of agitating against Mao as the Mao group were the targets of the purge in 1932, and Mao could not have taken back control of the Party in 1935 since he had not been in control in the first place. The interview was conducted by Falacci in English and Deng in Chinese with interpreting by Shi Yanhua, who also interpreted for Mao, but errors may have crept into the text as it was translated from English into Italian and it cannot be taken as clear evidence.

Although Deng was never afraid to exercise power and authority, he was personally a modest character and tended to play down his importance rather than indulge in self-aggrandisement. It was politically important for him to be able to associate himself with Mao at the crucial Zunyi Conference, but since Mao's status at the meeting is far from clear it is hardly surprising that the same has to be said for Deng. Was he there, did he misremember the room in which he sat, or did he confuse the Zunyi Conference with another meeting? These are possibilities, but they seem out of character for a man who was always mentally alert. It is more likely than not that he was present, but perhaps not precisely in the capacity that he or his supporters claim. Thomas Kampen, in a thorough examination of new Chinese sources on the Zunyi Conference that were made public in the 1990s, included Deng in a table of participants but lists him as 'other', that is, neither a full or an alternate member of the Politburo nor a representative of the military. That is probably as close as it is possible to get to the truth.

The Zunyi Conference took place during the Long March when the Chinese Communist Party was divided between different columns and only a section of the Party leadership was present. It is hardly surprising if memories and documentation are confused. What is fascinating is that this meeting was still such a bone of contention in the 1980s and this indicates the weight given to historical arguments in the evolution of the leadership and its policies. Much of the dispute about Zunyi was not really about 1935 but about the legitimacy of Mao Zedong's leadership and his legacy. Deng needed to be associated with that legacy to ensure the stability of his political position in the Party and the country, in spite of the fact that he was reversing almost all of Mao's economic policies, or rather to guarantee that he could reverse them, in the face of fierce opposition from those who were determined to adhere firmly to Mao's every word.[5]

1. Deng's birthplace in Paifang

2. The Deng museum in Paifang

3. Deng in France, 1921

4. Deng (top row, second from right) at the Chinese Socialist Youth Group conference, Paris, July 1924. Zhou Enlai is in the front row, fourth from left

5. Deng delivers a report in Yan'an, September 1937

6. Deng and his wife, Zhuo Lin, in the Taihang Mountains

7. Deng and Liu Bocheng of the 129th Division

8. Deng, Chen Yi and their families, Shanghai, 1949

9. Deng and Liu Bocheng, Chongqing, late 1949

10. The CCP Congress report on the Gao Gang and Rao Shushi case, March 1955

11. Deng and He Long engaging in 'manual labour' at Ming Tombs, 1958

12. Deng at Daqing oilfield, 16 July 1964

13. Deng and Zhou Enlai at Beijing airport, April 1974

悼念周恩来同志

毛泽东

14. Deng at a memorial ceremony for Zhou Enlai, January 1976

15. Chinese Communist Party 10th Central Committee Plenum, 27 July 1977

16. Deng and Peng Zhen, 1981

17. Deng on an inspection tour, spring 1983

18. Deng the calligrapher, spring 1984

19. Deng at Wuhan railway station on the Southern Tour, 1992

20. Deng in Shanghai on the Southern Tour

21. Deng playing bridge, 1990s

THE GREAT LEAP FORWARD, CONFRONTATION AT LUSHAN AND THE SINO–SOVIET SPLIT (1958–61)

Peng Dehuai's views at the [Lushan] meeting were correct. As a member of the Politburo it was in order for him to write to the chairman of the Politburo. Even if Peng had his faults, the way he was treated was completely wrong.[1]

In the late 1950s, the Chinese Communist Party was drifting away from its Soviet allies and its original core leadership was disintegrating: the two developments were closely connected. Early signs of the Sino–Soviet split were apparent in 1956; in 1960, it was an open secret and by 1963 a public propaganda war had broken out. Nikita Khrushchev, the first secretary of the Communist Party of the Soviet Union from 1953 and premier (chairman of the Council of Ministers) from 1958, was not as despotic as Stalin: he introduced some liberal reforms and led a de-Stalinisation programme. However, he was not willing to cede the primacy of the USSR in the international communist movement to China and to Mao. Khrushchev had as many doubts about Mao as Mao did about him and Mao's colleagues had their own doubts about their leader. The focus of these doubts both internally and externally was Mao's insistence on forging a distinctively Chinese model of development, exemplified by the Great Leap Forward.

GREAT LEAP FORWARD

Mao's Three Red Banners (*sanmian hongqi*) policy, launched in 1958, consisted of: the General Line for Building Socialism (*shehuizhuyi jianshe zong luxian*) to develop industry and agriculture using traditional and modern technologies; the Great Leap Forward (*Dayuejin*), to mobilise the necessary labour; and the People's Communes (*Renmin gongshe*) initially presented as a model for the collectivisation of the whole of Chinese society. These policies are usually known jointly as the Great Leap Forward and are blamed on Mao personally, especially the famine that followed, which, if not caused entirely by the Leap, was exacerbated by it. Unrealistically high targets were set for both agricultural and industrial production: local officials, out of fear or sycophancy, falsely reported inflated production figures; and senior officials persuaded themselves that the policies were working. Mao may have originated this collossal folly, but the rest of the leadership in Beijing, and in the provinces, must share the responsibility.

Little attention has been paid to Deng Xiaoping's role and his relationship with Mao during the Great Leap. As his role of general secretary dictated, he concentrated on organisational matters. As divisions emerged within the Central Committee, he remained behind the scenes, avoiding much of the rhetoric and ideological disputes. He went through the motions of public support for the mass mobilisation of labour and posed for a photograph with Marshal He Long at the site of the Ming Tombs Reservoir, which lies about 25 miles north of Beijing and supplies water and hydro-electric power to the capital and its region. The two are shown carrying out voluntary labour (*yiwu laodong*) using shoulder poles with baskets to move earth. The baskets are empty and Deng and He are attired in improbably crisp and clean white shirts and trousers: it was symbolic and it is unlikely that anyone was fooled.

PENG DEHUAI CONFRONTS MAO

Deng had no time for Mao's rhetorical extravagance, but there is very little evidence of him actively resisting. If he did try to restrain Mao his efforts were ineffective. Was Mao Zedong really unstoppable or could Deng have prevented the disaster that ensued? There was one individual who was prepared to challenge Mao on the tragedy that was unfolding. Peng Dehuai, like Deng, was a military man. He had risen to the rank of marshal of the People's Liberation Army and was minister of defence. Unlike Deng, he was a mainstream soldier rather than a political commissar and his experience was in combat command rather than military politics. From the end of November 1958 until the middle of August 1959, conflict within the political elite of the People's Republic of China over the organisation of the economy and society was epitomised by the dispute between Peng and Mao.

Peng's main source of independent information about the effects of the Great Leap Forward came from his military intelligence networks and his contact with his officers and – at least as important – the rank and file soldiers, the vast majority of whom were drawn from peasant families. An official visit that Peng made to the poor north-western province of Gansu in October 1958 (one of the provinces that Deng Xiaoping had visited briefly in 1957) gave additional credence to his existing concerns about the transformation to the commune system. He saw that the 'backyard furnaces' for producing steel were useless and were diverting labour from farming, with the result that crops were being left to rot in the field. Peng was the most courageous of all the leadership in his opposition to Mao, but even he was slow to voice his criticisms openly, even as late as the Sixth Plenum of the Central Committee in the winter of 1958 at which Mao agreed to step down as chairman of the PRC (but, crucially, not as chairman of the CCP). Peng eventually criticised Mao to his face at a later meeting, the Seventh Plenum of the Central Committee in Shanghai in April 1959, accusing the chairman of going against the wishes of the collective leadership of the Standing Committee of the Politburo. By this time Peng was no longer a lone voice and other senior CCP figures began to express their concerns, including Deng Xiaoping, Bo Yibo, the chairman of the State Economic Commission, and Li Xiannian, the minister of finance, who had previously been an enthusiastic supporter of the People's Communes. It was Peng's criticisms that affected Mao most and their political differences were exacerbated by bitter personal animosity.

The scene for the final and fateful confrontation between Mao and Peng was Lushan, a hill station and summer resort for senior cadres set in spectacular scenery near Lake Poyang in the north-east of Jiangxi Province. Two decisive meetings took place in Lushan in the summer of 1959, an enlarged meeting of the Politburo and the Eighth Plenum of the Eighth Central Committee. At the Poliburo meeting, Peng launched a devastating political attack on Mao, supported by Liu Shaoqi and Zhang Wentian, the old adversary of Mao in the 1930s and 1940s. Peng's attack on Mao and the Great Leap Forward was a *tour de force*. It was in turns emotional, sarcastic and mordant. He attacked the fanaticism of the frenzy to collectivise and the unreality of Mao's ambitions, but in particular he condemned the sycophancy and the craven performance of Party leaders who had encouraged the exaggeration of both targets and actual results. The majority of those present at the conference may have sympathised with Peng's strictures but his condemnation of the Great Leap Forward was not just an argument about policy: it was a direct assault on Mao and the nature and quality of his leadership. This was more than Mao could bear and his counter-attack was furious, vicious and personal. He linked Peng with 'revisionist' factions that he had defeated in the past and, in an extraordinary declaration, threatened that if Peng's criticisms were formally endorsed he would return to the countryside and create a new Red Army of peasants to overthrow the government.

Peng Dehuai and his supporters were sacrificed to appease Mao, but China was already moving into a new political phase and Mao was obliged to take a back seat. For all practical purposes, day-to-day government decisions were now in the hands of Liu Shaoqi and Deng Xiaoping, who benefited from the attack by Peng but did not suffer the political consequences. Peng Dehuai was obliged to make a humiliating self-criticism; he was forced to move out of the Zhongnanhai leadership compound; his glorious political and military careers came to an ignominious end and his rival, Marshal Lin Biao, was appointed minister of defence in his stead.

What was Deng Xiaoping's role in this critical altercation? There is no mention of him at the Lushan meetings and it is far from clear whether he attended. Some reports claimed that he injured his leg playing table tennis at Lushan and then left for treatment; alternatively he was said to be recovering from an injury sustained while playing billiards some months previously. These reports emanate from amateur Red Guard publications that are notoriously difficult to evaluate, but there must be a suspicion that this was a diplomatic absence: he did not wish to be involved in such a high-profile conflict, knowing that Mao would win. Another member of the Politburo Standing Committee, Chen Yun, a critic of Mao who was sympathetic to Peng Dehuai but in the 1980s opposed the way Deng's reforms were being implemented, was also absent from the Lushan meetings.[2]

BACK IN THE USSR

This internal conflict had serious repercussions for relations between China and the Soviet Union. Deng had trained in Moscow in the 1920s, but dealing with fraternal communist parties, part of his remit as general secretary, was still a challenge and he had to learn quickly. For Deng, as for Liu Shaoqi, it was not a simple matter. As the distance between the Chinese and Soviet Communist parties widened and the personal dispute between Mao and Khrushchev became more and more antagonistic, Deng's allegiances were complicated. He was personally loyal to Mao because of their shared history and because Mao was his patron, and he was also strongly inclined to back China against the Soviet Union for reasons of patriotism. However, his approach to practical domestic politics and his vision of the way China's economy should develop was much closer to the gradualist approach favoured by Khrushchev.

Deng had accompanied Mao Zedong to Moscow in November 1957 for celebrations of the fortieth anniversary of the October Revolution and a meeting of international communist parties. Mao made his celebrated speech asserting that the 'east wind was prevailing over the west wind', an oblique attack on Khrushchev's 'revisionism', China's pejorative description for Soviet policies with which it did not agree.

From 17 to 22 September 1960 Deng was back in the USSR, at the head of the first of two consultative missions designed to heal the breach in the world communist movement, and negotiated with a Soviet team led by Mikhail Suslov, the staid head of the Soviet delegation, a tall, thin bespectacled man. Deng's tough negotiating style made little progress with his Soviet counterparts but the visit ended with a tacit agreement that there could be further discussions. He then attended the Moscow Conference of 81 national communist parties in November 1960 as head of the Chinese delegation's drafting committee, determined to assert the principles of the CCP against Khrushchev's ideological backsliding. The delegation was led by Liu Shaoqi and during the meeting a 'heated dispute' erupted between the Chinese and Soviet delegates: this is often taken to be the first open acknowledgement of the Sino–Soviet split, although there had been major disagreements at a meeting in Bucharest the previous June after which all Soviet experts working in China were withdrawn and all aid to China cancelled by Moscow.

Two years previously in 1958, Mao had met Nikita Khrushchev during one of the Soviet leader's two visits to China and is said to have told him that he would be stepping down shortly as chairman of the PRC, which he did in the wake of criticism of his Great Leap Forward policies. Khrushchev asked who the possible successors were and Mao indicated that there were several, but at the top of the list were Liu Shaoqi, Deng Xiaoping and Zhou Enlai. He described Deng to Khrushchev as a complicated character, tough and principled but quick on his feet, a man of unusual talents. Khrushchev said that he had had dealings with Deng and agreed that he was a tough character. This amused Mao, who knew that Khrushchev had in fact consulted Deng when deciding how to handle the Hungarian crisis in 1956. Mao asked Khrushchev to be sure that in the future Deng was treated by the USSR in the same way that they had treated him, and Khrushchev formed the impression that, although Liu Shaoqi had been at the head of the original list, Mao was grooming Deng as his successor. In spite of this apparent exchange of political confidences Mao and Khrushchev were not at ease with each other.

At the September 1960 meeting, members of the Chinese and Soviet drafting committees frequently clashed, often ferociously, but Deng was self-possessed: he focused on what was important, simply ignored rhetoric and kept everything in perspective. As soon as he emerged from the meeting room he would chat in his usual cheerful and humorous fashion and when the members of the delegation met for meals in the Chinese embassy in Moscow there was an atmosphere of continuous laugher and relaxed chatter.

When another drafting committee (*qicao weiyuanhui*) was being prepared for the second CCP delegation to Moscow in November 1960, Mao proposed to the Politburo that Deng should manage it and this was unanimously approved. The head of the delegation was Liu Shaoqi and Deng was his deputy. Towards the end of August 1960, Deng arrived at the Diaoyutai state guest house and gave a pep talk to the members of the delegation. He explained that they had a heavy responsibility as it was their task to protect the unity of the international communist movement and the relationship between China and the Soviet Union. His staff listened intently and took notes scrupulously as is expected in such meetings. Deng insisted that they could not yield on any matters of principle and would have to attack the mistaken policies of Khrushchev and try to win over the other communist parties. When Deng and his team arrived in Moscow they were treated as a high-level delegation, probably because of the way Mao had spoken to Khrushchev about Deng in 1958, and were accommodated in a villa in the Lenin Hills that was used only for Soviet leaders and visiting foreign dignitaries. In the light of the worsening political atmosphere between China and the Soviet Union this was impressive hospitality, but the negotiations were doomed and the split between the two communist parties was never healed.[3]

INSPECTING SHUNYI COMMUNE

Shunyi County, to the north of Beijing, became a district of the city in 1958 and the now familiar Beijing Capital Airport was later built on nearby land. Due to its proximity to the airport it has become one of the most desirable residential areas in Beijing, but in April 1961 it was a poor farming area with little connection to the centres of power in Beijing. The people of Shunyi were desperately hoping for an improvement in their fortunes after the three dreadful years of poor harvests and hunger that had followed the Great Leap Forward.

Markets had continued to operate in rural areas, even during the famine years as long as there was anything to trade, but they were politically suspect for a long time and in the face of active opposition from the most enthusiastic supporters of Mao they had deteriorated. During the Great Leap Forward the People's Communes had been formed and in some of them the normal buying and selling of goods had been replaced by supplying the needs of the labour force according to the work points that they had earned. Communal kitchens, where peasant farmers and their families would eat, were also set up in some communes, but they were unpopular and the experiment did not last.

Although it was spring the weather was still cold when Deng visited Shunyi Commune between 7 and 21 April for a formal inspection and to 'direct work'. Shunyi had its own network of local markets that were supported by handicraft industries and family-run sideline occupations (*fuye*). According to villagers' accounts of Deng's visit, he took a great interest in the way the local economy operated, visiting many shops and learning about the local trade in country markets and temple fairs. On one occasion he called in to the retail department of a supply and marketing cooperative (*gongxiaoshe*) on Shunyi North Street just outside the old city gates. He asked the assistant to show him some of the small agricultural implements and everyday household necessities that the cooperative supplied. As he examined them he pointed out that people could not see what goods were available behind the wooden counter, which made it impossible for them to choose what they wanted. He also spotted that there was a burr on the edge of a metal wok that had not been properly polished flat (*daguang*) and on which somebody could easily cut their hand.

On 17 April Deng visited the temple fair that was traditionally held on the third day of the third month by the lunar calendar. He found it depressing as little business was being done, but he took a close interest in goods prices. At the restaurant he suggested that if they sold deep-fried dough cakes (*youbing*) at half price they would generate more business: peasants could be allowed to exchange an egg from their own hens for a dough cake, encouraging barter trade as ready cash was in short supply. Deng later told the commune leader that he could see possibilities for helping the market to flourish which would have a major impact on the income and the living standards of the peasant farmers. He suggested developing the production of *doufu* (tofu), shredded *doufu* (*doufusi*) and firm *doufu* (*lao doufu*), commonly used meat substitutes. More dough cakes and dough sticks (*youtiao*) – both popular snacks – could also be produced, especially at break-fast time. His educated interest in the detail of the markets impressed local people.

On 21 April Deng met cadres from the Shunyi Commune's industrial bureau, supply and marketing cooperative and handicraft cooperative, the officials responsible for managing the economy of the commune. Deng gave them the benefit of his 'penetrating analysis' (Deng's words are paraphrased in the original source) of why the local markets were in such a poor state:

> As far as the markets are concerned, business is hardly thriving in any area. The range of goods on sale is monotonous and they are few in number. In the case of small agricultural tools and everyday necessities that commune members need, there is shockingly little. Items needed to serve the people (*wei renmin fuwu de xiangmu*) have almost entirely disappeared, and this is because of problems with policy (*zhengce wenti*), circulation and communications (*liutong qudao wenti*). People used to care about these goods in the past but today no-one pays them any attention and things are just drifting. Handicrafts and household subsidiary occupations must under no circumstances be allowed to disappear as these can amount to one quarter of a family's total income. You cannot rely on grain production. The entire annual sale of grain in the county amounts to 40,000,000 *jin* (catties) and if you take away tax revenue and expenditure this yields an average per person over the whole county of just over 4 *yuan*. Although we must persist in the policy of making grain the priority in the countryside, all aspects of the economy should be developed.

In the final analysis, he continued, production had to be increased by economic methods and not political ones. The emphasis should be on household items such as reed and wickerwork, bricks and tiles, metalworking, leatherwork, earthenware and woodwork, *doufu* (clearly one of Deng's favourite topics), the raising of pigs, chicken, ducks and rabbits and vegetables in the kitchen gardens. Local markets were just as important as national ones: 'If there were more goods,' he went on, 'markets would be livelier, the lives of the commune members would be much easier and as the income of peasants increased they would be able to contribute more to the nation.' Stable prices in the free markets would allow people to be more relaxed and this would improve the political situation. This was a pragmatic rather than a utopian view. He was not setting unrealistic targets for developing free markets, just exhorting local leaders to encourage the villagers to produce what they knew how to, both from the farms or in the sideline handicraft production that was traditional in Chinese villages. He told the commune leaders that they must resolve the problem of the supply of raw materials and step up basic-level production before establishing complicated marketing structures. The supply and marketing cooperatives and commercial offices of the commune needed to learn how to manage the free markets and assist with the regulation of commodity prices.

He was concerned that under the communes there was a danger of traditional handicraft and sideline occupations disappearing in the dash for increased grain production. Shunyi, he pointed out, had a long tradition of pig rearing and the soil and water supply were good: one pig could bring in as much as 20 *yuan* and could also fertilise two or three *mu* of land and help increase agricultural production without the need for chemical fertiliser. Deng's views struck a chord with the local cadres and his support enabled Shunyi to develop handicraft and sideline occupations and raise the standard of living for local peasants. This was not because of the magical power of his message, which is often the implication of comments on interventions by Mao Zedong, but because his words could be used to defend the commune management against political opponents.

The Shunyi cadres were impressed that Deng did not arrive with a large retinue to show how important he was and did not expect a lavish reception. The villagers and their leadership were convinced that he had a genuine interest in the hardships that they were enduring. In the case of at least one of the villages Deng was able to intervene directly and arrange for a team to be sent out from the capital to drill wells so that they could have access to fresh water. After Deng's death in 1997, Shunyi people remembered this and also told the story that Deng had 'written a letter to Mao Zedong advising that their communal dining hall be disbanded'.[4]

By 1961, as the complete failure of the Great Leap became apparent to almost everyone in a position of responsibility in China (but not necessarily to Mao), attitudes towards markets began to change and Deng and Liu had already begun to implement policies to reverse some of the more crass decisions about commune management. Did Deng really say these things at this time or are they remembered in the light of his drive to expand the market economy after the death of Mao? Long before the CCP took power nationally in 1949 Deng had been involved in the detailed running of local economies in the Liberated Areas so this interest in the minutiae of local economic conditions was nothing new and completely in character. The level of detail recorded in these conversations adds to their credibility and it is important to remember once again that it has always been the normal practice for Chinese officials to take detailed notes in meetings.[5]

As the dust settled, Deng and Liu Shaoqi made full use of the bureaucratic machinery under their control, work seen as disloyal opposition to Mao and for which Red Guards would castigate them as the No. 1 and No. 2 'capitalist roaders'. They chose not to voice their opposition as openly and directly in meetings, speeches and articles as had Peng Dehuai. While echoing, or at least not opposing, Mao's rhetoric in public, they operated behind the scenes, drafting planning documents to counteract the disastrous effect of his policies. They did not consult Mao, who had every reason to feel undermined, marginalised and furious: the Cultural Revolution that he launched in 1966 was his response. As usual Deng was attempting to steer clear of ideological disputes. He was acting on the basis of what he saw as the practical needs of the country but this could not be ideologically neutral. Whether he liked it or not, by his actions if not his words, he was aligning himself with Liu Shaoqi and others who preferred the Soviet model of development.

11

REBUILDING THE ECONOMY (1962–5)

It is true that Mao Zedong said I took no notice of him, but it was not just me; other leaders did the same.[1]

Mao had stepped down as chairman of state (president) and in April 1959 was replaced at the National People's Congress by Liu Shaoqi, who held the post until the Cultural Revolution. Mao retained the chairmanship of the Chinese Communist Party. The government headed by Liu and Deng reverted to Soviet-style economic planning and political stability, but within the Party Mao continued the battle for his own vision of socialism in China.

Deng had become conscious, at an early stage, of the negative impact the Great Leap was having on industry, and had been raising the issue in meetings of the Secretariat as early as January 1959. At the ninth full session of the Eighth Central Committee in Beijing from 14 to 18 January 1961, Deng had taken responsibility, with Li Fuchun and Bo Yibo, for 'Regulations on the Work of State Industrial Enterprises' (the 'Seventy Articles'), a draft document circulated by the Central Committee on 16 September 1961. It set out measures for improving the management of state enterprises, creating representative councils of workers and office staff, establishing wage and salary structures, enforcing technical standards and improving accounting and financial control. This was not revolutionary but it was essential to undo the damage left by the Great Leap, and the process by which it was created indicates Deng's *modus operandi* and the problems he faced. Deng coordinated the work of the Secretariat, State Planning Commission and State Economic Commission and established 11 working groups based in Beijing, Shanghai, Tianjin, Taiyuan, Jilin and other cities to carry out investigations to inform the policy. Li Fuchun dealt with industrial enterprises in Beijing and Deng went out to the north-east to listen to reports from Liaoning Province. Between 3 and 6 May 1961, Bo Yibo held a conference in Beijing at which Party officials from the centre and Beijing, Tianjin, Liaoning, Heilongjiang, Jiangsu and other areas met to discuss the draft document. At the end of May and the beginning of June, responses from these reports and meetings were filtered through to the Central Committee. The evidence made grim reading. Industrial production was falling significantly, many basic construction projects had been forced to close down, there had been serious losses of equipment and many accidents. Rumblings of discontent and confused management risked paralysis in industrial production.

Bo Yibo was not optimistic when he addressed the Secretariat on 20 May and could not see how the report would solve the problems. Deng advised that they write 'some policy clauses dealing with the system of responsibility, technical policies and capital policies etc'. but the meeting was still unable to agree on how to proceed. This was Deng Xiaoping's favoured milieu – the committee room, the drafting of documents, the creation of a consensus, and the production of a policy document – and the difficulty the committee was having is an indication of the problems they faced. On 26 July Deng came back to the Secretariat with a report on the situation in the north-east as the possible basis for a policy.

The problems of industry were more intransigent than those of agriculture. A sudden decline in coal and steel production was adversely affecting the whole of Chinese industry and Li Fuchun suggested a separate group to analyse this problem. Bo Yibo travelled to the north-east with his Beijing working group and officials from the State Planning Commission. They consulted management and staff in Shenyang, Harbin and Changchun before revising the Seventy Articles.

When the Seventy Articles were finally completed in September 1961, Mao expressed his formal appreciation, even though the policy went directly against the spirit of his Great Leap Forward. The regulations on industry were part of a suite of political initiatives orchestrated by Deng and Liu Shaoqi as part of the second Five-Year Plan. Within a few years, supporters of Mao would be excoriating Liu and Deng for these initiatives as the two 'top party persons taking the capitalist road'.[2]

LIN BIAO AND 'MAO ZEDONG THOUGHT'

When Peng Dehuai was dismissed as minister of defence after the Lushan meetings, he was replaced by another marshal of the PRC with a distinguished war record, Lin Biao, who became increasingly committed to supporting Mao Zedong. Lin launched an ideological campaign in the People's Liberation Army to create a body of officers and other ranks who were personally loyal not just to the Chinese road to socialism and Marxism-Leninism but to 'Mao Zedong Thought' (*Mao Zedong sixiang*), a phrase that was becoming increasingly common. While there is much to criticise in Mao's theoretical writings and his attempts to be seen as a major Marxist philosopher, the version that was taught to uneducated and often barely literate peasant troops was inevitably a crude and simplistic version. It was, as Deng argued, a vulgarisation of Mao's theoretical writings which many Party members still valued as a distinctively Chinese contribution to Marxism-Leninism in a milieu that had been dominated by Stalin and other Soviet theorists. Soldiers had to memorise aphorisms and short texts which were published in May 1964 as *Quotations from Chairman Mao Zedong*, the infamous 'little red book'. Educated Chinese, including many in the Chinese Communist Party, ridiculed this vulgarisation and the idolatry of Mao that accompanied it, but it rapidly took hold in the military and then spread into schools, colleges and universities and more widely. Lin Biao is now blamed primarily for this vulgarisation, but it was condoned by Mao, and Lin had become his 'close comrade in arms' and heir apparent.

At an enlarged meeting of the Standing Committee of the CCP Military Commission (*junwei changwei*) on 12 September 1960, and then at the full meeting of the Military Commission (also enlarged to ensure support for Lin Biao's proposals) that ran from 14 September to 24 October, Lin Biao pressed the Party's military authorities to agree that political and ideological work, based on the adulation of Mao Zedong, should become the core of training in the PLA, at the expense of military or technical skills. The length of the meeting is an indication of the battle that was taking place. Tan Zheng, the director of the General Political Department of the PLA and a highly respected field commander during the Korean War, tried to resist Lin's ideological takeover but was severely criticised and eventually dismissed. Lin won the day and his proposals were approved not only by the Military Commission but by the Party's Central Committee on 21 December 1960.

Deng had consistently ridiculed the tendency to attribute any and every Chinese success story to 'Mao Zedong Thought'. When Rong Guotuan won the men's singles title in the 25th World Table Tennis Championship in Dortmund on 5 April 1959 – admittedly a significant achievement as it was the first world sports title ever won by a Chinese citizen – the press claimed that it was a victory for Mao's thought. Deng asked what would have happened if Rong had lost – would that have been a defeat for 'Mao Zedong Thought'? He expanded his ideas on this at a meeting in Tianjin on 25 March 1960, arguing that vulgarising Mao's ideas and neglecting the rest of the Marxist-Leninist tradition was self-defeating.

The tide was running against Deng. In April 1961, Lin Biao, while inspecting a unit of the PLA, proposed that *Liberation Army Daily (Jiefangjun bao)*, the official newspaper of the Chinese military, should carry quotations from Chairman Mao's works on a regular basis. The paper inserted its first quotation to the right of the masthead on 1 May 1961, with a comment by Lin Biao placed immediately below. This started an unstoppable trend – no-one was prepared to be the first to exclude quotations from the chairman. Luo Ronghuan, who had taken over as director of the PLA General Political Department, tried to resist this outbreak of sycophancy, arguing that the troops should be familiar with the arguments in Mao's writings and the spirit of his thinking but that they should not be parroting and memorising quotations 'like Buddhists monks reciting sutras'. Lin Biao ignored him, so Luo sent a formal report to Deng Xiaoping, as CCP general secretary, setting out his differences with Lin. Deng tabled the report for discussion at a meeting of the Secretariat and Luo Ronghuan's criticisms were supported by all present. It was to no avail and Lin Biao's politicisation of the army in Mao's name went ahead.

A decade later, after Deng had returned to Beijing from his Cultural Revolution exile in Jiangxi Province, he was staying in an official guest house when he met Luo Ronghuan's wife Lin Yueqin and their three children. He told the children that they should remember their father as someone who had supported the ideas of Mao Zedong (who was still alive at the time) but had resisted the vulgarisation and the campaign for the 'living use and living study of Mao Zedong Thought' (*huoxue huoyong Mao Zedong sixiang*) which encouraged people to apply Mao's aphorisms to every conceivable situation. He frequently commented on Luo's resistance to Lin Biao, conscious perhaps of his own political impotence in the wake of a movement that was beyond his control, but he blamed Lin Biao for the vulgarisation not Mao. Lin died in a plane crash after an abortive *coup d'état* in September 1971.[3]

PREPARING FOR THE SEVEN THOUSAND CADRES CONFERENCE (JANUARY–FEBRUARY 1962)

The CCP Central Committee held an 'enlarged working conference' in the Great Hall of the People between 11 January and 7 February 1962, ten days after the New Year celebrations and with a distinct chill in the air, meteorologically as well as politically, although the atmosphere was much warmer once the conference began. This conference, convened to entrench the political ascendancy of Liu Shaoqi and Deng Xiaoping, was enlarged to an unusual extent, even for an 'enlarged' meeting, a regular Party device for packing a conference hall to achieve agreement on difficult policies. Mao had been persuaded to extend what was originally intended as a working conference 'to ensure that the spirit of the conference would be implemented'[4] throughout the whole Party at all levels. It is usually referred to as the Seven Thousand Cadres Conference (*qiqianren dahui*): it was attended by 7,018 Party officials – there is a preference in China for large round numbers – representing provincial and local government and economic enterprises. In addition to its remarkable size, it lasted for a total of 28 days, a record at the time.

Wiser counsels were prevailing in the leadership of the CCP and there were regular meetings to discuss lessons to be learned from the failure of the Great Leap Forward. During 1961 the Central Committee had approved a long series of documents that one by one reversed the policies that Mao had espoused, although they were approved by Mao and retained some of his rhetoric. At working conferences of the Central Committee in May and June 1961, Mao had conceded that the country had paid a high price for 'going counter to objective laws' (*weibei keguan guilü*) but he tried to excuse the 'three lean years for the land, the people and animals', as mistakes on the road to socialism. The full Central Committee, meeting in ill-starred Lushan in September 1961, had decided on a period of economic retrenchment, reducing the targets for industrial and basic construction projects to give agriculture a chance to recover. In spite of the superficial consensus there was no unanimity within the Party – Mao did not approve of the changes.

Deng Xiaoping was given the responsibility of organising the enlarged conference. Wu Lengxi, the director of the Xinhua News Agency and editor-in-chief of *People's Daily*, recalled that Deng worked closely with Liu Shaoqi on the preparations. They drafted reports setting out the errors of the previous four years and measures to ensure the recovery of the national economy. What might seem to outsiders sensible and practical measues were highly sensitive political issues.

Although there was no intention of overthrowing Mao, it was essential – a matter of life and death for millions of Chinese suffering from famine – that these policies were approved. Even if Mao could not be won round, his opposition had to be neutralised.

In preparation for the conference, Deng and the Secretariat produced a situation report (*xingshi baogao*) based on documentation issued by the Central Committee since 1958. This report laid the blame primarily on the Central Committee and secondly on the provincial authorities and it set the tone for the Seven Thousand Cadres Conference. On 6 November 1961, Deng Xiaoping convened a meeting of officials who were working on drafts of the conference reports in Building 8 of the Diaoyutai State Guest House, which had been completed on the eve of National Day in 1959 to accommodate visiting heads of state and other international dignitaries. He gave them a clear framework as the basis for their reports.

The agricultural situation, he told them, was beginning to improve and although industrial production had been declining it was basically stable, so current policies of restructuring should be continued. It was essential to strengthen the centralised and unified leadership of the Central Committee and the system of democratic centralism. There needed to be clear agreement on policies without one faction dissenting. The Party working methods had to be improved: they should be practical and realistic (*shishi qiushi*), follow the 'mass line' (in this context take into account the real needs of the population) and respect internal Party democracy (*dangnei minzhu*). After prolonged discussions with Liu Shaoqi, Deng chaired a meeting on the first draft of the reports on 21 December 1961.

The degree of preparation is an indication of how Deng worked to exercise his authority, by controlling the agendas and attendees at meetings and, above all, the documents that emerged. Deng was able to carry out these mundane tasks and motivate his team to work in great detail and with great speed when necessary. By the time the conference opened, the final reports from the conference had been drafted. Democratic centralism in the Chinese Communist Party was more central than democratic.[5]

THE SEVEN THOUSAND CADRES CONFERENCE IN SESSION

The conference opened on 11 January 1962 with Mao presiding, but this was something of a formality. He was no longer at the political centre and it was Liu

Shaoqi who presented the written report on behalf of the Central Committee. From the opening ceremony until the morning of 29 January, the business of the conference revolved around Liu's report. The report had gone directly to the conference without going through the Politburo, which Mao could usually dominate. Since the vast majority of the delegates were lower-level cadres it was an opportunity to assess the views held by grass-roots cadres (*jisi guangyi*).

After meetings to discuss the minutiae of the reports, Mao presided over a plenary meeting on 27 January at which Liu expanded on the thinking behind the report. Liu said that in the past they had often weighed successes and failures in terms of 'the relationship between one finger and nine fingers' but that in the present situation it was more a case of 'the relationship between three fingers and seven fingers'. In some areas peasants were talking about 'three parts natural disaster and seven parts man-made disaster'. The use of the fingers to indicate the percentage (one finger equals ten per cent) of right and wrong or success and failure continued well into the 1970s and is still used to assess Mao Zedong's overall contribution to China's revolution.

Liu was making it clear that he and Deng regarded the Great Leap Forward as overwhelmingly a man-made disaster and one that was caused primarily by Mao. This was a turning point, not only in the conference, but also in the political culture of China, and was one of the high points of the conference. The original plan was that after speeches by the central leadership (*zhongyang zhuyao lingdaoren*) the conference would close. However, supporters of Mao made clear their dissatisfaction with the way Liu and Deng were dominating the conference and it was agreed that they should be allowed to speak. This dissipated the tension that had built up and was another high point of the conference.

On 30 January Mao made a long speech, and, in an unusually self-critical frame of mind, assumed personal responsibility for the mistakes of the Great Leap Forward. 'Whatever mistakes were made directly by the Central Committee they were my mistakes, the indirect ones I was partially responsible for as I was chairman of the Central Committee.' He appeared to be acknowledging that lack of internal democracy was to blame.

Deng Xiaoping addressed the conference on 6 February. He argued that the Party had the ability to lead the people towards 'victory in the construction of socialism' and shoulder its responsibilities in the wider world communist movement. However, there had been serious faults in the leadership and the work of the Party which had weakened the Party's tradition of excellence. The reasons for this were twofold: firstly insufficient study of Mao Zedong Thought with impractical tasks and slogans being proposed; secondly struggle within the party had produced deviations (*piancha*) which had harmed many Party cadres. Democratic centralism had not been properly exercised and there had been too many campaigns.

Dealing with Mao was the key problem for Liu and Deng and their strategy was to focus on 'democratic centralism' within the Party, which Mao had already raised. He reminded delegates that the CCP was now a ruling party (*zhizheng dang*), and a party in office was not the same as one in a revolution. Mao Zedong was still inclined to treat the CCP as if it was still a revolutionary party, arguing that the alternative was the way back to capitalism – as had already happened in the Soviet Union.

Deng maintained that there was a breakdown of communication between the top level of the Party and those below, and to counter this, supervision by Party committees or the Secretariat (which he controlled) was necessary. Liu Shaoqi suggested 'inner-party life' (*dangnei shenghuo*) meetings and they discussed how frequently such meetings should take place. It speaks volumes about problems within the leadership that even infrequent Party meetings had to be proposed at a special conference. Mao accepted that committees should 'inspect work, summarise experiences and exchange ideas' but the proposals on greater democracy found a powerful echo within the body of the conference. From 31 January to 7 February small working groups of provincial, central bureau, state organisation and central Party bodies discussed the implications of these points. Criticism and self-criticism of mistakes that had occurred in the work of the Party were made at all levels and provincial Party secretaries stood side by side with their county-level counterparts to apologise for their own part in the disastrous policies. The meeting became emotional and by all accounts cathartic. The Seven Thousand Cadres Conference was unprecedented in the way in which Party cadres at all levels spoke openly about the problems that China had been through. The degree of healthy criticism and self-criticism was seen as extremely positive and would allow the Party to forge ahead with a new unity and greater motivation; the conference ended on an optimistic note.

Only the speeches made by Lin Biao were out of step with this optimistic assessment. In sycophantic terms that were completely out of tune with the general tone of the conference, which should have sounded alarm bells in the minds of Deng and Liu's supporters, he stated bluntly that any mistakes were entirely the result of insufficient attention to Mao Zedong Thought. The implication was that if other leaders had slavishly followed Mao, there would have been no catastrophe after the Great Leap Forward. Since they had all deviated either to the left or the right and obstructed Mao, it was hardly surprising that there were mistakes. This was what Mao Zedong wanted to hear, and Lin's speech was a harbinger of Mao's attempt to wrest power back from Liu and Deng.[6]

MAO'S RESPONSE TO THE SEVEN THOUSAND CADRES CONFERENCE

Open divisions began to emerge almost immediately after the conference. Deng was positive about the way Mao had behaved, but there was a reversal during a meeting in July and August 1962 at Beidaihe, the Communist Party's favoured summer retreat on the coast of the Bohai Sea. Mao began to raise the issue of class struggle once again, although, back in Beijing at the Tenth Plenum of the Eighth Central Committee (24–27 September 1962), he acknowledged in public that class struggle should not interfere with the restructuring of the economy. Mao personally used the Four Cleanups (*siqing*) campaign, also known as the Socialist Education Movement (*shehuizhuyi jiaoyu yundong*) that was launched in his name to insist on the importance of class struggle. This campaign was essentially a trial run for the Cultural Revolution and emphasised a return to peasant values to eradicate 'bourgeois' attitudes in the Party, including the leadership. It also introduced China and the world to the bizarre cult of the proletarian hero-martyr, Lei Feng, a selfless 21-year-old soldier who was said to have died on duty when hit by a falling telegraph pole.

By late 1964 there were references in the media to 'people in authority taking the capitalist road' (*zou zibenzhuiyi daolu de dangquan pai*), and it was being said that there were two independent kingdoms in Beijing (*haishi chu Beijing you liang ge duli wangguo*). The economy had taken a turn for the better, but there had been no real resolution of the differences in the leadership. For all Deng Xiaoping's planning for the Seven Thousand Cadres Conference and its apparent success, the problem of Mao's ego and his personal and political ambitions had not been resolved.

Class struggle is central to any Marxist analysis of social and political change, but Mao applied it in an idiosyncratic fashion, although there are parallels with the way that Stalin used it in the USSR. From the mid-1950s onwards, Mao interpreted any opposition, either personal or to his policies, as evidence of the emergence of a new bourgeois class in China which the proletariat (of which he saw himself as the representative) must overthrow. This approach was behind the Anti-Rightist

Campaign of 1957 and the Cultural Revolution in 1966. It is clear that the establishment of the People's Republic of China had resulted in the creation of a new ruling elite, or a new class, as Milovan Djilas had argued in his analysis of similar regimes in the Soviet Union and Eastern Europe.[7] Mao presented himself as a principled outsider with the interests of the peasant masses at heart, but he was as much a part of that elite as any of the other leaders.

Liu and Deng were not interested in class struggle to continue the revolution but were planning the reconstruction of China. The only model that was realistically available to them in 1962 was the model that appeared to have worked in the Soviet Union. This was anathema to Mao.[8]

LEGACY OF THE 1929 GUANGXI UPRISING

As if the political negotiations, plots and intrigues were not enough, Deng discovered that his past was about to be used against him. The authorities in the Guangxi Zhuang Autonomous Region had planned a series of publications to celebrate a decade of the Communist Party's control over the province which had been designated an autonomous region in 1958, in deference to the minority Zhuang people who make up about a third of the region's population and whose language is distantly related to Thai.

The books planned included volumes on fiction, poetry and folk tales but *Reminiscences of the Revolution in Guangxi (Guangxi geming huiyi lu)*, which was issued on behalf of the Guangxi Military District, was the centrepiece of the whole project. It appeared in September 1959 with a dedication by General Zhang Yunyi who had fought with Deng Xiaoping in the Baise uprising of 1929 in Guangxi. There was no inscription by Deng, which was possibly a deliberate slight, but it was suggested that this was because of the tight publishing schedule.

Whatever the reason for the omission, it was thought necessary for Zhang Yunyi, who had worked in Guangxi from 1949 to 1955, to write personally to Deng with profuse apologies, asking him to contribute a calligraphic dedication that could be included in the second edition. Zhang's letter was taken to Beijing during the Spring Festival (Chinese New Year) of 1963 by Zhang Wu, a member of the editorial committee. Deng accorded this a high priority and produced within a week a brief inscription that contained conventional revolutionary nostalgia and exhortation in a hand that is elegant but not artistic. The publishers of *Reminiscences of the Revolution in Guangxi* soon found themselves in serious political trouble and the book was criticised as a 'poisonous weed', presumably on the instructions of Lin Biao. The publishers and authors, including military and local officials who had supported the idea of an inscription by Deng, were purged and sent to the countryside for re-education during the Socialist Education Movement. During the Cultural Revolution, Red Guards sealed up the cupboard in which the original manuscript of the book was stored (but with admirable political caution did not destroy it). Zhang Wu managed to preserve Deng's dedication and was rewarded for his efforts when the book was eventually published with the dedication in the 1980s. The story of this book indicates the links between the personal and the political and the way in which political rhetoric and judgements often masked vicious personal attacks.[9]

WU HAN

Wu Han was a distinguished historian and the author of an authoritative and readable biography of the first emperor of the Ming dynasty, Zhu Yuanzhang. He was also a bridge partner and close friend of Deng Xiaoping, who liked to call him 'professor'. Wu was a prominent member of the Democratic League, one of the non-Communist parties that was permitted to remain in existence after 1949 and possibly also a member of the Communist Party, although that was not made public until the Cultural Revolution. His reputation rests on a play that he wrote in the 1950s, *Hai Rui Dismissed from Office* (*Hai Rui baguan*), based on the life of an exemplary and honest official of the Ming dynasty. It was originally written in 1951 but was revised several times, and when it became popular as a Beijing opera in 1959 only the most obtuse reader or spectator could have failed to notice the parallels with the purging of Peng Dehuai during the Great Leap Forward. Criticism of this play by Yao Wenyuan, later notorious as one of the Gang of Four, was one of the first public signs that the Cultural Revolution was underway.

In 1965 Wu Han heard rumours that his play, *Hai Rui Dismissed from Office*, was likely to be criticised, and Peng Zhen wrote to Deng Xiaoping on his behalf. Peng Zhen was the mayor of Beijing and Wu Han, in addition to his academic and historical work, was also deputy mayor. Deng responded that he had seen the performance of *Hai Rui* starring the leading Beijing opera star Ma Lianliang (1901–66), and that there was really nothing to worry about; it was just a case of people 'trying to climb on the shoulders of others to rise to the top' and 'pulling pigtails when they only had a half-baked idea of what was going on'. 'Tell the professor', he said, 'that this is nothing out of the ordinary.' He also told Peng Zhen that politics and art should be kept apart; mixing them up was fraught with danger as it would stifle opportunities for expressing opinions. He was correct about the danger but he miscalculated the threat to Wu Han. He underestimated Mao's willingness to use cultural controversy to gain leverage in political faction fighting and he did not fully appreciate the growing authority of Jiang Qing in Shanghai cultural circles and her political machinations.

Later on, during a game of bridge with Deng, Wu Han threw in his hand and apologised, saying that he did not have the heart to play cards that day. Deng, much the tougher character, asked the 'professor' what he was afraid of, observing that the sky had not fallen in. Deng told Wu that he was 61 that year, had been through many ups and downs in his revolutionary career and had learned two important things. 'Firstly never be afraid and secondly be optimistic. Look ahead, look to the future and everything will work out.' He assured Wu Han that he and the Party would look after him and, somewhat reassured, Wu carried on with the game of bridge.

Wu Han should not have felt so reassured because the sky would eventually fall on him. As far back as the meeting of the Seventh Plenary Session of the Eighth Central Committee in Shanghai on 5 April 1959, in the context of a discussion on whether people had the courage to speak the truth and criticise him, Mao raised the question of Hai Rui. He said that he had read the original biography of Hai Rui in the *Mingshi* (*Ming History*), the multi-volume standard history of the Ming dynasty produced under the Manchu Qing dynasty. Mao had also sent a copy to Peng Dehuai, and had advised Premier Zhou Enlai to read it. He invited the assembled members of the Central Committee to tell him who among them had the kind of courage that Hai Rui possessed. Mao was clearly spoiling for a fight and after the meeting, Hu Qiaomu, who was also a historian and had been Mao's secretary during the 1940s, passed on the gist of Mao's remarks to Wu Han, suggesting that it might be politic for him to write something appropriate about Hai Rui. Wu Han hurriedly wrote an article 'Hai Rui criticises the Emperor' (*Hai Rui ma huangdi*) which appeared in *People's Daily* on 26 June 1959. He also published another article on 17 September, also in *People's Daily*, entitled 'On Hai Rui' (*Lun Hai Rui*), which had been checked and revised by Hu Qiaomu, who had responsibility for cultural matters. As the vicious Lushan meetings had just started, Wu Han carefully added a postscript criticising 'right opportunist elements' (which could only have referred to Peng Dehuai). At this point Ma Lianliang, who was not only a star performer but also the director of the Beijing Opera Company, asked Wu if he would turn his play on the heroic deeds of Hai Rui into a Beijing opera. Wu did not feel entirely comfortable about writing for that medium but thought it would be ungracious not to accept the offer. In March 1960 the new historical opera, *Hai Rui*, was completed but, at the suggestion of a friend, the title was changed to the now familiar *Hai Rui Dismissed from Office* and it was performed by the Beijing Opera Company at the beginning of 1961.

Defenders of Wu Han have argued that the history of the play indicates that it cannot have had any connection with the dismissal of Peng Dehuai after the Lushan meetings, but this seems a little disingenuous. Wu Han was sufficiently aware of the political tempest that was brewing up to have appended a cautious postscript to his articles; to rewrite the script and have it staged after Mao had drawn attention to the historical parallel between Peng Dehuai and Hai Rui in 1959 was, to say the least, risky. If Wu Han did not foresee problems surely Ma Lianliang should have done.

However, it was not until 1965 that the blow fell, when an article attacking the play appeared under the name of Yao Wenyuan, who was a close associate in Shanghai of Mao's wife, Jiang Qing, in the 10 November edition of the Shanghai newspaper *Wenhuibao*. This was followed in early 1966 by attacks on the *Notes from Three Family Village*, satirical newspaper articles by Wu Han, Deng Tuo and Liao Mosha, in which they had lampooned some of the grosser idiocies of the Great Leap Forward and which, together with Deng Tuo's *Evening Talks at Yanshan*, were popular with educated Chinese readers in the early 1960s. Wu Han was not the primary target but he was a convenient scapegoat and was arrested and interrogated, probably on the direct orders of Jiang Qing and Lin Biao, and died in prison on 11 October 1969. There were rumours that he had been forced to commit suicide but he may have been beaten to death or died from the recurrence of his tuberculosis and lack of adequate treatment. Deng Xiaoping could do nothing to save his friend, as by this time he had also been purged and sent to Jiangxi. Wu Han was not posthumously rehabilitated until 1979, partly at the instigation of Deng, who presided over a memorial meeting to help restore his good name.[10]

FINAL DAYS AS GENERAL SECRETARY

At the time of the Seven Thousand Cadres Conference in 1962, the major political obstacle to Deng Xiaoping and Liu Shaoqi was Mao Zedong. By 1965 the picture was becoming cloudier. Mao was in his early seventies and there were doubts about his health and mental stability. His wife, Jiang Qing, and his minister of defence, Lin Biao, were competing for influence and looking ahead to a possible succession contest.

That year saw the criticism and dismissal of Luo Ruiqing, the PLA chief of the general staff. Luo had resisted the politicisation of the army and the downgrading of military training and technical expertise, which inevitably resulted in conflict with Lin Biao. Luo was dismissed after meetings of the Central Committee and Politburo Standing Committee in Shanghai in December 1965, after having been accused by Lin Biao of anti-Party activities, although he did retain his position of deputy premier until the Cultural Revolution. Deng would not accept these accusations and made a coded speech at the end of the meeting defending the general. Deng then went to Luo's house with his wife Zhuo Lin and Zhou Enlai. While Deng and Zhou Enlai were talking to Luo, Zhuo Lin went upstairs to find Luo's wife, Hao Zhiping, told her how much they regretted what had happened and invited her to stay with them in Beijing. They flew to the capital in the same aircraft as the Dengs and Li Fuchun on 17 December 1965. The fact that Deng and Zhuo took care of the Luos would later form part of the indictment against Deng during the Cultural Revolution. It had become clear that Deng's influence was now insufficient to protect his political allies and friends.

INSPECTING THE NORTH-WEST

Deng's last major official duty, before the Cultural Revolution put an end to all normal political and administrative activity, was a tour of inspection to Xi'an, Lanzhou and Xining – the provincial capitals respectively of Shaanxi, Gansu and Qinghai – in March and April 1966. He arrived in Xi'an on 10 March with Li Fuchun and Bo Yibo, as part of a State Council delegation interested primarily in the progress of construction in this remote and poor region of China. In Xi'an he heard reports from local officials and made the usual round of visits to factories before leaving for Gansu. On 16 March at 3 o'clock in the afternoon the delegation arrived by special train in Lanzhou, where they were based for most of the month, taking particular interest in Gansu's oil and aviation industries. Photographs of Deng during this inspection trip show him as less relaxed and more formal than usual. The members of the delegation were all attired in the formal Sun Yat-sen jackets (*zhongshan zhuang*) favoured by Mao. Warm clothing was essential for protection against the wind and sand of this semi-desert region, but the suspicion must be that care was also taken to dress conservatively and formally for photo opportunities in a way that would not distinguish them from Mao and his acolytes. The factory visits and meetings were routine affairs but Deng took a particular interest in predicted production quotas as these had been such a controversial issue in the Great Leap Forward.

The delegation moved on to Qinghai on 29 March, where they stayed in the Victory Park Guesthouse before taking the train westwards, and Deng and his colleagues were briefed by local leaders in a compartment in the middle of the train. Qinghai, an ethnically mixed area on the borders with the Tibetan Autonomous Region and one of the least developed regions within the PRC, had suffered badly during the famines after the Great Leap Forward and it was not difficult for Deng, with his personal and political experience in the south-west, to see that the critical development issues were agriculture, herding and minority relations. Deng heard that the grain yields were recovering from the disastrous levels of 1961 and that the current year's figures were the best ever. The naturally sceptical Deng accepted that there had been much improvement.

Modern industry in Qinghai included mineral extraction but also nuclear installations, including the nuclear weapons development base at Jinyintan, deep inside the grasslands of Haiyan County. This reminded Deng of Maoergai, a town in Sichuan close to the border with Gansu which he had passed through with the Red Army on the Long March. As Deng inspected the nuclear facility he recalled that it had been built with Soviet assistance during the 1950s but that in 1960, when Moscow withdrew all of its technical aid, the CCP had decided to go it alone and continue to develop nuclear technology both for military and peaceful purposes. China's first atomic bomb was tested on 16 October 1964 and for China and for Deng this was a symbol of the country's modernity, strength and independence.

Deng's party returned to Lanzhou on 31 March to hear a report on the situation in Xinjiang from the first secretary of the Xinjiang Uyghur Autonomous Region, Wang Enmao, who presented a positive picture of satisfactory developments in agriculture, industry, the military and the militia, particularly commending the role of the Xinjiang Production and Construction Corps. Deng did not visit Xinjiang, but Lanzhou was the home of the military region which had the responsibility for control over Xinjiang. The final stopping point of the inspection tour was the old communist base area of Yan'an, which they reached on 3 April.

Deng's final visit, to Yan'an, provided an opportunity to see the Revolution Memorial Hall (*geming jinian guan*) that had been built on the outskirts of the city in 1950, and to visit the nearby cave complex of Yangjialing in which the

Communist Party lived and worked from 1936 to 1947. Deng was accompanied by Li Fuchun and Cai Chang, and his youngest daughter and biographer Maomao had also joined them in Yan'an. Cai Chang reminded them that Deng and Zhuo Lin had been married at the entrance to one of the caves at Yangjialing and Deng insisted that he remembered this well. They recalled who had lived in each cave: this tiny enclave had been home to Mao Zedong, Zhou Enlai and Liu Shaoqi and to Deng Xiaoping when he visited from the Taihang Mountains. This had been the core of the CCP leadership that had taken power in 1949 but had started to disintegrate and was now collapsing. Deng was well received by hundreds of officials and local people in the stadium.

The visit to the north-west had been productive and cheerful and the delegation discussed how to develop the region's economy, avoiding references to political tensions in Beijing. This came to a sudden end on 8 April 1966 when Kang Sheng telephoned Deng Xiaoping, recalling him immediately to Beijing. Kang Sheng was an aide to Mao Zedong and acted as his hatchet man, ready to attack any actual or potential rivals. Deng travelled back to the capital from Yan'an by a special flight: he was general secretary of the Chinese Communist Party, one of the most powerful individuals in the Party and the government, yet he had no idea that a convulsion on the scale of the Cultural Revolution was about to overwhelm the Party, the nation and the people, or that he personally would become the target of a mass campaign of hatred and vilification. Deng was one of the leaders most seriously affected by the Cultural Revolution and, although he was also a veteran of the Long March, the Japanese occupation and the civil wars, he would later freely acknowledge that this was one of the worst periods of his entire life.

RETROSPECTIVE: DENG XIAOPING FROM 1949 TO 1966

Deng's role in modernising China after 1978 is universally praised, perhaps excessively and at the expense of others who also played important roles, but on the whole with justification. As it is difficult to evaluate his role between 1949 and 1966 it is useful to consider his own evaluation of that period and his own performance. Deng took the view that the first seven years of the Peoples' Republic – up to about 1956 – had been broadly successful. This was a period of postwar reconstruction and included the period of the first Five-Year Plan, which was also positively evaluated by outside analysts; there was, however, severe repression of real or imaginary enemies of the regime. Deng argued that the process of socialist transformation of agriculture and industry was also successful, although at times the Party leadership had been too hasty.

He continued to believe that the Anti-Rightist Campaign of 1959 should still be assessed positively (*haishi yao kending*), but that after this campaign there were more and more mistakes (*cuowu yuelai yueduo le*). Mao's published speeches, 'On the Ten Great Relationships' and 'On the Correct Handling of Contradictions among the People', were basically fine (*shi haode*): his errors dated from the end of the 1950s. The Great Leap Forward was wrong (*bu zhengque*) as was the headlong rush (*yi hong er qi*) to convert all farms into People's Communes. The attempt (by Mao) to turn everything into large-scale public units in which everybody 'ate out of the same big pot' (*chi daguo fan*) was the cause of the disaster that followed. In the first half of 1959 these 'leftist' mistakes were corrected by a decision to decentralise the management of the communes and even at the beginning of the meetings at Lushan in the summer of that year there had been serious discussion of how to develop the economy. What followed, however, was a period of difficulties (*kunnan shiqi*).

Deng's response to these difficulties was a bureaucratic one as that was the area in which he was both able and had authority; he had been responsible for developing policies on industry and agriculture. He insisted that during the failed harvests and widespread famine, as a result of which tens of millions died, the Party responded to try to overcome those difficulties, but conceded that only certain sections of the party really did so. He also maintained that mistakes should not all be attributed to Mao since other members of the Central Committee were implicated. Deng also insisted that he had to take part of the responsibility for some of Mao's mistakes, even though he had the best of intentions and his conscience was clear. These comments by Deng date from about 1980, four years after the death of Mao Zedong and when he was finally and comfortably in command. It is worth recalling Mao's evaluation of Deng in 1956 when he was the chairman's candidate as general secretary. 'This man Deng is fair and reasonable (*gongdao*). Like me he has made mistakes but he is pretty fair. He is impartial (*gongzheng*) when he deals with problems and if he makes a mistake he is hard on himself.' This is an astute evaluation of Deng and also goes a long way to explain why he tried to remain loyal to Mao even as he was rejecting Mao's political perspective. Deng's political status and credibility depended on his association with Mao: during the 1960s he was performing a delicate balancing act, professing his loyalty to Mao while gradually distancing himself from what would eventually be accepted by the Party as a whole as the chairman's serious errors.[11]

12

CAPITALIST ROADER NUMBER 2 (1966–73)

In 1966 the Cultural Revolution began and it lasted for ten years. This was a great catastrophe. Many old cadres were persecuted, including me. After Liu Shaoqi, I was the Number 2 person in authority taking the capitalist road. Liu Shaoqi was the commander-in-chief and I was his deputy. In those ten years many strange things happened.[1]

Decades after it came to an end, the Cultural Revolution still defies simple categorisation. At heart it was an attempt by Mao to regain the power and prestige that he had enjoyed before the Great Leap Forward by mobilising support from the People's Liberation Army (PLA), students and secondary schoolchildren, and the poorest farmers. It was both a power struggle within the Communist Party leadership and a mass movement. Even its dates are confused: it is usually assumed to have been from 1966 to 1976 but the most violent phase ended in 1968 and by the Ninth Congress of the Chinese Communist Party (April 1969) the mass movement was over. The bitter internal political struggle continued beyond the death of Mao Zedong in September 1976 until the conclusion of the trial of the 'Gang of Four' in January 1981.

The Cultural Revolution started with a cultural enquiry, by the Mayor of Beijing Peng Zhen, in response to criticism from Jiang Qing and Lin Biao that contemporary Chinese culture was insufficiently proletarian. This became the focus of opposition to Liu Shaoqi and Deng Xiaoping, and a Central Cultural Revolution Group was formed of acolytes of Mao on 28 May 1966. Jiang Qing took control of this group and it soon replaced the Politburo and Secretariat as the most powerful body in the Party.

DENG AND THE LAUNCH OF THE CULTURAL REVOLUTION

In early June 1966, the CCP Central Committee, which was still more or less under the control of Liu Shaoqi and Deng Xiaoping, decided to send work teams into secondary schools and colleges in Beijing to gain support for their political approach and seize the initiative from Jiang Qing. They were powerless to stop the Cultural Revolution, so they had to try to take control of it. At this stage it appeared to be relatively innocuous, a drive to ensure that cultural productions were more relevant to the lives of ordinary Chinese and less obsessed with the vanished world of emperors and courtesans. Deng realised that there was more to it than met the eye: sinister forces were at work in the background and it could get out of hand.

It is not clear whether the Cultural Revolution was intended from the outset to be an attack on Deng and Liu Shaoqi or whether Mao and his allies came to realise that it was a highly convenient vehicle for a dishonourable and treacherous surprise attack on them. Deng may have been aware, as he had hinted to Wu Han over their game of bridge, that there was stormy weather ahead and there was nothing he could do but resign himself to his fate.

The Cultural Revolution emerged as a very public mass movement in the summer of 1966. On 18 August Mao Zedong stood on the rostrum over the Tian'anmen Gate of the Forbidden City, the very spot from which he had proclaimed the founding of the People's Republic of China in 1949, and took the salute of thousands of young Red Guards from across the whole country who had gathered in Tian'anmen Square to demonstrate their personal support for him. Within the Politburo and the Central Committee, the struggle between the two factions – Liu Shaoqi and Deng Xiaoping on the one hand and Mao Zedong, Lin Biao and Jiang Qing on the other – grew increasingly vitriolic, but it was not until the autumn that Liu and Deng would be attacked publicly by name. They were in a strong position in the Party hierarchy and the level of support for Mao was uncertain.

Initially the factional conflict was confined to Zhongnanhai, but political disputes intensified among the students and young workers, encouraged by Jiang Qing and Kang Sheng. On 24 July, Mao criticised the work teams for 'obstructing the movement', which was of course the object of the exercise. Liu and Deng made formal self-criticisms and on 28 July the Central Committee agreed that the activities of the work teams should cease.

This was not sufficient for Mao and he ordered a comprehensive relaunch of the movement. On 2 August 1966, during the Eleventh Plenum of the Eighth Central Committee, he issued his notorious instruction, entitled *Bombard the Headquarters: My Big Character Poster*. This was in support of an earlier 'big character poster' or wall newspaper (*dazi bao*) that had been put up on 25 May by Nie Yuanzi alleging that Beijing University was controlled by the bourgeoisie. This fitted neatly into Mao's view of a new class struggle and in his own document he declared that within the Central Committee there was also a 'bourgeois headquarters', a rival powerbase. Mao was referring to the day-to-day work of the Central Committee under Liu Shaoqi and Deng Xiaoping. Mao's poster did not name Liu and Deng, but Xie Fuzhi, the minister of public security, did accuse Deng in the Central Committee meeting of obstructing Mao's attack on the 'bourgeois reactionary line'. The Central Committee ended with a reshuffle of the leadership and although Deng remained in the Standing Committee of the Politburo, he was being sidelined politically.

PERSONAL ATTACKS ON DENG XIAOPING AND LIU SHAOQI

At a Central Committee Work Conference that met in Beijing from 9 to 28 October 1966, Chen Boda set out the argument that there were two opposed political 'lines' in the Cultural Revolution, and Lin Biao criticised both Liu and Deng by name as 'representatives of the incorrect line'. In a self-criticism that Deng was pressurised to make, he wrote that 'At the Eleventh Plenary Session Mao Zedong's big character poster was detonated in the headquarters of comrade Liu Shaoqi and myself': the transparent insincerity of the phrasing indicated clearly, if there were any remaining doubt, that he was not making the statement voluntarily: he may have been trying to protect his work teams by taking personal responsibility.

Mao was still treating the criticism of Liu and Deng as an internal Party matter and warned that posters attacking them should not be put up in the streets. 'If they have allowed mistakes to occur,' he said, 'we must allow them to correct their mistakes. Liu and Deng are being open, not secretive (*shi gao gongkai de, bushi mimide*). We must allow them to be revolutionary.' However, it was not long before some 'rebel groups at the instigation of Jiang Qing and others' went to Zhongnanhai to present Mao with a resolution demanding that the criticism of Liu and Deng should be made public. Bearing in mind the heavy security that has always surrounded Zhongnanhai, delegations from 'rebel groups' could not have approached the Party compound without the cooperation of a senior member of the Party.[2]

On 8 November 1966, Nie Yuanzi, the author of the 'first Marxist-Leninist big character poster', joined with a group of ten others to paste up a new poster, 'Deng Xiaoping is a person in authority within the party following the capitalist road' (*Deng Xiaoping shi dangnei zibenzhuyi daolu de dangquanpai*). The poster identified Deng as second only to Liu Shaoqi as leaders of the anti-Mao 'capitalist roaders' within the Communist Party leadership. From this point onwards slogans criticising Liu and Deng proliferated. On 18 December Zhang Chunqiao received the Qinghua University student activist, Kuai Dafu, at the west gate of Zhongnanhai demanding that Liu Shaoqi should be overthrown by force, and the first in a series of organised demonstrations calling for the downfall of Liu Shaoqi and Deng Xiaoping took place on 25 December 1966.

In August 1967, while Mao Zedong was conveniently absent from the capital, Jiang Qing organised renewed criticisms of Liu, Deng and and their families. Tao Zhu, the Party secretary of Guangdong Province, who had supported Mao at the beginning of the Cultural Revolution but turned against him after seeing the effects of his campaign, was also attacked. Deng was now branded the 'No. 2 capitalist roader' and forced out of his post of general secretary of the Communist Party. He was placed under guard and from September 1967 to October 1969 he was under house arrest in his residence in Zhongnanhai. There had been no trial or internal disciplinary hearing: he was being punished, silenced and segregated for political opposition to Mao, Jiang Qing and Lin Biao.

By 1969, many of the older generation of the leadership in the CCP, the government and the military had been forced out of their positions. Jiang Qing continued to consolidate her influence. Lin Biao used fears of tension on the border with the Soviet Union to justify putting the PLA, which he controlled, on a state of alert and deployed troops in Beijing 'so that they were combat-ready'. His 'Order No. 1' for the mobilisation of these troops also made provision for sending senior Party leaders, including Liu Shaoqi, Deng Xiaoping, Zhu De and Chen Yun, away from the capital to the provinces of Henan, Jiangxi, Guangdong and Anhui, where they would be placed under the supervision of the respective military districts. Strategic reasons were given for this dispersal, but there is no doubt that the leaders were moved away from the capital so that they were no longer able to obstruct the consolidation of power by Mao Zedong, Jiang Qing and Lin Biao.[3]

REPAIRING TRACTORS IN JIANGXI

For two years Deng had been living under guard in his own house in Zhongnanhai with his wife Zhuo Lin and his stepmother Xia Bogen; their children were not permitted to be with them because Deng was now a political pariah. Their eldest son, Deng Pufang, studying physics at Beijing University, was badly injured when he was hounded by Red Guards simply because he was Deng's son, and was left permanently disabled. The other children, Deng Lin, Deng Nan, Deng Rong and Deng Zhifang were sent to work in the countryside to be 'reformed'. On 25 October 1969, the three elder Dengs left Zhongnanhai to fly to Nanchang, the provincial capital of Jiangxi (and also the birthplace of the Red Army in August 1927), where they began a three-year period of exile and, for Deng, manual labour. They would be under the formal supervision of the local military district, but Zhou Enlai had made arrangements with contacts on the Jiangxi Province Revolutionary Committee (local government bodies had all been renamed revolutionary committees – *geming weiyuanhui*) for Deng to work at a tractor repair and spare parts workshop in Xinjian County in Jiangxi. The family would live in what was known as the General's Building (*jiangjun lou*), the accommodation of the former principal of the Nanchang Infantry School, General Xu Guangyou. It was a sizeable building, with six rooms upstairs and several downstairs, and his secretary Huang Wenhua and other staff were there to assist and guard him. It was exile from Beijing and from the political milieu in which he had been a successful and powerful operator, but it was an exile in which he could live and work with a degree of independence: he and Zhuo Lin were also able to avoid the worst excesses of the Red Guards.

After the Cultural Revolution, people who worked with Deng at the tractor plant insisted that they had never really seen him as the 'Number 2 capitalist roader' but as a genuine colleague. Once Deng had been restored to his Party and government positions a degree of sycophancy and hindsight might be expected, but he had never been overly conscious of his status and appears to have fitted in as well as he could.

Both Deng and Zhuo Lin made friends with their new neighbours, simple and honest country folk who were far less sophisticated than the people they mixed with in Zhongnanhai but fundamentally kind-hearted. These recollections may have been coloured by nostalgia and sentimentality for the peasant life. Xinjian County was not where he wanted to be, but in many ways it was a great improvement on his two years of house arrest. He was happy to be away from the poisonous atmosphere of Cultural Revolution-period Zhongnanhai with its vicious political infighting and Jiang Qing and Lin Biao's constant political attacks. Jiangxi is further east than Deng's home province of Sichuan, its mountains are complemented by a network of rivers and the Poyang Lake and the landscape is more watery than Sichuan. It was not an alien environment and southern Jiangxi had been the communist base before the Long March.

When Deng first arrived at the workshop he was solemn and taciturn, but after a few days he began to realise that the Party branch secretary, the director of the workshop and indeed the whole workforce were well disposed towards him. No-one was antagonistic or malicious towards him and the factory tried to make life as easy for the Dengs as possible. Zhou Enlai had chosen well and Deng, who had been more upset by the turn of events in Beijing than he was prepared to reveal, began to relax. He was not of course treated as an ordinary member of the team and his workmates would often suggest that he could rest if he were tired – he was 65 years old and had therefore reached what for most people would be the normal age for retirement – but he refused.

At first when Deng started his shift in the morning he used the main entrance of the tractor workshop, but this involved crossing a main road or making a detour of over 20 minutes. To save him time and to ensure that he had a safe route to work, his new workmates made a small gate in the wattle fence at one side of the workshop in which Deng worked, so that he had access to a narrow path through the fields at the bottom of a hill leading directly to the main gate of the Nanchang Infantry School where he was living. This was only about 2 *li* (1 kilometre) and considerably reduced Deng's journey time to and from work. They fixed a lock to the gate, gave Deng the key, flattened the path with hoes and cleared the undergrowth of thistles and thorns.

On one occasion he collapsed with a recurrence of an old problem with low blood pressure and hypoglycaemia: his colleagues looked after him and carefully took him home on a Fengshou model 27 tractor, as the plant was so small that it did not have a car or even a truck. The workers maintained that they saw Deng as a genuine colleague (*zhenzhi de gongyou*), but it is impossible to be certain whether their care for him was simply a human response and respect for an ageing revolutionary or if they were also concerned not to alienate someone who might soon be back in a position of authority. It is a salutary reminder that, although the exciting and hysterical rhetoric of the Cultural Revolution struck a chord with the young and impressionable, it was not well received by all. Many older and more sanguine workers who had seen military leaders and revolutionaries come and go were not impressed by the political rhetoric emanating from Beijing. All the accounts of Deng's period in Jiangxi indicate that he was well looked after by the local people, who helped the family in numerous small ways, including giving them medicine and showing them a special local way of grinding rice flour.

What could have been a bleak and depressing exile in Jiangxi was made tolerable by this relationship with neighbours and colleagues. Outside of work, one of the three things that Zhuo Lin knew made life worth living for Deng – his 'three loves' or passions (*san'ai*) – was reading: to keep him happy she tried to ensure that he had a good supply of books. His other two passions were playing bridge and mah-jong and having plenty of hot peppers in his food. Chillies are not such a major feature in the normal diet of people in northern Jiangxi as they had been in Deng's native Sichuan, although after the harvest, the flat roofs of rural houses throughout Jiangxi are always adorned with bright red peppers drying in the sun.

Deng used much of his spare time to read, and could often be seen at his desk bent over books late into the night. There were few books available in rural Jiangxi, but he eventually managed to get approval from Beijing to have his collection sent to Xinjian County. He read the works of Marx and Lenin, but he never tired of reading and rereading the classic texts of early Chinese history, particularly the *Historical Records* (*Shiji*) of Sima Qian (died 104 BC). The *Historical Records*, also known as the *Records of the Grand Historian*, is a solid work of history which includes chronological accounts of the reigns of emperors, biographies of notable individuals and monographs on such practical topics as rituals, astronomy, the calendar and taxation. Deng read this and the other standard histories that followed it.

In 1970, although the Cultural Revolution was far from over, there was welcome news for the culture-starved readers of China. Deng saw a newspaper announcement that the People's Literature Publishing House was about to issue new editions of well-known traditional works of fiction. Deng approached Zhao Zichang, the secretary of one of the Party offices in Jiangxi, and asked for a set to be bought for him. Zhao went to some trouble and finally acquired sets of the four most famous, *Romance of the Three Kingdoms*, *Dream of the Red Chamber*, *Water*

Margin and *Journey to the West*, a total of 11 volumes. These novels, which are written in a transitional form of the Chinese language that is basically classical but incorporates the spoken vernacular, had been popular for centuries, but they were banned during the Cultural Revolution – although Mao was also a great enthusiast for them. Some were fictionalised versions of history that did not fit into simple-minded black-and-white analyses of good and evil or right and wrong, and most featured stories about upper-class families. *Journey to the West* (better known outside China as *Monkey*), is a fantastic account of a Buddhist pilgrimage to India. These were unacceptable to the crude and nervous cultural commissars of the Chinese Communist Party. The publication of these books and others that followed came as a breath of fresh air to Deng as to many other educated Chinese.

The children were finally allowed to visit them as the paranoia of the Cultural Revolution began to subside. The separation from their sons and daughters was hard for both of the Dengs, but it was particularly painful for Zhuo Lin. When the children arrived in Jiangxi and the Dengs were able to recreate some of the family atmosphere that they all remembered from their time in Beijing, they were often regaled with tales of what their parents had been reading. They formed the opinion that Deng in particular was using the opportunity to catch up on books that he had not had enough time for in his busy revolutionary and military life. When he returned to Beijing he kept up the habit of reading and it sustained him after his formal retirement in the 1990s.

When Deng was eventually recalled to Beijing they left on good terms and he and Zhuo Lin distributed gifts of sweets, cakes and cigarettes. Later when he met the Jiangxi Province Party secretary at the crucial meeting of the National People's Congress in 1978, Deng ensured that his former colleagues at the tractor factory were given additional funding to build a new workshop and improve their conditions of work and for some official cars. Deng and Zhuo Lin attempted to keep in touch with their friends in Jiangxi through letters and when visitors came to Beijing. This was increasingly difficult after Deng took over the reins of power, but in 1985 Zhuo Lin made a point of inviting to their home a woman with whom she had worked in Jiangxi.[4]

TRAGEDY OF DENG PUFANG

The Cultural Revolution had caused great distress to the family, but neither Deng nor his wife had been physically harmed, unlike Liu Shaoqi, the 'No. 1 capitalist roader', who died in 1969 at the age of 70 after he had been refused medical treatment and abused by Red Guards during his incarceration. The Dengs' eldest son, Pufang, was not so fortunate.

Deng Pufang had been an outstanding student in the Department of Physics at Beijing University (*Beida*) when in 1968, at the height of the violent conflict between Red Guard factions, he was attacked by a Red Guard group led by Nie Yuanzi, the 'madwoman of the age of chaos' (*luanshi kuangnü*), solely because he was the son of Deng Xiaoping. There is some dispute about precisely what happened, but he was either pushed out of a window or jumped to try to escape from his pursuers: his back was broken. A member of the support staff at the university helped him and may have saved his life, but he was paralysed from the waist down and has used a wheelchair ever since. Life during the Cultural Revolution was difficult for everyone but exceptionally difficult for someone who was disabled. Deng Xiaoping heard that his son had been taken into hospital in Beijing but was powerless to help so he wrote to Mao Zedong asking for Pufang to be sent to stay with them in Jiangxi. The letter was sent to Mao via Wang Dongxing, commanding officer of 8341 Special Regiment, which provided protection for Mao and other senior leaders of the CCP. Wang was born in Yiyang in northern Jiangxi, not far from where the Dengs were living, and had been personally responsible for Mao's security since the 1940s. Before Deng had been expelled from Beijing under the provisions of Lin Biao's Order No. 1, Wang Dongxing had indicated that Deng could communicate with him through his relatives in Jiangxi. In January 1971 Deng Pufang came to stay at the general's house. Caring for him was a considerable undertaking as he was unable to stand up, dress or keep himself clean without assistance and they had no professional help. In addition to Deng's work at the tractor plant, he and Zhuo Lin grew vegetables and kept hens for eggs, which they were able to give to Pufang, and by this time they had their own library from Beijing which he could also use.

In the early 1970s even the best medical care in China lagged far behind what was available in the West and this was even more the case in rural areas, such as in northern Jiangxi, where the legendary 'barefoot doctors' – usually trained and often highly motivated paramedics – were the only medical personnel available to treat serious illness and injury, with little in the way of medicines or facilities. Deng Pufang's condition did not seem to be improving and his parents became so concerned that they felt they had no alternative but to write again to Beijing, this time a joint letter to the Central Committee asking for help. In 1972 Zhou Enlai, on behalf of the Central Committee, issued a directive that Deng Pufang should be treated at No. 301 Hospital and Pufang, assisted by his younger sister, boarded a train to Beijing. The Deng family felt that, in spite of Zhou's intervention, their son still did not receive the treatment that he needed soon enough. This was blamed on the continuing influence of supporters of Jiang Qing whom the doctors at No. 301 Hospital were afraid of offending. When the Dengs finally returned to Beijing in March 1973 Pufang's condition had not improved and in the summer of 1974 Zhuo Lin was able to identify specialists in Shanghai who had been sent down to the countryside and had just been 'liberated'. They came to Beijing to consult with doctors at No. 301 Hospital: it was too late to reverse the paralysis and Deng Pufang remains a wheelchair user, but he has become a symbol and a spokesman for disabled people in China.

For the Deng family, as for so many others, the Cultural Revolution was not just a theoretical struggle about ideas, a political battle lost, or an opportunity for young Red Guards to enjoy themselves travelling around the country. They suffered distress and disruption in their personal and professional lives and, with the injury to Deng Pufang, a family tragedy.

Did Deng Xiaoping undergo a spiritual or political crisis during the Cultural Revolution? Neither Deng nor the Chinese sources choose to analyse his response to the catastrophe in that way. Vogel argues that, even as he set out for Jiangxi, Deng had come to the conclusion that the problems China faced had been produced by 'deep flaws in the system' and was determined to change that system as soon as the opportunity presented itself. He never gave up hope that this change was possible and his exile in Jiangxi gave him 'time to ponder' on both the problems and their solution. Although it may not have seemed so at the time, it proved to have been a blessing in disguise as he avoided the poisonous factional disputes that tore apart the capital and was able to think carefully about strategies for reform.

Deng came to the conclusion that in the future the CCP should continue to praise Mao, in spite of all his faults, but that he should not be put 'on a pedestal'. His teachings should be interpreted, 'not as a rigid ideology but as a successful adaptation to the conditions of the time', in Ezra Vogel's words. This would give Deng and those who thought like him the latitude that they needed to adapt Mao's thinking to the new challenges that China faced and assist them in dealing with those within the Party who were devoted to the Mao cult. There is no evidence that Deng came to reject his Marxist training or the world view of a communist, but the climate of opinion had changed and it was necessary to adapt this training to the new circumstances. Much of the population of China had experienced trials and tribulations similar to those endured by the Dengs and one of the results of the Cultural Revolution was a profound abhorrence of factional battles and a deep distrust of rigid ideology. Deng, the natural pragmatist, was in the right place at the right time to take advantage of this new mood of scepticism.[5]

13

RETURN FROM THE COWSHED (1973–5)

In 1973 Premier Zhou Enlai was seriously ill. He brought me back from my cowshed in Jiangxi and to begin with I carried out some State Council business on his behalf.[1]

On 10 March 1973 the Central Committee 'on the suggestion of Mao Zedong and Zhou Enlai decided that it was time to reappoint Deng Xiaoping'.[2] In fact the decision had been taken earlier and Deng had already been in Beijing since late February 1973 after three and a half years of exile in rural Jiangxi. Deng's recall to national politics was primarily the work of Zhou Enlai rather than Mao and it was a slow process that was achieved in the face of bitter opposition. Nevertheless, it indicated a major reversal in the internal politics of the leadership. Mao was ailing and Zhou had been actively trying to re-establish his own authority, especially since the occupation of the Ministry of Foreign Affairs by Red Guards in August 1967 had damaged China's international standing.

Lin Biao had risen to prominence during the Cultural Revolution by pledging the support of the PLA for Mao. At the 1969 CCP National Congress he was described as Mao's 'close comrade in arms' and anointed his heir-apparent. However, on 13 September 1971 he fled towards the Soviet Union in an aircraft which crashed over Mongolia, killing him and several members of his family. This drama has never been satisfactorily explained, but the official position is that Lin had been plotting a military coup against Mao. There was little enthusiasm for the idea that Jiang Qing, Lin's sometime ally but fierce rival, should succeed Mao, but she and her three key supporters among the Shanghai radicals (later excoriated as the Gang of Four) wielded enormous power.

Zhou Enlai was the only member of the Central Committee with sufficient authority to oppose Jiang Qing; however, he was also a sick man and would die on 8 January 1976, eight months before Mao. Zhou had known Deng since their days in France in the 1920s and, although they were very different in personality and temperament, they had a mutual respect and shared a preference for organisation and order over theatricality, mass movements and perpetual revolutionary rhetoric. Zhou needed someone to assist him and Deng was the obvious, possibly the only, choice. Deng's return to political life was not immediately made public because of the struggle between Jiang Qing and the Zhou–Deng axis. Gradual hints were dropped in the press that Deng was back and there were many anecdotes: he was spotted dining in a Beijing restaurant and fellow diners applauded him. Deng, whose sense of humour had not deserted him in his years of exile, applauded them in return (in the conventional Chinese manner) and called out, 'Carry on criticising Deng' (*jixu pi Deng*).

A COMMUNIQUÉ AND A CELEBRATORY DRINK

Deng Xiaoping was a tough and disciplined soldier and politician but he was not a puritan and he was partial to an occasional drink, especially the powerful distilled Five Grain Liquor (*wuliangye*). This is distilled from millet, two types of rice, corn and wheat in Yibin, a city in the south of his home province, Sichuan, and yields a drink of 45 per cent alcohol. After Deng was rusticated to Jiangxi his government salary was no longer paid, but he was allowed some living expenses. The family's monthly income was reduced from 500 *yuan* (*renminbi*) to 200 *yuan* and that income had to support the two Dengs, his stepmother, and as far as possible their children. Deng had lowered his standards and started to drink common-or-garden rice wine (not unlike Japanese sake), which is much weaker and much cheaper than Five Grain Liquor. He even learned to make home-made rice wine, with help from his supervisor at the tractor workshop who showed him where to get yeast, sugar and other ingredients.

1 October 1971 was the twenty-second anniversary of the People's Republic. All the political luminaries normally appear for the National Day celebration but on this occasion one luminary was missing – Lin Biao, the deputy commander-in-chief (*fu tongshuai*). Even in far away Jiangxi Province, Deng Xiaoping's finely tuned political antennae sensed that something unusual was happening in Beijing, but he judged it best to be cautious and said nothing. On the morning of 5 November, he and Zhuo Lin received a summons to attend a meeting in a hall at the tractor plant where the workforce was to hear local officials read out an important Central Committee document that had been relayed through the usual Party channels. By the time they reached the hall, many of the workers were already there and the hall was in silence. Deng found a seat at the back but the Party secretary, Luo Peng, spotted him and shouted, 'Old Deng, you had better come and sit at the front as your hearing is not that good'.

Deng did as he was asked and sat to attention, concentrating and hardly moving for over two hours as the entire communiqué was read out. At the end he went over to Luo Peng and asked if he could look at the document himself as there were passages that he had not heard clearly. This was highly irregular as documents of this nature were intended only to be read out by the authorised Party official but these were not normal times and Deng was not just a regular member of staff. Luo Peng agreed without hesitation and just asked him to take care of the document. Deng and Zhuo Lin did not return home until lunchtime, which worried his stepmother and his daughter who had just arrived. When they saw the expressions on the faces of the couple they were relieved, but because their bodyguard was still present they dared not say anything. Zhuo Lin motioned her daughter into the kitchen and, with her finger, traced on her daughter's palm the four characters, 'Lin Biao is dead' (*Lin Biao sile*). Their immediate reaction, which may have been as symbolic as it was practical, was to go up to their rooms and put in a more powerful light bulb that flooded the room with light. Zhuo Lin cooked a celebratory meal. Deng broke open a bottle of Maotai (the sorghum spirit that is used at state banquets and is even more highly valued than his favourite Five Grain Liquor). They toasted each other with the Maotai, 'Lin Biao is dead, thank heavens' (*Lin Biao bu si, tianli nanrong*). As the news spread other colleagues joined them and rumour has it that by lunchtime Deng and the older workers had managed to drink at least another five bottles of celebratory Maotai between them.

With the death of Lin Biao the political atmosphere cooled down. In Beijing, the day-to-day running of the Central Committee was in the hands of Zhou Enlai – officially with the support and assistance of Mao Zedong – and one of Zhou's first acts was to order the release of a group of 'old cadres' (*lao ganbu*) who had been imprisoned on the orders of Mao or his acolytes. Although Zhou had executive authority he still felt it necessary to secure Mao's imprimatur in sensitive matters, to prevent his orders being countermanded by Jiang Qing.

APPLYING FOR HIS OWN JOB

Deng judged that the time had come to write to Beijing expressing his wish to return to work 'for the party, the people and the state'. The letter was written to Mao, but it went via Zhou Enlai, who not only saw that it was placed before the chairman immediately but ensured that the response was the one that Deng wanted.

Mao's response was a written instruction:

> After Premier [Zhou] has read this, please refer it to Director Wang [Dongxing, Director of the Central Committee General Office and Head of the 8341 Special Regiment, the leadership bodyguard] for printing and distribution to other comrades. The errors that Comrade Deng Xiaoping has committed were grave, but should be distinguished from [those made by] Liu Shaoqi. (1) He was criticised (*aizheng de*) in the Central Soviet, that is he was one of the four offenders, Deng, Mao, Xie and Gu, the chiefs of the so-called Mao faction. For the documents attacking him, refer to 'The Two Lines' and 'Since the Sixth Congress' [...] (2) There are no historical issues involving him, that is, he never surrendered to the enemy. (3) He provided capable assistance to Comrade Liu Bocheng during the war and his military exploits were distinguished. In addition, after [we] entered the cities [to set up the PRC administrations after 1949], everything that he did was positive, for instance when leading delegations to Moscow, he did not yield to pressure from the Soviet Union. These are matters that I have referred to previously.

This instruction rings true as it refers to Deng's personal loyalty to Mao that went back to the early 1930s and Deng's undeniable contributions during the Japanese occupation. The convoluted style in which the original is written, including the use of double negatives, could be interpreted as a forced and grudging admission that Deng should at last be readmitted to the political centre. It is not unlikely that this statement was dragged out of Mao by Zhou Enlai, who needed the political support of Deng in Beijing. Whatever the truth, Mao's agreement was still essential before Zhou could go to the Central Committee with a proposal to rehabilitate Deng.

Zhou Enlai instructed the Central Committee General Office (*zhongyang bangongting*) to circulate copies, together with copies of Mao's instruction and Deng's original letter, to members of the Politburo and followed this up by convening a special meeting of the Politburo. He also contacted the Jiangxi Provincial Party Committee, in the name of the Central Committee, to inform them that the supervision and monitoring (*jiandu*) of Deng had ended and that his 'party organisation life' (*dang zuzhi shenghuo*) had been restored. He asked the Jiangxi Party secretary to make arrangements for Deng to undertake a tour that would combine sightseeing (*canguan fangwen*) with inspection and study (*diaocha yanjiu*).

The Party secretary, Huang Zhizhen, who had only recently been restored to his own posts, decided that he would travel to Xinjian County to pass on the good news in person. Deng indicated that he wanted to travel within Jiangxi and specifically to revisit the sacred revolutionary bases (*geming shengdi*) of Jinggangshan and Ganzhou (formerly in the Jiangxi Soviet) where the CCP and the Red Army had been based before the Long March. This was approved by the Central Committee at the end of September 1972.

It was a most unusual request and required careful management as Deng's position was ambiguous to say the least. He was still officially labelled as the 'Number 2 party person taking the capitalist road' and he had not been reappointed to any of his former positions. Party committees in the places that he wished to visit and other towns and villages en route were telephoned with instructions on how to deal with this visitor, whose status had suddenly altered, even though it was not clear to anyone precisely what that new status was. Detailed instructions for the protocol to be observed on his tour were relayed to local officials by telephone:

1. He is to be received according to his treatment by the main leadership of the Provincial Party Committee. On meeting him he can be addressed as 'Comrade Xiaoping' or 'old senior cadre' (*lao shouzhang*).
2. When Comrade Xiaoping arrives at each location, he must be received and accompanied in person by the leadership.
3. When reporting on their work to Comrade Xiaoping, officials at each location should only refer to the excellent situation of industry and agriculture following the 'internal party struggle of the ten lines' (*dangnei*

shici luxian douzheng) [struggles between the 'correct' line of Mao Zedong and all his opponents from Li Lisan in 1930 to Lin Biao in 1971].

4. When receiving him no requests are to be made and no photographs taken.
5. Security must be absolutely guaranteed, especially security of transport.
6. His reception must be warm and enthusiastic and preparations must be thorough.

There were even more detailed instructions, including an insistence that the cotton quilts provided for Deng should not exceed 5 kilograms in weight and that the rooms in which the Dengs were to stay should be equipped with twin beds, two large towels etc. It was also emphasised that slogans on the route must be carefully checked and, although it was not stated so crudely, it must have been obvious that this meant cleaning up or covering any slogans from the Cultural Revolution that still remained, especially if they attacked Deng by name. In some areas of north-eastern Jiangxi, as in much of rural China, it was still possible to see the remnants of Cultural Revolution slogans well into the 1980s, especially in the more remote villages. The orders also made it clear that absolute secrecy had to be maintained over Deng's itinerary, security had to be strict wherever he was received and it was even forbidden to discuss any arrangement for his visit by telephone: the local authorities were ordered to use messengers instead.

The extraordinary security arrangements for Deng Xiaoping's tour seem more appropriate to a clandestine operation conducted by the military or security services than the visit of a senior politician. This reflects the sensitivity and uncertainty of Deng's position, which in 1972 was far from resolved, and the paranoia after the death of Lin Biao. At the highest level there was tension between Zhou Enlai, who was running the government, and Mao Zedong, who was formally head of the Party, but who was known to be physically and mentally fragile. Mao's instructions were often mediated by Jiang Qing, an implacable opponent of Zhou and Deng, which added another layer of confusion. Deng was in political limbo: the supervision and control order may have been lifted, but he had no official position. However, the nature of the instructions transmitted from the Central Committee (Zhou Enlai) to Jiangxi Party officials were such that only the dimmest and worst-informed local official could possibly have failed to grasp the message that momentous changes were about to take place and that Deng would be playing an important role.[3]

PILGRIMAGE TO JINGGANGSHAN

After three years, Deng was finally free from the Party's supervision and monitoring and he embarked on a highly symbolic visit to Jinggangshan and Ganzhou. He had joined Mao Zedong and Zhu De after they established the Jiangxi Soviet in Ruijin and had not previously been to Jinggangshan. He had always wanted to go there, partly because this poor mountainous region was home to long-established Hakka communities similar to his own in Sichuan, but after 1949 his duties in the Party and government had made such a visit impossible. On one level, the 1972 visit was a tour of inspection, a step forward in his rehabilitation; it was part of his painfully slow return to active political life and perhaps a token of recompense for his years of exile and restriction. In a sense it was also an act of penance and a pilgrimage during which Deng became reconnected with the roots of the Communist Party, a rite of passage that had to be observed before he could return to high office. Deng had chosen his itinerary with care and it had significant parallels with a journey that Mao Zedong had made to Jinggangshan in 1965 on the eve of the Cultural Revolution. By making a similar journey Deng was acknowledging Mao and his place in the history of the Chinese Communist Party, but also asserting his own right to succeed Mao who was ill but still alive.

At about 10 o'clock in the morning of 12 November 1972 Deng, his wife Zhuo Lin, his personal secretary Huang Wenhua, his bodyguard Li Shulin and five other members of staff set forth in a grey Russian Volga car. They headed south and the first stop was at the county town of Qingjiang which is now called Ganshu City. Ganshu is the source of ingredients used in traditional remedies and the locals call it Medicine Capital (*Yaodu*); Deng remembered this from his time in Jiangxi in the 1930s.

The Dengs, both wearing grey Sun Yat-sen jackets, were met at the guest house (*zhaodaisuo*) of the local Revolutionary Committee and went into the main reception room. Deng selected a chair facing east: in the fraught atmosphere of the Cultural Revolution when 'The East is Red' was the unofficial Maoist anthem, this may have been a political statement of loyalty to the CCP or even to Mao: it might just have been a comfortable chair. The Dengs were introduced to the former deputy Party secretary, Chen Zhichuan, who had lost his position at the beginning of the Cultural Revolution for the crime of being a 'faithful executor of the Liu and Deng line' and had only recently been 'liberated' and returned to the County Revolutionary Committee. The choice of Chen was highly symbolic, but he followed the instructions from the centre and restricted himself to briefing Deng

193

about recent developments, mostly about agricultural and industrial production, although he did allow himself a few words on 'excellent' ideological and political changes since the Cultural Revolution.

Visiting the Jiangxi Salt Mine in the southern outskirts of Qingjiang, Deng was enthusiastically received by five or six hundred miners and office staff, some of whom should have been taking a regular day off. The manager and Party secretary, in defiance of strict instructions from above, had spread the word that Deng was coming and had led a cleaning party to make the area around the mine fit for an exceptionally important visitor. The mine had been opened in 1970 with only rudimentary equipment, but it provided Jiangxi with a useful supply of salt. Deng inspected the machinery and processes and recalled that the former lack of salt had been a serious problem for the Red Army when it was based at Jinggangshan. He and Zhuo Lin spent part of the afternoon with Chen Zhichuan and other officials, taking lunch and drinking the local Four Special liquor (*sitejiu*) which Deng declared to be very much to his taste. At the end of the meal, in spite of protests from their hosts, the Dengs insisted that they cover the cost and they also handed over a ration coupon. Deng was actually and symbolically continuing the old Red Army tradition of not being a burden on the local population: the stub of the ration coupon (no. 0005776), dated 12 November 1972, is retained to this day in the mine office as a souvenir. Ration coupons for food grain had been introduced in the mid-1950s to stabilise the grain market. They were still in use in the 1980s, but by the 1990s had been discontinued as market reforms became firmly established.

After a brief visit for Deng to pay his respects at the Four Special distillery, the party continued southwards on the Nanchang-Ganzhou Highway and, at about 4 o'clock in the afternoon they arrived at the town of Ji'an. Ji'an is approximately halfway between Nanchang and Ganzhou and is close to the Jinggangshan mountain range, after which the district was temporarily renamed in 1972. Jinggangshan is now a county-level city subordinate to the prefectural-level city of Ji'an. Deng was welcomed enthusiastically and was told that he would be staying in the house which Mao Zedong had occupied on his 1965 visit. It is on the outskirts of the town by the banks of the Gan River and is now the No. 1 Building of the Ji'an Guesthouse. It also lies close to one of Ji'an's most treasured monuments, the Egret Academy (*Bailu shuyuan*), built in the Southern Song dynasty (1127–1279) for Zhu Xi and other distinguished Neo-Confucian scholars to lecture in..

Deng took his evening walks along the banks of the Gan River and could often be seen gazing across to Egret Island and its ancient monument. The evenings also provided opportunities to talk to Cui Yongming, a senior member of the

Jinggangshan (Ji'an) District Party Committee who was also deputy political commissar of the Ganzhou Military District. In 1942 and 1943 Cui had been an intelligence and reconnaissance officer in a security unit of the 129th Division political section when Deng was the regimental political commissar. Cui relished the opportunity to play host to his old commanding officer. When he briefed Deng on local conditions, Cui's clear Shanxi accent took Deng back to his days of fighting in the Taihang Mountains. The lamps in Deng's room burned late into the night as Cui described life in the province during the Cultural Revolution. Deng also discovered that Lin Biao had tried to rewrite the history of the Jinggangshan period, downplaying the role of Zhu De and exaggerating his own contribution.

They visited the site of the battles to establish the Jinggangshan base on 13 November, arriving at about 9 o'clock in the morning, and then continued along rugged tracks over heavily forested mountains to the village of Sanwan where in 1927 Mao Zedong had reorganised units of the Red Army in a clearing under the maple trees. Officials in this part of Jiangxi had taken the security precautions seriously and local people had been told to expect a 'foreign guest from South-East Asia'. When a lively, short chap appeared wearing a grey Sun Yat-sen jacket and an old pair of black shoes, he seemed strangely familiar: as soon as he spoke, his Sichuan accent gave him away. The news soon spread and villagers flocked to see him. Although he had been aware of the dreadful conditions in the mountain villages of Jiangxi since the Great Leap Forward, this was his first direct contact since the 1930s. He was surrounded by desperately poor people wearing thin home-made clothes in spite of the fact that it was early winter and already cold. Few of them owned the padded jackets and trousers that are essential in northern Chinese winters.

Rushing through some of the smaller villages because of their tight schedule, Deng's party eventually arrived at the Octagon (*bajiao lou*) in Maoping. Maoping is close to the border with Hunan and was the scene of a battle between the communist and nationalist forces. The building, which has octagonal skylights, was the headquarters of the Red Army, which survived the attack during the CCP withdrawal as it had been owned by a doctor who was on good terms with both the parties. It is now a museum, and a magnet for the 'red tourism' industry catering for Chinese people wishing to visit the 'sacred sites of the revolution'.

Deng alighted from his car at a temple close to the Octagon, strode across and quickly climbed the steps. The ground floor had been Zhu De's living quarters and the site of a meeting that combined two communist military units and helped establish the Jiangxi Soviet. It was always known as the 'Zhu–Mao joint talks' (*Zhu*

Mao huishi), but during the Cultural Revolution had been renamed the 'Mao–Lin joint talks' (*Mao Lin huishi*). Lin Biao, recently and safely dead, was blamed personally for this falsehood, although it is just as likely that a local sycophant was responsible. Deng had listened in silence but said emphatically, 'Lies are lies and truth is truth'. Mao Zedong's former quarters were on the second floor and Deng inspected the display, which included the bed, ink block and lamp that Mao had used and two works of Mao's that had been written in the Jinggangshan period, 'How can Red Political Power Exist' and 'The struggle in Jinggangshan'. He also visited the former hospital and the sanatorium where wounded Red Army troops had been housed.

Local cadres were not forthcoming about the current economic situation in the area, either for fear of offending him or because of their instructions. Deng made a point of acknowledging that in many ways the villagers of the Jinggangshan region were as poor as they had been in 1929 and promised better times ahead. The party drove further south to Ciping and in the evening Deng and Zhuo Lin arrived at the Jinggangshan Guesthouse. On 14 November they spent the morning at the Jinggangshan Revolutionary Museum (*Jinggangshan geming bowuguan*) in Ciping and in the afternoon visited Mao Zedong's former residence and the Martyrs' Memorial. The following day, as the earlier fog had lifted, they were able to return to Huangyangjie, where the Red Army had successfully defended a key mountain pass. Mao mentioned Huangyangjie in his verses and it was there, in the autumn of 1928, that he composed *Jinggangshan*, one of his better known poems.

This stage of Deng's tour in the wooded mountains of Jinggangshan is especially redolent of a political pilgrimage. His status may have been insecure but his political acumen was as sharp as ever. In addition to giving ammunition to his supporters in Beijing, Deng also wished to strengthen his association with Mao's revolutionary legacy, one of the main sources of legitimacy of the CCP, in spite of the damage Mao had done to him personally. He also demonstrated a determination to correct any misrepresentations of CCP history. The man who from the 1980s onwards came to be seen as the antithesis of everything that Mao Zedong stood for was not trying to distance himself from Mao. It is impossible to judge whether this reflected a personal commitment to Mao or political expediency.

On 17 November 1972, immediately after breakfast, Deng's party left Jinggangshan for Taihe County on the west bank of the Gan River. The Taihe Revolutionary Committee had been hosting a south China conference on agricultural mechanisation and Deng, fresh from his recent experience of the tractor repair and spares plant, took a particular interest in the small-scale machinery produced in the country. One witness to this visit to Taihe was Chi Long, a former PLA Air Force officer who had been designated a counter-revolutionary because he had offended the commander-in-chief of the air force, Wu Faxian, a protégée of Lin Biao. Chi had been sent to work on a farm in Shandong but had left his children with relatives in his home town of Taihe. After the death of Lin Biao, Chi had been able to leave Shandong and had returned to collect his children. When a new guest arrived on 17 November Chi was determined to find out who it was. When he learned that it was Deng he asked to meet him and this was agreed. Chi greeted Deng with a military salute and shook his hands firmly, explaining that he had been in the old 1st Front Army and with Deng on the Long March as part of a signals unit. Deng appeared to recognise him, possibly being diplomatic, and the two sat and talked for over two hours. Chi took off his coat and showed Deng an injury that he had received, not during these battles but in the Cultural Revolution, and Deng responded that they had both been forced out by Lin Biao's 'Order No. 1'. On 19 November Deng and his party left Taihe to visit a joint military-civilian production brigade in a commune close to Ji'an. He questioned the management in detail about the grain they were producing and the pigs they were rearing and so brought to an end his ten-day, 2000 *li* trip to southern Jiangxi. He had missed no opportunity to inform himself about local problems and assess the attitude of the local Party leadership to the Cultural Revolution, to Mao and to himself.[4]

RETURN TO BEIJING

After their tour of southern Jiangxi, Deng Xiaoping and Zhuo Lin returned to Xinjian County: their unplanned sojourn in Jiangxi was finally coming to an end. On 17 February 1973 the Jiangxi Provincial Revolutionary Committee office received a telephone call from Wang Dongxing, the director of the Central Committee's General Office (and also the commanding officer of the 8341 Special Regiment, the leadership bodyguard), who informed the Jiangxi leadership that the Central Committee had approved Deng's recall: moreover, Wang was insistent that Deng should return to Beijing immediately. This was, said Wang, 'according to instructions from Mao Zedong, personally arranged by Zhou Enlai' (*genju Mao Zedong de zhishi, you Zhou Enlai qinzi anpaide*), leaving little room for doubt that the decision had been made by Zhou. Wang instructed the Jiangxi leadership to take Deng and his family by car to Yingtan, a major rail hub in eastern Jiangxi, and put them on a train to Beijing; he gave strict instructions that absolute secrecy and the security of the Deng family were of paramount importance. At 10 o'clock in the morning of 18 February 1973 the Jiangxi Provincial Revolutionary Committee secretary, Huang Zhizhen, telephoned his subordinate Wang Ruiqing in Shangrao District to convey the news of Deng's recall and instruct him to organise the reception for the Dengs at Yingtan. Wang in turn contacted the local officials who would be meeting the Dengs at Yingtan and, to avoid possible misunderstandings, added that the reception should be warm and considerate. Deng was no longer *persona non grata*.

At ten minutes to five on the afternoon of 18 February 1973 the Deng family and their staff arrived at the town guesthouse at Yingtan in two official cars. Conscious of the great change that was about to take place in his life at the age of almost 70, Deng was unable to sleep and caused the guesthouse staff and the guard some consternation when he insisted on walking outside alone in the cold night air. It was a long wait as the train to Beijing, Express 46, en route from Fuzhou, did not pass through Yingtan until 11 o'clock on the morning of 20 February. Deng was seen off with proper ceremony and headed north towards the capital.

Zhou Enlai convened a special meeting of the Politburo on 10 March 1973 to discuss Deng Xiaoping's return. The Central Committee then issued a formal document, 'Decision on the reinstatement of Comrade Deng Xiaoping in the organisational life of the Party and in his position as Deputy Premier of the State Council'. On 12 April, a little over a month after his return from Jiangxi, Deputy Premier Deng Xiaoping appeared with Premier Zhou Enlai at a grand banquet in the Great Hall of the People to welcome the Cambodian leader Prince Sihanouk and his wife on a state visit to China, the first public acknowledgement that Deng Xiaoping had been officially rehabilitated.

He was still far from being in control. Preparations were underway for the Tenth National Congress of the CCP in August 1973 and key supporters of Jiang Qing were already being manoeuvred towards positions on the Central Committee, which was as divided as ever. It would be another five years before Deng could begin his great economic reform programme.[5]

TENTH NATIONAL CONGRESS OF THE CCP (AUGUST 1973)

The Ninth National Congress of the CCP had been held in Beijing in April 1969 at the height of the Cultural Revolution to legitimise the ruling elite around Mao and Lin Biao after the purge of Deng and Liu Shaoqi. By the Tenth Congress, held in the summer of 1973, Lin Biao was dead and Deng Xiaoping had been rehabilitated. At the congress, key allies of Mao and his wife Jiang Qing, based on her political clique in Shanghai, were elected to the Central Committee, but so were Deng and other 'long-standing veteran cadres who had been persecuted' during the Cultural Revolution. Deng was not elected to the Politburo. The strains in the congress and the bitterly divided Central Committee are exemplified by the fact that the opening political report was given by Zhou Enlai and a report on the revision of the Party's Constitution was given by Wang Hongwen, a former Shanghai Red Guard who Jiang Qing wished to replace Zhou as premier and was later to be condemned as one of the Gang of Four. On 12 December 1973 at a meeting of the Politburo Mao proposed that Deng should now take a leading role in the Central Committee and the powerful Central Military Commission and also be appointed chief of the general staff of the PLA. Although the Central Committee issued a circular on his new roles on the same day, the military appointments were not ratified until 5 January 1975 and he did not become deputy chairman of the Central Committee until three or four days later. The delay was simply the result of obstruction by Jiang Qing and her supporters.

OFFICIAL VISITS: PIERRE TRUDEAU AND THE UNITED NATIONS

In spite of his precarious position Deng embarked on a series of high-profile official activities, beginning in October 1973 with the visit to China of the Canadian Prime Minister Pierre Trudeau and his wife. Deng accompanied them for their entire visit, which included the cities of Luoyang, Zhengzhou and Guilin, only recently opened to foreign visitors. Arriving back in Beijing he paused only to attend a meeting on the protection of the environment in the valley of the Li River in Guangxi (which he had just visited) before setting off again, this time to pay his respects at Shaoshan in Hunan Province, Mao Zedong's birthplace. He arrived in Shaoshan on 19 October and on 22 October moved on to Handan in Hebei in an area where he had fought against the Japanese in 1938, adding to the political symbolism for his fightback.

In international terms the most important of his official engagements was his speech at the Sixth Special Session of the United Nations in April and May 1974 to discuss conflict in the Middle East and the 'oil crisis' that profoundly affected the costs of energy and the world economy. Deng's speech emphasised the need for unity among developing countries and echoed ideas that Mao Zedong had begun to formulate in 1973: Mao believed that there was 'great disorder under heaven' that favoured the rise of developing countries. There was no sign of the pragmatism and diplomacy that was later to mark Deng's international activities. Deng was presenting the official views of the Central Committee, which was dominated by Mao. His speech had been approved personally by Mao on 4 April 1974 and he delivered it on the afternoon of 10 April in front of over 100 international delegates.

Deng had been formally nominated by Zhou Enlai, who wanted Deng to deputise for him as he was already terminall ill. Although Deng was not a Politburo member he had foreign and diplomatic experience that others did not have, but his nomination had to be pushed through the Central Committee in the face of such bitter opposition by Jiang Qing and other 'leftists' that the first meeting to discuss the nomination was inconclusive. Zhou ignored Jiang Qing's opposition, reported to the Foreign Ministry that Deng's nomination had been approved and then submitted the programme drawn up by the ministry to Mao and carefully selected members of the Politburo. Jiang Qing flew into a rage and tried to get the decision rescinded. Mao sent word to Zhou Enlai that Deng was his candidate and added, 'if not all Politburo members agreed, that is tough' (*ru zhengzhiju tongzhi dou bu tongyi, na jiu suanle*). Zhou was delighted to be able to pass this on to Wang Hongwen. On 26 March at another meeting only Jiang Qing opposed Deng's appointment; she became hysterical and Mao had to write ordering her not to oppose Deng.

On 6 April 1974 Zhou Enlai went to the airport in person to send the delegation on their way, backed by 4,000 Party members who had been mustered as a major public demonstration of support for Deng. In a photograph taken as Deng was about to board the aircraft, the illness that was to end Zhou's life in January 1976 is clearly reflected in his face, but it does not take much imagination to discern in the expressions of both men a feeling of grim satisfaction at having outwitted Jiang Qing. Deng's speech to the United Nations does not stand up to close inspection. It lacked depth or subtlety, but his strategy of consulting widely and using the language and political position of Mao shielded him from further attack.[6]

CONFRONTING JIANG QING AND THE CAMPAIGN AGAINST LIN BIAO AND CONFUCIUS

Deng slowly consolidated his position. He was supported openly by Zhou Enlai, who also had a popular following, and was opposed both openly and furtively by Jiang Qing, who was becoming a figure of hate. A major confrontation erupted on 4 October 1974 when Mao agreed, on the advice of Zhou Enlai, that Deng should be appointed first deputy premier of the State Council. This would make him Zhou's immediate deputy and his natural successor, an important consideration in view of the severity of Zhou's illness. Jiang Qing was predictably furious and railed at Deng during a Politburo meeting on 17 October 1974. The other members of what Mao had started to refer to as a 'small faction of four' made strenuous efforts to have Deng's promotion rescinded and tried to form a 'cabinet' of their own. Mao Zedong was not in Beijing at this time and on 18 October Wang Hongwen, on Jiang Qing's instructions, travelled to Changsha to persuade him not to approve Deng's appointment. Wang was rebuffed and told in no uncertain terms that the four should not act as a faction but should rally around Deng. On 12 November Mao wrote to Jiang Qing warning her not to set up an independent 'cabinet', like the Shanghai cabal that had operated in the 1960s. The atmosphere in Zhongnanhai and in Diaoyutai, the state guesthouse in Beijing's Haidian district where Jiang Qing also operated, was increasingly poisonous. In their desperation to prevent Deng from wielding the authority that he was steadily acquiring, Jiang Qing and her supporters used every trick in the book, including lies, innuendo and attempts to manipulate Mao.

Mao, although very ill, was not easily fooled and in January 1975 decided that it was time for Deng to be named not only first deputy premier but also deputy chairman of the Communist Party and the Central Military Commission, and chief of the general staff. These decisions were ratified by the Central Committee when it met in Beijing from 8 to 10 January 1975 to prepare for the upcoming Fourth National People's Congress. The outcome of the machinations was precisely the opposite of what Jiang Qing intended. Deng had now become the major stumbling block to her political ambitions, the 'tiger blocking the road' (*lanlu hu*). Jiang's opposition was personal and vindictive, but it was conducted in language of such overwrought invective and fantastic hyperbole that it was difficult to take seriously. In any case her primary target appeared not to be Deng, which would have been rational in view of his increasingly powerful position, but the ailing Zhou Enlai, against whom she had a deep and abiding personal animus. Her antagonism towards Zhou reached its height in a campaign to criticise Lin Biao and Confucius (*Pi Lin pi Kong yundong*) which was bizarre even by the standards of the Cultural Revolution. The campaign was a joint character assassination, beginning as an attack on Jiang Qing's erstwhile ally, the deceased Lin Biao, and then redirected against Zhou Enlai (represented by Confucius). It sought spurious justification in lessons purportedly drawn from various episodes in Chinese history, exacerbated political uncertainty and paralysed the government when China desperately needed stability.[7]

14

RUNNING CHINA
(JANUARY 1975)

In 1975 I took charge of the day-to-day business of the Central Committee.[1]

The Fourth National People's Congress (NPC), the first since 1964 and thus the first after the Cultural Revolution, met in Beijing from 13 to 17 January 1975. The NPC is the nearest that China has to a parliament but it is not openly elected or representative of the population as a whole. Zhou Enlai delivered the 'Report on the work of the government' and set out plans for the development of the Chinese economy based on the modernisation of agriculture, industry, national defence and science and technology. These 'four modernisations', as they became known, were Zhou's legacy and the foundation of the reform programme that Deng was to implement after Zhou's death. The congress elected what was effectively a 'cabinet' of Zhou Enlai, Deng Xiaoping and other like-minded politicians, frustrating Jiang Qing's ambitions to control the government. As Premier, Zhou Enlai was responsible for the day-to-day business of government but he was so frail that Deng Xiaoping had to deputise for him. Mao's formal approval had to be acknowledged, but for all practical purposes Deng was now running China although his success was not a foregone conclusion.

Jiang Qing remained Deng Xiaoping's most vociferous opponent. Following her conviction, imprisonment and death in prison in 1991 (presumed to have been suicide), she has been condemned, almost unanimously, as a vindictive and divisive individual who tried to use her position as Mao's wife to seize power. Even bearing in mind the common prejudice against women exercising political power in China (the most notable example being the Empress Dowager Cixi) it is difficult to argue that she made any positive contributions to Chinese political life. Towards the end of Mao's life her support metamorphosed into manipulation and she became his political gatekeeper. It was difficult for anyone to know whether instructions genuinely originated with Mao or with his wife.[2]

CONVERSATIONS WITH HU QIAOMU AND COMPREHENSIVE REORGANISATION

Jiang Qing may have been Deng's most unpleasant antagonist after his return to Beijing from internal exile but she was not his most serious political opponent. The political opposition that caused Deng most difficulty was from established Communist Party intellectuals, respected figures able to argue rationally but resolutely on the basis of Marxist theory, theory that Deng had also studied although he was no theorist. Two of the most implacable were Hu Qiaomu and Deng Liqun, both influential in propaganda and the media. Hu Qiaomu (Mao's secretary from 1941 to 1966) and Deng Liqun (Liu Shaoqi's former secretary) were adamantly opposed to Deng Xiaoping's plans for economic reform and they represented a considerable body of opinion in the leadership of the Communist Party, nationally as well as in Beijing. Although Deng Xiaoping was able to secure the agreement of the Third Plenum of the Eleventh Central Committee on the need for economic reforms in 1978, it was not until the conclusion of his Southern Tour of 1992 that the opposition of Hu Qiaomu, Deng Liqun and their supporters was finally overcome.

Deng's disagreements with these two theorists, Hu Qiaomu in particular, were on a different level from those with Jiang Qing. Their opposition was based on their genuine but different understanding of Marxist theories: it was not vindictive and there was little personal antagonism. Between January 1975 and January 1976 Deng Xiaoping had 24 'conversations' (*tanhua*) with Hu Qiaomu and other members of what would eventually become the State Council Political Research Office (*Guowuyuan zhengzhi yanjiushi*), 15 of these conversations were with Hu alone. Records of these discussions were published by the editorial group for the biography of Hu Qiaomu which was led by Deng Liqun, and they illustrate in detail the struggle that Deng Xiaoping had in reorganising (*zhengdun*) the Communist

Party and overcoming resistance to reform. The establishment of the Political Research Office was formally ratified by the State Council in June 1975 and became operational at the beginning of the following month. Deng Xiaoping had effectively taken over the day-to-day running of the Central Committee, following the formal approval of the Second Plenum of the Tenth Central Committee and the Fourth National People's Congress (Beijing, 13–17 January) and with the support of Zhou Enlai and (at least nominally) the ageing and infirm Mao Zedong. Deng's ascent to power continued to be a slow and tortuous affair and would still take many more months of both delicate negotiations and bitter battles.

Deng was walking an ideological tightrope. Although his aim was the fundamental reform of the economy, he had to find a way of presenting it as consistent with the three basic theoretical principles laid down by Mao: 'opposing and defending against revisionism' (*fanxiu fangxiu*), 'stability and unity' (*anding tuanjie*) and 'improving the national economy' (*ba guomin jingji gaoshangqu*). Deng and Zhou drew on these principles selectively, only paying lip service to Mao's strictures on revisionism; they also ignored much of the background rhetoric that related to class struggle and the dictatorship of the proletariat. Mao was clinging to these slogans while supporting the practical work done by Deng and Zhou: the 'three principles' were a useful flag of convenience as they drove through their reform proposals.[3]

REORGANISING THE MILITARY

Navigating this doctrinal minefield Deng set about his reforms, beginning with the military and the economy. Establishing his authority over the military was his top priority. On 25 January 1975, immediately after his appointment as chief of the general staff and deputy chairman of the Central Military Commission, he spoke to senior officers. He told them that the military was in a chaotic state; many valuable traditions had been lost under Lin Biao; and restoring the over-staffed and cumbersome PLA to pre-1959 effectiveness and confidence was a formidable task. The Central Military Commission convened in an enlarged session from 24 June to 15 July to discuss Deng's reform proposals. On 14 July Deng set out what he required the PLA to do: recover the old traditions; turn their backs on the days when it was swollen, dispersed, conceited, extravagant and lazy (*zhong, san, jiao, she, duo*); avoid factional disputes and follow orders from the Party. This was easier said than done as it was not clear who was authorised to issue orders on behalf of the Party. Deng's proposals met with general approval in the forces and were followed up by swift and resolute reorganisation of command in the major units and a new policy on cadres to stabilise the military.

REVIVING THE NATIONAL ECONOMY

Once Deng had the military behind him and was in control of the State Council he could work on revitalising the economy. On 10 February 1975 he had the Central Committee issue a 'Communiqué on the National Economic Plan for 1975', which 'called on the entire party to rally all those who could be rallied (*yaoqiu quan dang tuanjie yiqie keyi tuanjie de ren*) and muster all active elements to improve the national economy'.

The Chinese economy was in a truly parlous state: all sectors had been severely damaged during the Cultural Revolution and in the first half of 1974 many sectors and individual enterprises had not only under-performed against their planned targets but were seriously in debt. Production had dropped, revenue had also decreased, but expenditure was still increasing. There had been a slight increase in agricultural production, but industrial production had stagnated and, crucially, steel and coal production had declined. These problems were deep-seated and the result of ingrained attitudes and habits. It was difficult to know where to start, but a comprehensive overhaul (*zhengdun*) of the economy was imperative: piecemeal reforms would not work.

Nevertheless, there had to be priorities: industry and communications were Deng's main concern and within that sector he rapidly identified the most urgent tasks to be the railways, iron, steel and coal. Restructuring was a daunting prospect. Deng began by examining the leading cadres in the organisations that ran these sectors, redeploying where necessary, rooting out factional plots and intrigues, and reinstating structures and rules and regulations with a proven track record.

RESTRUCTURING THE RAILWAYS

The railways were a high priority as the main artery of communications for the vast distances that had to be covered in China. Deng, as a Sichuanese, was conscious of the part played by railways in China's history. Towards the end of the Qing dynasty the Railway Protection Movement in Sichuan had attempted to prevent railway development from falling into the hands of foreign banks, and their protests contributed to the downfall of the dynasty. When Deng became secretary of the South-Western Bureau, he championed the construction of a rail link between Chengdu and Chongqing, the first new line built after 1949. Sichuan was not fully connected to the national rail network until the late 1970s and Deng identified the railways as an obvious weak link in the economy.

On 28 January 1975 Deng summoned Wan Li, the minister of railways, to his office for a briefing. Wan had been deputy mayor of Beijing before the Cultural Revolution. He had only been in his new post for ten days, yet he tried to give Deng a report that was as blunt and unvarnished as possible, knowing that this was what Deng would expect. This did not come as a great surprise to Deng, but it did give him serious cause for concern. The level of freight (*yunshu shengchan*) being transported had fallen dramatically from 500,000 freight trucks per day in 1965 to about 400,000 by 1975. The level of accidents was alarming: there had been ten times more serious accidents in 1975 than in 1965. Damage to locomotives and rolling stock was a great cause for concern and the rate of building new locomotives was only 60 per cent of the previous figure. There were also serious blockages at important railway hubs such as Zhengzhou and Xuzhou, which adversely affected the entire network. Without railway restructuring the rest of the economy could not function.

Deng called a meeting of Party secretaries responsible for industry at provincial, municipal and autonomous regional level to attack this critical issue. It ran from 25 February to 8 March 1975 and on 5 March Deng gave his keynote speech to a packed hall. Officials had arrived early, desperate for something to give them hope for the future of the railways and a boost to the economies of their regions. Deng hurried into the room and waved at the audience, but would not shake hands with the provincial leaders who rushed forward, telling them that he would only do so once the economic situation had improved. Some delegates were taken aback by the lack of opportunity for ritual sycophancy, but it helped Deng to persuade them how serious the position was and how urgently they needed to ensure that the material base (*wuzhi jichu*) of the economy was improved.

In the language of the Cultural Revolution, leading officials had 'grasped revolution but had not grasped production', creating a serious crisis. The Central Committee approved the 'Decision on Improving the Work of Railways' (*Document No. 9*) which had been drafted by Wan Li in consultation with Deng. The main provisions were the restoration of order to a chaotic network and new regulations emphasising security and punctuality. Deng's speech and

Document No. 9 were the 'emperor's sword' (*shangfang baojian*) that confered authority on Wan Li, and he circulated them as widely and swiftly as possible. Wan led work teams to Xuzhou, Taiyuan, Zhengzhou, Changsha and other key railway towns to implement the reorganisation. It was not simply a matter of waving the new documents: tough meetings were necessary to underline the seriousness of the situation and the urgent need to combat factional strife. Miscarriages of justice had to be redressed; managers were ordered to put discipline, unity and the needs of the nation first; and pre-Cultural Revolution regulations had to be reinstated. The new order was first applied to the section that operated out of Xuzhou, and by April monthly targets were reached ahead of schedule. There was overwhelming genuine support for Deng's reforms: employees and management were desperate to escape from the chaos and rhetorical battles and concentrate on their jobs.

IRON AND STEEL

Iron and steel provide the basic material for industrial and consumer products, not least locomotives, rolling stock and railway track. Deng addressed the ruinous position of the industry at a symposium that ran from 8 to 29 May in Beijing that was attended by provincial industrial officials and the directors of the 11 largest iron and steel plants. Wan Li outlined his experience in reorganising the railways and Ye Jianying, Li Xiannian, Gu Mu and other senior figures lent their support. This was essential as Deng's reform enterprise was still far from plain sailing and were not to be seen as the policy of one man. Jiang Qing and her supporters were organising a political campaign attacking 'empiricism', a conventional code word for pragmatism and a preference for economic reforms over ideology.

Deng's most important contribution to the symposium was his speech on 29 May, 'Problems that need to be resolved in the current iron and steel industry'. Realising that he was not entirely preaching to the converted he framed it around Mao Zedong's 'three principles' of a Marxist approach; stability, unity and improving the national economy. He passed over the first and emphasised the practical needs of the industry, echoing his earlier thoughts on railway reorganisation. A Central Committee document based on this speech, 'Directive on striving to fulfil the 1975 Plan for iron and steel production' (*Document No. 13*), was issued on 4 June 1975 and the State Council established a specialist Iron and Steel Industry Leading Group. Within a month the industry was already showing signs of improvement, not because Deng had administered a miracle cure but because his strategy had enabled management and staff to resume their normal work without fear of constant political criticism.

SCIENCE, TECHNOLOGY AND EDUCATION

The Cultural Revolution had adversely affected all areas of China's economy and society, but in no field was it more serious than in education, science and technology. The universities and colleges had been the battleground of Red Guards all claiming to represent the true policies of Mao. Formal education simply stopped for most secondary, college and university students and was replaced by the study of Mao Zedong's works, which was safer. As a result, an entire generation missed out on genuine education.

Many scientific and technical research institutes were closed down or paralysed, unable to carry out research for lack of funds or fear of political criticism. Some scientists had continued to carry out their work in secret as if they were criminals and the entire scientific community felt defeated and dejected. Technical advance was essential for defence projects as well as economic development. In 1975 the Seventh Ministry of Machine Building (*qi jibu*) was created to develop a Chinese space programme, but it lacked the necessary technical knowledge.

In September 1975 Hu Yaobang, who had been working under Hu Qiaomu at the State Council Political Research Office, produced his 'Outline report on the work of the Academy of Sciences' that emphasised the central role of science and technology in economic production. He rejected the idea that there could be 'forbidden zones' that academics should not touch and criticised the management of the Academy of Sciences for blocking specialist research. Deng Xiaoping was enthusiastic about Hu Yaobang's report, seeing it not only as a template for running the Academy of Sciences but as a blueprint for science, technology and education more generally. He failed to secure Mao Zedong's imprimatur as he had hoped but, although the report was never formally accepted, it formed the basis for the future direction of science and technology in China.

REORGANISING THE PARTY

The time had come to reorganise the CCP. In a speech at a Central Committee Study Class, entitled 'Strengthen the leadership of the party and overhaul the party's work style', that Deng gave on 4 July 1975, he expressed concern at the failure of local Party organisations to re-emerge after the Cultural Revolution. He insisted that unified leadership must be created at provincial level: even if two factions had been acceptable at the beginning of the Cultural Revolution they were not now and Mao's strictures on stability and unity should be observed. The persecution and injustice of the Cultural Revolution was a running sore throughout the Party and, although Mao had accepted that 'special cases' of rehabilitation of wrongly purged cadres should be speeded up, overall the process was slow. At the end of April 1975 Deng and Zhou Enlai had pushed through the Central Committee measures to allow the release of people incarcerated for political reasons, with the exception of a few cases including those associated with Lin Biao. Over 300 senior cadres were released and many were reassigned jobs.[4]

HU QIAOMU AND THE POLITICAL RESEARCH OFFICE OF THE STATE COUNCIL

Deng and Zhou Enlai had successfully frustrated the attempts of Jiang Qing and her supporters to set up their own independent 'cabinet' in 1974 but in the spring of 1975 her supporters had launched a campaign under the slogan of 'anti-empiricism' (*fan jingyan zhuyi*) to obstruct the reforms. The press was under the control of Jiang Qing, who had a group of writers to act as her 'mouthpieces [*chuigushou*] and weapons [*gunzi*]'. Deng was happiest dealing with practical policies and pragmatic decisions but he understood that he needed his own ideological special forces for close combat (*duanbing xiangjie de zhengduo*) with these 'ideological commandos' of the Gang of Four.

In early 1975 he initiated a series of discussions with Hu Qiaomu, a former secretary to Mao Zedong and expert drafter of documents. Hu Qiaomu also understood how Mao thought and reacted and, if there was any possibility that Mao Zedong Thought could be manipulated so that it appeared to permit the practical changes that Deng required, Hu's expertise would be essential. Although Hu was to remain fundamentally opposed to Deng's economic reforms, he was no supporter of the Gang of Four: he had been purged during the Cultural Revolution, although he was protected by Mao from the brutal treatment that had been meted out to many of Mao's opponents. When Deng Xiaoping returned to Beijing in March 1973, Hu Qiaomu had only been 'liberated' for a short time and he did not appear in public for the first time until the celebrations for National Day in October 1974.

In spite of their differences Deng and Hu worked well together against the common enemy of Jiang Qing and her Shanghai clique. They decided that in light of this ideological struggle they would take the opportunity offered by the editorial work on the fifth volume of Mao Zedong's *Selected Works* (*Mao Zedong xuanji*) to create a State Council Political Research Office (*Guowuyuan zhengzhi yanjiushi*) which would be led by Hu Qiaomu with the assistance of six other senior Party members – Wu Lengxi, Hu Sheng, Xiong Fu, Yu Guangyuan, Li Xin and Deng Liqun. This body was initially proposed in January 1975 but was blocked by Jiang Qing's associates, Zhang Chunqao and Yao Wenyuan, who retained a great deal of influence over the CCP's ideology even though they were no longer in control of the day-to-day running of the Party or the government. The proposal was finally approved by the Central Committee in June 1975.

Mao Zedong's *Selected Works* were the bible for members of the Communist Party (although they were temporarily superseded by *Quotations from Chairman Mao Zedong* during the Cultural Revolution) and the first four volumes, which contain officially approved texts of Mao's articles and speeches up to 16 September 1949, had been published in Chinese in 1960. They are authoritative but incomplete and were heavily edited; other editions by scholars in Europe, the United States and Japan have since been compiled to produce a fuller and more accurate version of Mao's ideas. Control over Volume 5 of *Selected Works*, which contained Mao's writings after the foundation of the PRC, was important for establishing the ideological tone of the post-Mao era, which all knew was rapidly approaching, and Deng had secured this control. The fact that his Political Research Office, which was going to provide the ideological justification for his reform programme, was also responsible for Mao's *Selected Works* provided political leverage, credibility, ideological cover and sufficient intellectual continuity with the Mao era for a defence against opponents who wished to argue, not without justification, that Deng was intent on overturning everything that Mao had stood for. Deng was not in a position to make a clean break from Mao and could only implement changes if he could claim the authority of Mao for them.

The Political Research Office became the field headquarters for Deng's ideological resistance to the Gang of Four. It has been characterised as a think tank, but that seems a tame and inadequate description in light of its pioneering and embattled role in a period of such bitter conflict. This research group was headed by the seven 'leading cadres' chosen to bridge the gap between Deng's pragmatism and the theories of Mao, and had up to 40 other members of staff. In the words of Teiwes and Sun, 'Deng not only placed high importance on the Research Office, he also personally directed its activities'.[5] The day-to-day running of the office, which occupied two buildings in Zhongnanhai (one to work on Mao's *Selected Works* and the other for investigation, research and policy), was the responsibility of Hu Qiaomu, but he reported to Deng and only to Deng. Within four months of starting work in early July 1975, in addition to the work on the fifth volume of Mao's *Selected Works* (which was eventually published in the spring of 1977), the members of the Research Office had developed four key project areas to advise and assist the Central Committee and the State Council.

First, they reported on the negative effect that the Gang of Four were having on cultural production. They had blocked films, the publication of Lu Xun's correspondence and a novel about the life of Li Zicheng, a rebel at the end of the Ming dynasty who became a popular folk hero. As a result of the war of attrition waged by the Political Research Office, many of these decisions were overturned on Mao's instructions. The Political Research Office staff also supported a campaign to criticise the dominant position of 'revolutionary model operas', Jiang Qing's pet project, and put her on the defensive. This campaign effectively undermined the stranglehold that Jiang and her coterie had on the arts in the early 1970s.

Second, they redrafted and revised existing crucial State Council documents, which was of course Deng Xiaoping's forte. Among the most significant were 'Questions on the Speeding up of Industrial Development' (*Twenty Points*) and the 'Outline Report on the Work of the Academy of Sciences' (*Outline Report*). Between them, these two documents set out in detail the policies that Deng wished to follow to achieve rapid industrialisation and the scientific and educational basis that was necessary for it to succeed. The commentaries also provided an incisive critique of obstruction by Jiang Qing and her supporters.

Third, the Political Research Office rewrote a theoretical document, 'General Principles on the Work of the Whole Party and the Whole Nation' (*General Principles*), Deng Xiaoping's manifesto for reform within the framework of Mao Zedong's three basic theoretical principles on anti-revisionism, stability and economic development. The *General Principles*, which was the last straw for Jiang Qing, together with the *Twenty Points* and the *Outline Report*, were described by Jiang Qing and her clique as 'three poisonous weeds' (*san zhu da ducao*) in a new 'campaign to criticise Deng Xiaoping and fight back the rightist attempts to reverse correct verdicts'. This began in earnest on 3 November 1975 and Deng's reforms were opposed and undermined by fair means or foul – mostly foul.

Fourth, the Political Research Office supported the Philosophy and Social Science Department of the Chinese Academy of Sciences in establishing a new journal, *Ideological Front* (*Sixiang zhanxian*) to provide an alternative to the quasi-academic publications over which the Jiang Qing faction had control.[6]

JIANG QING'S RESISTANCE

The fact that Deng was appointed to senior Party, government and military posts was a 'heavy blow' (*chenzhong de daji*) to Jiang Qing: it was a clear sign that Mao acknowledged Deng as his successor. The Jiang Qing group (*Jiang Qing yihuo*) opposed Deng at every possible opportunity, and succeeded in blocking or delaying many of his political initiatives.

In August 1975, the 'Campaign to Criticise Lin Biao and Confucius' was revived as a debate in the media about the popular and highly respected historical novel of the Ming dynasty, *Water Margin* (*Shuihuzhuan*). Jiang Qing and her acolyte Yao Wenyuan felt more comfortable arguing in a pseudo-cultural field than in direct political discussions, and the debate, based on an aside by Mao that the book was an example of political capitulation, focused on whether one of the key characters Song Jiang, the leader of an outlaw band was guilty of capitulating to imperial authority. The debate was, of course, nothing to do with Song Jiang or *Water Margin* but a transparent assault on the policies of the dying Zhou Enlai and his close colleague, Deng Xiaoping.

A more tangible field of attack was a debate on the Dazhai Commune which had been held up as the model for agricultural organisation during the Cultural Revolution and was the subject of Mao's well-known instruction, 'in agriculture learn from Dazhai' (*nongye xue Dazhai*). On 15 September 1975 a National Conference on Learning from Dahzai in Agriculture opened in Xiyang County, Shanxi where Dazhai Commune was located and later continued in Beijing. It was organised by Hua Guofeng who was vice-premier and a member of the Politburo, and was thought to be close to Zhou Enlai in his views on modernising the Chinese economy. Chen Yonggui, the Party secretary of Dazhai and Politburo member, who had been lionised during the Cultural Revolution as the ideal peasant leader, took the podium with a self-serving speech on the importance of the experience of his commune for the development of China's agriculture. When Hua introduced Deng Xiaoping, who was due to speak on agricultural modernisation, there was thunderous applause in the hall and the more Deng tried to indicate that the clapping should stop the louder it became. In the audience were many 'old cadres' who had been incarcerated during the Cultural Revolution and had only recently been 'liberated' on the instructions of Deng and Zhou Enlai. Deng argued that agricultural reform was the key to the 'four modernisations' that he and Zhou were putting forward as the road ahead for China. He pointed out that in some counties and districts the amount of grain being produced was less than it had been before 1949, and this produced an angry response from Jiang Qing who interjected that he was just citing one or two atypical cases. Deng responded sharply with figures on the value of grain produced in Guizhou, the poorest province, and Sichuan the second poorest which appeared to silence his adversary temporarily. Deng outlined other problems in agriculture that required reorganisation and reform and insisted that this would only be possible with comprehensive reform of the military, local government, industry, commerce, science, technology, education and culture (which Jiang Qing regarded as her personal bailiwick). Deng called for good and capable people to be appointed to leadership positions in the rural areas and argued that any study of Dazhai should be genuine rather than a fake or partial study – it should examine Dazhai warts and all.

Jiang Qing, without waiting to be called to speak as the etiquette of the meeting required, interjected that Mao was being misrepresented, complained that agriculture was being marginalised as provincial Party first secretaries were not in attendance (although that was a decision that had been made by the Central Committee) and went on to make irrelevant remarks about the *Water Margin* campaign which had been used to attack Zhou Enlai and Deng Xiaoping. She demanded that her speech be published and circulated at the conference, but Mao apparently did not authorise this.

There is little reliable evidence for what Mao thought or did at all at this time. There were no independent observers and the political actors contending for his crown, including Deng, Zhou Enlai and Jiang Qing, all claimed his support. Mao had high regard for Deng's ability as a political leader and may have hoped that he would eventually accept that the Cultural Revolution had been necessary. Jiang Qing and her supporters, more realistically, saw that Deng was biding his time until he could safely reject the Cultural Revolution and reverse the verdict (*fan'an*) on its legacy and, by implication, on them and on Mao.

Mao was torn between his chosen successor and his wife and demanded a closed meeting of a small group of Politburo members to resolve the position. Mao's nephew Mao Yuanxin, who was close to Jiang Qing's faction, was the main contact between Mao Zedong and the Politburo as Mao's Alzheimer's disease worsened and on the evening of 2 November 1975 he called Deng, Chen Xilian and Wang Dongxing to a meeting. Deng was not prepared to acknowledge the 'mistakes' that were put to him, so a 'courtesy' meeting (*da zhaohu huiyi*) of the Central Committee was convened in Beijing for the end of November to consider a document, 'The rightwing trend of reversing verdicts denying the Great Proletarian Cultural Revolution', that had been prepared by Mao Yuanxin and approved by Mao Zedong as a counter-attack against Deng. This attack had some credibility because it had Mao's name behind it, but it is not possible to say whether he was really in a fit state, physically or mentally, to have approved the statement.

Jiang Qing and her supporters regarded the Political Research Office as one of the major obstacles to their ambitions and it was attacked publicly by Jiang Qing and in articles in *People's Daily*, which was controlled by her acolyte, Yao Wenyuan. The documents that the office produced were attacked as recipes for bringing back capitalism and in August 1976 were criticised in pamphlets which the Jiang faction circulated nationwide. With hindsight, Jiang and her confederates were uncannily accurate in their analysis of the long-term implications of the policies that Deng was espousing, but ironically the pamphlets and the campaign may have had precisely the opposite effect to that intended as they introduced many of Deng's ideas and policy proposals to a wider audience. The relationship between the seven leading lights of the Political Research Office was inevitably strained by the campaign of criticism and innuendo and by allegations that the office had spread rumours and falsehoods and leaked confidential Party and government documents. In spite of the pressure and serious differences of political opinion the seven held together remarkably well, recognising that their overriding priority must be to fight off the Jiang Qing clique. Hu Qiaomu later offered to apologise in writing for criticising Deng in the heat of battle but Deng insisted that no apology was necessary.[7]

Deng's period as the leader of China is often said to have begun in 1975, but he was opposed and obstructed to such an extent that by the end of that year he had still not been able to implement his reforms. This situation took at least two years to resolve.

15

ATTAINING POWER (1976—8)

I did not get back to work and take part in Central Committee meetings until July 1977, nine months after the smashing of the 'Gang of Four'.

Realistically I was in the seeking truth from facts faction.[1]

For China, and for Deng Xiaoping, 1976 was a year of destiny. A succession of high-profile political deaths cleared the way for modest changes in the political system, and structural changes in the economy became possible for the first time in decades. This was not a straightforward process. For insiders, dispirited after the 'ten catastrophic years' (*shinian haojie*) of the Cultural Revolution, the two years that followed – 1976–8 – were dominated by a life-and-death struggle during which the very existence of the Chinese Communist Party and its state hung in the balance. This conflict is often represented as a struggle between two political slogans: 'seek truth from facts' (*shishi qiushi*) and the 'two whatevers' (*liang ge fanshi*). Slogans such as these seem bizarre and meaningless outside China and their implications were not necessarily clear, even to informed Chinese who tried to follow the twists and turns of elite politics in Beijing. The 'seekers of truth from facts' were Deng and his supporters, determined to do what was practically necessary for China irrespective of ideological considerations – and for which they had been ferociously criticised as 'empiricists'. The 'two whatevers' were whatever Mao Zedong had said and whatever Mao Zedong had done; these indicated Mao's revolutionary line and that was what China must follow. The 'two whatevers' were the touchstones for the supporters of Jiang Qing.

Zhou Enlai died on 8 January, depriving Deng Xiaoping of his oldest, most powerful and most trustworthy political ally. Hua Guofeng was appointed as acting premier in Zhou's place: he sided with Jiang Qing's faction and insisted that criticism of Deng Xiaoping was still official policy. The next towering historical figure to leave the stage was Zhu De, Mao's military counterpart in the early years of the Chinese revolution, who died on 6 July. Although Zhu had long ceased to wield any direct political influence his death was another potent symbol of the passing of an era.

TIAN'ANMEN SQUARE DISTURBANCES

Although the mention of disturbances in Tian'anmen Square usually calls to mind the suppression of the Democracy Movement on 3–4 June 1989, there was a precedent in 1976. Zhou Enlai had died on 8 January and his passing was accompanied by genuine grief as well as ritual mourning. Zhou was revered as an able elder statesman and as a humane communist who, during the Cultural Revolution, had succeeded in limiting the damage caused by the vendettas of Mao and Jiang Qing. He had protected Deng Xiaoping, whose sojourn in Jiangxi Zhou had monitored. Deng survived the Cultural Revolution whereas Liu Shaoqi was ill-treated by Red Guards in Kaifeng and died in November 1969. Whether Zhou's conduct during the Cultural Revolution genuinely justifies his beatifica-tion by the more liberal members of the Communist Party and Chinese intellectuals in general must be a matter for another time and another place. Be that as it may, in the spring of 1976 he became the focus for those who wished to express their opposition to the continuation of Mao's policies by Jiang Qing and her faction.

The occasion for this was the traditional Chinese festival of Qingming ('clear and bright'). It is often referred to as tomb-sweeping day as it is the custom to commemorate the dead by cleaning the graves of the family ancestors during the festival. Qingming falls in early April, 15 days after the spring equinox: in 1976 it was on 5 April. Crowds gathered to remember Zhou in Tian'anmen Square, the great public space in front of the Imperial Palace (Forbidden City) that had been created in 1958–9 to construct a rival to Moscow's Red Square. The focus of the demonstrators was the Monument to the People's Heroes, which was completed in

1958 and commemorates all who died during China's revolutionary wars. Wreaths paying tribute to Zhou had appeared on and around the monument during March 1976 but the spark for political conflict was a wreath laid on 1 April by 80 young workers from the Beijing Chemical Fibres Factory, praising Zhou Enlai and attacking Jiang Qing. When Jiang Qing's supporters removed this wreath it was replaced by other wreaths and placards and also posters condemning the campaign that Jiang and her supporters had mounted against Deng Xiaoping. Young people began to recite poetry composed in Zhou's memory and crowds of students, workers and government officials flocked to the square. Wang Hongwen and Zhang Chunqiao (two of the soon to be arrested Gang of Four) watched with mounting horror from the Great Hall of the People on the west side of the square as the demonstrations grew, and on 4 April they ordered the removal of all the wreaths and placards. This incensed the demonstrators and a crowd of at least 10,000 'surged into the square', overturning a police car from which a loudspeaker was being used to order demonstrators to disperse. By midday the number of people in the square may have been as high as 100,000 and some of the demonstrators announced that they had created a 'committee of the people of the capital for commemorating the premier'. Wang Hongwen organised supporters of the Cultural Revolution radicals to shout slogans denouncing Zhou Enlai and Deng Xiaoping and some of the crowd created banners with slogans denouncing the Empress Dowager Cixi and India's first woman prime minister, Indira Gandhi. Demonstrators did not feel that they could attack Jiang Qing directly but she would not have been amused by these parallels.

Police cars and a police post were set on fire, and there were violent clashes between demonstrators and police in which many were injured. Hua Guofeng, after a period of hesitation and indecision, referred the issue to Mao and then deployed troops and militia to suppress the demonstrators. There were more injuries and deaths including, it is reported, children of prominent members of the CCP and the PLA. The campaign against Deng Xiaoping by Jiang Qing's faction was intensified and Deng was blamed for instigating the demonstrations, although they were as spontaneous as any in this period of Chinese history. Hua Guofeng played a prominent role in the campaign against Deng, following what were said to be Mao's views at the time, but the Jiang Qing faction distrusted his cautious and moderate approach and he became alienated from them. Articles began to appear in the press, which was controlled by the Cultural Revolution radicals, accusing Hua of being part of the Zhou and Deng faction. As Mao's physical and mental capacities declined, it became less and less credible to cite instructions that purported to come from him. The campaign against Deng and his modernisation policies could no longer be attributed to Mao: it was now attributed to the unpopular Jiang Qing, and her influence waned considerably.

DEATH OF MAO ZEDONG

On 28 July an earthquake of magnitude 7.5 devastated the city of Tangshan in Hebei province; it also affected a much wider area and caused the deaths of over 250,000 people. Some superstitious Chinese citizens would subsequently interpret this natural disaster as a heavenly portent, a warning of the death of an emperor. Mao Zedong died on 9 September, three months before his eighty-third birthday. He had been physically and mentally frail for many years and it was unclear to what extent he had been able to influence the affairs of state. There was no legitimate constitutional process in place to indicate how a successor should be chosen and a battle between Jiang Qing's radicals and supporters of Deng began in earnest. Hua claimed the right to succeed Mao on the strength of what he claimed were the chairman's deathbed instructions to him: 'With you in charge, I am at ease' (*Ni banshi wo fangxin*). Hua did not have the confidence of the Shanghai radicals and Jiang Qing presented herself as the only genuine inheritor of Mao's revolutionary policies. Deng was marginalised and had withdrawn to Guangzhou for his own safety.

Hua Guofeng became the official leader of China, but one of the Shanghai radicals subsequently known as the Gang of Four, Wang Hongwen, set up his own office in the Zhongnanhai political compound and ensured that it was manned 24 hours a day, in an attempt to put himself or another member of Jiang Qing's faction in a postion of power. Confusion reigned in Beijing until on 6 October Jiang Qing, Zhang Chunqiao, Yao Wenyuan and Wang Hongwen were arrested by troops of the 8341 Special Regiment, commanded by Wang Dongxing, who was responsible for providing security for the senior leadership. The decision to arrest the Gang of Four was made when:

> the Political Bureau of the Central Committee with Hua Guofeng, Ye Jianying and Li Xiannian as the nucleus, took drastic measures and put Jiang Qing, Zhang Chunqiao, Yao Wenyuan and Wang Hongwen in custody for investigation, thus smashing the Jiang Qing counter-revolutionary clique.[2]

For many people this was an indication that the Cultural Revolution was finally over, but it was by no means the end of the battle for control of China. Deng Xiaoping was out of office and not directly implicated. Hua Guofeng was one of the prime movers and he was appointed chairman of the Central Committee and the Central Military Commission the following day: he was only to last as leader for nine months.

HUA GUOFENG INTERREGNUM

Supporters of Deng have argued that in 1976 there was a demand from cadres at all levels to redress the 'leftist' wrongs of the Cultural Revolution and they criticise Hua because he failed to respond to this and chose to rely on the memory of Mao through the policy of the 'two whatevers'. The situation was even more complicated. Many Party and government cadres were aware of what would later be acknowledged as Mao's 'errors', particularly in the way that he acted in the last years of his life, but in the general population there were many who had blind faith in Mao and almost worshipped him. The 'two whatevers' policy was first set out in an article published on 7 February 1977 in *People's Daily*, *Red Flag* and *Liberation Army Daily* on the instructions of Hua Guofeng. Simultaneous publication in the three most powerful press organs emphasised the authority of the article.

The immediate political purpose of this article was to prevent Deng Xiaoping from returning to work and to block any attempt to reclassify the Tian'anmen Square protests as a revolutionary, rather than a counter-revolutionary, incident. Since Mao had formally approved both the continuing criticism of Deng in late 1975 and the counter-revolutionary nature of the Tian'anmen Square incident it was difficult to repudiate these judgements. The longer-term effect of the 'two whatevers' was to deify Mao and to turn his writings and his life into a dogma which could not be questioned. This may have been the only way that Hua could retain his position, but it prolonged many of the injustices of the Cultural Revolution, prevented many cadres from returning to their jobs and in particular restricted the activity of educated Chinese, the 'stinking old ninth' (*chou lao jiu*) category of intellectuals, whose support was so desperately needed for economic and technological reforms. The name derives from a Cultural Revolution list of nine 'black' categories, classes of people who were likely to be opposed to the 'red' Mao and his thought: intellectuals were right at the bottom.

Deng was out of office and out of favour and he had little opportunity to oppose directly the 'two whatevers', which he identified as the major barrier to the development of China. Like-minded colleagues, including Chen Yun, Wang Zhen and Deng Liqun, continued to speak on his behalf at Party meetings, notably a working conference of the Central Committee held between 10 and 22 March to plan political work for the year ahead. Their arguments that Deng should be reinstated did not appear in the formal printed documents that were published after the conference. Hua Guofeng appeared to be firmly in control of the CCP, but on 10 April, after the Tian'anmen Square demonstrations, Deng wrote a formal letter to the Central Committee attacking the 'two whatevers' as a doctrine that was not only contrary to the spirit of Mao Zedong but also to the entire Marxist way of thinking. Marx, Engels, Lenin, Stalin and Mao, argued Deng, would never have insisted that 'whatever' they said should be the policy. It was only by arguing on the basis of the CCP's understanding of Marxist theory and the relationship of Mao Zedong's 'thought' to this theory that Deng was able to persuade recalcitrant senior colleagues of the correctness of his views.

On 3 May 1977 Deng's argument was finally accepted by the Central Committee and his letter was circulated formally throughout the Communist Party. Few people had the nerve to argue openly that Mao had been guilty of errors, but during April and May 1977 the balance of power within the Central Committee was beginning to shift in favour of Deng's more critical approach. Deng's Marxist argument against the 'two whatevers' was reinforced in a speech that he gave on 24 May; it is not recorded where this speech was given or to whom, but Wang Zhen and Deng Liqun were among those present. Hua Guofeng did not surrender easily and tried to use a major conference (20 April to 13 May) on lessons from the Daqing oilfield (which, together with the Dazhai Commune, was one of Mao's revolutionary exemplars) and an article in *People's Daily* on 1 May 1977 to bolster his position. By the time of the Third Plenum of the Tenth Central Committee from 16 to 21 July 1977, the shift of power was more evident. Hua Guofeng retained his key positions as chairman of the Central Committee and the Central Military Commission but Deng was reinstated as deputy chairman of the Central Committee and Central Military Commission and deputy premier of the State Council as well as chief of the general staff of the PLA. This looked like an uncomfortable compromise with two individuals who could not possibly work together, but it was a face-saving exercise: Hua Guofeng retained his status, but his authority had evaporated. Formally Deng may have been Hua's deputy, but Deng was dictating policy. On 30 July Deng made a symbolic public appearance at the closing ceremony of the International Football Friendship Invitation Tournament at the Beijing Workers Stadium. Xinhua News Agency reported his attendance and the sustained applause, confirmation that Deng was back in power.

At the Third Plenum, Deng spoke of the need to use Mao Zedong Thought 'correctly and comprehensively', and this underpinned his strategy. He had made this final and permanent return to power on the basis of arguing that his own interpretation of Mao's ideas was correct. He diverged radically from Mao's idea of development but was unable to make a clean break from arguing within the framework of Mao's ideology. This partially explains why China's economic transformation has not been accompanied by political reforms.

When the Eleventh National Congress of the CCP was held in Beijing from 12 to 18 August 1977, both Hua Guofeng and Deng Xiaoping made policy speeches. At the end of the conference even Deng's most ardent supporters conceded that the 'two whatevers' problem (Hua) had not been resolved, although they argued that those who supported the 'seek truth from facts' approach (Deng) were steadily growing in influence. The tide had turned, but this could not be openly acknowledged. The transition to a party and government firmly under Deng's control was slow and convoluted. On one level he controlled day-to-day business but on another he was obliged to accept the formal authority of Hua Guofeng. While this political and ideological struggle remained unresolved he behaved as if he were the national leader, visiting North Korea and carrying out an inspection tour of the North-East (Manchuria). On 19 September he visited the city of Tangshan that had been devastated by the earthquake of July 1976 and gave his personal backing to the reconstruction work and the building of a 'New Tangshan' for the Deng era.

HU YAOBANG AND THE CENTRAL PARTY SCHOOL

An obscure but critical ideological battle based on 'tests for truth' (*zhenli biaozhun*) was waged behind the scenes by Deng's supporters, particularly Hu Yaobang from his base at the newly-restored Central Party School. The success of this ideological battle was essential in paving the way for a less constrained style of debate and discussion: in the idiom of the period, it 'liberated' Chinese thinking. Hua Guofeng was only too willing to permit criticism of the errors of his rivals in the 'Gang of Four', but he was not willing for this to extend to criticism of what were beginning to be called the 'errors of Mao Zedong's later years' (*Mao Zedong wannian de cuowu*).

The campaign became public with an article, 'Practice is the sole criterion for testing truth' (*shixian shi jianyan zhenli de weiyi biaozhun*), that appeared in *Guangming Daily*, the newspaper favoured by China's educated professionals, and in Xinhua News Agency press releases on 11 May; it is often referred to simply as the 'practice' (*shi*) article. This article originated in discussions at the Central Party School, under the Deputy Principal Hu Yaobang. The school was one of the props of Deng Xiaoping's ideological struggle against the intransigent elements who insisted on living by the revealed truth of every word that Mao had ever uttered.

Although Hu was deputy principal, he was in practice the head of the Central Party School and responsible for its day-to-day running: the principal was nominally Chairman Hua Guofeng and the first deputy principal was Wang Dongxing, Mao's former bodyguard whose troops had arrested the Gang of Four. The school, known as the Advanced Party School (*gao dangxiao*) between 1955 and 1966, had then come under the political control of Kang Sheng, a close ally of Mao who was the main persecutor of the chairman's enemies and rivals, with the assistance of his wife, Cao Yi'ou, who taught at the school. Kang's authority had been used ruthlessly during the Anti-Rightist Campaign that began in 1957 and targeted non-conformist intellectuals. The school was suspended during the Cultural Revolution although its nucleus continued to operate as the Leading Group of the Central Party School May 7th Cadre School (May 7th Cadre Schools were a Cultural Revolution institution designed to bring to heel recalcitrant Party intellectuals). The Central Party School had effectively been wrecked by Kang and had to be reinvented.

When Hu Yaobang took over it had only recently been reopened, although CCP sources are coy about the precise date: a formal opening ceremony (*kaixue dianli*) was held on 9 October 1977 but discussions about rebuilding the school and its intellectual impact on CCP thinking began earlier than that. In 1977, Ye Jianying, a PLA general who was deputy chairman of the National People's Congress and effectively acting head of state, invited Hu Yaobang to his house in the Western Hills outside Beijing and asked him if he would return to political duties. Most posts in Beijing were considered too sensitive for Hu as he was too closely associated with Deng Xiaoping, whose position was still precarious. Ye suggested that Hu should take responsibility for rebuilding the Central Party School as deputy principal in charge of the everyday running of the institution (*changwu fu xiaozhang*), flattering him that his talents and ability would be perfect for this post. Ye argued, somewhat disingenuously, that as the school was out in the western suburbs of Beijing there would be very little conflict. The school was later moved into the university district of Haidian and there was considerable conflict.

The formal Politburo decision to revive the Party School was made on 3 March 1977 and Hu Yaobang moved to his new job, taking with him one secretary, Liang Jinquan. On the morning of 9 March, Hu met the school's leading group (*lingdao banzi*) about whose political loyalties he had serious doubts. He nevertheless insisted that the 'exposure and criticism' (*jiepi*) of the Gang of Four applied to the Party School as much as anywhere else. On 25 March he addressed a meeting of the whole body of staff and cadres to pass on the substance of documents issued by a Central Committee working conference that met between 10 and 22 March but had not accepted the formal reinstatement of Deng Xiaoping. The Party School staff had crammed into the Eastern Lecture Hall and many had arrived early. Hu arrived with his secretary Liang Jinquan, walked to the speaker's rostrum alone and announced calmly that he had begun work. He was greeted with warm applause and announced that there would be 'rectification' (*zhengfeng*) meetings to eradicate any vestiges of Cultural Revolution period thinking in the school.

This revival of the Central Party School illustrates the complexity, the fluidity and the paradoxes of the political situation after the death of Mao Zedong. Ye Jianying, who had persuaded Hu to take over the running of the Central Party School, had been one of the prime movers behind the arrest of the Gang of Four, possibly the most important. He had also been a supporter of Hua Guofeng, who was determined to prevent the return to office of Deng Xiaoping, Hu Yaobang's mentor, but was reconsidering his position. The Central Party School was to provide the intellectual support and ideological justification for Deng's policies, the rejection of the 'two whatevers', and ultimately the political demise of Hua Guofeng.

'PRACTICE' VERSUS 'WHATEVER'

Raising the intellectual and educational level of Party members was a top priority. Hu Yaobang insisted that the study of the history of the Chinese Communist Party, both at the Central Party School and more broadly, must observe two principles: the thorough and accurate understanding of relevant instructions issued by Mao Zedong; and the use of 'practice as the sole criterion for testing truth'. Like Deng Xiaoping he was treading carefully and testing the waters, not moving far away from the Maoist formula but gradually giving priority to practical reality as the only way of determining the efficacy of theory.

The 'practice' campaign began to take shape early in April 1978 when the newly appointed editor-in-chief of *Guangming Daily*, Yang Xiguang, who was also attached to the Central Party School, asked a member of staff of the Philosophy Department of Nanjing University, Hu Fuming, to revise an article that he had submitted to the newspaper, and to make it more timely and more focused. The article was entitled 'Practice is the criterion for testing all truth' (*shixian shi jianyan yiqie zhenli de biaozhun*). Hu Fuming had begun the piece as an attack on the Gang of Four and the philosophy of the 'two whatevers' and had worked on the article heroically while sitting with his wife who was seriously ill in hospital in Nanjing, fanning her to relieve the heat of high summer in one of China's 'furnace cities' and then going out into the hospital corridors to read and correct his draft. Yang also approached Sun Changjiang of the Central Party School Theory Research Department, who had been working on a similar topic, and invited him to assist. The article that was eventually published in *Guangming Daily* was the result of this collaboration with only a slight change of wording in the title. It was approved by Hu Yaobang and appeared first in the Party School's internal publication *Theoretical Trends* (*Lilun Dongtai*) on 10 May and in *Guangming Daily* the following day under the byline 'Special Commentator'. It was then published in *People's Daily* and *Liberation Army Daily* on 12 May 1978.

The delay of 24 hours in releasing the article in the most powerful media outlets indicates the amount of uncertainty and tension that still characterised the highest levels of the CCP. The 'practice' article provoked widespread comment, much of it highly critical, as there were many who argued that it was an attack on the legacy of Mao – which in many ways it was.

Deng was not directly involved in the discussions that led to the publication of this article. He was after all no theoretician and preferred to leave that type of work to the specialists. When he became aware of the controversy, he realised that it resolved many of the issues that he was trying to overcome in promoting the 'four modernisations'; he pronounced it to be 'Marxist' and adopted it as a statement of his own position. He referred to it in discussions with Hu Qiaomu towards the end of May 1978 and, in a meeting with senior officials of the CCP's Propaganda Department on 21 July, he insisted that there should be no 'forbidden areas' in discussing the questions raised by the 'practice' article. He met Hu Yaobang on 22 July and congratulated him on the article.

In September 1978 Deng made an official visit to North Korea and then undertook an inspection tour of China's north-east (Manchuria). During the tour he made a number of formal speeches insisting that the CCP had to 'hold high the banner of Mao Zedong Thought' (*gaoju Mao Zedong sixiang de qizhi*) but also adhere to the principle of 'seeking truth through facts' (*shishi qiushi*), the phrase with which he is most associated. These speeches were made available to senior officials across China in October and November and Deng's endorsement of this new approach gave great impetus to the ideological shift that had been promoted by the 'practice' article. Together they paved the way for his political triumph at the Third Plenum of the Eleventh Central Committee in December 1978 that was to change the face of China within a generation.

The debate about the 'practice' article raged within the Party well into the autumn, but the official theoretical journal of the CCP, *Red Flag* (*Hongqi*) was still hedging its bets. The editorial staff had officially taken the position of 'non-involvement' (*bu juanru*) in this debate, but this effectively supported the 'two whatevers' position of Hua Guofeng. In November 1978 the veteran political commissar and member of the Central Committee Tan Zhenlin was invited by *Red Flag* to write an article commemorating the eighty-fifth anniversary of the birth of Mao Zedong and took the opportunity to promote the 'practice' article. He was sufficiently senior that editorial staff could not alter his text and on 16 November the manuscript was submitted to the Standing Committee of the CCP's Central Committee. Deng saw the draft manuscript and wrote in response:

> In my opinion this article is fine. At any rate there are no errors. If *Red Flag* does not want to publish it after minor editorial changes, it can be published in *People's Daily*. Why does *Red Flag* have this policy of non-involvement? It should be involved and should publish articles with different points of view. It seems as if [the journal] does not want to become involved but perhaps it should be.

Li Xiannian, who had been a supporter of Hua Guofeng but was now backing Deng, also wrote in support of Tan Zhenlin, and the editors of *Red Flag* had no choice but to publish Li's article as well. Between them Deng and Li had ended *Red Flag*'s policy of 'non-involvement' and removed one of the major obstacles for open discussion of the idea that 'practice' was the main criterion for deciding whether or not a policy was correct.

The carefully constructed commentary of 'practice is the sole criterion for testing truth' offered a casuistic model that senior officials were able to use to demonstrate that they were following the ideological tradition of the leaders of the revolution – primarily Mao – but that simultaneously they were also formulating theory and policy that accorded with the practical needs of China at the time.

Deng's genius was to understand, even though he was no theoretician, that such a theoretical model was essential. He had entrusted the task of contriving the necessary model to the staff of the Central Party School, which was run by his disciple Hu Yaobang, and to intellectuals who had only recently re-emerged as *personae gratae*. The model was effective enough to enable Deng's supporters to repudiate the 'two whatevers' incantation favoured by Hua Guofeng. Hua was gradually sidelined, eventually losing the CCP chairmanship in 1981 when he made a formal self-criticism acknowledging that the 'two whatevers' had been a mistake: he finally bowed out of front-line politics in 1982.

For anyone who was not brought up in the intense and highly politicised atmosphere of China during the 1960s and 1970s, or has not been immersed in the minutiae of the history and politics of that era, it is not easy to understand why creating such a theoretical model was necessary. Why did Deng not just say that he was going to follow a pragmatic policy and implement it? The simple answer is that he would not have been allowed to get away with it. There was still considerable support within the Chinese Communist Party nationally, both openly expressed and privately felt, for the slogans and the quasi-military values of the Cultural Revolution period and for Mao personally. If Deng had tried to discard the rhetoric of this period, and by implication Mao's political legacy, he would almost certainly have been pushed aside yet again. The man who carried his Marxist ideology lightly was obliged to create a theoretical cloak to conceal his pragmatism.[3]

16

ECONOMIC REFORM AND OPENING TO THE WORLD (1978–9)

Personally I like a game of bridge but China is not keen on political gambles.[1]

The Third Plenary Session solved a series of major problems left over from the recent history of the Party in order to rally the whole Party and army and our people of all nationalities to march forward towards the grand objective – the four modernisations.[2]

1976 might have been China's year of destiny – as the death of Mao Zedong cleared the way for a fundamental change of direction – but 1978 was the year in which that change became a political reality. From December 1978 it is possible to say with some confidence that Deng Xiaoping had finally emerged as the political leader of China. There remained some caveats: Hua Guofeng was still chairman of the Communist Party until June 1981, but well before that date his power and influence had evaporated. Foreign observers began to refer to Deng as the 'paramount leader' of China, not a title used by the government or the CCP, but a form of words which acknowledged that he ruled China but was not chairman. Deng did not have absolute control even after 1978, as is demonstrated by his decision in 1992, at the age of 88, to embark on a strenuous tour of the south to defeat organised opposition to his economic reforms. Within the CCP a significant body of opinion feared that the reforms endangered the authority of the party.

In spite of these caveats, Deng's achievement in ensuring the necessary level of political support for his economic reforms is impressive. In 1978 he had to pilot these policies through two meetings of the Central Committee in which sat many of his colleagues who were either suspicious of, or actively opposed to, the changes that he was proposing. The early stages of the battle to create this political support were in a working conference of the Central Committee which lasted for over a month – from 10 November to 15 December 1978. This was followed by a shorter, but politically more authoritative, meeting of the full Central Committee, officially known as the Third Plenum of the Eleventh Central Committee but universally referred to simply as the Third Plenum (or plenary session), which endorsed the changes in a formal meeting from 18 to 22 December 1978. In these two conferences the personal authority of Deng Xiaoping and the future of his economic reforms were at stake, as was the authority and credibility of the Central Committee and its ability to operate in an unfamiliar political atmosphere.

Two previous full sessions of this Eleventh Central Committee, the first since the death of Mao, had already taken place. The first, on 19 August 1977, followed the CCP's Eleventh National Congress and did little more than elect Hua Guofeng as chairman and approve a list of deputy chairmen, including Deng Xiaoping, and the names of members of the Politburo and its standing committee. The second full session from 18 to 23 February 1978 was preoccupied with preparations for the Fifth National People's Congress. Hua Guofeng presided over both sessions, but they were dominated by the personality and policies of Deng. By the close of the Third Plenum on 22 December 1978, Deng Xiaoping was firmly established as the *de facto* leader of China, although without the title of chairman. Hua Guofeng had the title but was a lame duck and there were no other contenders.[3]

ONTO THE WORLD STAGE: JAPAN

Even before the Third Plenum, Deng had made an appearance on the international stage and acquired an unexpected level of personal popularity outside China, which also boosted his status within the country: this was something that Mao Zedong had never achieved, in spite of the wave of enthusiasm for his theories of revolution in parts of the developing world. Deng gave every indication that he enjoyed the international exposure. Before 1978, apart from his youthful sojourn in

France, his experience of the world outside China had been restricted to the communist bloc, principally the Soviet Union and North Korea, but his new role as leader of a nation that was officially opening up (*kaifang*) to the outside world, as well as reforming (*gaige*) took him to two countries that had been no friend to China in the recent past – Japan and the United States.

On 22 October 1978 the special aircraft carrying Deng arrived at Narita Airport for an official visit to Tokyo, a city he said that he had long hoped to visit. Deng was the first Chinese leader to visit Japan while in post. Sun Yat-sen had spent time in Japan, but as an exiled revolutionary. Chiang Kai-shek had studied at the *Tōkyō Shinbu Gakkō*, a preparatory school for Chinese students aiming to join the Japanese Imperial Military Academy, from 1907 to 1909 and after graduation had served with the Takada Regiment, although this was a part of his life that he did not choose to dwell on when he headed the National Government and faced a Japanese military invasion. Mao, who was not enthusiastic about foreign travel at the best of times, never visited Japan. However, he did meet the Japanese Prime Minister Tanaka Kakuei when Tanaka visited Beijing from 25 to 29 September 1972 and an agreement was reached to establish diplomatic relations between the two countries.

Japan was a problem for the Chinese Communist Party. It had been the aggressor since the late nineteenth century and had gradually colonised parts of Chinese territory. It took control of Taiwan in 1895, and Manchuria in 1931, while expanding its economic and political influence from the treaty ports and leased territories, especially in Shandong province. When the Imperial Japanese Army began the invasion of the Chinese interior on 7 July 1937 Japan became the principal enemy of the CCP. Resistance to Japanese aggression was a central part of the strategy and doctrine of the CCP until the surrender of the Tokyo government on 2 September 1945 at the end of World War II. Indeed this war is always known to the Chinese, at least on the mainland, as the War of Resistance against Japan (*kang Ri zhanzheng*). The Japanese occupation of China was exceptionally brutal, even in the context of savage twentieth-century warfare: the rape of Nanjing and the inhumane way in which millions of Chinese peasants were treated by the occupation forces is remembered to this day in histories of the period, in literature and in film. Deng had served in CCP military units for long enough to be more aware than most of the significance of this reputation.

However, in the 1970s Japan was not only one of China's closest neighbours, but also a highly developed, sophisticated and successful capitalist economy. China was looking for sources of inward investment and modern technology that could be transferred easily to China. Japan shared many cultural traits with China, notably the traditional forms of social thinking that are loosely referred to as Confucianism: this emphasises social hierarchies and groups rather than individuals, and values conformity. The Japanese language is unrelated to Chinese but because of close historical ties to China it had adopted Chinese written characters by the fifth century AD and these remain in use today, although much modified and with the assistance of additional syllabic scripts. These differences were the subject of some amusement when Deng and Prime Minister Fukuda met. The superficial similarity of the written languages has led to assumptions of a greater degree of cultural identity than actually exists: in Japan the idea of 'same script same race' (*dōbun dōzoku*) was popular with expansionist politicians before World War II. Historically Japan was the 'younger brother', in the Confucian sense, learning from China. This changed dramatically in the late nineteenth century when Japan responded far more successfully than China to the pressure of Western powers by learning from them and modernising more effectively than China.

It was therefore an event of some historical significance when the aircraft with the five red stars motif on its tail fin taxied to the stand at Narita airport where the Japanese Foreign Minister and member of the conservative Liberal Democratic Party Sonoda Sunao was waiting at the end of a red carpet to greet the honoured guests. Sonoda had been conscripted into the Imperial Japanese Army in 1938; he served in China and later in the Pacific where he trained as a kamikaze pilot. His wartime experiences left him determined to prevent further conflict with China and he had actively promoted the idea of normalising diplomatic relations during the early part of his parliamentary career.

Deng's visit to Japan took place before the Third Plenum of December 1978 and he was still only the deputy chairman of the CCP and the deputy premier of the State Council, but he was treated almost as if he were the head of state. Autumn in Tokyo means red leaves, but the crisp weather and clear autumn sky (*qiugao qishuang*) were also reminiscent of the weather of Beijing and it was hoped that the similarities augured well for the visit. As soon as the airport gantry arrived, Sonoda abandoned all protocol and rushed up the steps to greet Deng and Zhuo Lin in the passenger cabin. Deng did not give him a chance to speak but grasped his hand and said, 'Well, here I am' (*Wo haishi laile*). Sonoda welcomed him by thanking him for the bright sunny weather that they had brought with them. These may have been banal formalities but they had great significance for the parties involved. Earlier, on 8 August Sonoda had flown to Beijing to conclude the Treaty of Peace and Friendship between China and Japan, arriving in the

Chinese capital after a long period of drought. As he landed Beijing experienced a spectacular thunderstorm and Huang Hua, China's foreign minister and highly respected diplomat who received Sonoda, thanked him for bringing them rain. The treaty was signed on 12 August and the purpose of Deng's September visit was to cement the alliance.

When Deng reached the State Guesthouse at Akasaka where he and his wife were staying, he remarked, recalling his time in France, that it was a miniature version of Versailles. The Akasaka palace belongs to the estate of the imperial family and was built for the Crown Prince in the first decade of the twentieth century: it was the home of Crown Prince Hirohito (later the Shōwa Emperor, 1926–89) and his family for five years in the 1920s. It was renovated and became the State Guesthouse in 1974 and is indeed referred to as Japan's Versailles. When the Japanese Prime Minister Tanaka had been in Beijing in September 1972 to discuss the normalisation of Sino–Japanese relations he had spoken of the renovation of the palace and expressed the wish that Premier Zhou Enlai would be the first foreign guest in the new State Guesthouse. Zhou had said that he would be delighted as long as the treaty between the two countries had been signed. However, this was not to be: Zhou died on 8 January 1976 and it was not until 1978 that negotiations to complete the signing of the treaty were complete, so it was Deng's destiny to be, if not the first foreign guest, the first Chinese leader to stay there. On the morning of 23 October Prime Minister Fukuda Takeo held a formal ceremony at the State Guesthouse to welcome Deng and his party, just as if Deng had been head of state. They talked informally after the reception and Fukuda, whose war had been spent in the Ministry of Finance and the Cabinet Office, expressed a wish to visit China, which he had only known before the war.

Deng also visited the Imperial Palace where he and Zhuo Lin were received by the Shōwa Emperor (Hirohito) and the Empress. This was the Emperor's first meeting with a Chinese leader since the end of World War II and was highly symbolic. The expansion of the Japanese empire, and the invasion of China in the 1930s, had been carried out in the name of the Emperor: in the eyes of many Chinese, and indeed many Westerners, the Emperor was blamed personally for the horrors of World War II. This meeting with Deng was a powerful sign of the wish for reconciliation between the peoples of two states that were divided by political ideology and by the alliances that had been forged during the Cold War. The Japanese side had naturally been apprehensive about the visit and feared that Deng might take the opportunity to reflect the feelings of many Chinese towards Japan and the Emperor. They were pleasantly surprised that everything went smoothly.

Deng was at his most pragmatic and statesmanlike when at noon on 23 October, wearing the Sun Yat sen jacket that was *de rigeur* for Chinese on formal occasions, he shook hands with the Emperor, who was wearing a western-style suit. Their conversation was appropriately diplomatic and uncontroversial: both stressed the importance of the new treaty that the two states were signing and the Emperor referred to 'unfortunate matters' (conveyed in Chinese as *buxing de shijian*) between China and Japan but hoped that these were now in the past. The conduct of all meetings with the Emperor and the text of statements released had been approved in advance by palace officials and the Japanese Foreign Office. Kyōdō, the influential Japanese News Agency, reported that the wording was intended to be an indirect expression to the Chinese people of the responsibility that the Emperor acknowledged for World War II. Deng naturally approved.

The following morning, 24 October, Deng met Tanaka Kakuei, the former prime minister of the liberal Democratic Party who had played a vital role in the normalisation of relations between Japan and China. Tanaka had been one of the signatories, together with his opposite number Zhou Enlai and their foreign ministers Ohira Masayoshi and Ji Pengfei, of the joint communiqué signed on 29 September 1972 in Beijing that established formal diplomatic relations between the two countries. That same afternoon Deng met members of both houses of the Japanese Diet and pointed out that, although a formal peace treaty had now been signed, much work still needed to be done. He gave a reception for the Japanese press, visited temples and factories in Tokyo and Osaka, and returned to Beijing on 29 October at the end of an eight-day visit. Thirty-three years after the defeat of Japan in World War II, fences were being mended and bridges were being built. The former enemy was now to be, if not a political ally, at least an economic partner in China's drive for modernisation. Deng's visit had been delayed for six years after the original 1972 communiqué, but the immediate effect, to everyone's relief, was what was referred to in Beijing as a 'China fever' (*Zhongguo re*) in Japan or, as the Japanese press and politicians preferred, a 'Deng Xiaoping whirlwind' (in Chinese, *Deng Xiaoping xuanfeng*).[4]

ONTO THE WORLD STAGE: SOUTH-EAST ASIA (NOVEMBER 1978)

Deng's visit to Thailand, Malaysia and Singapore began on the afternoon of 5 November 1978 when he travelled by air to Bangkok with his wife Zhuo Lin. The problems of the Chinese economy were clearly on his mind as he had invited Hu

Qiaomu to his residence the previous day to discuss economic projects that were run by either the People's Communes or their Production Brigades. In Thailand he met the Prime Minister, General Kriangsak Chamanan, visited agricultural and freshwater fish cooperatives and a major air force base, and met members of ethnic Chinese communities in Thailand. On 9 November he left Bangkok for routine political and cultural engagements in the Malaysian capital, Kuala Lumpur, and then onwards to Singapore on the morning of 12 November.

Deng's 1978 visit to Japan and his subsequent journey to the United States of America in 1979 made international headlines. In contrast, the impact of his visit to Singapore just before the Third Plenum is often underestimated, although not by Lee Kuan Yew who was then prime minister of Singapore. Lee, like Deng, is of Hakka descent and remained active in the Singapore cabinet as minister mentor until 2011. Although brought up and educated in an English and Malay-speaking environment, Lee is intensely proud of his roots in China and assiduously promoted the speaking of Mandarin (known in Singapore as *Huayu*). Lee Kuan Yew visited China for the first time in 1976 and has always been proud of the advice that he offered to Deng on the opening of China's economy, claiming that he was Deng's chief mentor on economic development. This may be an exaggeration, but there are good reasons for concluding that Singapore, more than any of the other countries that Deng visited before the Third Plenum, was the most influential model for China's reforms.

In Thailand and Malaysia (and indeed Indonesia, which Deng did not visit), ethnic Chinese are in the minority, albeit in communities that are economically and politically significant. By contrast almost 75 per cent of the population of Singapore is Chinese-speaking and its Malay and Indian communities are in a minority. Singapore was a British colony, as one of the Straits Settlements, but gained internal self-government within the Commonwealth in 1959 and independence as part of Malaysia in 1963, before breaking away as a republic within the Commonwealth in 1965. It was therefore a predominantly Chinese community that had achieved independence and in which a version of Confucianism was respected if not universally practised. It is a small city state, the area of the urban part being merely 274 square miles, but it has an impressive track record for economic growth that qualified it as one of the four Asian tigers (with Hong Kong, South Korea and Taiwan) by virtue of the speed of its industrialisation. It is also noted for its stability and the importance attached to social order, and there is a degree of conformity that has also raised questions about human rights, freedom of speech and civil liberties for minorities and dissenters. Although it is technically a multi-party democracy, one party, the People's Action Party, has won all elections since 1959. There are striking parallels with the conditions from which the modernisation of China emerged after the 1978 Third Plenum. Singapore had achieved economic success without slavishly copying Western democracy and it had done so within a restricted area. The Special Economic Zones, based on southern cities (for example Shenzhen, which has an urban area of about 160 square miles), resemble a cluster of budding Singapores created within the People's Republic of China.

At a formal banquet arranged by Lee Kuan Yew on the evening of 12 November, Deng praised the successes of the Singaporean economy and the adherence of its government to policies of non-alignment while actively participating in ASEAN and actively seeking trade and other links with developed economies. He assured the Singapore people of China's peaceful intentions and Beijing's determination to oppose the intimidation of small states by larger ones. China, he added, was not a hegemonic power and would not seek hegemony as its economy developed and would never seek to 'invade, interfere in, control, threaten or subvert' other states. This was designed to allay concerns of the Singapore government that had arisen since the late 1960s. In a meeting with Lee on the afternoon of 13 November he and Deng discussed the thorny issue of the relationship between Singaporean Chinese and the mainland and Deng restated his opposition to a suggestion, not supported by Lee, that they should have dual citizenship. The following day, 14 November, Deng spoke to representatives of Chinese business groups in Singapore and discussed proposals that had been received from Japan for joint venture banks, arguing that China should use Japanese capital and Japanese technology. He reminded them that China was still poor and indicated that even though the PRC would soon be celebrating its first 30 years the celebrations would be low key and not over-elaborate. Chinese should not fool themselves by building superficially attractive developments which were empty inside. Agriculture was underdeveloped in China and so was technology: these should be addressed but China should not impose unnecessary restrictions. Deng was thinking aloud, reacting to what he had seen in Japan and in Singapore; and formulating his own attitude to alternative ways of running the economy and their implications for China.

The experience of an industrial park in Suzhou, the town in Jiangsu Province that is famed for its gardens, canals and history of silk production, provides more concrete evidence of the lasting effect that Deng's visit to Singapore had on China's modernisation. After Deng's visit, Singapore became a regular destination for

Chinese delegations looking for inspiration and investment, but it was many years before Singaporean investment in Suzhou became a reality. According to the management of the industrial park:

> Deng was greatly impressed by the beautiful, clean, and dynamic garden city, especially its urban construction and the Build-To-Order (BTO) system. During his southern inspection tour in 1992, Deng said: 'Singapore's social order is good. Its leaders exercise strict management. We should learn from their experience, and we should do a better job than they do.' Since then, Chinese socialist construction has been closely related to Singaporean experience.

Singapore, in the eyes of the Suzhou developers, had been the model for China's reform and opening-up in general, not just for the Suzhou Industrial Park. Lee Kuan Yew had impressed Deng by his detailed account of Singapore's development and in particular the ways in which it had succeeded in attracting foreign investment. The argument that 'Singapore managed to shut the door to possible negative impacts from the Western world and to maintain national cohesion, ethnic harmony, social stability, and cultural dignity' also impressed Deng. The agreement to create what was initially going to be called the Singapore Industrial Park was signed on 26 February 1994 by Lee Kuan Yew and Li Lanqing, Deputy Premier of the PRC, who had special responsibility for foreign investment. It attracted many businesses, but it was later the subject of a major scandal after heavy losses were incurred by Singapore companies. Even so, the influence of the Singapore model on the development in China is not in any doubt.[5]

CENTRAL COMMITTEE WORKING CONFERENCE (NOVEMBER–DECEMBER 1978)

In September 1978 the Central Committee (that is Deng Xiaoping) decided to set up a preparatory 'working conference' (*gongzuo huiyi*) to ensure the smooth running of the more formal Third Plenum of the Eleventh Central Committee that was planned for December. These two meetings are of critical significance for Deng's reforms. Although they were conducted in the normal bureaucratic manner of the CCP, there were differences, and it is worthwhile to examine them closely.

The working conference met from 10 November to 15 December 1978 in the Jingxi Hotel. This hotel, which is in the Haidian district of Beijing, is owned and run by the People's Liberation Army and is one of the most secure in the capital: it is a favoured location for high-level private meetings of Party and government officials and it does not accommodate foreigners. The conference had plenary meetings on 13 and 25 November and the remainder of the time was spent in small group discussion, with delegates grouped according to the regions of China that they represented: northern, north-eastern, eastern, south-central, south-western and south-eastern regions. The closing ceremony was on 13 December, with speeches by Deng Xiaoping, Ye Jianying and Hua Guofeng, but there were another two days of discussion and the conference did not finally conclude until 15 December.

The 219 delegates (some sources say 212 out of a possible 218) to this working conference were acutely conscious that a major change in the political climate was underway. They included the most senior Party, government and military officials working in Beijing but also senior cadres from the provinces and military districts. These were the people who mattered, who had to be convinced in private and in secure surroundings that Deng's course of action was correct before the policies were placed before the full Central Committee. The contribution of the military to policy discussions is rarely referred to openly, but their views had to be taken into account. Ten years previously the PLA had effectively put China under martial law, had prevented the collapse of the government and made possible the convening of the Ninth Party Congress in April 1969 that marked the beginning of the end of the Cultural Revolution.

By this time the majority of Party committees throughout the country had formally declared themselves in favour of the 'practice' article. It had been widely circulated, together with Deng's comments, and the supporters of the 'two whatevers' were isolated and marginalised. From the beginning of the meeting the delegates strayed from the original agenda, which was intended to focus on the economy. Wu Guoyou of the Central Committee's Party History Research Office has argued that, although in his opening speech on 13 December, Hua Guofeng formally accepted the need for the Party to change course economically, he had not fully appreciated the ideological shift that had taken place in the Party.

Among the issues discussed at this working conference were six crucial topics:

1. The Party's shift towards economic modernisation about which there was little disagreement;
2. The resolution of problems bequeathed by history, that is the legacy of the Cultural Revolution including the 1976 Tian'anmen Incident;
3. Agriculture, originally intended as the main agenda item;

4. Party ideology, 'truth as the basis' (*zhenli biaozhun*), versus the 'two whatevers' of Hua Guofeng;
5. Economic tasks and reform and opening, Deng's flagship policies;
6. Organisational matters, confirming Deng's authority.

Many of the delegates wanted to focus on criticism of Hua and the 1976 Tian'anmen Incident. There was a general agreement that the economic reforms could not succeed without these political reforms being implemented and the mood of the meeting was strongly for Deng and against Hua.

ONTO THE WORLD STAGE: DIPLOMATIC RELATIONS WITH THE UNITED STATES

On 16 December 1978, as the Working Conference came to an end, and delegates prepared for two days' break to recuperate and read and revise their conference papers, it was announced that diplomatic relations were to be established between the United States and China with effect from 1 January 1979. A joint statement was issued simultaneously in the name of President Carter in Washington and in Beijing by Hua Guofeng, who was nominally the head of state. Saving face and the need to preserve diplomatic niceties partially explains why Hua was able to retain this position until 1981. The timing of the announcement was spectacular: when the Central Committee sat down at the Third Plenum, they had to digest not only Deng's radical economic policies, but a relationship with the old enemy, the imperialist United States of America, that had previously been inconceivable.[6]

THIRD PLENUM OF ELEVENTH CENTRAL COMMITTEE (18–22 DECEMBER 1978)

The Third Plenum, held from 18 to 22 December 1978, formally endorsed and made public the message that China was now on a new course. This much shorter conference – five days rather than in excess of a month for the working conference – clarified the policy for the general population of China, the majority of whom were not members of the Communist Party and had for years been receiving conflicting signals from the press and the radio, both of which were controlled by the Party. It also notified the wider world of the changes, most importantly those countries and corporations whose capital and technological input was essential to stimulate the country's economic growth.

Like the Working Conference, the Third Plenum took place in the Jingxi Hotel and the delegates sat tightly packed behind long desks in the conference room with little elbow room for the essential note-taking. The Third Plenum followed shortly after the Working Conference, which was convenient as many of the 281 delegates attending the Central Committee meeting were already in Beijing if not in the hotel. The agenda of the Third Plenum, unlike the working party that preceded it, was dominated by the need for what was now being called 'socialist modernisation'(*shehuizhuyi xiandaihua*). Long-standing ideas associated with Mao were discarded together with the now discredited 'two whatevers' of Hua Guofeng. Two large photographs of Mao and Hua dominated the meeting hall, but although it may have looked like an old-fashioned meeting of the Central Committee, the nature of the debate had changed fundamentally. Mao Zedong Thought could not be discarded completely but it was replaced by the need to 'correctly understand Mao Zedong Thought as an integral whole': these mentions of Mao were essentially a sop to the old guard and the meeting marked the end of the serious application of Mao's analysis to the real problems faced by China. The unjust treatment of former senior Party officials was formally repudiated, especially the case of Peng Dehuai who had opposed Mao's handling of the Great Leap Forward in 1959 and for whom a memorial ceremony was held on 24 December 1978. Peng had died in 1974 and his ill-health at the end of his life was blamed on ill-treatment during the Cultural Revolution.

Supporters of Deng Xiaoping were elected to the Central Committee, the Politburo and the Central Commission for Discipline, the three Party bodies that exercised the greatest authority. Among the new faces were prominent reformers including Chen Yun and Hu Yaobang. Hua Guofeng still remained in post as chairman, but he no longer had any authority. Hua's military aide, Wang Dongxing, who had been instrumental in the arrest of the Gang of Four, was dismissed as director of the Central Committee's General Office, although he was permitted to remain as an alternative member of the Central Committee.

The discussion at the Third Plenum focused on five central issues:

1. The strategic shift towards economic reform from January 1979;
2. How the Party should lead this economic work;
3. Strengthening the Party's internal democracy and establishing democratic structures and regulations;

4. Restoring a version of Marxism based on 'seeking truth from facts';
5. Augmenting healthy leading forces within the Party.

The aim underlying these discussions was to put the Chinese Communist Party on an entirely new footing. The Third Plenum repudiated policies of the Cultural Revolution and earlier that were now characterised as 'left' errors. It was also rejecting a view of social change based on class struggle in favour of one based on economic construction, and moving from a closed towards a more open system. Whether this still constituted a Marxist approach is a moot point, but it was Deng's approach and he had at last persuaded the central leadership of the Party and enough of the national membership that it was the right approach.

In the words of Wu Guoyou of the Central Committee's Party History Research Office, at the Third Plenum the Party had begun the process of 'restoring order from chaos' (*bo luan fan zheng*) that was eventually completed at the Sixth Plenum in June 1981 when Hua Guofeng was finally ousted. Such had been the twists and turns of China's political history since the late 1950s that no-one could be certain how permanent this change was going to be, so to protect the reform programme, Deng reminded local Party organisations that 'theories should be based on reality' and insisted that educational programmes must be created to ensure that this was done.[7]

TWO MEETINGS: AN INSIDER'S VIEW

In 1978 Zhu Jiamu was secretary to Hu Qiaomu, then President of the Chinese Academy of Social Sciences and one of Deng Xiaoping's closest advisers but also a critic. Zhu, who later became deputy director of the Academy, attended both the Working Conference and the Third Plenum with his chief and 30 years later set out his personal recollections to supplement the mass of publicly available material. He identified three important characteristics of the meetings and, as the Third Plenum was almost a continuation of the Working Conference, he considers them together.

First, in both cases the discussions departed significantly from the original agendas. The Working Conference was originally set up to discuss communes and the speed of agricultural development; the national economic plans for 1979 and 1980; and a speech that Li Xiannian had made at a State Council ideological sub-committee. Even before discussions opened on this formal agenda the conference spent over two days discussing the implications of the great shift towards economic reform for Party and government work. However, the great majority of delegates also wanted to talk about other matters: the historical problems left over from the Cultural Revolution; the 'truth and practice' debate; the political position of certain 'responsible comrades' and the 'adjustment of senior central personnel'. In short this was a collective criticism of the fact that Hua Guofeng was still nominally chairman of the CCP and a demand that the position of Deng Xiaoping should be formally resolved. What was significant to Zhu, the observer, was that delegates were breaking through the ideological cotton wool and their views were being taken seriously. At the Third Plenum the first agenda items – the establishment and compostion of the Central Discipline Inspection Commission – were dealt with first, but then the tenor of the conference rapidly shifted to confirming the discussions that had taken place at the Working Conference, especially those on the central leadership structure.

Second, the length of both meetings was extended. The Working Conference was initially planned to last for 20 days with a short break before the Third Plenum began: in fact it lasted for 36 days. Because of the thoroughness of the discussion and the level of detail covered in the Working Conference there was very little new to take to the Third Plenum, but that meeting was also extended from the planned three days to five. The Central Committee and their advisers and staff were in meetings for a total of 41 days. Hu Qiaomu had requested a break between the two in spite of the time that had already elapsed so that there was time for staff to revise documents, and if that is taken into account, together with the additional day that was allocated at the end of the Third Plenum to prepare and agree the final public statement, the whole exercise lasted for 45 days.

Third, Zhu was impressed by the lively atmosphere of the meetings. Discussions were animated, delegates were enthusiastic and they felt free to express what was on their minds. The formal reports, timely and thorough, that were given by delegates were listened to carefully and copious notes were taken. There was an attempt by the platform early on in the proceedings to try to exclude some reports but, after complaints from delegates, this was rapidly overturned. Zhu noted that, since the Working Conference of March 1977 that failed to reinstate Deng Xiaoping, there had been a fundamental change in the balance of forces in the Party and in the attitudes of senior members. The longer the meetings went on the livelier they became in spite of the length of time they were taking. Zhu considered that if these meetings were not unprecedented they were extremely unusual.

The change in the mood was such that even Hua Guofeng, the originator of the 'two whatevers' doctrine, found himself obliged to discuss the role of 'practice as the sole criterion for testing truth'. He conceded that articles in the press supporting this view should not be interpreted as attacks on Mao Zedong, but he was still desperately clinging to power.

In the closing stages of the Working Conference there were speeches by Ye Jianying, Hua Guofeng and Deng Xiaoping, but the principal report from the meeting, which also set the agenda for the forthcoming Third Plenum, was Deng's final speech. Deng had prepared this speech in October, with the assistance of Hu Qiaomu, and had not been present at the opening of the Working Conference because of his travels abroad. He arrived back in Beijing from Singapore on 13 November and joined the conference the following day, although he was absent from time to time for meetings and to perform other official duties. On hearing how the discussions had been progressing, he made significant changes to his original draft. Deng emphasised the need to implement the shift to economic modernisation as rapidly as possible and called for the 'liberation of thought' and 'seeking truth through facts' as essential for progress. There was a sense of urgency in his address: it was essential, he argued, that the leadership grasp this historic opportunity to implement the 'four modernisations' that he and Zhou Enlai had espoused. If there was one point in the 1970s at which Hua's approach and authority can be said to have been replaced by Deng's, it was during the discussions at the Working Conference rather than in the more public and better-known Third Plenum.[8]

XIAOGANG VILLAGE AND THE DEMISE OF THE PEOPLE'S COMMUNES

Discussions on agriculture and the reform of the commune system may have been sidelined at the Working Conference and Third Plenum but they were still a high priority. Some farmers were already taking the initiative. The town of Fengyang is a county town in a deprived part of the northern Anhui Province: the county, and particularly the village of Xiaogang, shot to fame in 1978 when local farmers took the law into their own hands to reverse the system of communes and collective farming that had dominated China since the 1950s. By doing so they put pressure on the government to institute reforms on a nationwide basis and also provided evidence of popular support for Deng's policies. The breadth of this support helped to persuade doubters in the Central Committee that Deng's reforms should be endorsed. The 'household responsibility system' which was devised in Xiaogang became the formula for the transformation of collectively managed enterprises into what were essentially family farms, while retaining the legal fiction that the spirit of collectivisation was being maintained.

Anhui is not one of the most underdeveloped provinces in China but Xiaogang had been bypassed by new roads and rail links and other economic developments: before 1978 it was desperately poor and begging was commonplace. In December 1978, following a devastating summer drought, a group of 18 peasant families, in courageous defiance of the existing policies of collectivisation, initiated what they termed a responsibility system (*dabao gan*). This handed over the management of agricultural production to individual families, in a desperate attempt to increase the amount of food available. The farmers sealed their agreement by impressing the prints of their hands dipped in red ink on a contract. This contract and other mementoes of their struggle are displayed in a memorial hall that opened on 19 June 2008. The 18 rebels could not have known how local officials would react to this defiance, but the timing of the farmers' independent protest was opportune. Unknown to them, the Third Plenum was about to set the whole of China, including the management of farms, on course for reform. The responsibility system that they had devised was in tune with this new mood: it spread across the country, was adopted officially and eventually received the all-important imprimatur of Deng Xiaoping.[9]

THE FIVE ELDERS AND A NEW ERA FOR INDUSTRY

It is one thing to secure political approval for a reform policy, immense challenge though that was: it is another to implement it. On 16 January 1979 Rong Yiren, Hu Juewen, Hu Zi'ang, Gu Gengyu and Zhou Shutao, former industrialists and businessmen who had not seen each other for over a decade, all received the same message: Deng Xiaoping wanted to see them. They were excited at the prospect of meeting the leader and gathered at Rong's house that evening to consider what he would want to discuss with them and what proposals they might put forward for the reconstruction of the Chinese economy. Gu Gengyu worked late into the night to fashion their thoughts into a coherent document. At 10 o'clock on the morning of 17 January, Deng met the five men in the Great Hall of the People and said he wanted to hear from them what was needed to revive the economy. He spoke frankly to them about the political position. The Third Plenum had decided to shift the entire focus of the Party's work to constructing 'socialist modernisation' and they could not afford to lose any more time: the problem was how it should be done. At all costs they must avoid repeating the errors of the Great Leap Forward. There were methods open to them now that were not available in 1958: they had access to foreign capital and technology and there were Chinese experts, either living temporarily overseas or citizens of other countries, who were willing to return to run factories. Attracting foreign capital could be done by compensatory trade (payment in goods rather than in cash) and by setting up joint ventures, but initially it was necessary to select the sectors with fast capital turnover to attract investors.

This was a new language and a new dispensation and the Five Elders (*wu lao*) responded enthusiastically. Hu Zi'ang insisted that they should develop existing talent, beginning with those who already had experience of business, and if such people proved suitable they should be given official positions. Deng agreed, acknowledged that they were more familiar with the problem than he was, but also suggested that capable individuals in the tourist industry, for example, could be appointed as company managers, or alternatively as consultants if they were not ready to manage. He also asked the five to recommend individuals with special technical expertise and experience of management to run the enterprises, especially in new sectors. They should, he said, consider outsiders as well as Chinese citizens, as long as they were able, committed and patriotic. When the discussion turned to the question of workable policies for former industrialists and businessmen, Gu Gengyu handed over the draft list of proposals that he had prepared the night before. Deng took the draft and responded:

> Appropriate policies are necessary and these must include [ideas on how] their [industrialists] descendants should be treated. The most important thing is that they should not continue to be exploitative. Apart from that there is no reason why they should continue to be stuck with the label of capitalist. When the policies are in place and if there is money available, some people can run a couple of factories to earn some profit in foreign currency and invest in the tourist industry. However, it is not right to allow them to keep money idle. You will have to be selective but money and personnel should be used.

The thinking behind this appears to be that it was acceptable for businessmen to use their skills to develop industries but that profits should be used, reinvested, rather than accumulated by the businesses and their owners. In the light of the level of capital accumulated by commercial organisations since the introduction of the market reforms, these reservations appear quaint and naive.

With these Five Elders, Deng was able to get things off his chest and talk frankly in a way that was not possible with his colleagues in the Central Committee and the Politburo, where he had to adopt a completely different idiom. His guests were also able to speak candidly. Deng inspired confidence in these former industrialists who had been out in the cold for at least a decade and were being brought back to carry out reforms in the face of determined opposition from some members of the CCP. He had courage, resourcefulness and energy, and more importantly he had the skill to motivate people, however impossible the task appeared. Their work was completed by lunchtime and Deng took them to a restaurant where they sat round a boiling Mongolian hotpot, one of Deng's favourite dishes. Ten years later Gu Gengyu would remember the occasion as 'one hotpot, one great performance' (*yi zhi huoguo, yi tai daxi*).[10]

RONG YIREN AND CITIC: OPENING CHINA'S ECONOMY TO THE WORLD

A major consideration in Deng's plans was the requirement to attract foreign capital to China. In the late 1970s China was poor and underdeveloped and one of the factors blocking the modernisation of the economy was a severe shortage of capital. At the conclusion of his meeting with the Five Elders, Deng charged one of them, Rong Yiren, with the responsibility of attracting and managing foreign capital. It was one of the most important decisions that Deng took in his struggle to change the way that the Chinese economy was managed.

Rong had a background in business and in the 1940s had run his family's flour and cotton mills in the city of Wuxi in Jiangsu Province. Rong's father Rong Desheng had been one of the wealthiest industrialists in China before World War II, and in 2000 Rong Yiren would be named as China's richest individual. Rong Yiren had chosen to stay on the mainland after the CCP's victory in 1949, unlike many business owners who moved, with their assets, to Hong Kong or Taiwan. This decision was judged to have been patriotic and he was one of the few pre-1949 industrialists who worked closely with the government of the People's Republic. During the 1950s Rong was closer to Mao Zedong and Zhou Enlai than to Deng Xiaoping, but he came to Deng's attention when he contributed to the cost of aircraft during the Korean War and cooperated with the CCP when large private businesses were brought under state control. He became deputy mayor of Shanghai in 1957 and in 1959 Deng even recommended him for the post of deputy minister with responsibility for the textile industry. Rong was criticised severely during the Cultural Revolution but may have been protected from the worst excesses of Red Guards by the intervention of Zhou Enlai.

In 1978 Deng realised that in order to transform the Chinese economy they needed to be able to draw on the experience, talent and insight of people who were not members of the Communist Party and bring them 'down from the mountains' (*chushan*). This new group of political supporters would be able to 'explore, experiment, and open up new fields of activity' (*qu tansuo, qu shiyan, qu kaichuang xin tiandi*). It is to Deng Xiaoping's credit that not only was he able to recognise his own limitations, he was also able to recognise the limitations of the Communist Party and its leadership. He did not believe dogmatically that all wisdom lay within the Party and its ideologues. Deng initially brought Rong into the Beijing political elite by inviting him to take on the role of deputy chairman of the Chinese People's Political Consultative Conference (CPPCC), the national forum for people and groups outside the Communist Party.

In the spring of 1979 the United Front Department of the Communist Party convened a meeting of representatives of industrial and commercial bodies and leaders of the 'democratic parties' in Beijing to prepare for a conference. These 'democratic parties' (*minzhu dangpai*) are eight non-communist parties that were allowed to continue in existence after 1949 as they were deemed to have behaved in a patriotic manner in the war and civil war. The little influence that they had in the early 1950s was eliminated during the Anti-Rightist Campaign of 1957 when many of their senior members were sent to the countryside for re-education. In 1979 Deng invited several of these representatives to meet him, and Rong Yiren played a pivotal role.

Deng was beginning to assemble the personnel he needed and asked Rong to set aside all his other business interests and to concentrate his efforts on rebuilding China's national economy. Deng emphasised that whatever methods and instruments were used internationally in capitalist countries should be brought to China. On Deng's instructions, Rong began work to create a new inward investment organisation operating on the basis of modern international financial principles rather than political doctrine. This would eventually become the China International Trust and Investment Corporation (*Zhongguo zhongxin jituan gongsi*), CITIC. It would be Rong's job to find the right people, manage the business and take responsibility for the whole enterprise. No such body existed in

China and Deng wanted a report to the Central Committee as soon as possible. Rong had no assistants and spent many late nights in the study of his traditional Beijing courtyard house working, creating the concept and working out how it would operate, with his wife, Yang Jianqing, acting as his unofficial secretary.

The Central Committee received the report and rapidly approved it. Deng Xiaoping, Chen Yun and Li Xiannian were unequivocally enthusiastic, but there was still doubt and even outright opposition to the 'reform and opening' (*gaige kaifang*) policy. Deng tried to smooth Rong's path and remove predictable obstacles: he warned Rong against allowing other bodies to take over his respons- ibilities and insisted that he and CITIC should not become bureaucratised. Deng kept a watching brief on Rong and his organisation, conscious of the fact that a non-Party person must have real power in order to be effective – he must be seen to be the bearer of the emperor's sword (*shangfang baojian*). Only with the public support of Deng would Rong be able to complete his task.

The preparatory group of what would eventually become CITIC was established on 8 July 1978, the same day that a law on Chinese–foreign joint ventures was promulgated: this was an indication of the strength of China's resolution to open to the world economy. CITIC came into being formally on 4 October the same year and immediately attracted international interest: it was eventually based in the Chaoyang District of Beijing in a building on Jianguomenwai Avenue that was briefly the tallest building in Beijing. CITIC developed into a powerful financial and industrial conglomerate with extensive international connections. It has functioned as the government's investment banking arm and was China's key link to the international capital market and the means through which foreign investment reached the Chinese economy.

One of Rong Yiren's major assets was that he had over 400 relatives scattered about the world in various locations where the Chinese diaspora had settled. Many of these were well known in the commercial, technical or scientific fields. In the immediate past such foreign contacts would have been suspect, to say the least. In the new Deng era they were vital for bringing China into contact with the rest of the world. In June 1986, over half of this extremely extended family – 200 overseas members of five generations of the Rong clan and 20 who still lived in China – travelled to Beijing for what turned out to be a cross between a family reunion and a political rally. Members of the clan had travelled from many countries including the United States, Canada, Australia, Brazil, West Germany and Switzerland. This reunion was unprecedented in the history of the Rong clan and it brought together many whose business and professional interests had already brought them to

China – or back to China – since the Nixon visit of 1972. On 18 June 1986 Deng met representatives of Rong's huge family at a reception in the Great Hall of the People in Beijing. Later that afternoon they were joined by another veteran communist who had been persecuted in the Cultural Revolution, the former mayor of Beijing, Peng Zhen. The overseas Rongs stayed in Beijing for three days before embarking on a tourist itinerary that took in Xi'an, the family ancestral home of Wuxi and Shanghai.

The reunion was a personal triumph for Rong Yiren, whose authority was strengthened by the direct involvement of Deng, and for the worldwide Rong family. For Deng, it could be presented as a public acknowledgment of the patriotism of the diaspora and their commitment to the development of the motherland. It was also a necessary symbol that attitudes to the business and professional classes had genuinely changed. In 1949 many educated Chinese professionals who had been studying or working overseas had returned to the mainland determined to contribute to the creation of 'New China' following the years of war and occupation. Their hopes had been dashed at the end of the 1950s when a series of increasingly repressive campaigns culminated in the Anti-Rightist campaign, the main target of which was the technical and professional intelligentsia. In the 1980s the leadership of another 'New China', this time entering a period of economic reforms, was seeking to persuade diaspora Chinese, most of whom still had firm ties to their family's place of origin (*guxiang*) in China even after decades of emigration, to return to the motherland. Many of these had been successful in their new homes and were people of some standing in their communities. Some had also become extremely wealthy and their capital, and that of their business partners in their home countries, was a potential asset for China's future develoment. Superficially, the CCP's determination to attract people like the Rong family was a complete reversal of policy. In fact it was a return to the original concept of a broadly based political structure known as New Democracy that existed briefly in the early 1950s but which lost out to a more authoritarian and narrow system.

Although Rong Yiren worked closely with the government and the CCP – Deng was reputed to have called him his 'red capitalist' – it was assumed that he had remained outside the Communist Party: rumours persist that he did eventually join (some say in 1985) but that there was an agreement that this would not be revealed during his lifetime. An obituary in a news release in Chinese from the New China News Agency (Xinhua) on 27 October 2005 referred to him as a 'fighter for communism' (*gongchanzhuyi zhanshi*) but did not claim that he was a member of the CCP. Rong served as deputy chairman of the National People's Congress from 1988 to 1993 and as vice-president of China from 1993 to 1998, but he had been so closely identified with the investment body that he had created that, right up to his death, he was often referred to as Mr CITIC. As so often happened in the Beijing political elite, the political relationship also led to more personal links: the Deng and Rong families became close, their children played together and grew up together, especially the youngest daughters of each family, who were both known as Maomao, an affectionate nickname often given to small girls.[11]

ONTO THE WORLD STAGE: UNITED STATES OF AMERICA (28 JANUARY TO 5 FEBRUARY 1979)

During the 1930s and 1940s, China's great adversary was Japan. After the outbreak of the Korean War, and certainly by the 1960s, it was the United States or rather 'American imperialism' (*Meidiguozhuyi*). This Chinese term has now almost vanished, but during the Cultural Revolution the plain name for the United States (*Meiguo*) was rarely used on its own. Such was the animosity between the two governments that creating normal diplomatic relations in the new Deng era required a fundamental readjustment in attitudes, both in Beijing and in Washington.

After the dramatic fall from power of Lin Biao in September 1971 and his death, apparently while fleeing to the Soviet Union, Beijing had decided that the threat from Moscow was so great that China must come to a rapprochement with the United States. Thus began a dramatic and bewildering diplomatic *volte face* that took the world, and the Chinese population, completely by surprise.

The Chinese seat in the United Nations had been occupied by Taiwan since 1949. Since all sides insisted that there could only be one China, the People's Republic of China was excluded from the UN. On 25 October 1971, after fierce lobbying, and with the sponsorship of the United States and its ally Japan, the United Nations General Assembly finally voted to award the Chinese seat to the PRC and to exclude Taiwan. The first delegation from Beijing to the UN arrived at UN headquarters in New York on 11 November. The People's Republic of China was finally able to participate in international diplomacy.

The most public manifestation of the new relationship was the official visit by the President of the United States, Richard M. Nixon, who arrived in Beijing on 21 February 1972. Nixon had long discussions with the Chinese leadership, mostly with Zhou Enlai. Much of the detailed business was carried out by his Secretary of State for Foreign Affairs, Henry Kissinger, whose exploratory trip the previous year had made the visit possible, and by the Deputy Foreign Minister of China, Qiao Guanhua. The United States and China did not finally establish normal diplomatic relations and exchange ambassadors until 1 January 1979, primarily because of disputes over the status of Taiwan. Until that had happened, Deng Xiaoping's return visit – the first of a leader of the PRC to the United States – could not take place. Mao Zedong and Zhou Enlai had been formally invited but it was Deng's destiny to make the journey. Deng had visited the United States before he became leader, as the head of the Chinese delegation to the United Nations in April 1974.

On 28 January 1979, the first day of New Year in the traditional Chinese calendar, Deng and Zhuo Lin climbed the steps of a China Airlines Boeing 707 in Beijing and were flown to Andrews Air Force Base outside Washington. In a temperature of 38°F (3°C) following a heavy snowfall, the Dengs were welcomed by Vice-President Walter Mondale and Secretary of State Cyrus Vance – Deng may have been the acknowledged leader of China, but he was not the president and indeed never would be. They did not stay at a state guesthouse of the status of Diaoyutai, which was where a high-level visitor to China would be accommodated, but at the suburban residence of Zbigniew Brzezinski. Brzezinski, who was a scholar of international relations of Polish origin, was from 1977 to 1981 President Jimmy Carter's National Security Adviser. Brzezinski had met Deng in Beijing in May 1978 to discuss the final arrangements for establishing diplomatic relations and had promised him a home-cooked supper when he visited the United States. The promise was fulfilled with a roast beef dinner *chez* Brzezinski: Deng was being given a taste not only of the roast beef but also of the American way of life. Deng took to the occasion and the repartee like a duck to water. This was not what Americans had come to expect from communist politicians.

Deng met President Jimmy Carter at the White House on the morning of 29 January and on two subsequent occasions during his Washington visit, but each meeting was relatively short and their conversations were formal – the most serious and detailed discussions were with Brzezinski. The presidency (1977–81) of Jimmy Carter (1924–) is often underestimated and Carter's performance has been much maligned, largely because of his administration's handling of the Iran hostage crisis that began in the winter of 1979: his enlightened social views were not favoured by illiberal sections of the US media. Deng and Carter signed a series of accords which provided for technical and cultural exchanges between China and the United States, but it is unlikely that either of the statesmen could have foreseen the scale of exchanges that was to follow. In spite of the success of this visit it was not until 1 March 1979 that full diplomatic relations were in place and embassies were established in Beijing and Washington. The decision to move to full diplomatic recognition was made under the Carter administration, but this vital development did not have the glamour or the drama of the Nixon visit.

Deng visited Atlanta and Seattle and in Texas he toured the Johnson Space Centre, attended a rodeo and was photographed wearing a ten-gallon hat. This was not necessarily politically significant but it did provide effective public relations copy, both for the United States, which could demonstrate how Deng was being seduced by American culture (which he was not) and for the Chinese side who could demonstrate that the affable, confident and relaxed Deng Xiaoping was popular wherever he went and was obviously enjoying being in what might have been expected to be an alien environment. The Dengs left the United States on 6 February 1979 and flew home via Japan, where they spent two days, and Deng held talks with Prime Minister Masayoshi Ohira. The brief stopover in Japan made sense logistically and geographically, but it was also politically significant as the normalisation of relations with Japan was ultimately dependent on progress in establishing diplomatic relations with the United States.[12]

DEMOCRACY WALL AND FOUR CARDINAL PRINCIPLES (1978–9)

The central conundrum of Deng Xiaoping's time in power is the contrast between his tenacious commitment to the transformation of the Chinese economy (from a man who before 1978 had very limited exposure to the Western capitalist world) and his equally resolute refusal to countenance any political reform that might appear to resemble Western multi-party democracy. The key to unravelling this conundrum lies not only in his early training and experience but also in the tightrope that he walked in the Politburo and the Central Committee between economic and political reform. The more contacts China developed with the Western world the more fraught this issue became. The most obvious manifestations of this conundrum were the political contortions that Deng had to perform with his affirmation in 1979 of the 'four cardinal [or basic] principles' that governed the operation of the CCP after Mao.

The elucidation of the four fundamental principles emerged from a special meeting of the Central Committee between 18 January and 3 April 1979, a 'meeting to discuss guidelines for theoretical work' (*lilun gongzuo wuxu hui*). This meeting was unusually long: it lasted for approximately six weeks, and the length of the meeting is an indication of the difficulties the Party leadership faced. (A historical parallel is the back-to-back meeting of the Politburo and Central Committee in Lushan from 2 July to 16 August, which was the arena for the battle between Mao Zedong and Peng Dehuai and lasted for just over six weeks.) At the March 1979 meeting the new leadership was attempting to reconcile the practicalities of a root and branch reform programme that gave back much of the initiative to private capitalists with an ideological tradition that the Chinese Communist Party and Deng were committed to.

Different schools of thought had emerged within the Party and some of these alarmed Deng. A small minority of members still clung to the rhetoric of Lin Biao and Jiang Qing and completely opposed the overall thrust of political changes put forward at the Third Plenum. Others exaggerated the faults of the past and took the opportunity of the political flux to propose the complete rejection of the Party leadership and the legacy of Mao and Mao's Thought, presenting themselves as 'opponents of famine, persecution and upholders of human rights and democracy'. Some of these individuals began to form organisations and issue their own publications. For Deng and the new Party leadership this was going too far. The organisations and publications that these individuals created were deemed illegal and their originators were accused of 'inciting widespread disturbances and attacks against the organs of the party centre and the government'. Some were also accused of collaborating with foreign enemies of China and plotting to provoke more serious incidents – activities which, if allowed to continue, would 'damage the political arrangements that provided the stability necessary for the construction of China's socialist modernisation'.

The appearance of the 'Xidan Democracy Wall' (*Xidan minzhu qiang*) was a more troublesome issue. The background to this was the appearance of political posters, originally on Wangfujing Road in Beijing, but later on Xidan Road on the opposite side of the Imperial Palace and closer to the Party compound of Zhongnanhai. The wall on Xidan was soon dubbed Democracy Wall and became a forum for the free expression of ideas by dissenting activists. They had been encouraged by the new freedoms that were anticipated as a result of the Third Plenum and particularly by the decision of the Beijing Municipal Committee to reverse the verdict on the violent demonstrations in Tian'anmen Square that had taken place on 5 April 1976. The committee declared, with the support of the Standing Committee of the Politburo, that the demonstrations honouring Zhou Enlai and attacking Jiang Qing and her supporters should now be treated as a revolutionary and not a counter-revolutionary event. This encouraged dissidents and democracy activists to demonstrate afresh in Tian'anmen Square and, in addition to the official slogan of 'four modernisations' (agriculture, industry, science and technology, and defence), activists argued for a fifth modernisation, 'democracy'. The best known of these activists was Wei Jingsheng, whose poster was put up on Democracy Wall on 5 December 1978. Demonstrations and a wave of new and creative publications continued into the following year in what is sometimes called the Beijing Spring (although there were similar manifestations of dissent in Shanghai and other cities).

Supporters of Deng were willing to tolerate the movement as long as it criticised his opponents such as Jiang Qing, but the demands for greater democracy were soon regarded as a serious threat to the authority of the CCP. Ironically Deng had lauded the new democratic life that was now possible both within and outside the Party in a speech at a meeting of the Central Committee.

Wei Jingsheng was imprisoned on 16 October 1979, having been convicted of passing military secrets to foreign journalists and diplomats: this was a powerful signal that the wave of dissidence would no longer be tolerated. The Xidan wall was cleared and an alternative venue established in the Temple of the Sun (*Ritan*) Park, which lies some distance to the east of the most sensitive areas of central Beijing. Access to the park was restricted by police who demanded to see identity cards and, not surprisingly, Democracy Wall ceased to exist. Wei served a total of 18 years in prison and was only finally released, to exile in the United States, in 1997.

On 30 March 1979, towards the end of the discussions in the Central Committee, Deng gave the keynote speech, 'Uphold the Four Cardinal Principles' (*Jianchi si xiang jiben yuanze*), after extensive consultations with Hu Yaobang, Hu Qiaomu and other aides. Much of the speech set out his thinking on where China and the Communist Party now stood and the tasks that faced them. The four principles emphasised in this speech were: the socialist path (*shehuizhuyi daolu*), dictatorship of the proletariat (*wuchanjieji zhuanzheng*), leadership by the Communist Party (*gongchandang de lindao*) and Marxism-Leninism Mao Zedong Thought (*Ma Lie zhuyi Mao Zedong sixiang*). These were not new, merely a restatement of the Party's traditional principles and as such considered inviolable. They resulted from a compromise with those who doubted the wisdom of Deng's reforms and were intended to provide reassurance that, whatever changes might take place in the economy, the political status quo, with the Communist Party controlling the state, would not be at risk.[13]

Is it possible to know what Deng really thought of the Democracy Wall, the criticism that was being levelled at his new leadership and the demands for greater and more genuine democracy inside and outside the Party? There are no written records to answer this conclusively, but from what we know of his character, it seems unlikely that he would have been nervous about demands for democracy. He always gave the impression of being tough, and he had been down and out politically in the past. He was no stranger to criticism, but he was not prepared to countenance any threat to his reform programme. It was a programme that, in one form or another, he had been working on for over 20 years since he had collaborated with Liu Shaoqi during the 1950s. Once he had secured the support of the Third Plenum in 1978 he was not prepared to countenance any danger to what might be his last opportunity to see his project through.

Whatever his private thoughts, Deng was not able to be a dictator even if that was what he had wished. He could only work within the parameters of the party bureaucracy. Deng was an influential voice in the two most powerful bodies, the Central Committee and the Politburo, but he was not in a position to control them. Although he had managed to secure support for the economic reforms, the opposition was still formidable: those who were most suspicious of the economic reforms were even more distrustful of demands for greater democracy. If Deng had defied his critics and insisted on a parallel programme of wider political reform, it is unlikely that he would have secured sufficient support: the consistent opposition that he faced over his economic policies and the length of time that was needed to hammer out a compromise sustain this view. By allowing any concessions to Western multi-party democracy, he could have jeopardised the economic reforms. When preparing his speech to that fraught meeting of the Central Committee, he consulted two of his advisers, whose views could not have been more different: Hu Yaobang, who would later become an icon for the reform tendency in the CCP, and Hu Qiaomu, a determined doctrinaire opponent of reform. The only possible conclusion is that in the end it was his pragmatism that won: he made the only decision that he believed would work at that time, saved his economic reforms and allowed the demands for political democracy to be silenced, or at least shelved, for another time and another generation.

CHAPTER 17

RETREATING TO ADVANCE: FROM THE GANG OF FOUR TO THE DEMOCRACY MOVEMENT (1980–92)

This [historical] resolution took a year to write and in that time it was discussed by 4,000 people; then by a few dozen and the enlarged meeting of the Politburo. The present discussions at the preparatory meeting for the Sixth Plenary Session [of the Central Committee] are the fourth round. In my opinion the resolution is conscientious, serious and cautious.[1]

By 1980 there was little doubt about Deng's personal authority, but his status and official positions did not reflect this. The greatest anomaly was that, in spite of the fact that he was widely acknowledged at home and abroad as China's political leader, Deng was merely first deputy premier while Mao's protégé, Hua Guofeng, was both premier and chairman of the CCP's Central Committee. A series of political moves were made to rectify this position in 1980, but they did not entirely clarify Deng's formal position and in some ways created more confusion.

DENG AND HUA GUOFENG RESIGN (SEPTEMBER 1980)

The Eleventh Central Committee held its Fifth Plenary Session in Beijing between 23 and 29 February 1980 and significant organisational reforms were enacted. The Central Committee Secretariat, which had been in abeyance since the Cultural Revolution and had previously been Deng Xiaoping's powerbase, was reconstituted. Hu Yaobang was nominated as general secretary of the CCP, and Wan Li and ten others were appointed as members of the Secretariat. Hu and Zhao Ziyang were appointed to the Standing Committee of the Politburo. Former President Liu Shaoqi, who had been purged during the Cultural Revolution and died after illtreatment by Red Guards on 12 November 1969, was formally rehabilitated. This did nothing for Liu, but it was a highly symbolic move because he had been Deng's closest collaborator in government during the 1950s. When the Central Committee held a meeting in Liu's memory in the Great Hall of the People on 17 May 1980, it was chaired by Hua Guofeng but Deng gave the formal memorial speech.

The Fifth National People's Congress met in Beijing for its Third Session from 30 August to 10 September 1980. Much of the agenda was devoted to bread and butter issues such as legislation on marriage and joint venture enterprises, but there were also major and dramatic personnel changes. Hua Guofeng, who had only recently attended the funerals of President Josip Broz Tito in Yugoslavia and the Japanese Prime Minister Ōhira Masayoshī, who had died in office, was relieved of his post of premier and Zhao Ziyang appointed in his place: two of the most prominent supporters of Deng's reforms, Zhao and Hu Yaobang, were now in powerful positions. Deng had decided to resign his post of deputy premier, and he took with him several 'revolutionaries of the older generation', including Li Xiannian, Chen Yun, Xu Xiangqian and Wang Zhen who had also been persuaded to resign their posts as deputy premiers: other senior politicians also stood down from the National People's Congress. This 'voluntary' resignation of such senior members of the leadership enabled Deng, by sacrificing a status that had meant little in terms of authority, to remove actual and potential obstacles to reform. It also signalled an end to the system in which party and state leaders remained in post for life, unless they were purged.

Hua Guofeng still remained chairman of the Chinese Communist Party, but this was purely a face-saving device. For the writer Ye Yonglie, Hua was a chairman in name only, a 'phony chairman' (*kongtou zhuxi*), although he was not finally 'faded out' until the end of June 1981.[2] For months there had been broad hints that Hua was on his way out, notably an article by a 'special commentator' in *People's*

Daily on 4 July 1980. The newly restored Secretariat also directed that photographs of leaders should not be displayed routinely: Mao's image had been ubiquitous during the Cultural Revolution and this was an indication that the much-photographed Chairman Hua was not Mao's successor.

These changes in personnel did nothing to clarify Deng's ambiguous and paradoxical position. He had resigned from a second-tier post but in practice had been behaving as head of both the CCP and the state: this was acknowledged both within China and internationally. His resignation increased his authority while removing the threat from actual or potential opponents. He preferred to leave day-to-day politics to the younger generation, while retaining great authority behind the scenes, and only intervened in exceptional circumstances. He was 76 years old and appeared tireless, but he needed successors. In Hu Yaobang and Zhao Ziyang he had found two reliable supporters of his economic reforms, although within a few years they would differ profoundly on issues of political change.[3]

GANG OF FOUR TRIAL AND 'HISTORICAL RESOLUTION' (1980–1)

The trial of ten of the surviving Cultural Revolution radicals, aggregated as the 'Lin Biao and Jiang Qing counter-revolutionary clique' but always known in the West as the Gang of Four, began on 20 November 1980. On 25 January 1981 a Special Court under the jurisdiction of the Supreme People's Court finally brought forward its judgments. Jiang Qing and Zhang Chunqiao were sentenced to death with a reprieve of two years (usually seen as the equivalent of a life sentence without parole) and Wang Hongwen and Yao Wenyuan, the other two members of the 'Gang of Four', were sentenced to life imprisonment. Others who had been associated with them or with Lin Biao were sentenced to various long terms of imprisonment.

Deng Xiaoping was not directly involved in the legal process, although it must be assumed that the conduct of the trial and the verdicts met with his approval. The remnants of the opposition to Deng's policies were now either serving lengthy prison sentences or were dead. Hua Guofeng was powerless and isolated. Although many supporters of Mao's policies and rhetoric remained the rank and file of the Party, the way ahead for Deng's reforms was almost clear.

The power struggle with Hua was virtually over, but a resolution of the ideological conflict behind it was necessary to mollify the Party faithful and provide political cover for the reforms. This was achieved through the 'Resolution on certain questions on the history of our party since the founding of the People's Republic of China', usually abbreviated in Chinese as the Historical Resolution (*lishi jueyi*), which was approved by the Sixth Plenum of the Eleventh Central Committee when it met in Beijing from 27 to 29 June 1981. Unlike Mao Zedong, Deng had never sought to establish himself as a major Marxist theoretician and he avoided ideological debates wherever possible. In the case of the Historical Resolution, however, he took a close interest from the outset, produced a 'clear draft' of what he expected to see in it and on a number of occasions offered 'exhaustive guidance' (*xiangjin zhidao*) on its structure and contents.

The decision to draw up the Historical Resolution had been made after the historic Third Plenum and was seen as a high priority which would 'unify the thinking of the whole party, nation and people' (*shi quan dang quan guo quan renmin tongyi sixiang*). In essence its function was to create a narrative of the history of the Chinese Communist Party since the foundation of the People's Republic of China in 1949. This narrative, constructed according to the perspective of Deng and his supporters, would explain what had happened, why it had been like that and what this meant for the future of the Party. The most cynical interpretation is that people were to be told what to remember and how to forget all the interpretations that they had previously been given. Deng insisted that this document should be drawn up as quickly as possible, arguing that it was expected both at home and abroad as a sign that China was genuinely unified and looking towards a new common future. Under the direct supervision of Deng Xiaoping and Hu Yaobang, a small committee reporting to the Politburo and the Secretariat began to produce early versions of the document in November 1979.

From the outset Deng laid down three guiding principles:

1. Mao Zedong's status in history must be established and Mao Zedong Thought must be upheld and developed.
2. Major issues in the 30 years since 1949 should be analysed according to the principle of 'seek truth from facts', to establish which are correct and which erroneous, including a fair evaluation of the merits and faults of responsible comrades.
3. This resolution must make a fundamental summary (*jiben zongjie*) of the past.

Deng insisted that these guiding principles were inextricably linked and a resolution that did not incorporate all of them would not be effective and would therefore be unacceptable. The first on Mao and his thought was the core, the second the foundation, and the third the objective. Once the resolution had finally been approved, Deng argued, there would be clarity and unanimity among the people of China when they discussed these great historical issues. Deng paid special attention to the structure of the document, setting out exactly how it should be written and how much space should be given to specific topics. He insisted that, although it should conclude that the CCP was of great importance, it should encourage everyone to confront their errors and redress them. Naturally the drafting committee followed Deng's suggestions and he actively sought comments from a number of individuals before it was revised and improved to his satisfaction. Deng implemented some of these suggestions, especially Chen Yun's proposal that the Party's history before 1949 should also be covered.

The Historical Resolution is a long and complex document written in bureaucratic Marxist language, but it undoubtedly has the imprimatur of Deng Xiaoping. He may have been no theoretician but his propaganda work in the 1930s, and his time as general secretary in the 1950s, had taught him the importance of producing the right document at the right time. It is simultaneously an apologia, a defence of Deng's position, and an attempt to reclaim the fundamental values and policies that the CCP had espoused in the early 1950s – the period known as New Democracy – but from which it had subsequently strayed so far.

The document that Deng had so carefully managed through the drafting committee was naturally approved unanimously at the Sixth Plenum of the Eleventh Central Committee at the end of June 1981, and the official history of the first 30 years of the People's Republic was preserved in political aspic, at least for a time. The more concrete decisions made by this full session of the Central Committee were to do with personnel. Hua Guofeng's resignation from his only remaining positions as chairman of the CCP Central Committee and Central Military Commission was accepted, in the light of his 'left deviationist mistakes': he was no longer Chairman Hua. When a new Central Committee leadership was elected, Hu Yaobang was appointed chairman, and both Zhao Ziyang (a close supporter of Deng's) and Hua Guofeng (his long-standing opponent) were named as deputy chairman – a promotion for Hu and a humiliating demotion for Hua. Hua was also allowed to remain on the Standing Committee of the Politburo with Hu Yaobang, Zhao Ziyang, Ye Jianying, Deng Xiaoping, Li Xiannian and Chen Yun, but he was completely outnumbered. Deng's only formal position other than on the Standing Committee was as chairman of the Central Military Commission: that was a powerful role normally held by the party chairman and it is interesting that Deng continued to hold the position. Another victim of Mao Zedong's paranoia, Xi Zhongxun, was brought into the Secretariat during this round of appointments: his son, Xi Jinping, would become chairman of the CCP and president of China in 2013.

DENG'S ANALYSIS OF CHINESE HISTORY AFTER 1949

The link with Mao Zedong was not, and could not be, completely broken. It was the ideological lifeline (still symbolised by Hua Guofeng lurking in the Standing Committee) that Deng needed to provide cover for his economic reforms; reforms that were the antithesis of Mao's policies. It was only by preserving Mao's 'historical status' (*lishi diwei*) that Maoist policies could be reversed with the minimum of opposition. To this end it was necessary to arrive at a correct and appropriate conclusion on Mao's positive contributions to China's development and his errors, avoiding both the 'rightist' analysis of throwing the baby out with the bathwater and concluding that everything Mao did was wrong; and the 'leftist' analysis that refused to countenance any serious criticism at all.

Deng insisted that the Chinese people needed a thorough understanding of the different periods of its history since 1949. The first seven years of the PRC, from 1949 to roughly 1956, he argued, were accepted by all as having been broadly successful. This was the period of the first Five-Year Plan; it was also a time of harsh campaigns to suppress any opposition movements, but Deng tended to think of success only or at least primarily in economic terms. The 'socialist transformation' of China was proceeding according to plan, essentially along Soviet lines. There were, he acknowledged, some problems and errors, the major political issue being the purge of Gao Gang and Rao Shushi, whose crime he stated baldly was to try to overthrow Liu Shaoqi (his mentor and colleague) by underhand means: for that reason the struggle against them was correct.

The following period, the ten years before the Cultural Revolution, was also, Deng believed, basically sound, although there were twists and turns and some major errors – the Anti-Rightist Campaign (1957), the Great Leap Forward (1958) and the Lushan Plenum (1959) – which were all criticised as errors in the Historical Resolution. Deng still considered the Anti-Rightist Campaign to have been basically correct: it was necessary at that time to counter those who were 'opposed to socialism and still had bourgeois ideas' as they constituted a powerful force. 'If there had not been a counter-attack progress would not have been possible.' He did, however, concede that there had been errors in the way that its scope had been extended. In his comments in 1982 he appears to make a distinction between the ideological trend that should be attacked and the attacks on individuals which caused so much damage to the careers and lives of so many educated Chinese. It is not at all clear that he made these distinctions at the time of these campaigns.

Deng's criticisms of the next period, the Cultural Revolution which began in 1966, were unsurprisingly more robust and were made with fewer qualifications. The mistakes of the Cultural Revolution were, in his view, far more serious than anything in the previous 17 years. The errors were far more comprehensive and the effects more serious, lasting as they had into the 1980s. Even then he argued that during the Cultural Revolution there had been positive features. A move against the Central Cultural Revolution Group that was called at the time the 'February Counter Current' of early 1967 was, he argued, a positive struggle against Lin Biao and the Gang of Four. 'In spite of the conflict', he argued, China's international standing increased during this period because of the successes of work that was being done in foreign relations.' This is of course a reference to Zhou Enlai's extraordinary performance in maintaining control of the Foreign Ministry and developing diplomatic relations, at least from 1971 onwards, in spite of the political and social chaos that swept the country. It had been argued that the Chinese Communist Party ceased to function during the Cultural Revolution or, at the very least, that meetings held in its name were illegal. Deng rejected this argument and pointed to the Eighth Plenum of the Twelfth Central Committee (13–31 October 1968) and the Ninth Party Congress (1–24 April 1969) as legitimate Party meetings, even though these were meetings at which he was heavily criticised. He was not prepared to acknowledge that there had been a political hiatus: it was essential to demonstrate the continuity of the CCP's rule, however erroneous some of its policies might have been, to guarantee its present and future legitimacy.

The difficult issue of the role of the military during the Cultural Revolution was summed up in the slogan that was then in vogue – 'three supports and two militarys' (*sanzhi liangjun* – support industry, support agriculture, support the broad masses of the left; military control and political and military training). Deng said that support for the military had been laid on too thickly (*dai gao maozi*) to flatter the army. It had been necessary for the army to intervene during the Cultural Revolution or the situation would have got out of hand (*weichi jumian*). However, the policy also damaged the prestige of the PLA and cost it much trust and popular support.

Finally, when considering the two years since the 'smashing of the Gang of Four', it was necessary to criticise the 'two whatevers' attitude and point the finger at Hua Guofeng who was primarily responsible for this. Hua had been China's main leader (*zhuyao lingdao*) so even people who had serious doubts were reluctant to criticise his ideas. People who had previously supported Lin Biao or Jiang Qing were now supporting Hua and it was necessary for the good of the whole Party and the whole nation to point out Hua's errors.

Deng emerges from these accounts as someone who did not base his judgements on personal grievances, even though in many cases he had every reason to feel aggrieved. His judgement on the historical periods of China since 1949 is balanced and interesting and he forces us to consider whether even during the Cultural Revolution, which almost everyone in China now rejects completely, there were positive developments. His attitude towards the 1950s is positive: he refuses to condemn out of hand the repressive Anti-Rightist Campaign although he does criticise its excesses and, when he was in a position to do so, he remedied many of the injustices that had been done to individuals during that campaign.[4]

ELDERS AND CENTRAL ADVISORY COMMISSION

Just as the traditional Chinese year is marked out by festivals in the agricultural calendar, so is the life of the People's Republic inevitably measured out in meetings, congresses and conferences. The Twelfth National Congress of the Chinese Communist Party was held in Beijing from 1 to 11 September 1982. In his opening speech Deng Xiaoping harked back to the Seventh and Eighth Party Congresses to compare them with the current state of the Party. The Seventh Congress in 1945 marked the beginning of the CCP's push for victory against the Guomindang. The Eighth Congress in 1956 was the last one with which Deng could identify: 'its line was correct.' This correct line did not last long because soon afterwards 'we suffered serious setbacks although we also achieved many successes in socialist construction'. In trying to correct the mistakes that had been made from 1957 onwards, Deng – in the 1980s – was to a large extent trying to re-create the working style of the early 1950s with a broad-based coalition and a Constitution, a period that reformers within the CCP still regard with nostalgia.

By the 1980s China was in uncharted waters. The Soviet model could no longer be followed: after border clashes between Russian and Chinese forces in 1969 and the flight of Lin Biao in 1971, the USSR and China had become estranged and were potential enemies rather than allies. Although Deng could not know it in 1982, Mikhail Gorbachev's reforms were on the horizon with *perestroika* (reconstruction, of which Deng would approve) and *glasnost* (openness, about which Deng would be less enthusiastic). There was less than a decade left before the USSR would collapse. It was not to the USSR that Deng turned during his drive for reform but to the capitalist world, unthinkable in the 1950s. The combination of nostalgia for bureaucratic 1950s Party life and Western-style capitalist reform was incongruous, fraught with conflict and perilous. By the time of Deng's speech to the Twelfth Congress, China's 'socialist modernisation' (*shehuizhuyi xiandaihua*) had become 'socialism with Chinese characteristics' (*you Zhongguo tese de shehuizhuyi*) and, to the consternation of many CCP members, it soon began to resemble Western capitalism. It was later termed a socialist market economy (*shehuizhuyi shichang jingji*) but, whatever name was used, it was completely alien to the old guard of the CCP.

Behind the scenes Deng consulted a small group of the 'older generation of revolutionaries', whose outlook was conservative and cautious, and who maintained constant vigilance for any reforms that they considered were going too far. The symbol of this older generation was an unofficial cabal known as the Eight Elders (*ba da yuanlao*), also irreverently known as the Eight Immortals (*ba xian*) after the great sages of the Daoist tradition. These Elders were Deng Xiaoping, Chen Yun, Li Xiannian, Peng Zhen, Yang Shangkun, Bo Yibo (father of Bo Xilai who was disgraced in 2012), Wang Zhen and Song Renqiong. In addition to this small elite group, there were many senior members of the Communist Party and the PLA in the provinces whose entire lives had been devoted to the policies of Mao and who were not easily persuaded that the new-fangled ideas coming from Beijing were necessarily an improvement. To many of the reformers the Elders represented the dead hand of history, a conservative obstacle that frustrated enthusiastic supporters of economic progress. However, paradoxically, they also served to protect the economic reforms from other conservatives, many of whom remained nostalgic for the quasi-military and bureaucratic organisations of the Mao era.

At the CCP congress in September 1982, not only was a new Central Committee (*zhongyang weiyuanhui*) elected, as was the normal practice, but a new Communist Party committee was created. This was the Central Advisory Commission (*zhongyang guwen weiyuanhui*, CAC) which operated until 1992. The Chinese term (*weiyuanhui*) is generally translated as 'committee' but, beginning in the 1980s, official translations into English began to use 'commission' for some of these bodies, although not for the Central Committee, presumably because that term had historical links with Lenin's Communist Party.

The Elders and the membership of the Central Advisory Commission (CAC) were not identical although there was some overlap. The CAC was established by Deng, he was named its chairman and he then entrusted its operation to one of his closest allies, Bo Yibo, the senior of the deputy chairmen, who was indeed one of the Elders. Speaking at the first full session of what he described as a 'transitional organisation' that would probably last for ten, or at most 15 years, Deng outlined the purpose of the CAC:

> The Central Advisory Commission is something new. Established in the light of the circumstances of the Communist Party of China, it is an organisational form that will enable new cadres to succeed the old ones in the central leading organs of the Party. The purpose of establishing this commission is to lower the average age of the members of the Central Committee and at the same time to make it possible for some elderly comrades who have retired from the forefront of affairs to play a certain role.

The CAC was an interim body but it was unprecedented in the history of the CCP. The creation of the CAC was on one level a formal device to enable older members of central bodies to be 'kicked upstairs', in an analogy with the more cynical interpretation of membership of the House of Lords in the parliamentary system of the United Kingdom. If they were offered a title and a role they might be more willing to make way for the younger generation. Deng had also raised at various meetings the problem, as he saw it, that the leadership of the CCP was ageing and that the number of senior officials who had not been through the war and revolution would soon outnumber his own generation who had.

Members of the CAC would have access to the Central Committee and could also attend plenary sessions of the committee as observers. They would have considerable influence, if only to caution, advise and possibly obstruct. Deng envisaged that the vice-chairmen of the CAC (Bo Yibo, Xu Shiyou, Tan Zhenlin and Li Weihan) and members of its Standing Committee would have the same status as members of the Politburo, but he insisted that the CAC should advise; they should not 'hinder the work of the Central Committee' or abuse their prestige and status to interfere with it or with lower-level organisations. This might be a counsel of perfection but it established parameters for good intentions and best practice.

Another body, the Central Commission for Discipline Inspection (*zhongyang jilü jiancha weiyuanhui*, CCDI) was reconstituted after the Third Plenum in December 1978. It was legitimised by the Twelfth Party Congress and headed by Chen Yun, another elder who was an aide of Deng's but sceptical about his reforms. The CCDI had existed before the Cultural Revolution, when it was known as the Central Control Commission, but had fallen into disuse. It had, in the words of Kenneth Lieberthal, 'the task of ferreting out violations of rules in the Party'.[5] It acted as an internal policing and security body which could be used either to deal with breaches of party discipline or for excluding those whose political views or activities were considered undesirable. The scope of its activities can be seen in a Central Committee Circular of 30 December 1982 which ordered the removal of individuals in 'leading bodies' or 'key posts' who remained in their jobs or were being promoted in spite of their association with supporters of Jiang Qing, or their undesirable behaviour. The Central Commission for Discipline Inspection remains in existence and it continues to exercise considerable power over Party officials under Wang Qishan, a member of the Politburo Standing Committee since 2012.

In 1982 the post of deputy chairman of the Central Committee was abolished: this had been held by Hua Guofeng, who remained an ordinary member of the Central Committee, a mere back-bencher, a position he held until 2002. Hua was not purged, charged with any political offences or imprisoned – he was simply allowed to sink into political oblivion. On 4 December 1982 the Fifth Session of the National People's Congress that sat from 26 November to 10 December approved the sixth Five-Year Plan for economic and social development and ratified a new Constitution. This was Deng's Constitution: it was the fourth Constitution of the PRC, superseding those of 1954, 1975 and 1978 and it remains in force, although with some revisions. Deng Xiaoping had finally triumphed over Hua Guofeng.[6]

HU YAOBANG AND ZHAO ZIYANG

Hu Yaobang and Zhao Ziyang were not only supporters of Deng's economic reforms but were also relatively open-minded and tolerant on political and social issues. They were Deng Xiaoping's protégées and had been groomed to succeed him: Deng often referred to them as his left and right hands. Throughout the decade they were at the head of either the Communist Party (as general secretary) or (as premier) of the government, which is subservient to the Party. Zhao held both positions. Their rise and subsequent fall, and the attitudes of those who succeeded them, illustrate the complexities of often irreconcilable relationships at the highest level of Chinese politics in the Deng era.

They were only able to operate independently to a limited extent as Deng Xiaoping, the Elders and the Central Advisory Commission restricted their room for manoeuvre. Openly published sources are, to say the least, reticent on such matters and Deng's Chinese biographers prefer to concentrate on his meetings with foreign dignitaries in this period. These well-publicised encounters played an important role in enhancing China's international profile and status, but they reveal little about how the country was governed or what part Deng played in its governance. This is unfortunate because the first serious attempt to introduce political reforms, including proposals for the separation of the Party from the state, were made during this period and Hu and Zhao were in turn both removed from the political leadership for their pains. The decade ended with the Democracy Movement and its brutal suppression in Tian'anmen Square by the military on 4 June 1989. It is possible to infer what Deng's role was in this failed experiment for democracy but it is more difficult to adduce clear evidence of his direct involvement.

Hu Yaobang became chairman of the Chinese Communist Party in 1981, replacing Hua Guofeng. When the Party chairmanship was abolished to give a clear signal of a complete break with the Mao period after the Twelfth Congress in 1982, Hu served as its general secretary. He was obliged to resign on 15 January 1987 after criticisms of his leniency towards pro-democracy demonstrators and his willingness to build closer ties with Japan.

Zhao Ziyang, who had been Premier since 10 September 1980, replaced Hu as general secretary on 1 November 1987. Zhao also continued as Premier until 24 November 1987 when he was succeeded by the more conservative Li Peng. Zhao served as general secretary until 23 June 1989, when he was forced to stand down in the wake of the military suppression of the Democracy Movement in Beijing on 4 June and was replaced by Jiang Zemin, who had been secretary of the Communist Party Committee in Shanghai. After 1989 Zhao was effectively under house arrest for the remainder of his life.

TWIN PEAKS AND TWO POLES: POLITICAL CONFLICT IN THE 1980s

Yang Jisheng is best known for *Mubei* (*Tombstone*), his masterly treatment of the famine that followed the 1958 Great Leap Forward. As a journalist, working for the official Xinhua News Agency from 1966 to 2001, he was also a close – and increasingly sceptical – observer of the struggles within the Party and the government during the early years of Deng's reforms. Yang has analysed these years in terms of 'twin peak politics and the clash of two poles' (*shuangfeng zhengzhi he liangdian pengzhuang*), an analogy that reflects both an early exposure to Marxist dialectics and a nod in the direction of the history of guerrilla warfare. The 'twin peaks and the two poles' are the political redoubts and opposing points of view of the forces of Deng Xiaoping on the one hand and, on the other, Chen Yun, his one-time supporter who became an important political critic in the 1980s. This is reminiscent of the 'struggle between the two lines' of the 1950s and 1960s, with Mao Zedong on one side and Liu Shaoqi and Deng Xiaoping on the other. Like that earlier political divide, it was blurred rather than clear cut and, because it has never been possible to declare openly the existence of factions inside the CCP, the struggle had to be fought out in a disorderly manner without a formal framework.

Deng and Chen had very different ideas on the way to implement economic reforms and often found it difficult to communicate with each other. Deng's tactic on some of these occasions was to fail to convene a meeting of the Politburo Standing Committee, on the grounds that there was no point as they would not be able to reach agreement. Hu Yaobang claimed that the Standing Committee did not meet very often precisely for that reason. Instead Deng approached Hu or Zhao Ziyang directly with instructions, leaving Chen with no opportunity for input. Chen then had to instruct his coterie to take up issues with Deng's subordinates, which created considerable conflict. Deng did not want open conflict with Chen, as that might have impeded the reforms. Chen was not an unpleasant or difficult individual: on the contrary he had the reputation of being a mild and flexible politician who often did not like the way things were going but was deprived of any way of saying so. There is no evidence that he had any plan to replace Deng, but he did want his opinions to be taken into consideration. The result was a personal awkwardness, not on the same level as Deng's conflict with Jiang Qing, but one which made the implementation of policies more difficult. Not only were the general public kept in the dark about these disagreements, even those working on economic policy in the central leadership were confused and frequently found themselves in a difficult and dangerous position, trying to determine which policy statements from the centre were authoritative.

Yang has argued that the years of the late 1970s and the 1980s follow a consistent pattern: an even-numbered year of positive action on reform was followed by an odd-numbered year dominated by negative reaction. Although this approach is somewhat mechanistic it does help to illuminate the political swings between reform and reaction caused by the internal conflicts of this period.[7]

1976: Gang of Four arrested

1977: 'Two whatevers' slogan created

1978: Third Plenum approves economic reforms; Xidan Democracy Wall

1979: 'Four basic principles' speech given to appease conservatives; Democracy Wall suppressed

1980: Hu Yaobang becomes general secretary of CCP Central Committee; Deng Xiaoping speech 'On the reform of the system of party and state leadership' is published; reform-minded intellectuals emerge; *Guangming Daily*, the preferred newspaper of the intelligentsia, publishes articles by liberals (*ziyoupai renshi*)

1981: Chen Yun counter-attacks against 'bourgeois liberalisation'

1982: Twelfth Party Conference; 'whatever' faction loses posts to reformers; relaxed political atmosphere; deputy editor of *Peoples' Daily* publishes articles on 'socialist alienation' (*shehuizhuyi yihua*) and 'abstract humanism' (*chouxiang de rendaozhuyi*), previously forbidden ideas

1983: 'Theory of alienation' attacked in campaign against 'spiritual pollution'. Economist Liu Guoguan's proposal of 'guiding plan' (rather than mandatory Five-Year Plan) criticised

1984: Deng Xiaoping inspects the Special Economic Zones of Shenzhen and Zhuhai; Central Committee and the State Council agree to open 14 coastal cities; Third Plenary Session of the Twelfth Central Committee discusses 'planned commodity economy'

1985: Chen Yun demands determined struggle against 'mistakes counter to communist ideals and ethics'; CCP National Congress, Chen emphasises need to maintain a planned economy

1986: Deng speech on political reform; 'high tide' of reform demands by CCP 'liberal faction' (*ziyoupai*); December demonstrations demand political reform

1987: Hu Yaobang, general secretary of the CCP, falls from grace (*luoma*); 'leftists' mount new 'restoration of order' (*bo luan fan zheng*); liberal party members expelled

1988: Fang Lizhi criticises government's aggressive tone; Beijing liberals organise research associations, discussion groups and 'salons' criticising government and political system; 'democracy movement' emerges

1989: Martial law declared; 'Democracy movement' suppressed on 4 June; Zhao Ziyang steps down as CCP general secretary; 'leftist' current takes over; this state of affairs persists until Deng Xiaoping's Southern Tour in 1992; suppressing demonstrations was given the same level of priority as economic construction.

It is easy to pick holes in Yang's cyclical analysis and point to pro-reform trends in odd numbered years and vice versa, but as a broad-brush depiction of the ebb and flow of the political battle in the 1980s it works well enough. Two important points emerge from this. Firstly, Deng Xiaoping had to negotiate and compromise constantly with powerful political opponents to ensure that his policy priorities were implemented. Secondly, the 1980s are often presented as a struggle over political reform and demands for greater democracy. While this is true it is not the whole truth. There was also a battle for economic reform. Chen Yun had been a supporter of Deng and was one of the senior Party people who demanded Deng's rehabilitation after the death of Mao Zedong. When Deng did return to power, Chen Yun chaired the newly created Economic and Financial Commission, with Li Xiannian as his deputy, and should be credited with some of the successes of the reform programme, as he was responsible for all the detailed planning. Chen Yun was appointed chair of the Central Advisory Commission by Deng in 1982 but his initial enthusiastic support for the economic reforms changed as a result of some of the concomitant social and intellectual changes, of which he vigorously disapproved. Zhao Ziyang, who was close to Deng, effectively replaced Chen as the lead in economic policy, but Chen was still in a position to criticise and obstruct.

BOURGEOIS LIBERALISATION

Chen Yun had complained about what he saw as creeping 'bourgeois liberalisation' (*zichanjieji ziyouhua*) as early as 1981. Bourgeois liberalisation was the catch-all phrase for new ideas and trends – specifically those influenced by the capitalist world (the West and Japan) – of which the conservatives in the CCP, often described as 'leftists', deeply disapproved. It was the subject of a well-publicised campaign in 1987 but was the watchword of the conservatives throughout the 1980s and Hu Qiaomu and Deng Liqun were the main protagonists.

In a study of ideological movements in China since 1949, Li Honglin identifies the initial phase of the movement against bourgeois liberalisation with observations made by Chen Yun on the rise of the Solidarity trades union in Poland in 1980, and Hu Qiaomu's suppression of a reincarnation of the pre-war journal *Life* (*Shenghuo*) later the same year. The second phase was from 1982 to 1984, the third from 1985 to 1987, and the fourth from 1987 to 1991. The movement was ostensibly aimed at social and cultural phenomena which the conservatives considered inimical to traditional communist values and everything or anything could be included. However, it also affected the progress of the economic reforms because, either explicitly or implicitly, the reforms were deemed to be responsible for all new and unfamiliar fashions and behaviour (especially among the young). The campaign against bourgeois liberalisation was not just a series of empty slogans: it informed the public that there was powerful opposition to Deng and the reforms within the Chinese Communist Party and inhibited discussion of reform, especially political reform. It was partly responsible for the downfall of Hu Yaobang in 1987 and Zhao Ziyang in 1989.

Between the suppression of the Democracy Movement in June 1989 and 1991, Yang Jisheng's rule of alternating years of reform and reaction is not as helpful. There were three consecutive years of a 'leftist counter-offensive' (*zuopai fangong*), which means a conservative reaction to the reforms, and this reaction was not reversed until Deng Xiaoping's Southern Tour of 1992 finally established his objective of a socialist market economy (*shehuizhuyi shichang jingji*), the term that remains in force to describe China's booming industrial and commercial expansion.[8]

TIAN'ANMEN SQUARE (4 JUNE 1989)

One of the most traumatic and controversial episodes of China's modern history was the military intervention on the night of 3–4 June 1989 that brought to an end the demonstrations in Tian'anmen Square and crushed the Democracy Movement. The use of the military to suppress peaceful protests and the carnage that ensued have had a profound and mainly negative impact on Deng Xiaoping's reputation both within and outside China. There are conflicting accounts of what happened and estimates of how many demonstrators were killed and injured by the PLA range from a few hundred to thousands. Many were killed and injured in Tian'anmen Square but the greatest number of casualties probably occurred as troops marched from the west of the capital through Muxidi towards the square, and then southwards away from it into the Qianmen district. There is also confusion about who gave the orders in the military and precisely what political authorisation was given for the military action. At the time the blame for the ultimate political decision to authorise an attack on unarmed civilians was laid at the feet of two people: Li Peng, the premier, and Deng Xiaoping, who, it was assumed, had ultimate authority within the political leadership, as 'paramount leader'. This term has never had any official standing in China but it has become widely used and has led people to believe that Deng had become the ultimate authority and the final arbiter of political decisions, which is far from the case. After the event more people wished to distance themselves from the attack than were willing to take responsibility and that is reflected in the confusing and inconsistent evidence that is offered in published accounts of the tragedy.

The protests of 1989 were a continuation of the nationwide upsurge of student demonstrations in 1986 that resulted in the dismissal of Hu Yaobang, the protégé of Deng Xiaoping, who wanted to go further with political reform than his mentor. Political discussion groups and salons continued to demand greater freedoms and on 6 January 1989, the distinguished astrophysicist and political activist, Fang Lizhi, sent an open letter to Deng Xiaoping asking for an amnesty for all China's political prisoners. Fang highlighted the case of Wei Jingsheng, the democracy activist who had been sentenced to 15 years in prison in 1979; for his pains Fang was prevented from attending a reception organised by the American President George Bush (Senior). Fang's open letter attracted widespread popular support, but he was expelled from the Communist Party in 1987, sought asylum in the US Embassy in Beijing on 5 June 1989, and subsequently went into exile in the United States, where he died on 6 April 2012.

Hu Yaobang died on 15 April 1989 from natural causes, but there were persistent rumours that his fatal heart attack was brought on while he was arguing the case for reform with members of the Politburo. Students paid tribute to him in Tian'anmen Square and by 20 April thousands had gathered outside the gates of the secure CCP headquarters in Zhongnanhai. Police were deployed to disperse the demonstrators and several were injured. A hunger strike began and other Beijing residents began to participate. By mid-May, there were demands for the dismissal of Premier Li Peng and Deng Xiaoping who were identified by the demonstrators as the main obstacles to political reform.

The crisis came to a head on 15 May during the visit to Beijing of Mikhail Gorbachev, the general secretary of the Communist Party of the Soviet Union and chairman of the Supreme Soviet. Gorbachev met Deng Xiaoping, Li Peng and other senior Chinese leaders and the two governments issued a communiqué proclaiming the resumption of normal diplomatic relations, but what should have been the announcement of a triumphant breakthrough, a renewal of political relations that had been broken off in the early 1960s, was completely overshadowed by the turmoil on the streets of Beijing.

The Politburo was divided on how to respond and this division continues to be reflected in subsequent Chinese accounts of the crisis. Zhao Ziyang, general secretary of the CCP, argued for a peaceful resolution but he was sidelined after 17 May and eventually dismissed from his Party and government posts. On 20 May, Li Peng, the premier and acting as the sole government authority, issued an Order of the State Council declaring martial law in Beijing. Units of the PLA moved into Beijing during the night of 3–4 June. Official figures given later by the Chinese government claimed that 200 civilians had been killed, including 36 students, and that over 3,000 had been injured. Independent sources estimate the numbers to be far higher. The formal removal of Zhao Ziyang from his post of general secretary and from the Politburo and its Standing Committee was announced at the Fourth Plenary Meeting of the Thirteenth Central Committee, which convened in Beijing from 23 to 24 June. Li Peng introduced a 'Report on Comrade Zhao Ziyang's mistakes in the Anti-Party, Anti-Socialism Turmoil' which severely criticised the former general secretary for taking the side of the demonstrators and splitting the CCP. Zhao was not allowed to defend himself and that report marked the end of his political career – he was put under house arrest until his death in 2004. Zhao's successor as general secretary of the party was Jiang Zemin, formerly head of the CCP in Shanghai, where he had dealt with pro-democracy demonstrations without resorting to violence.

Zhao Ziyang clearly resisted the use of force against the student and citizen demonstrators and was dismissed for his pains. There is no doubt that Li Peng issued the formal instructions declaring martial law which permitted the military to suppress the movement. Deng Xiaoping's role is much less clear. He was not the head of the government: that was Premier Li Peng. He was not the general secretary of the Party which theoretically outranks the premier: that was Zhao Ziyang, but he had effectively been ousted on 17 May and Jiang Zemin did not take up the post until 24 June so there was no-one actively operating in that role. Deng's only formal position was as chairman of the Party's Central Military Commission.

This is a position that notionally carries considerable weight, but it is usually held concurrently by the chairman of the Chinese Communist Party; in that case the question of a conflict of authority would not normally arise and it is usually assumed that under those circumstances the authority is derived from the chairmanship of the party rather than the military commission. Deng was not and never had been the chairman of the Chinese Communist Party. The situation is further complicated by the fact that, in addition to the CCP Central Military Commission, there is also a PRC Central Military Commission, although the two normally worked and met as one body, chaired by Deng.

The key issue that has to be addressed is whether Deng's role with the Central Military Commission was a real one with genuine authority, or merely a nominal and honorary position to acknowledge his seniority. Deng was in his mid-eighties and had retired from most of his official posts. He was not involved in day-to-day decision making, either for the Party or for the government, although he was often consulted either as an individual or through the Central Advisory Commission. Li Peng was aged 60: he had been premier for almost two years by 4 June 1989 and he remained in that post until 1998. Li had a reputation as a conservative and had been a determined opponent of Zhao Ziyang's proposals for more market reforms, believing that they would undermine the authority of the CCP.

Deng Xiaoping's attitude to the demonstrators was ambiguous. In an article published in *People's Daily* on 26 April 1989, before the crackdown, he appears to criticise them for inciting 'anti-party and anti-socialist turmoil', but Zhao Ziyang insisted that these remarks were taken from a private conversation with Li Peng and that they were published without Deng's authorisation. 'Deng was not happy about how Li Peng had made his remarks public. Deng's children were also displeased that Deng had been put in the position of being in direct confrontation with the public.' Zhao recounts how on 19 April, just before leaving for an official visit to North Korea, he had visited Deng. He insists that during that meeting Deng agreed with him that the demonstrations should be handled carefully and that, although criminal acts should be prosecuted, 'bloodshed must be avoided at all costs'.

Li Peng called a meeting of the Politburo Standing Committee, which he was entitled to chair during Zhao's absence in North Korea. At this meeting, Li Ximing, the secretary of the Beijing Party Committee and Chen Xitong, the mayor, exaggerated the militancy of the demonstrators and the extent of their criticism of Deng. Premier Li Peng and President Yang Shangkun went to see Deng on 25 April to report on the outcome of that meeting and to try to persuade him to agree to a swift solution to the problem. Both Li Peng and the Beijing Communist Party Committee had decided that they required Deng's imprimatur before authorising military intervention.

A crucial decision to impose martial law (but not to send in the troops to clear the square) was made at a meeting between Li Peng and Deng at Deng's home on 17 May. 'Don't repeat this as you did before', Deng is said to have insisted, 'Don't say that it was I who made the decision to impose martial law'. Li Peng agreed that he would not: Deng appears to have been reluctant, rather than enthusiastic, about the prospect of using the military in the square.

If Deng had not been persuaded to give his approval to the imposition of marital law it is conceivable, although not certain, that the massacre might never have taken place. Deng Xiaoping was elderly, although age alone should not be considered a defence and he is credited with the political success of the Southern Tour which took place almost three years later. However, he was probably not in possession of all the necessary information and, in the absence of Zhao Ziyang, was manipulated by Li Peng, Yang Shangkun, Li Ximing and Chen Xitong. Deng was an old military man who had not hesitated to take life-and-death decisions during wartime, but his track record in power speaks of a man who valued consensus, rather than unnecessary conflict, and who certainly did not want a repetition of the violence and persecution of the Cultural Revolution years. He cannot be absolved of blame for the massacre; he should have been better informed and may have been unwise. However, the responsibility for the military intervention and the deaths lies primarily with his duplicitous and manipulative colleagues – Li Peng and Yang Shangkun of the central government, and Li Ximing and Chen Xitong of the Beijing Communist Party Committee.

Some accounts, including those in the *Tian'anmen Papers* on which Ezra Vogel relies heavily for his own analysis of Deng's role in the massacre (although he also uses an unpublished manuscript of Li Peng's diaries), take a different view. In this alternative perspective Deng was far more positive about the need for martial law, took the lead in key meetings and should therefore take more of the blame for the subsequent massacre, even though he had issued explicit instructions that there should be no bloodshed.

The problem with this account is that the authenticity of the original documents that are translated and edited in the *Tian'anmen Papers* cannot yet be conclusively substantiated. What are offered as *bona fide* transcripts of meetings that portray Deng Xiaoping as more confrontational in his approach to the demonstrators must be treated with considerable caution. One of the most trenchant critics of the *Tian'anmen Papers*, Alfred L. Chan, is completely dismissive of the value, and even the authenticity, of the documents:

> Authentic Chinese internal documents matter greatly as historical records that illuminate our understanding of Chinese politics. Yet careful scrutiny shows that the Chinese book version of the *Tian'anmen Papers* is part fiction and part documentary history based on open and semi-open sources and document collections. The alleged transcripts of top-level meetings are basically stitched together ex post facto (even by the admission of the editors) and then presented as secret documents. Furthermore, the English translation is a heavily retouched version of the Chinese with differences in claims of authenticity, translation, citation and style. There is little evidence that any real secret documents are in the hands of the Chinese author, and even if they were, the two books under consideration are really secondary sources, steps removed from the originals. The editors strongly vouch for the authenticity of these two books, but their efforts are inadequate and unconvincing.

While most historians would not necessarily go as far as Chan, doubts about the authenticity and reliability of the documents remain and even the editors have accepted that they were producing the papers in circumstances of considerable difficulty. The *Tian'anmen Papers* cannot therefore be taken as the definitive and authoritative account of the decision-making process within the CCP elite in the weeks before 4 June 1989.

In the aftermath of the disastrous failure of the attempt to resolve the Tian'anmen crisis by the use of martial law and military intervention, it is not surprising that the prime movers, Li Peng and Yang Shangkun, and their political supporters wished to spread the responsibility and invoke the authority of Deng Xiaoping. Equally it must be conceded that those with great respect for Deng's reputation prefer to follow Zhao Ziyang and continue to distance Deng from the final decision to occupy Tian'anmen Square and the carnage that followed.[9]

RESIGNATION FROM CENTRAL MILITARY COMMISSION

Deng Xiaoping was almost 85 years old when the military moved into Tian'anmen Square in June 1989 and nearly 88 when he embarked on his Southern Tour in the spring of 1992; he would live to the age of 92. He had not been involved in day-to-day political matters for many years, although he was often consulted and his suggestions were respected if not always followed. Organised opposition to his reforms had reduced and, after the passing of Chen Yun in 1995, the focus of the Party and the government had moved from ideological disputes and concerns over demonstrations and instability to the development of the economy, Deng's overriding priority.

The *Selected Works of Deng Xiaoping* (1938–65) was published on 20 August 1989. It is a collection of 39 articles and speeches from before the Cultural Revolution and its contents are dull and unenlightening. This is not entirely surprising: Deng's actions made him such an important figure, not his writings. He was a master of the pertinent and effective bureaucratic document but by no means a great writer or an original or compelling political thinker, even by the standards of modern Chinese Marxism.

Deng attended a mass rally in Tian'anmen Square on 1 October 1989 to celebrate National Day – the fortieth anniversary of the founding of the People's Republic – which could hardly have been celebrated in unhappier circumstances. His name does not appear on the official list of those who celebrated the anniversary in the Great Hall of the People on 29 September, an occasion presided over by Yang Shangkun and Jiang Zemin, the replacement for Zhao Ziyang as CCP general secretary. Martial law in the capital was formally ended on 30 October when troops guarding key intersections and overpasses were removed and replaced by members of the People's Armed Police. On the surface, Beijing was returning to normal.

The Politburo met from 30 October to 3 November 1989 and was followed by the Fifth Plenum of the Thirteenth Central Committee between 6 and 9 November. Deng had written to the Politburo on 4 September requesting that he be allowed 'to resign from his post as Chairman of the Military Commission of the Central Committee', the only official position that he still held. The Central Committee approved his request:

> The session highly appraised Deng's outstanding contribution to the founding of the party and the new China. The session paid high homage to Deng for having set an example for the state leaders to stop the practice of holding their posts lifelong. It held that Deng had proceeded from the fundamental interest of the Party and the state to resign from his present post when he was still hale and hearty.[10]

Was this reference to Deng's good health intended to demonstrate that he had been fully *compus mentis* when he agreed to the imposition of martial law? This would ensure that he shared the blame for the disastrous results of the military intervention that followed. The text of the official announcement indicates as clearly as possible that the Politburo were only too ready to allow him to leave. Deng also formally resigned from the parallel PRC Central Military Commission the following year.

The new chairman of the military commission was Jiang Zemin. Yang Shangkun and Liu Huaqing were appointed first and second deputy chairmen and Yang Baibing its secretary-general. Jiang Zemin who had previously been CCP secretary in Shanghai, had not been involved in the suppression of the Tian'anmen protests; President Yang Shangkun had persuaded Deng to approve the martial law order; Admiral Liu Huaqing had been in overall command of the troops deployed to enforce martial law in Beijing; General Yang Baibing, the half-brother of Yang Shangkun, had been political commissar of the Beijing Military Region and director of the General Political Department of the PLA.

In terms of the Constitution, the Central Military Commission, from which Deng had resigned, exercised political control over the People's Liberation Army on behalf of the Central Committee, but it is often viewed as the ultimate authority because of its ability to issue orders to the military. Although the new commission had a civilian chairman with no military experience, Jiang Zemin, it was now dominated by senior military men who were implicated in the military intervention of 3–4 June. It began to look as if the gun was commanding the Party rather than, in Mao Zedong's stricture, the Party commanding the gun.

It is impossible to say whether Deng was anxious to leave the Central Military Commission because of its associations with the 4 June tragedy or whether he was persuaded to write a letter of resignation so that the military men could ensure that they had control over the commission. On 13 November Deng received a delegation of the Japan–China Economy and Trade Association in the Great Hall of the People. Many foreign businesses and governments had evacuated their staff during or after the 4 June clampdown, fearing a civil war, and the Japanese were the first foreigners to return to China and resume normal business. In his address to the trade association, Deng told the visitors 'I want to take this opportunity to bid farewell to my political career. Yours is the last official delegation I'll meet. Retirement must be a true one so that new leaders will not feel embarrassed in their work'.[11]

CHINA AND THE INTERNATIONAL SITUATION (1989–91)

For observers in the West, particularly those of a conservative outlook, developments in the international situation between 1989 and 1991 were almost entirely positive. The Berlin Wall, a hated symbol of the division of Europe, had fallen in 1989 and the Soviet Union tottered for several years and finally collapsed in 1991. As far as the United States and much of Western Europe was concerned, this was the end of the Cold War and communism had been defeated. However, for orthodox communists, including the leadership of the Chinese Communist Party, the outlook was grim. A period of industrial and political unrest in Poland and East Germany had spread to Hungary, Czechoslovakia and Romania. After the collapse of the USSR there was a great fear within the Beijing political elite that China might follow suit. This was also the hope of some reactionary observers in the West. China's leaders had been looking over their shoulders at events in Eastern Europe since well before 1989 and were determined that they should remain in power. They believed that if the power of the CCP broke down in the same way as the collapse of Soviet power, it could only end in an outbreak of chaos (*luan*) or even a return to the warlord conflicts of the 1920s. These anxieties had been exacerbated by reaction within the Party to demands made by the democracy protesters.

Some conservatives in the CCP took the opportunity to revive fears that Deng's reforms were most likely to precipitate collapse and chaos and that the government should backpedal on these. Deng resisted, arguing that only economic reform could prevent China from suffering the same fate as the other communist states. However, he added, the reforms had to be accompanied by a continuation of strong state control over Chinese society.

DEATH AND THE LATER DENG PERIOD

By the 1990s, nature and biology were in command in Zhongnanhai, rather than politics. Li Xiannian, who had been a supporter of Deng's but became increasingly conservative and backed the military action in Tian'anmen Square, died on 26 June 1992. Hu Qiaomu, another close colleague, but also a determined opponent of further reforms, followed on 28 September, and Wang Zhen passed away on 21 March 1993. Yao Yilin, another uncompromising member of Chen Yun's camp, died on 11 December 1994. Chen Yun had been seriously ill since the end of 1994 and he died on 10 April 1995. The Chen Yun camp was no more, the struggle between the 'twin peaks and the two poles' was over, and from 1994 until Deng Xiaoping's death on 20 February 1997, China had entered what Yang Jisheng refers to as the Later Deng (*hou Deng*) period – connoisseurs of early Chinese history will not need to be reminded that the great Han dynasty (206 BC to 220 AD) is often divided into the Former and the Later Han. In Yang Jisheng's view the Later Deng period, in which there was no effective political opposition to reform, can be extended to include the Jiang Zemin, and Hu Jintao periods.

With no opposition, the rapid development of the socialist market economy continued apace. The four basic principles had to be upheld, but in time the idea of 'three representations' (*sange daibiao* – also translated, even less grammatically, as 'three represents'), associated with Jiang Zemin, was introduced and this to some extent weakened the authority of the four principles. The theory of 'three representations' (often ridiculed) was that the CCP should represent 'advanced productive forces', 'advanced culture', and 'the fundamental interests of the overwhelming majority of the people in China'. The mechanical class analysis that had been the foundation for the political rhetoric for generations of Chinese communists was quietly being jettisoned.

Politicians became increasingly enthusiastic as economic development began to benefit them personally, but new social forces and social problems were arising. Increased prosperity became more widespread but the unequal distribution of wealth, new forms of corruption and other social evils began to cause concern. After its entry into the World Trade Organisation in 2001, China was increasingly integrated into global systems and unfamiliar political, ideological and cultural influences flooded into the country. Yang Jisheng has argued that the standard-bearers of truth were no longer the rulers but the common people of China and the intellectuals who spoke up for them. This may be wishful thinking, but in spite of regular clampdowns, it is possible to publish and discuss a far wider range of topics in the twenty-first century than it was in the late twentieth. Perhaps most significantly, China had moved from 'strong man politics' to a politics that was closer to the man and woman in the street. The most senior leadership is no longer composed exclusively of Party members tempered in battle and the revolution, but is emerging on the basis of opportunity, character and ability as well as connections. Leaders cannot any longer base their arguments solely on high ideals from the era of struggle and resistance but have to engage with practical day-to-day issues.[12]

SOUTHERN TOUR AND THE DENG LEGACY (1992–7)

I never expected the development to be so quick but when I saw it my confidence increased.[1]

One of my big mistakes was not including Shanghai in the Special Economic Zones.[2]

My life has been devoted to the party and the nation; after I retire I will continue to devote myself to the cause of the party and the nation.[3]

In November 1989 when Deng retired as chairman of the Central Military Commission, his remaining official position, it was reasonable to assume that this marked the end of his political influence. He had passed his eighty-fifth birthday and appeared to be happy spending more time with his family, not to mention his passion for playing bridge. President Jiang Zemin and his colleagues may have thought that they had seen the last of him. They had not.

JOURNEY TO THE SOUTH: DENG XIAOPING'S VALEDICTORY CAMPAIGN

In January 1992 Deng embarked on what has become known as his 'Southern Tour' (*nanfang zhi xing* or *nanxing*). This tour, a political mission in defence of his economic reform policies, lasted just over a month, from 17 January to 21 February 1992 and has become something of a legend: it has been compared, rather fancifully, to the imperial progresses of the Qing dynasty emperors, Kangxi and Qianlong.

On 2 January Deng was pictured posing for a commemorative photograph with other competitors in the ninth 'strategy for health' bridge competition, a safe and suitable activity for an elderly retired leader. Two weeks later on the afternoon of 17 January he set off from Beijing by special train to carry out a tour of inspection which was to take him to Wuchang, Shenzhen, Zhuhai and Shanghai. It is not clear whether the political leadership realised the full implications of this mission. Deng did not do things without a reason and what could have been just a valedictory tour became a memorable finale in his political career.

His first engagement was on the morning of 18 January at Wuchang railway station in Wuhan, Hubei Province where Guan Guangfu, a member of the Central Committee and secretary of the Hubei Provincial Party Committee, reported to him formally on the local situation. By the afternoon he had crossed the provincial border into Hunan and at Changsha station heard another report from Xiong Qingquan, the Hunan Party secretary who was also a Central Committee member. Xiong brought him up to date on the natural disasters that had affected the province in 1991: the north had experienced severe flooding which left large areas waterlogged; whereas the south had been badly affected by drought. This was a reminder, if one was necessary, of the size and complexity of the individual provinces and how vulnerable rural China is to the weather. In his report to Deng, Xiong insisted that only China's superior socialist system, which depended on the leadership of the Communist Party, could have successfully dealt with and overcome (*zhansheng*) a disaster on this scale. Although this is recorded factually and without comment, it contains a coded warning that the central government should not tamper too far with the political system.

The next stage and the main objective of the tour was Shenzhen, which he reached by the morning of 19 January. Shenzhen was one of the initial five Special Economic Zones (SEZ) – the others were Zhuhai, Shantou, Xiamen and Hainan Island – that were established on 16 May 1980 when the Central Committee and the State Council formally issued its important reform document, 'Summary of the Conference of Guangdong and Fujian Provinces'. Sixteenth May is a date with some resonance in Chinese political culture: it was the date of the 16 May Circular of 1966 which effectively launched the Cultural Revolution. The irony of the date on which the SEZs were created would not have been lost on Deng as they were the antithesis of Mao's plans for China's economy.

Shenzhen, in Guangdong Province, lies in the Pearl River Delta just to the north of Hong Kong; it was the first of the SEZs to develop and was a flagship for the whole reform programme. Immediately on arriving in Shenzhen, Deng insisted on going with Xie Fei, the Guangdong Party secretary and Li Hao, the Party secretary of Shenzhen City to see how it had developed since his last visit over eight years previously. He admitted that when they had decided to set up the SEZs he had never expected the development to be so fast. Shenzhen was catching up with Hong Kong, Zhuhai with Macao and Xiamen with Taiwan; Shantou (Swatou), a city in which many inhabitants had relatives living overseas, was also catching up with Taiwan. Without the SEZs, he argued, in what was for Deng an unusually self-congratulatory mood, who knew how long economic modernisation would have taken? He concluded his perambulation with an inspection of Huanggang, one of the river ports of Shenzhen that also links the city with Hong Kong and 'stood on the great bridge over the Shenzhen River, gazing out at Hong Kong opposite'. Deng's family have said that he longed to see the return of Hong Kong to China but it did not happen until several months after his death.

The following day, 20 January, again with Xie and Li, he went up to the 5th floor of the Shenzhen International Trade Centre (*Shenzhen guomao daxia*) for a bird's eye view of the region. The trade centre was the tallest building in Shenzhen when it was completed in 1985. After viewing plans of the SEZ and hearing the obligatory formal reports from local officials he made a speech. The lessons from the Soviet Union and Eastern Europe, he told them, indicated clearly that China must proceed along the socialist road: the alternative would be chaos and a disaster for the country. However, China was on its way to achieving modest prosperity (*xiaokang*) by the end of the century and there was reason to believe that it could catch up with at least the middle-ranking developed countries. Time was short, he stressed, and international markets were highly competitive. On 21 and 22 January he visited companies throughout the Shenzhen region and planted a commemorative tree. In the afternoon with President Yang Shangkun he held a reception for members of the Shenzhen Communist Party Committee, Government, People's Congress, People's Political Consultative Conference and Discipline Inspection Committee at which he gave a speech to what was the broadest possible spread of influential people in Shenzhen political circles.

On the morning of 23 January, accompanied once again by Xie Fei but on this occasion also by Liang Guangda, who was both mayor and Party secretary of Zhuhai city, Deng travelled by hydrofoil to Zhuhai, another of the Pearl River Delta SEZs, which has a relationship with Macau to its south, similar to that of Shenzhen and Hong Kong. The journey was used of course for an exchange of information about conditions in Guangdong. Peasant incomes were still extremely low in international terms but natural disasters had been dealt with successfully and the province was benefiting greatly from the decade or more of reform. During the obligatory tour of factories on 24 and 25 January Deng emphasised the need for Chinese people to have more consumer goods available: it was essential for China to develop its own brands if it were not to lose out in competition. Science, technology and the development of suitably qualified personnel were, he argued, the key to success, a sentiment that was applauded in Zhuhai, which had already made a name for itself in high technology production including electronics, computers and biotechnology. Although he had been out of front-line politics for some time, Deng had clearly kept abreast of current economic developments and was able to deliver his main message with conviction: the past decade had seen tremendous changes but in the next decade the pace would have to be even faster. He received more officials from Zhuhai and visitors from the cities of Foshan and Zhongshan in the morning of 29 January and in the afternoon left Zhuhai for Guangzhou, where he bade a formal farewell to the official Guangdong delegation, and in the evening entrained for Shanghai. En route the train stopped at Yingtan, the major railway junction in the east of Jiangxi Province from where he and Zhuo Lin had returned from exile in 1973. He was met by the Provincial Party secretary and the governor and heard of the difficulties that the province was having with the pressure on granaries because of its high grain production.

Deng's train arrived in Shanghai in the early morning of 31 January 1992 for a more leisurely visit. On 3 February Deng celebrated the New Year with President Yang Shangkun and carefully selected local people, and the following evening enjoyed playing bridge with the Shanghai team. On 7 February he inspected a different type of bridge, the Nanpu crossing, which had been opened in 1991 and the Yangpu, which was still under construction. The following day he took an evening cruise on the Huangpu River, on which Shanghai's importance as a port relies, to see the city by night. He was accompanied by Wu Bangguo, who was the Shanghai Municipal Party secretary and Huang Ju, the mayor. Deng spoke of the need to develop and promote younger, more courageous officials for the twenty-first century that was fast approaching. Visiting factories and outlying areas during the remainder of his Shanghai sojourn, he made it clear that Pudong, like Shenzhen, was an important model and that both would be judged on how they contributed to socialism. His train left Shanghai and made brief stops at Nanjing and Bengbu where Deng met local Party leaders and expressed his concern that China was in danger of losing the initiative if it did not speed up reforms. They must 'grasp the opportunity' (*zhuazhu shiji*), he told them. This was the *raison d'être* of the tour: he was deeply concerned that the impetus for rapid development was being lost and that conservative forces would take the opportunity to scale down or even roll back the reforms. By 21 February Deng and his entourage had returned to Beijing.

The Southern Tour was a *tour de force* of political theatre. It may have lasted for only a month but its influence endured and its impact was immediate. However, there was a delay in reporting his progress in the mainstream media. This is an indication of the resistance of the more conservative elements within the Communist Party leadership, and, in Deng's eyes, was confirmation that the campaign had been necessary. It had parallels with his tour of Jiangxi in November 1972 when he was about to be rehabilitated, and there is an ironic echo of Mao's journey to Shanghai and other parts of southern China in 1965 to appeal for political support before he launched the Cultural Revolution. The real impact of Deng's Southern Tour was not initially on the central Party machinery and the media in Beijing, but on the provincial CCP leaders and industrialists, and the local media that had covered their meetings with Deng. He had succeeded in impressing on the provinces the need for deepening and continuing economic reforms in spite of the reservations of some officials and had highlighted the success of reform in the provinces on which he could now report back to the party centre.

DOCUMENT NO. 2

On 28 February the Central Committee issued a summary of the key points that Deng had made in his speeches during the tour as *Document No. 2* (1992), for immediate distribution to all Party members and cadres. This paper, a version of which later appeared in the third volume of his *Selected Works*, had six sections which began with the following slogans or exhortations: (1) Reform is a liberation of the forces of production, as was revolution; (2) Reform and opening require courage, including the courage to experiment; (3) Seize the time, develop yourself but the key is the development of the economy; (4) It is necessary to keep grasping with both hands – with one hand grasp reform and opening, and with the other grasp the attack on all types of criminal activities; (5) The correct political line depends on its being guaranteed by the correct organisational line.

Document No. 2 is couched in the customary convoluted and bureaucratic language and its message is hardly profound, but it was appropriate for the target audience – conservative doubters in the Party in Beijing and across the country. Even at this relatively late stage in the reform and opening process, Deng felt it necessary to defend his case on an ideological basis, placing reform within the context of the CCP and China's revolution. It is all too readily assumed that, after the death of Mao Zedong, the reforms promoted by Deng were immediately accepted. This was not the case: acceptance came only with protracted debates and strife within the Party hierarchy. In what was almost a Faustian pact, the soul of economic modernisation was bought at the price of political reform. Deng understood that to inist on political change risked generating such a level of opposition within the CCP that the economic reform programme might fail. This battle has continued even after Deng's death.[4]

THE RISE OF ZHU RONGJI: DENG MARK 2?

With the resolution of the Central Committee and the dissemination of *Document No. 2*, the leadership had more or less returned to the politics of reform after the period of indecision and loss of direction that followed the trauma of June 1989. Deng's intervention in support of his reform programme during the Southern Tour was endorsed at a full meeting of the Politburo on 9 and 10 March 1992, a meeting which had been called by Jiang Zemin specifically for that purpose. The Politburo agreed that Deng's conversations with local leaders during his Southern Tour contained important and enduring lessons for the Party that should be studied by all. Deng Xiaoping's authority had recovered from a low point in June 1989 to the extent that Jiang Zemin and other members of the Standing Committee of the Politburo felt obliged to defer to him once again.

The composition of the central political leadership that had emerged under Jiang Zemin was changing. The Standing Committee of the Politburo which ruled from 1992 to 1997 – the last five years of Deng's life – included three uncompromising opponents of reform: Li Peng, the conservative premier who had declared martial law in 1989; Qiao Shi, whose main responsibilities were security and internal party discipline, and Liu Huaqing, the commander-in-chief of the PLA Navy who had directed the troops enforcing martial law in Beijing. Two other members were the then unknown Hu Jintao and a cautious reformer, Li Ruihuan, but for Deng Xiaoping's reform project, the most important addition to a less than dazzling line-up was Zhu Rongji.

Zhu, an engineering graduate from Qinghua University, worked in the State Planning Commission in the 1950s but was purged as a 'rightist' in 1959 for criticising Mao's Great Leap Forward policies. He returned to work in the 1960s but was not fully rehabilitated until after the Cultural Revolution. In 1979, on the specific orders of Deng, who was actively recruiting technically competent and experienced staff for his reform programme, he began work at the State Economic Commission. This was the successor to the State Planning Commission and was responsible for developing China's 'socialist market economy'. Zhu later served as mayor of Shanghai from 1989 to 1991, where he presided over the development of the ultra-modern Pudong district and moved to Beijing as deputy premier in 1991, just before Deng's Southern Tour. From 1993 to 1998 Zhu was a member of the Standing Committee of the Politburo and after Deng's death he served as premier from 1998 to 2003. After leaving office, Zhu maintained a low profile and rarely spoke in public, but in September 2013 a video recording was issued of his appearance at the launch of *Zhu Rongji on the Record: The Road to Reform 1991–1997* – an English translation of four volumes of speeches that he had made while serving as deputy premier and premier.

Zhu Rongji's financial acumen, his experience at the State Economic Commission and his personal commitment to reform provided vital support for Deng. Zhu was respected for his toughness, pragmatism and determination to root out corruption, all of which increased popular support for the policies of reform. Like Deng, Zhu never held the most senior appointment of Party leader and president, but the longest period of sustained growth in China's GDP began during his time in office. In 1997 Jiang Zemin, who had never been either confident or competent in managing the Chinese economy, effectively devolved the responsibility for economic development to Zhu; in many ways it was Zhu, rather than Jiang, who inherited the mantle of Deng Xiaoping.

The brief interlude in the 1980s during which Hu Yaobang and Zhao Ziyang seemed to represent the rise of a more open and humane leadership of the Chinese Communist Party had ended abruptly with the suppression of the Democracy Movement on 4 June 1989. Hu and Zhao had been chosen personally by Deng as his successors but their democratic sensibilities had proved too much for conservatives in the leadership, and for their mentor, and they were dismissed. If subsequent senior members of the CCP felt any sympathy for the two purged leaders, they mostly kept it to themselves, but it was always safe to invoke the name of Deng Xiaoping.

DEATH OF A GIANT

Deng Xiaoping's passing was hardly unexpected. He was 93 and rumours of his declining health had been circulating for some time. Indeed for a man who had been through the trials and tribulations of China's revolutionary upheaval, including the Long March and the Cultural Revolution, it is extraordinary that he not only survived and remained active for so long, but that he also retained so much of his influence and authority when so many of his contemporaries had long since retired or died.

Deng died in Beijing on 19 February 1997. Local people strolling in Tian'anmen Square, who noticed the national flag at half-mast and speculated that a senior leader must have died, did not immediately realise that it was Deng whose passing was being marked. The news had initially been made public in the early hours of the morning in a press release from Xinhua News Agency that was broadcast on Chinese Central Television's Channel 4 News, the international service directed at viewers outside the People's Republic. It took some time for news of his death to percolate through to the general public in China and it was only at about 7.00 am the following morning, some ten hours after Deng's passing, that the nation was officially notified in a news bulletin on CCTV Channel 1, the main domestic terrestrial television channel. The newsreader wore a dark-blue suit and a grey tie with a black check and, in an appropriately mournful and respectful tone, read out an obituary which lasted half an hour and concentrated on Deng's contributions to China's reform. He concluded with, 'Comrade Deng Xiaoping is now immortal'.

Behind the delay in announcing Deng's death lay uncertainty and anxiety. What would be the effect of the death of such a powerful political personality, and would the leadership be able to maintain the stability and somewhat fragile unity that had existed within the Party and government since 1989, and which Deng was credited, at least partly, with having created? This anxiety seems strange in view of the fact that Deng held no official post and had not been at the centre of Chinese politics for many years, but it is a measure of the strength of his personality, his moral authority and his role as the embodiment and the conscience of China's reforms that there were such concerns about the consequences of his death. In 1989 the Democracy Movement and the tragedy of 4 June had begun with commemorations of the death of Hu Yaobang and, although Deng – unlike Hu – was not a great friend of liberal intellectuals, there was always the possibility that his death could result in demonstrations and a rekindling of demands for political democracy.

Television and radio interviews with passers-by in Beijing were predictably positive about his contribution to China's modern economy. One interviewee said, 'He was a little bloke but he was a giant'. Close observers of Zhongnanhai watched for signs of the emergence of a new strong man, but Deng may have been the last of this type of Chinese politician. There were no emotional demonstrations of the type that followed Zhou Enlai's death in 1975, but a few demonstrators carrying placards praising Deng expressed their concern that after his death the bad old days might return. The police dispersed any gatherings that began to form: even expressions of appreciation of Deng might conceal criticisms of Li Peng's government.

On 24 February there were formal ceremonies to mark his death, Premier Li Peng led a three-minute silence and flags flew at half-mast for a week. Thousands of mourners lined the streets of Beijing as Deng's coffin was taken to the cemetery at Babaoshan, but the simple funeral was private and focused on his immediate family, although it was televised and broadcast across the country. The banner over his ashes which lay in state in the Great Hall of the People read simply 'Memorial meeting for comrade Deng Xiaoping'. There was no mention of his previous titles; it was not necessary.[5]

DENG'S CONTRIBUTION TO CHINA'S MODERNISATION

The modernisation of China did not of course begin with Deng Xiaoping. China had a burgeoning commercial sector in the Song and Ming dynasties, but merchants never acquired the economic and political power that they did in Europe. The country's transition from a predominantly agricultural society began with localised industrialisation, mostly associated with foreign-dominated Treaty Ports in the late nineteenth century. The process continued into the twentieth century during the Republican period and also, ironically, during the Japanese occupation, especially in Manchuria. Nevertheless, when the CCP took power in 1949, China had a very low level of modern industrial development and industrialisation was the main economic priority.

Industrialisation is not of course the same as modernisation, but it is an important component and initially the model that the CCP followed was the Soviet one, developing heavy industry owned by the state and managing it as part of the five-year planning process. Private commerce and industry continued to exist, although major enterprises were nationalised (socialised) early in the 1950s and only small-scale operations were left in private hands. Even these came under attack during the political campaigns of the Great Leap Forward and the Cultural Revolution, but private production did re-emerge briefly in the early 1960s. After the Cultural Revolution there were increasing demands for markets and private commercial businesses. The introduction of free markets was very slow: for example in 1983, four years after the Third Plenum which legitimised their reintroduction, free markets in Nanjing were a new and exciting phenomenon that local sociologists were avidly studying.[6]

The pressure to commercialise did not come solely from outside the CCP. Many open-minded members of the Party had disapproved of the blanket ban on private businesses and Deng's track record in the liberated areas in the 1940s and in the south-west after 1949 indicate that he was of that mind. Even so there has also been resistance at the highest levels in the CCP and the process of developing private sector commerce and industry was slow and far from smooth. There was a serious setback after the Tian'anmen protests in 1989 that was not overcome until Deng's Southern Tour in 1992. Deng lived to see the beginning of the new face of China, but many of the now familiar cityscapes emerged after his death.

TWENTY YEARS AFTER THE SOUTHERN TOUR: REFORMERS ASSESS DENG'S LEGACY

Seventeen years after his death, Deng is still revered in China, and by many outside, for his pivotal role in generating the development that dragged millions out of poverty and turned China into a major global economic power. His family's former home, in Paifang village, Sichuan Province, has been turned into a museum honouring his life and achievement.

Chinese political history from 1949 is often over-simplified by contrasting the heroic Deng with the villainous Mao Zedong. This is erroneous and dangerously misleading. Deng had been a close comrade and a supporter of Mao since the 1930s and worked with him in both the government and the Communist Party in the 1950s and 1960s, although by the middle of the 1950s their paths began to diverge. Mao developed his own radical political perspectives, preferring grand gestures and populist appeal to revolutionary sentiment. Deng and his close colleague and political chief, Liu Shaoqi, persisted in the slow and prosaic backroom work of economic planning. Deng may have been the greatest champion of economic reform but he was by no means a democrat or a liberal; he remained resolutely opposed to any political reform that might undermine the supremacy of the Chinese Communist Party which, he believed, was the only institution that could deliver the economic development that China so desperately needed.

His political life since the foundation of the People's Republic of China in 1949 exemplifies the paradoxes and inconsistencies in the life of the nation. He did not oppose the repression of dissenting voices during the Anti-Rightist movement of 1957, although he later acknowledged that the campaign had gone too far. In the mid-1960s he fell foul of Mao, who regarded his collaboration with Liu Shaoqi as a betrayal of the spirit of the revolution, and he was banished to the countryside.

Deng returned to power as Mao was nearing the end of his life and did so with the support of Zhou Enlai, the ultimate *éminence grise* who had remained personally loyal to Mao in spite of the fact that he had little sympathy with the chairman's policies. Deng briefly allowed the use of the Democracy Wall in Beijing for the airing of independent and dissident views but then proscribed it when criticism became directed at the Communist Party. He acquiesced in the resignation of Premier Hu Yaobang in 1987 after Hu was accused of being too sympathetic to student demonstrators; Deng was not willing to back his ideas for political reform, although he allowed the appointment of another relatively liberal figure, Zhao Ziyang, to replace him. Deng was also criticised for not preventing the military assault on student and citizen demonstrators occupying Tian'anmen Square on 4 June 1989, and agreeing to the dismissal of the liberal Premier Zhao Ziyang who had attempted to resolve the crisis by negotiation.

In the traditional Chinese calendar, 2012 was the year of the water dragon, a sign traditionally associated with progress and good fortune, but there was still no complete agreement on the relationship between economic modernisation and political democracy. The contest for the selection of the next generation of political leaders preoccupied observers and commentators in China and abroad. Xi Jinping and Li Keqiang, who were virtually unknown outside China, emerged in 2007 as the front runners for the posts of president and premier respectively and their appointments were confirmed in the Eighteenth Communist Party Congress that took place in November 2012 and the National People's Congress that followed in March 2013. Both Xi and Li have been influenced in their political careers by the reformist ideas of Hu Yaobang and Zhao Ziyang, but they are also aware that openly espousing anything that appears to be similar to a Western multi-party system of democracy is anathema to many senior Party figures, who can only countenance Deng Xiaoping's approach of economic modernisation without political change.

On Wednesday 18 January 2012, Hu Yaobang's eldest son, Hu Deping, convened a forum to put the case for political reform on the twentieth anniversary of Deng Xiaoping's Southern Tour. This meeting was attended by reform-minded academics, retired public servants and the sons and daughters of former senior Party and government officials. Hu Deping, an economist who chairs the Chinese National Chamber of Commerce and Industry, commended the way in which recent protests in the village of Wukan in Guangdong against land confiscation and corruption had been handled by negotiation and compromise rather than the use of overwhelming force. He then argued that the time was right to extend 'reform and opening', Deng Xiaoping's key slogan, into the political sphere. It remains to be seen whether the new leadership of Xi and Li will move in this direction and allow, however slowly, a degree of political reform or whether, whatever their private feelings, they will take refuge in the security of Deng's legacy and concentrate on the economy.[7]

CHINA'S GREAT REFORMER: A PROVISIONAL ASSESSMENT

Whatever else is said or written about Deng Xiaoping, he will always be remembered primarily for the economic reform programme that he intiated, and doggedly sustained until the end of his life; and for the dramatic transformation that these reforms brought about in China's fortunes and its physical appearance. His political legacy is less straightforward and uncomfortable questions remain about his attitude to democracy, openness and freedom of expression. Could Deng have done anything other than he did? Given his years in the highly disciplined milieu of the Chinese Communist Party and its army could he possibly have been more open, liberal and democratic as some of his admirers might have wished? Or is it remarkable enough that someone from his background had the vision to see the necessity and the possibility of economic reform in China and also had the drive to push it through in the teeth of serious and obdurate opposition, opposition that was couched in terms of the same ideological principles in which Deng had been schooled since his teens?

It is possible that someone else in his position in the 1970s and 1980s could have combined Deng's authority and his commitment to economic reform with a similar dedication to political change. It is difficult to see who that person might have been. Another powerful leader might not have been able to drive through the reforms at all, or, if political reform had been attempted, would probably have fallen by the wayside in the manner or Hu Yaobang and Zhao Ziyang. Deng was no dictator: he ruled China, insofar as he ruled it at all, by consent. It was not the consent of the majority of the population: he never sought this consent directly, although there is no doubt that many of that great majority revere him for the changes that he brought about. The consent that he sought, and had to win, was the consent of his colleagues in the central Chinese Communist Party leadership and of those further down the hierarchy in the vast and scattered provinces; these were local political leaders whose careers and lives depended on the Communist Party and who were not prepared to see it collapse because of reckless policies. Without the support of the rest of the leadership and indeed of the wider Communist Party, China's economic transformation could not have taken place.

Deng could not do it alone: he had to carry the institution with him, or at the very least neutralise most of the opposition. Deng walked a tightrope and his balancing act was largely successful. He protected the economic reforms against those who wished to reverse them, or slow them down, but the price for doing this was the preservation of the 'dictatorship of the proletariat' – permanent rule by the CCP – and the exclusion of anything resembling Western multi-party democracy.

If Deng had been able to bring about democratic change in addition to the economic reforms that were his highest priority, would he have done so? The answer has to be that this would not necessarily have seemed important to him. There is nothing in his background, in his writings or speeches, or in his actions to suggest that he secretly harboured the desire for a more open and liberal political culture. He was an army man by training and adoption; he understood and valued unity, loyalty and discipline above all. He was a man of his time, and his time was really the war against the Japanese and the Guomindang in the 1930s and 1940s. What is remarkable is that he was able to continue in political life well beyond that time and to continue in a way that was relevant and fresh so that, by the time of the death of Mao Zedong in 1976, he was able to transcend the limitations of his upbringing and his early career and assimilate a new worldview and a new way forward for China. Ironically, the frustrations of the wasted years of the 1960s, when he saw China taking a disastrously wrong direction and was powerless to do anything about it, had a profound and positive effect. When he surfaced from internal exile in 1973, he seems to have emerged with a new vigour and a new vision, a determination to ensure that a catastrophe like the Cultural Revolution could never happen again. Even if he did not know exactly what sort of China he wanted to materialise – and neither he nor anyone else could really know at that point – he at least had a clear understanding of what he did not want for China.

None of this means that his failures or his short-sightedness in political and intellectual spheres can be completely ignored. There was no possibility that he would consider genuine autonomy for Tibet or Xinjiang. He never acknowledged that the Anti-Rightist campaign of 1957 was fundamentally wrong, only that it went too far, even after his own career and life were turned upside down by its successor, the Cultural Revolution. Between 1978 and 1981, he probably had the authority to permit an extension of free speech and open publication but he did not do so. Perhaps he was correct to judge that if he had conceded demands for the 'fifth modernisation' – democracy – he would have lost the first four that permitted the reform of the economy, but there is no evidence that he was troubled by this. In June 1989, if he had used his remaining formal authority as chairman of the Central Military Commission to insist that troops should not be sent in to remove pro-democracy protestors from Tian'anmen Square (and if that authority had been respected, which is far from certain), there might not have been any deaths among the student and citizen demonstrators; China, the Communist Party and Deng might then not have suffered the international opprobrium that followed. He may have been misled or badly advised on the nature of the threat to the government in the summer of 1989; it is possible that he came to the wrong decision for what he felt were the right reasons – the preservation of the state and rule by the Communist Party. Whatever the truth, in addition to being lauded as the godfather of economic reform, Deng Xiaoping will always be associated personally with China's most public episode of repression.

Deng Xiaoping's true monument is China as it is today, warts and all. It is a monument that includes the futuristic cities, the Special Economic Zones and the increasingly prosperous population, but it also includes the nation's strained political structures and its restricted freedom of expression. Looking at this monument, it is only proper for the reader to pause and reflect whether any other individual at the same time, in the same place and with the same resources – people, organisations and materials – at his disposal could have done more, or even as much.

For the Chinese Communist Party Deng remains an iconic figure. In August 2014, on the 110th anniversary of his birth, the theoretical journal of the Central Committee, *Qiushi*, devoted no less than five articles to Deng's political legacy. President Xi Jinping, emerging that month from a successful conclave at the Party's summer retreat of Beidaihe, after having consolidated his personal control over the leadership, was hailed as the new Deng Xiaoping.

APPENDIX: KEY PERSONALITIES IN DENG XIAOPING'S POLITICAL CAREER

Bo Gu (also Qin Bangxian, 1907–46) Leading member of CCP '28 Bolsheviks', the Moscow-trained majority CCP faction in the early 1930s in opposition to Mao Zedong. General Secretary 1931–5 and succeeded by Zhang Wentian. Died in air crash en route from Chongqing to Yan'an in 1946.

Bo Yibo (1908–2007) Member of the Central Committee until the Cultural Revolution and then critical supporter of Deng Xiaoping. Also father of Bo Xilai, who was disgraced in 2012.

Braun, Otto (also Li De, 1900–74) German Comintern military adviser during early Long March and opponent of Mao Zedong's guerrilla tactics.

Cai Chang (1900–90) Early CCP member and sister of Cai Hesen. Active in All-China Women's Federation and member of Central Committee. Married to the socialist economic planner Li Fuchun.

Cai Hesen (1895–1931) Early CCP member in France and China, married to Xiang Jingyu.

Chen Duxiu (1879–1942) May Fourth Movement intellectual, founder member of CCP and general secretary until ousted in 1927.

Chen Jitang (1890–1954) Nationalist officer in Guangxi and Guangdong and *de facto* Guangdong warlord in 1930s.

Chen Xilian (1915–99) PLA officer in Fourth Front Army and Eighth Route Army, active in war against Japan and civil war. Party secretary and mayor of Chongqing in 1950, senior PLA commander and politician, rising to power in the Cultural Revolution. Purged by Deng Xiaoping in 1980.

Chen Xitong (1930–2013) Politburo member. Mayor of Beijing during 4 June 1989 military crackdown. Imprisoned for corruption in 1998.

Chen Yi (1901–72) Early CCP member and New Fourth Army officer. Mayor of Shanghai and vice-premier and foreign minister 1958–72, survived the Cultural Revolution.

Chen Yun (1905–95) Economic planner, political ally of Deng Xiaoping but opponent of a move away from planned economy. Chaired State Planning and Finance and Economic commissions.

Deng Fa (1906–46) Principal of CCP Central Party School 1939–42.

Deng Liqun (1932–92) Liu Shaoqi's former secretary. Propaganda chief behind the campaign against spiritual pollution and worked closely with Hu Qiaomu in Political Research Office.

Deng Nan (1945–) Second daughter of Deng Xiaoping. deputy minister of state Science and Technology Commission.

Deng Pufang (1944–) Son of Deng Xiaoping, disabled in 1968 after conflict with Red Guards in Cultural Revolution. Active in national organisations for the disabled.

Deng Rong (also Deng Maomao, 1950–) Youngest daughter of Deng Xiaoping. Diplomat, government official and author of *Deng Xiaoping, My Father.*

Deng Shaochang (also Deng Wenming, 1886–1936) Deng Xiaoping's father.

Deng Yingchao (1904–92) CCP activist, especially in women's organisations. Wife of Zhou Enlai.

Fei Xiaotong (also Fei Hsiao-tung, 1910–2005) Eminent anthropologist and sociologist, attacked as a rightist in the late 1950s and then unable to teach or research for over 30 years. Rehabilitated after Deng Xiaoping emerged as the new leader of the CCP and credited with re-establishing sociology as a modern discipline in China.

Feng Yuxiang (1882–1948) Shaanxi warlord, also known as the 'Christian General' after conversion to Protestantism, allied with the Guomindang and later Wang Jingwei. Later critical of GMD and close to CCP.

Fukuda Takeo (1905–95) Japanese Liberal Democratic Party leader and prime minister 1976–8.

Gao Gang (1905–55) Chairman of Northeast People's Government in 1947, and of State Planning Commission in 1952. Expelled from CCP, with Rao Shushi, in the first purge after 1949.

Hu Qiaomu (1912–92) Marxist ideologue and Mao's secretary during the 1940s. First president of the Academy of Social Sciences and supporter of Deng Xiaoping, but then an intransigent opponent of economic reform.

Hu Yaobang (1915–89) Protégé of Deng Xiaoping and supporter of his economic reform policies. General secretary of the CCP 1982–7 and purged for his overly liberal political attitudes. His death in 1989 led to the Democracy Movement.

Huang Zhizhen Jiangxi Provincial Revolutionary Committee secretary. Purged during the Cultural Revolution and later a member of the Twelfth Central Committee.

Jiang Jingguo (1918–88) Son of Jiang Jieshi (Chiang Kai-shek). Studied in Moscow and responsible for economic management in Shanghai. After 1949 president of Taiwan and credited with major role in both the economic success and the democratisation of the island.

Jiang Qing (1914–91) Actress and CCP activist in the 1930s and wife of Mao Zedong. Active in cultural politics in the PRC and in the Cultural Revolution Group. Tried as member of Gang of Four in 1980–1 and died in prison.

Jiang Zemin (1926–) Shanghai CCP secretary and, after the military suppression of 4 June Democracy Movement, general secretary of the CCP. Derided for his 'Three Represents' theory – that the CCP should represent advanced productive forces, advanced culture and the interests of the majority. Criticised by Deng Xiaoping for lack of enthusiasm for economic development, but his move to bring business people into the CCP strengthened its political base. Retired when Hu Jintao was elected general secretary in 2002 but remains an influential *éminence grise*.

Jin Weiying Deng's second wife who divorced him in 1933 when he was the target of political criticism.

Lee Kuan Yew (1923–) Prime minister of Singapore, secretary general of the People's Action Party 1959–90, and subsequently senior minister and minister mentor. Often referred to as the 'father of Singapore'. Key figure behind Singapore's economic success and authoritarian social policies.

Li Fuchun (1900–75) Early member of CCP in France and China and married to Cai Chang. Long-term senior figure in CCP organisation and after 1949 chair of State Planning Commission and member of Politburo and Secretariat. Criticised during Cultural Revolution as revisionist but rehabilitated in 1971.

Li Lisan (1899–1967) Influential in CCP leadership 1929–30 and blamed for 'Li Lisan line' which advocated military attacks on cities in expectation of workers risings which failed to materialise. He was the major opponent of Mao Zedong's strategy of peasant guerrilla warfare.

Li Peng (1928–) Premier of CCP 1987–98 and blamed for military suppression of 4 June Democracy Movement in 1989. Allegedly adopted by Zhou Enlai after father executed by the Guomindang and rose through government as a qualified engineer before advancement in the CCP sponsored by Chen Yun.

Li Weihan (1886–1984) Principal of CCP Party School in 1930s. After 1949 held posts in National People's Congress and CPPCC. Purged during Cultural Revolution and rehabilitated under Deng Xiaoping.

Li Xiannian (1909–92) President of the PRC 1983–8 and then chairman of the CPPCC. CCP member from 1927 and became vice-premier to Zhou Enlai in 1954. Worked closely with Zhou and was instrumental in the arrest of the Gang of Four after the death of Mao Zedong in 1976. Remained influential and was one of the elders blamed for the suppression of the Tian'anmen demonstrations in 1989.

Li Ximing (1926–2008) Beijing CCP secretary at the time of the Tian'anmen demonstrations who advocated a military solution to the crisis from behind the scenes.

Li Xuefeng (1907–2003) CCP political commissar who prospered during the Cultural Revolution as a supporter of Chen Boda and Lin Biao but was rehabilitated during the Deng Xiaoping years.

Li Zongren (1890–1969) Guangxi warlord and acting president of the Chinese Republic of Taiwan in 1947.

Lin Biao (1907–71) Decorated PLA general from the war against Japan and the civil war and vice-premier who replaced Peng Dehuai as minister of defence in 1959. Became a devoted acolyte of Mao Zedong, politicising the PLA to lend him support in the Cultural Revolution. Died in 1971 when an aircraft carrying him crashed en route to Russia after an unsuccessful military coup.

Liu Bocheng (1892–1986) Senior military officer and marshal of the PLA. Commanding officer of 129th Division and close associate of Deng Xiaoping who had been his political commissar. Supported Deng in the Cultural Revolution but retired with health problems in 1982.

Liu Huaqing (1916–2011) Commander of the PLA Navy and moderniser. Commanded PLA units enforcing martial law in Tian'anmen Square on 3–4 June 1989.

Liu Shaoqi (1898–1969) Chairman of the PRC (president) 1959–69. Had a history of underground revolutionary and trades union activity for the CCP and took over as head of state when Mao relinquished some of his powers in 1959. As a pragmatist and bureaucrat, his conflict with Mao led to the Cultural Revolution. Purged and died after ill-treatment at the hands of Red Guards.

Lu Dingyi (1906–96) Minister of culture and vice-premier of the PRC, purged during the Cultural Revolution. Rehabilitated by Deng Xiaoping in 1979 and joined Central Advisory Commission.

Luo Ronghuan (1902–63) Senior CCP military officer and marshal of the PLA, close to both Mao Zedong and Lin Biao.

Luo Ruiqing (1906–78) PLA chief of staff attacked during the Cultural Revolution. Deputy minister of defence under Lin Biao but, as an advocate of military professionalism rather than political loyalty, parted company with his chief.

Mao Yuanxin (1941–) Son of Mao Zemin (the younger brother of Mao Zedong who worked in Xinjiang in the 1930s and 1940s and died a martyr's death). Had a career in the military as a political commissar and in 1975 was the main contact between Mao Zedong and the Politburo (as the chairman's Alzheimer's disease worsened and he was increasingly unable to attend meetings). Was close to Jiang Qing's faction, was sentenced to 17 years in prison at the trial of the Gang of Four, and is believed to have worked in a factory from his release in 1993 until retirement.

Mao Zedong (1892–1976) Chairman of the Chinese Communist Party from some point between 1935 and 1942 and also chairman of the PRC (head of state 1949–59). Masterminded the strategy of peasant revolution and guerrilla warfare that brought the CCP to power in 1949 and, though lacking dictatorial powers, was deferred to by many other senior revolutionaries. His radical policies of the Great Leap Forward and Cultural Revolution are now universally acknowledged as disasters but he is still venerated as the founding father of the PRC. He was opposed by Liu Shaoqi and Deng Xiaoping but their more pragmatic and reformist policies could not be implemented until after his death in September 1976.

Nie Rongzhen (1899–1992) Senior CCP military officer and marshal of the PLA. Purged during the Cultural Revolution but after Mao's death became deputy chairman of the Central Military Commission. Played a key role in the Korean War and the development of China's nuclear weapons. Reportedly opposed the use of military force against demonstrators in Tian'anmen Square in June 1989.

Peng Dehuai (1898–1974) After a distinguished career as a battlefield commander in the CCP Red Army, was commander-in-chief of the Chinese Peoples'

Volunteers during the Korean War. Best known as the minister of defence who confronted long-term ally Mao Zedong at the Lushan meetings of 1959 and criticised his Great Leap Forward policies which had impoverished the peasants and contributed to the millions of deaths that resulted from the famine of 1959–62. Purged and replaced by Lin Biao but remains an icon for reform-minded Chinese.

Peng Zhen (1902–97) Early member of CCP in Shanxi, mayor of Beijing from 1951 to 1965 and one of the first senior leaders to be purged in the Cultural Revolution. Rehabilitated under Deng and chairman of NPC Standing Committee from 1983–8. Although committed to the rule of law, he opposed the liberal approaches of Hu Yaobang and Zhao Ziyang and played a key role in the political demise of both.

Qin Bangxian *see* **Bo Gu**

Qu Qiubai (1899–1935) Essayist, critic, translator from Russian and prominent member of League of Left-wing Writers. Succeeded Chen Duxiu as general secretary of CCP in 1927. Served in the governing body of the Jiangxi Soviet and was executed by Guomindang in 1935.

Rao Shushi (1901–75) Chairman of East China Military and Administrative Committee based in Shanghai after 1949. Together with Gao Gang criticised for establishing 'independent kingdoms' and expelled from CCP in 1954.

Ren Bishi (1904–50) Veteran CCP military and political leader with experience in Hunan and on the Long March. Became a senior member of the Politburo and died aged only 46.

Rong Yiren (1916–2005) From a wealthy Jiangsu business family. Chose to remain in the PRC after 1949 and became deputy mayor of Shanghai, but was attacked during the Cultural Revolution. Deng Xiaoping appointed him to lead CITIC (which played a leading role in attracting foreign investment) and he became vice-president in 1993 in spite of having opposed the use of force against Tian'anmen Square demonstrators in June 1989. It is not known for certain whether he joined the CCP.

Song Renqiong (1909–2005) CCP soldier and political commissar with Deng Xiaoping's 129th Division. Director of the CCP Organisation department from 1978–83, member of the Politburo from 1982–5, and one of the Party's influential elders during the Deng period.

Sonoda Sunao (1913–84) Foreign minister of Japan 1977–9 and active in promoting the normalisation of Sino-Japanese relations. Conscripted into the Imperial Japanese Army in 1938 and served in China and later in the Pacific.

Tanaka Kakuei (1918–93) Rose through the Liberal Democratic Party and became prime minister of Japan from 1972 to 1974. In 1972 met Zhou Enlai to initiate the process of normalisation of relations between the PRC and Japan. Later years were tarnished by the Lockheed bribery scandal, but he remained in the Japanese Diet until 1989.

Wang Jingwei (1883–1944) Leader of Left Guomindang administration in Wuhan from 1927 and of a puppet government based in Nanjing during the Japanese occupation.

Wang Zhen (1908–93) One of the Eight Elders who supported Deng Xiaoping on his return to power in the 1970s. Led PLA units into Xinjiang in 1949 and established the first CCP administration there. Although supportive of Deng's economic reforms, he was an intransigent political conservative who was implicated in the moves to have Hu Yaobang dismissed.

Wei Jingsheng (1949–) Democracy Wall activist and editor of the journal *Beijing Spring* in 1978. Led demands for a 'fifth modernisation' – democracy. Imprisoned on charges of passing state secrets to foreigners, released and then imprisoned again. Finally released in 1997 and allowed to move to the United States.

Wu Bangguo (1942–) Shanghai Municipal Party secretary, vice-premier, member of Politburo Standing Committee and chairman of the NPC Standing Committee until 2013.

Wu Faxian (1915–2004) PLA Air Force general associated with Jiang Qing and Lin Biao faction in the Cultural Revolution. Arrested after Lin's death.

Wu Han (1909–69) Historian, member of the Democratic League and deputy mayor of Beijing. His play, *Hai Rui Dismissed from Office*, was criticised at the beginning of the Cultural Revolution. Purged alongside the mayor, Peng Zhen.

Wu Lengxi (1919–2002) Director of the Xinhua News Agency and concurrently editor-in-chief of *People's Daily* 1958–66. Became a member of the Central Committee and minister of radio and televison in 1982.

Xi Zhongxun (1913–2002) Communist guerrilla leader and one of the first generation of CCP leaders in power after 1949. Became a deputy premier but was purged in 1962 after supporting a book that Mao objected to. Rehabilitated in 1978 and became governor and first secretary of Guangdong Province. His son, Xi Jinping, became CCP chairman in 2013.

Yan Xishan (1883–1969) Japanese-educated independent warlord who ruled Shanxi province from 1912 to 1949. He was nominally allied to the Guomindang but also cooperated with the CCP.

Yang Shangkun (1907–98) Member of Politburo 1982–7, vice-chairman of Central Military Commission and president of PRC 1988–93. Played key role in decision to crack down on Tian'anmen Square protesters in June 1989.

Ye Jianying (1897–1986) Marshal of PLA and member of the Central Committee. Remained in power during the Cultural Revolution but organised the arrest of the Gang of Four after the death of Mao Zedong.

Zhang Wentian (1900–76) CCP general secretary 1935–43, although this role was played down during the Mao era. Ambassador to Soviet Union in 1950s, but purged after supporting Peng Dehuai at the 1959 Lushan Conference. Rehabilitated after Mao's death with belated recognition of his earlier contributions to the Party.

Zhao Ziyang (1919–2005) Economic reformer in Sichuan from 1975. Replaced liberal Hu Yaobang as CCP secretary in 1987. As a reformist, he was sympathetic to the demonstrators in Tian'anmen Square and as a result was dismissed. Spent the following fifteen years under house arrest, in increasingly poor health.

Zhou Enlai (1898–1976) Enigmatic, cultured and ruthless statesman and premier of the PRC 1949–76. Joined the Chinese communist movement in France and studied at the Huangpu (Whampoa) Military Academy. Survived the Cultural Revolution because of his close personal relationship with Mao Zedong (although Jiang Qing became a bitter enemy) and was a consummate diplomat.

Zhu De (1886–1976) Close military associate of Mao Zedong from 1928. Was the most senior of the marshals of the PLA after 1949. Survived the Cultural Revolution because of his reputation and connection with Mao and remained, albeit ineffectually, on the Politburo Standing Committee.

NOTES

PRELIMS

1   Ezra F. Vogel, *Deng Xiaoping and the Transformation of China* (Cambridge, Massachusetts: Belknap Press at Harvard University Press, 2011).
2   Fang Lizhi, 'The Real Deng (Review of *Deng Xiaoping and the Transformation of China* by Ezra F. Vogel)' *New York Review of Books* (10 November 2011).
3   Deng Maomao, *Deng Xiaoping, My Father* (London: Harper Collins, 1995).

1. FAVOURED SON OF SICHUAN: GROWING UP IN PAIFANG (1904–20)

1   Zhao Xiaoguang and Liu Jie, *Deng Xiaoping de san luo san qi* (*The Three Falls and Three Rises of Deng Xiaoping*) (Shenyang: Liaoning renmin chubanshe (Liaoning People's Press, 2011), p. 3.
2   Luo Guangbin and Yang Yiyan, *Hongyan* (Beijing: Zhongguo qingnian chubanshe, 2011/ 1961).
3   Liu Jianhua and Liu Li, *Deng Xiaoping jishi* (*Chronicle of the Life of Deng Xiaoping*) (Beijing: Zhongyang wenxian chubanshe, 2011, two volumes), pp. 2–14; Deng Maomao, *Deng Xiaoping, My Father*, pp. 40–1.
4   Observations by author, Paifang, October 2011; 'Tafang Deng Xiaoping guju Sichuan sheng Guangan shi Xiexing zhen de Paifang cun', Xinhua News Agency (4 July 2003); *China Daily* (14 August 2004); *China Economic Net* (20 February 2009).
5   Liu and Liu, *Deng Xiaoping jishi*, pp. 2–14; Deng Maomao, *Deng Xiaoping, My Father*, pp. 34–41.

2. À LA RECHERCHE DU DENG PERDU: THE ROOTS OF CHINESE COMMUNISM IN PROVINCIAL FRANCE AFTER WORLD WAR I (1920–6)

1   Zhao and Liu, *Deng Xiaoping de san luo san qi*, p. 10.

2   Information from Dr. Wang Peiwen, President of the Association Amitié Chine-Montargis, Montargis, September 2011; the website of the China-Montargis Friendship Association is www.montargis.fr. For a description of these waterways and bridges, see the tourist information leaflet *Circuit of Bridges,* Montargis: Office de Tourisme de l'AME. Available at www.tourisme-montargis.fr (accessed 14 April 2014). See also Francis Cachon, *Montargis* (St-Cyr-sur Loire: Alan Sutton, 2006), pp. 84, 86, 127; Francis Cachon, *Montargis Tome II* (St-Cyr-sur Loire: Alan Sutton, 2011), pp. 74, 76, 81; and *Une page d'histoire: Découvrez comment la Chine est entrée dans l'histoire de Montargis.* Montargis: Agglomération Montargoise et Rives du Loing. Available at www.agglo-montargoise.fr (accessed 14 April 2014).

3   Its successor is the Lycée Agricole Le Chesnoy at Amilly.

4   Liu and Liu, *Deng Xiaoping jishi*, pp. 27–35; Geneviève Barman and Nicole Dulioust, 'Les années françaises de Deng Xiaoping', *Vingtième Siècle Revue d'Histoire*, 20 (1988), pp. 17–34; *Une page d'histoire: Découvrez comment la Chine est entrée dans l'histoire de Montargis*; Marilyn A. Levine, *The Found Generation: Chinese Communists in Europe during the Twenties* (Seattle: University of Washington Press, 1993), pp. 3–8; Ye Xingqiu and Jiang Jingshi, *Faguo yizhan lao huagong jishi (Chinese Labourers in France During the First World War)* (Paris: Pacifica, 2010).

5   'Les Schneider, Le Creusot: Une famille, une enterprise, une ville (1836–1960)', exhibition organised by the Réunion des Musées Nationaux and the Musée d'Orsay, 27 February–21 May 1995. (*Le petit journal des grandes expositions*, Hors série.)

6   See Deng Maomao, *Deng Xiaoping, My Father*, pp. 75–103. Deng Xiaoping's registration form is held in the Montargis archives. *Les Schneider, Le Creusot: une famille, une enterprise, une ville*; Zhao and Liu, *Deng Xiaoping de san luo san qi*, pp. 12–14; Liu and Liu *Deng Xiaoping jishi*, pp. 15–35.

7   Rod Kedward, *La Vie en bleu: France and the French since 1900* (London: Allen Lane, 2005), pp. 154–6

8   See Zhao and Liu, *Deng Xiaoping de san luo san qi*, pp. 12–16; Liu and Liu, *Deng Xiaoping jishi*, pp. 15–35; Marilyn A. Levine and Chen San-Ching, 'Communist-Leftist control of the European Branch of the Guomindang, 1923–1927', *Modern China* 22/1 (January 1996), pp. 62–92; Chae-Jin Lee, *Zhou Enlai: The Early Years* (Stanford: Stanford University Press, 1994), pp. 157–167; Kedward, *La Vie en bleu: France and the French since 1900*, pp. 154–6; François Ferrette, *La Véritable Histoire du Parti Communiste Français* (Paris: Demopolis, 2011), pp. 69–74 and *passim*; Deng Maomao, *Deng Xiaoping, My Father*, pp. 75–103; N. Bukharin and E. Preobrazhensky *The ABC of Communism* (London: Penguin, 1969)

3. MOSCOW AND THE CHINESE REVOLUTION (1926–31)

1   Zhao and Liu, *Deng Xiaoping de san luo san qi*, p. 15.

2   Jane L. Price, *Cadres, Commanders and Commissars: The Training of the Chinese Communist Leadership, 1920–1945,* (Folkestone: Dawson, 1976) p. 93

3   Party History Research Centre of the Central Committee of the Chinese Communist Party, *History of the Chinese Communist Party: A Chronology of Events (1919–1990)* (Beijing: Foreign Languages Press, 1991), pp. 46, 52–3; Zhao and Liu, *Deng Xiaoping de san luo san qi*, pp. 24–30, 33–7; Liu and Liu, *Deng Xiaoping jishi*, pp. 48–92; Xinhua.net 'Ba qi huiyi (1927 nian)', no date; Deng Maomao, *Deng Xiaoping, My Father*, pp. 197–9; David S. G. Goodman, *Deng Xiaoping and the Chinese Revolution: A Political Biography* (London: Routledge, 1994), pp. 30–33.

4   Party History Research Centre, *A Chronology of Events (1919–1990)*, pp. 46, 52–3; Zhao and Liu, *Deng Xiaoping de san luo san qi*, pp. 24–30, 33–7; Liu and Liu, *Deng Xiaoping jishi*, pp. 48–92; Xinhua.net 'Ba qi huiyi (1927 nian)', no date; Deng Maomao, *Deng Xiaoping, My Father*, pp. 197–9; Goodman, *Deng Xiaoping and the Chinese Revolution*, pp. 30–33.

5   Zhao and Liu, *Deng Xiaoping de san luo san qi*, pp. 17–23; Liu and Liu, *Deng Xiaoping jishi*, pp. 36–45; Jane L. Price, *Cadres, Commanders and Commissars: The Training of the Chinese Communist Leadership, 1920–1945*, pp. 89–99 and *passim*.

6   Party History Research Centre, *A Chronology of Events (1919–1990)*, pp. 46, 52–3; Zhao and Liu, *Deng Xiaoping de san luo san qi*, pp. 24–30, 33–7; Liu and Liu, *Deng Xiaoping jishi*, pp. 48–92; Xinhua.net 'Ba qi huiyi (1927 nian)', no date; Deng Maomao, *Deng Xiaoping, My Father*, pp. 197–9; Goodman, *Deng Xiaoping and the Chinese Revolution*, pp. 30–33.

7   Party History Research Centre, *A Chronology of Events (1919–1990)*, pp. 46, 52–3; Zhao and Liu, *Deng Xiaoping de san luo san qi*, pp. 24–30, 33–7; Liu and Liu, *Deng Xiaoping jishi*, pp. 48–92; Xinhua.net 'Ba qi huiyi (1927 nian)'; Deng Maomao, *Deng Xiaoping, My Father*, pp. 197–9; Goodman, *Deng Xiaoping and the Chinese Revolution*, pp. 30–33.

8   Liu and Liu, *Deng Xiaoping jishi*, p. 52

9   Party History Research Centre, *A Chronology of Events (1919–1990)*, pp. 46, 52–3; Zhao and Liu, *Deng Xiaoping de san luo san qi*, pp. 24–30, 33–7; Liu and Liu, *Deng Xiaoping jishi*, pp. 48–92; Xinhua.net 'Ba qi huiyi (1927 nian)'; Deng Maomao, *Deng Xiaoping, My Father*, pp. 197–9; Goodman, *Deng Xiaoping and the Chinese Revolution*, pp. 30–33; Yu Boliu, *Weiren zhi jian: Mao Zedong yu Deng Xiaoping (Between Great Men: Mao Zedong and Deng Xiaoping)* (Nanchang: Jiangxi renmin chubanshe, 2011), pp. 2–5.

10   Party History Research Centre, *A Chronology of Events (1919–1990)*, pp. 46, 52–3; Zhao and Liu, *Deng Xiaoping de san luo san qi*, pp. 24–30, 33–7; Liu and Liu, *Deng Xiaoping jishi*, pp. 48–92; Xinhua.net 'Ba qi huiyi (1927 nian)'; Deng Maomao, *Deng Xiaoping, My Father*, pp. 197–9; Goodman, *Deng Xiaoping and the Chinese Revolution*, pp. 30–33.

11   Party History Research Centre, *A Chronology of Events (1919–1990)*, pp. 46, 52–3; Zhao and Liu, *Deng Xiaoping de san luo san qi*, pp. 24–30, 33–7; Liu and Liu, *Deng Xiaoping jishi*, pp. 48–92; Xinhua.net 'Ba qi huiyi (1927 nian)'; Deng Maomao, *Deng Xiaoping, My Father*, pp. 197–9; Goodman, *Deng Xiaoping and the Chinese Revolution*, pp. 30–33; Sophie Quinn-Judge, *Ho Chi Minh: The Missing Years 1919–1941* (London, Hurst: 2003), pp. 36, 140, 159; Huynh Kim Khanh, *Vietnamese Communism 1924–1945* (Ithaca and London: Cornell University Press, 1982), pp. 63–89.

4. SOLDIER AND COMMUNIST: TRIUMPH OVER ADVERSITY IN JIANGXI (1931–4)

1   Zhao and Liu, *Deng Xiaoping de san luo san qi*, pp. 24, 31.

2   Zhao and Liu, *Deng Xiaoping de san luo san qi*, pp. 33–7.

3   Liu and Liu, *Deng Xiaoping jishi*, pp. 93–100, 100–5; Zhao and Liu, *Deng Xiaoping de san luo san qi*, pp. 38–45; Tony Saich, *The Rise to Power of the Chinese Communist Party* (New York: M.E. Sharpe, 1996), pp. 509–13, 530–5, 652 n. 39, 701; Deng Maomao, *Deng Xiaoping, My Father*, pp. 199–204; Trygve Lötveit, *Chinese Communism 1931–1934: Experience in Civil Government* (Lund: Scandinavian Institute of Asian Studies, 1973), pp. 98–105.

4   Liu and Liu, *Deng Xiaoping jishi*, pp. 104–5; Lötveit, *Chinese Communism 1931–1934*, pp. 185–209.

5   For a local perspective from Ningdu county see www.ningdu.gov.cn/ndgk/xqjj/200810/
     t20081022_8426.htm (link no longer working); Deng Maomao, *Deng Xiaoping, My Father*,
     pp. 204–217; Zhao and Liu, *Deng Xiaoping de san luo san qi*, pp. 151–168; Liu and Liu,
     Deng Xiaoping jishi, pp. 105–8; Gregor Benton, 'The "Second Wang Ming Line"', *China
     Quarterly*, 61 (March 1975), pp. 61–94; Gregor Benton, *Mountain Fires: The Red Army's
     Three-Year War in South China, 1934–1938* (Berkeley: University of California Press,
     1992), pp. 132–4; Thomas Kampen, *Mao Zedong, Zhou Enlai and the Evolution of the
     Chinese Communist Leadership* (Copenhagen: Nordic Institute of Asian Studies, 2000),
     pp. 49–65; Yu, *Weiren zhi jian*, pp. 22–30, 32–44.
6   Liu and Liu, *Deng Xiaoping jishi*, p. 111.
7   Liu and Liu, *Deng Xiaoping jishi*, pp. 109–19; Deng Maomao, *Deng Xiaoping, My Father*,
     pp. 218–224; Yu, *Weiren zhi jian*, pp. 47–53.

5. REVOLUTION AND RESISTANCE: THE LONG MARCH, YAN'AN AND THE TAIHANG MOUNTAINS (1934–45)

1   Zhao and Liu, *Deng Xiaoping de san luo san qi*, pp. 38, 46.
2   Liu and Liu, *Deng Xiaoping jishi*, p. 120
3   Liu and Liu, *Deng Xiaoping jishi*, pp. 119–32; Kampen, *Mao Zedong, Zhou Enlai*, pp. 68–9.
4   Tony Saich and Hans J. Van de Ven (eds), *New Perspectives on the Chinese Communist
     Revolution* (New York: M.E. Sharpe, 1997), pp. 238–9.
5   Theodore H. White and Annalee Jacoby, *Thunder Out of China* (New York: Sloane, 1946),
     p. 129.
6   Tian Youru, '*Zhongguo kang Ri genjudi fazhan shi*', in Liu and Liu, *Deng Xiaoping jishi*,
     pp. 148–154.
7   Liu and Liu, *Deng Xiaoping jishi*, pp. 138–46, 148–54, 158–65; Deng Maomao, *Deng
     Xiaoping, My Father*, pp. 265–8, 280–93.
8   Zhao and Liu, *Deng Xiaoping de san luo san qi*, pp. 46–58; Deng Maomao, *Deng Xiaoping,
     My Father*, pp. 291–93.
9   Liu and Liu, *Deng Xiaoping jishi*, pp. 166–72; Deng Maomao, *Deng Xiaoping, My Father*,
     pp. 273–9, 280–93.
10   Liu and Liu, *Deng Xiaoping jishi*, pp. 172–7, 178–82; Zhao and Liu, *Deng Xiaoping de san
     luo san qi*, pp. 46–58; Deng Maomao, *Deng Xiaoping, My Father*, pp. 319–20.
11   Liu and Liu, *Deng Xiaoping jishi*, pp. 188–96; Party History Research Centre, *A Chronology
     of Events (1919-1990)*, pp. 128–40.
12   Liu and Liu, *Deng Xiaoping jishi*, pp. 205–16, 223–8; Deng Xiaoping, *Selected Works of
     Deng Xiaoping, Vol. 1 (1938-1965)* (Beijing: Foreign Languages Press, 1992), pp. 73–84,
     85–93. Stuart Gelder, *The Chinese Communists* (London: Victor Gollancz, 1946), pp. 200–
     204; Yu, *Weiren zhi jian*, pp. 63–83.

6. CIVIL WAR AND NEW CHINA (1945–9)

1   Zhao and Liu, *Deng Xiaoping de san luo san qi*, p. 151.
2   Liu and Liu, *Deng Xiaoping jishi*, p. 264.
3   Liu and Liu, *Deng Xiaoping jishi*, pp. 242–52, 264–302; Wang Shuzeng, *Jiefang zhanzheng
     (shang): 1945 8 yue–1948 9 yue (War of Liberation Volume 1: August 1945–September 1948)*
     (Beijing: Renmin chubanshe, 2011, two volumes), pp. 26–35; Party History Research
     Centre, *A Chronology of Events (1919–1990)*, pp. 164–5; Lionel Max Chassin, *The

Communist Conquest of China: A History of the Civil War 1945-9 (London: Weidenfeld and Nicolson, 1966), pp. 139–41; Deng Xiaoping, 'A review of the history of the Second Field Army', in *Selected Works of Deng Xiaoping, Vol. 3 (1982-1992)* (Beijing: Foreign Languages Press, 1992), Deng Maomao, *Deng Xiaoping, My Father*, pp. 388–406.

4   Liu and Liu, *Deng Xiaoping jishi*, pp. 317–21; Deng Xiaoping, 'The situation following our triumphal advance to the Central Plains and our future policies and strategy', 'Some suggestions concerning our entry into new areas in the future', in *Selected Works, Vol. 1 (1938-1965)*, pp. 103–14, 132–7.

5   Liu and Liu, *Deng Xiaoping jishi*, p. 326.

6   Liu and Liu, *Deng Xiaoping jishi*, pp. 323–8; Party History Research Centre, *A Chronology of Events (1919-1990)*, p. 196.

7   Liu and Liu, *Deng Xiaoping jishi*, pp. 328–35.

8   Liu and Liu, *Deng Xiaoping jishi*, pp. 339–45, 349–52, 355–61; Party History Research Centre, *A Chronology of Events*, pp. 182–6, 205; Deng Maomao, *Deng Xiaoping, My Father*, pp. 430–55.

7. LIBERATING SICHUAN AND RULING FROM CHONGQING (1949–52)

1   Shi Quanwei, *Shihua shishuo Deng Xiaoping (Straight Talking about Deng Xiaoping)* (Beijing: Zhongguo qingnian chubanshe, 2011, two volumes), p. 7.

2   Zhao and Liu, *Deng Xiaoping de san luo san qi*, p. 121.

3   Liu and Liu, *Deng Xiaoping jishi*, pp. 364–375; Shi, *Shihua shishuo Deng Xiaoping*, pp. 2–9, 10–14, 15–20, 21–7; Zhonggong Chongqing shiwei dang shi yanjiushi, *Zhongguo gongchandang Chongqing lishi, diyi juan (1926-1949)* (Chongqing: Chongqing chubanshe, 2011), pp. 552–63; Zhonggong Chongqing shiwei dang shi yanjiushi, *Zhongguo gongchandang Chongqing difang jianshi* (Chongqing: Chongqing chubanshe, 2006), pp. 104–22; Chassin, *Communist Conquest of China*, p. 236; Deng Maomao, *Deng Xiaoping, My Father*, pp. 456–67.

4   Liu and Liu, *Deng Xiaoping jishi*, pp. 364–375; Shi, *Shihua shishuo Deng Xiaoping*, pp. 2–9, 10–14, 15–20, 21–7; *Zhongguo gongchandang Chongqing lishi*, pp. 552–63; *Zhongguo gongchandang Chongqing difang jianshi*, pp. 104–122; Chassin, *Communist Conquest of China*, p. 236; Deng Maomao, *Deng Xiaoping, My Father*, pp. 456–67.

5   Liu and Liu, *Deng Xiaoping jishi*, pp. 379–83, 409–12; Shi, *Shihua shishuo Deng Xiaoping*, pp. 2–9, 10–14, 15–20, 21–7; Fei Hsiao-tung, *Peasant Life in China* (London: Routledge and Kegan Paul, 1980/1939); Fei Hsiao-tung and Chih-yi Chang, *Earthbound China: A Study of Rural Economy in Yunnan* (London: Routledge and Kegan Paul, 1948).

6   Liu and Liu, *Deng Xiaoping jishi*, pp. 364–75; Shi, *Shihua shishuo Deng Xiaoping*, pp. 2–9, 10–14, 15–20, 21–7; Luo and Yang, *Hongyan*; *Zhongguo gongchandang Chongqing difang jianshi*, pp. 96–9; *Zhongguo gongchandang Chongqing lishi*, pp. 519–29; Chassin, *Communist Conquest of China*, p. 236; Deng Maomao, *Deng Xiaoping, My Father*, pp. 456–67; Peter Townsend, *China Phoenix: The Revolution in China* (London: Jonathan Cape, 1955), pp. 381–6.

7   Liu and Liu, *Deng Xiaoping jishi*, pp. 423–4; Shi, *Shihua shishuo Deng Xiaoping*, pp. 2–9, 10–14, 15–20, 21–7.

8. BEIJING AND ZHONGNANHAI (1952–6)

1   Zhao and Liu, *Deng Xiaoping de san luo san qi*, p. 145.

2   Liu and Liu, *Deng Xiaoping jishi*, pp. 433–5.

3   Ibid., pp. 433–7; Deng Maomao, *Deng Xiaoping, My Father*, pp. 210–17; Party History Research Centre, *A Chronology of Events (1919–1990)*, p. 245.

4   Zhao and Liu, *Deng Xiaoping de san luo san qi*, p. 145.

5   Shi, *Shihua shishuo Deng Xiaoping*, pp. 52–4; Liu and Liu, *Deng Xiaoping jishi*, pp. 435–7; Frederick C. Teiwes, *Politics at Mao's Court: Gao Gang and Party Factionalism in the Early 1950s* (New York: M.E. Sharpe, 1990), p. 297, fn. 59; 'Guanyu 1954 nian guojia cao'an de baogao', in Zhonggong zhongyang wenxian yanjiushi (ed.), *Jianguo yilai zhongyao wenxian xuanbian* (Beijing: Zhongyang wenxian chubanshe, 1994), Vol. 5, pp. 294–314.

6   Liu and Liu, *Deng Xiaoping jishi*, p. 439

7   Zhao and Liu, *Deng Xiaoping de san luo san qi*, pp. 135–6, 145–6; Liu and Liu, *Deng Xiaoping jishi*, pp. 438–45; Shi Jian, *Gao Gang 'fandang' zhenxiang* (Hong Kong: Wenhua yishu chubanshe, 2008), pp. 225–30 and *passim*.

8   Liu and Liu, *Deng Xiaoping jishi*, pp. 438–45; 'Zhonggong zhongyang guanyu jiaqiang dui zhongyang renmin zhengfu caizheng jingji bumen gongzuo de jueding', in *Jianguo yilai*, Vol. 4, pp. 180–3.

9   Party History Research Centre, *A Chronology of Events (1919–1990)*, pp. 259–60.

10   Party History Research Centre, *A Chronology of Events (1919–1990)*, pp. 259–61.

11   Zhao and Liu, *Deng Xiaoping de san luo san qi*, pp. 135–44.

12   Shi, *Shihua shishuo Deng Xiaoping*, pp. 55–8; Zhao and Liu, *Deng Xiaoping de san luo san qi*, pp. 135–44.

13   Zhao and Liu, *Deng Xiaoping de san luo san qi*, pp. 135–44, p. 139.

14   Zhao and Liu, *Deng Xiaoping de san luo san qi*, pp. 135–44; Kuang Chen, Pan Liang (ed.) *Women de 1950 niandai* (Beijing: Zhongguo youyi chubangongsi, 2006), pp. 94–6. The text of Deng's speech can be found in *Jianguo yilai*, Vol. 9, pp. 118–67.

15   Party History Research Centre, *A Chronology of Events (1919–1990)*, p. 260; Laszlo Ladany, *The Communist Party of China and Marxism 1921–1985: A Self-Portrait* (London: Hurst, 1988), pp. 214–19; Jürgen Domes, *The Internal Politics of China 1949–1972* (London: Hurst, 1973), pp. 57–8; Deng Xiaoping, 'Report on the Revision of the Constitution of the Communist Party of China', 16 September 1956, in *Selected Works, Vol. 1 (1938–1965)*, pp. 217–55.

16   Liu Jintian and Zhang Airu, *Deng Xiaoping* (Hong Kong: Sanlian, 2003), cited in Liu and Liu, *Deng Xiaoping jishi*, pp. 450.

17   Zhao and Liu, *Deng Xiaoping de san luo san qi*, pp. 135–50; 'Guanyu xiugai dang de zhangcheng de baogao', in *Jianguo yilai*, Vol. 9, pp. 118–67; Liu and Liu, *Deng Xiaoping jishi*, pp. 450–1; Shi, *Shihua shishuo Deng Xiaoping*, pp. 55–8; Harold C. Hinton, 'The Eighth Congress of the Chinese Communist Party', *Far Eastern Survey* 26/1 (January 1957), pp. 1–8.

9. CAMPAIGN AGAINST RIGHTISTS AND INTELLECTUALS (1956–7)

1   Deng Xiaoping, 'The Communist Party must accept supervision', 8 April 1957, in *Selected Works*, Vol. 1, p. 270.

2   Zhao and Liu, *Deng Xiaoping de san luo san qi*, p. 147.

3   *People's Daily*, 19 October 1957, in Ladany, *Communist Party of China and Marxism*, pp. 233–4 and Domes, *Internal Politics of China*, pp. 85, 89; *Jianguo yilai*, Vols 1–17; Mu Fu-sheng, *The Wilting of the Hundred Flowers: Free Thought in China Today* (London: Heinemann, 1962), pp. 172–3; Chi Hsin, *Teng Hsiao-ping – A Political Biography* (Hong Kong: Cosmos Books, 1978), pp. 35–6; Party History Research Centre, *A Chronology of*

Events (1919–1990), pp. 263–4, 267; Roderick MacFarquhar, *The Origins of the Cultural Revolution 1: Contradictions among the People* 1956–7 (New York: Columbia University Press, 1974), pp. 281–9, 402–3.

4   Liu and Liu, *Deng Xiaoping jishi*, pp. 454–66; 467–70; Party History Research Centre, *A Chronology of Events (1919–1990)*, p. 267; David Bachman, *Bureaucracy, Economy, and Leadership in China: The Institutional Origins of the Great Leap Forward* (Cambridge: Cambridge University Press, 1991), p. 141; Roderick MacFarquhar, Timothy Cheek and Eugene wu (eds) *The Secret Speeches of Chairman Mao: From the Hundred Flowers to the Great Leap Forward* (Cambridge: Harvard University Press, 1989), pp. 273–96; Mao Zedong, *Mao Zedong xuanji (Selected Works)*, Vol. 5 (Beijing: Renmin chubanshe, 1977), pp. 267–88.

5   Liu and Liu, *Deng Xiaoping jishi*, pp. 471–4; Kampen, *Mao Zedong, Zhou Enlai and the Evolution of the Chinese Communist Leadership*, pp. 69–75 and *passim*; Stuart Schram (ed.) with Nancy Jane Hodes, *Mao's Road to Power: Revolutionary Writings 1912–1949* (New York: M. E. Sharpe, 1992), pp. xxxvii–viii; Harrison Salisbury, *The Long March: The Untold Story* (London: Macmillan, 1985), p. 371 n. 20; Liu Ying 'Nanwang de sanbai liush jiu tian' *Liaowang* Issue no. 41, 1986; Oriana Fallaci, *Intervista con il Potere* (Milan: Rizzoli, 2009), pp. 456–92. Fallaci's original reads: *Mi accuse di sobillargli contro il gruppo di Mao Tse-tung, mi defenestrò, e dovetti aspettare tre ani per essere riabilitato. Cosa che avenne nel 1935, durante la Grande Marcia, al congresso di Zuen Yi. Perché, a Zuen Yi, gli opportunisti dell'estrema sinistra vennero sconfitti, Wang Min messo da parte, e Mao Tse-tung riprese in mano il partito facendomi segretario generale.*

10. THE GREAT LEAP FORWARD, CONFRONTATION AT LUSHAN AND THE SINO–SOVIET SPLIT (1958–61)

1   Zhao and Liu, *Deng Xiaoping de san luo san qi*, p. 147.
2   Jürgen Domes, *Peng Te-huai: The Man and the Image* (London: Hurst, 1985), pp. 77–106; Domes, *Internal Politics of China 1949–1972*, pp. 110–13; Roderick MacFarquhar, *The Origins of the Cultural Revolution 2: The Great Leap Forward* 1958–60 (Oxford: Oxford University Press, 1983), pp. 228–33, 407.
3   Liu and Liu, *Deng Xiaoping jishi*, pp. 474–81, 482–4; Party History Research Centre, *A Chronology of Events (1919–1990)*, pp. 285–7; Chi, *Teng Hsiao-ping*, pp. 36–7; Mark Frankland, *Khrushchev* (London: Penguin, 1966), pp. 171–87; Isaac Deutscher, *Russia, China and the West: A Contemporary Chronicle 1953–1966* (London: Penguin, 1970), pp. 202–233 and *passim*.
4   Liu and Liu, *Deng Xiaoping jishi*, pp. 500–1.
5   Liu and Liu, *Deng Xiaoping jishi*, pp. 497–501, 501–3.

11. REBUILDING THE ECONOMY (1962–5)

1   Zhao and Liu, *Deng Xiaoping de san luo san qi*, p. 179.
2   Liu and Liu, *Deng Xiaoping jishi*, pp. 485–503; Party History Research Centre, *A Chronology of Events (1919–1990)*, pp. 294–5.
3   Liu and Liu, *Deng Xiaoping jishi*, pp. 485–503; Party History Research Centre, *A Chronology of Events (1919–1990)*, pp. 278, 286; David Shambaugh, 'The Soldier and the State in China: The Political Work System in the People's Liberation Army', in Brian Hook

(ed.) *The Individual and the State in China* (Oxford: Oxford University Press, 1996), pp. 116–17.

4 Liu and Liu, *Deng Xiaoping jishi*, p. 504

5 Zhang Suhua, *Bianzhu: qiqianren dahui shimo (1962 nian 1 yue 11 ri – 2 yue 7 ri)* (*Critical Moment: Seven Thousand Cadres Conference 11 January to 7 February 1962*), pp. 7–33, 34–44 and *passim*; Liu and Liu, *Deng Xiaoping jishi*, pp. 504–12.

6 Zhang Suhua, *Bianzhu: qiqianren dahui shimo (1962 nian 1 yue 11 ri – 2 yue 7 ri)* (*Critical Moment: Seven Thousand Cadres Conference 11 January to 7 February 1962*) pp. 46–86; 192–200 and *passim*.

7 Milovan Djilas, *The New Class: An Analysis of the Communist System* (London: Unwin Books, 1957).

8 Liu and Liu, *Deng Xiaoping jishi*, pp. 504–12, 512–15; Zhang Suhua, *Bianzhu: qiqianren dahui shimo (1962 nian 1 yue 11 ri – 2 yue 7 ri)* (*Critical Moment: Seven Thousand Cadres Conference 11 January to 7 February 1962*) (Beijing: Zhongguo qingnian chubanshe, 2006), pp. 34–45, 192–200; Party History Research Centre, *A Chronology of Events (1919–1990)*, pp. 289–97, 301–2; Larry M. Wortzel and Robin D. S. Higham, *Dictionary of Contemporary Chinese Military History* (Santa Barbara: ABC-CLIO, 1999), pp. 303–4; Michael Schoenhals and Brewer S. Stone, 'More edited records: Liu Shaoqi on Peng Dehuai at the 7,000 Cadres Conference', *CCP Research Newsletter* No. 5 (1990).

9 Liu and Liu, *Deng Xiaoping jishi*, pp. 504–12, 512–15; Party History Research Centre, *A Chronology of Events (1919–1990)*, pp. 289–97, 301–2; Wortzel and Higham, *Dictionary of Contemporary Chinese Military History*, pp. 303–4; Djilas, *The New Class*; Schoenhals and Stone, 'More edited records'.

10 Liu and Liu, *Deng Xiaoping jishi*, pp. 518–22.

11 Liu and Liu, *Deng Xiaoping jishi*, pp. 522–39; Zhao and Liu, *Deng Xiaoping de san luo san qi*, pp. 149–50.

12. CAPITALIST ROADER NUMBER 2 (1966–73)

1 Zhao and Liu, *Deng Xiaoping de san luo san qi*, p. 179.

2 Liu and Liu, *Deng Xiaoping jishi*, p. 547.

3 Liu and Liu, *Deng Xiaoping jishi*, pp. 544–9;

4 Liu and Liu, *Deng Xiaoping jishi*, pp. 549–63;

5 Liu and Liu, *Deng Xiaoping jishi*, pp. 549–63, 563–7; Party History Research Centre, *A Chronology of Events (1919–1990)*, pp. 323–34; Ezra F. Vogel, *Deng Xiaoping and the Transformation of China* (Cambridge, Massachusetts: Belknap Press at Harvard University Press, 2011), pp. 44–5, 49–61; Endymion Wilkinson, *Chinese History: A Manual (Revised and Enlarged)* (Cambridge: Harvard-Yenching Institute, 2000), pp. 501–7.

13. RETURN FROM THE COWSHED (1973–5)

1 Zhao and Liu, *Deng Xiaoping de san luo san qi*, p. 191.

2 Party History Research Centre, *A Chronology of Events (1919–1990)*, p. 359.

3 Liu and Liu, *Deng Xiaoping jishi*, pp. 549–54, 568–71, 571–84.

4 Liu and Liu, *Deng Xiaoping jishi*, pp. 571–84; *People's Daily*, 4 July 2002; Mao Zedong, *Poems of Mao Tse-tung* (translated and edited by Wong Man), pp. 8–9. For an account of

Mao's journey, see Ma Shexiang, *Qianzou: Mao Zedong 1965 nian chong shang Jinggangshan* (*Prelude: Mao Zedong's repeat ascent of Jinggangshan*).

5   Liu and Liu, *Deng Xiaoping jishi*, pp. 571–84, 584–595
6   Liu and Liu, *Deng Xiaoping jishi*, pp. 595–602
7   Liu and Liu, *Deng Xiaoping jishi*, pp. 605–619.

14. RUNNING CHINA (JANUARY 1975)

1   Zhao and Liu, *Deng Xiaoping de san luo san qi*, p. 191.
2   Liu and Liu, *Deng Xiaoping jishi*, pp. 584–7, 587–619; Party History Research Centre, *A Chronology of Events (1919–1990)*, pp. 359, 360–1, 364–5, 366; Deng Xiaoping internet archive, available at www.marxists.org/reference/archive/deng-xiaoping/1974/04/10.htm (accessed 14 April 2014).
3   Hu Qiaomu zhuan bianxiezu (ed.), *Deng Xiaoping de ershisi ci tanhua* (*Twenty-Four Conversations with Deng Xiaoping*) (Beijing: Renmin chubanshe, 2004), pp. 1–7.
4   Liu and Liu, *Deng Xiaoping jishi*, pp. 605–619; Deng Xiaoping, 'Some problems outstanding in the iron and steel industry', in *Selected Works (1975-1982)*, pp. 18–22; Deng Xiaoping 'Dangqian gangtie gongye bixu jiejue de jige wenti', *Deng Xiaoping wenxuan (1975-1982)*, pp. 8–11.
5   Frederick C. Teiwes, and Warren Sun, *The End of the Maoist Era: Chinese Politics During the Twilight of the Cultural Revolution, 1972–1976* (Armonk, New York: M.E. Sharpe, 2008), p. 319.
6   Teiwes, Sun, *The End of the Maoist Era*: pp. 315–324
7   Hu Qiaomu zhuan bianxiezu (ed.), *Deng Xiaoping de ershisi ci tanhua*, pp. 1–7 – this book also contains the key documents drafted by the Political Research Office; Liu and Liu, *Deng Xiaoping jishi*, pp. 605–19; David M. Finkelstein and Maryanne Kivlehan (ed.), *Chinese Leadership in the Twenty-First Century: The Rise of the Fourth Generation* (New York: M.E. Sharpe, 2002), pp. 153–4; Party History Research Centre, *A Chronology of Events (1919–1990)*, pp. 366–74; Kenneth G. Lieberthal and Bruce J. Dickson, *A Research Guide to Central Party and Government Meetings in China: 1949–1986* (New York: M.E. Sharpe, 1989), pp. 235–6; Teiwes and Sun, *The End of the Maoist Era*: pp. 282–91, 315–24.

15. ATTAINING POWER (1976–8)

1   Zhao and Liu, *Deng Xiaoping de san luo san qi*, pp. 215, 220.
2   Party History Research Centre, *A Chronology of Events (1919–1990)*, pp. 377.
3   Liu and Liu, *Deng Xiaoping jishi*, pp. 622–8; Party History Research Centre, *A Chronology of Events (1919–1990)*, pp. 377, 380–6; Ting Wang, *Chairman Hua: Leader of the Chinese Communists* (London: Hurst, 1980), pp. 100–21 and *passim*; Teiwes and Sun, *End of the Maoist Era*, pp. 324–48; Hu Deping, *Zhongguo weishenme yao gaige: siyi fuqin Hu Yaobang* (*Why China Needs Reform: Remembering my Father Hu Yaobang*) (Beijing: Renmin chubanshe, 2011), pp. 86–129; Han Hongghong, *Hu Yaobang zai lieshi zhuanzhe guantou (1975–1982)* (*Hu Yaobang at a Turning Point in History (1975–1982)*) (Beijing: Renmin chubanshe, 2009), pp. 81–115; Zhonggong zhongyang dangshi yanjiushi, *Zhongguo gongchandang lishi, di er juan (1949–1978) xiace* (*History of the Chinese Communist Party, Volume 2 (1949–1978), Part 2*) (Beijing: Zhonggong dangshi chubanshe, 2010), pp. 1022–

37; Yu Wei and Wu Zhifei, *Deng Xiaoping de zuihou ershi nian* (Beijing: Xinhua chubanshe, 2008) pp. 13–18.

16. ECONOMIC REFORM AND OPENING TO THE WORLD (1978–9)

1   Zhao and Liu, *Deng Xiaoping de san luo san qi*, p. 243.
2   Deng Xiaoping, 'Uphold the Four Cardinal Principles', in *Selected Works, Vol. 2*, 1975–1982, p. 166.
3   Party History Research Centre, *A Chronology of Events (1919–1990)*, pp. 383–7, 393–5.
4   Liu and Liu, *Deng Xiaoping jishi*, pp. 661–78; S.I. Hsiung, *The Life of Chiang Kai-shek* (London: Peter Davies, 1948), pp. 54–62; Editorial Committee for 'Records of Deng Xiaoping's meetings with heads of state and journalists', *Deng Xiaoping yu waiguo shounao ji jizhe huitan lu* (*Records of Deng Xiaoping's meetings with heads of state and journalists*) [Beijing: Taihai Press, 2011], pp. 49–81; Zhong Wen and Wen Fu, *Deng Xiaoping waijiao fengcai shilu* (*Veritable Records of Deng Xiaoping's Elegant Diplomacy*) (Beijing: Renmin chubanshe, 2004), pp. 85–129; Yu and Wu, *Deng Xiaoping de zuihou ershi nian*, pp. 25–48; Party History Research Centre, *A Chronology of Events (1919–1990)*, pp. 393–5.
5   Leng Rong and Wang Zuoling (chief eds), *Deng Xiaoping nianpu 1975–1997* (*Chronicles of Deng Xiaoping 1975–1997*) (Beijing: Zhongyang wenxian chubanshe, 2004, 2 vols), pp. 419–30; Ben Dolven, 'Suzhou project: wounded pride', *Far Eastern Economic Review* (8 July 1999).
6   Party History Research Centre, *A Chronology of Events (1919–1990)*, p. 393.
7   Wu Guoyou, *Zhonggong zhizhengdang jianshi shi (1978–2009)* (*History of the Construction of the Chinese Communist Party as a Ruling Party*) (Shenyang: Liaoning renmin chubanshe, 2011), pp. 32–47; Ye Yonglie, *Deng Xiaoping gaibian Zhongguo: 1978 Zhongguo mingyun da zhuanzhe* (Nanchang: Jiangxi renmin chubanshe, 2008), pp. 402–40; Zhu Jiamu, *Wo suo zhidao de shiyi jie sanzhong quanhui* (*The Third Plenum of the Eleventh Central Committee That I Knew*) (Beijing: Dangdai Zhongguo chubanshe), 2009, pp. 70–94 and *passim*; Leng and Wang, *Deng Xiaoping nianpu 1975–1997* (*Chronicles of Deng Xiaoping 1975–1997*), pp. 427–56.
8   Wu, *Zhonggong zhizhengdang jianshi shi (1978–2009)*, pp. 32–47; Ye, *Deng Xiaoping gaibian Zhongguo*, pp. 395–400; Zhu, *Wo suo zhidao de shiyi jie sanzhong quanhui*, pp. 70–94; Leng and Wang, *Deng Xiaoping nianpu 1975–1997*, pp. 427–56.
9   'Hundreds mourn head of China's "reform cradle village" Xinhua News Agency (8 November 2008); In December 2008, the Fengyang County government website (www.fengyang.gov.cn) carried illustrated articles about the anniversary and the opening of the memorial hall; Yu and Wu, *Deng Xiaoping de zuihou ershi nian*, pp. 51–6; Chen Guikang and Chun Tao, *Xiaogangcun de gushi* (Beijing: Huawen chubanshe, 2009), pp. 27–43 and *passim*.
10   Liu and Liu, *Deng Xiaoping jishi*, pp. 684–6.
11   Liu and Liu, *Deng Xiaoping jishi*, pp. 679–86; 'Former Vice-President Rong dies at age 89 in Beijing', Xinhuanet.com (27 October 2005). Available at http://news.xinhuanet.com/politics/2005-10/27/content_3690438.htm (accessed 14 April 2014).
12   Liu and Liu, *Deng Xiaoping jishi*, pp. 690–711; Leng and Wang, *Deng Xiaoping nianpu 1975–1997*, pp. 475–87; Cheng, Jin, *A Chronology of the People's Republic of China 1949–1984* (Beijing: Foreign Languages Press, 1986), p. 72; Xiong Xianghui, 'Dakai Zhong Mei guanxi de qianzou: 1969 nian siwei laoshuai dui guoji xingshi de yanjiu yu jianyi' ('The prelude to the opening of Sino–US relations: 1969 study of the international situation by

four veteran commanders'), in *Xin Zhongguo waijiao fengyun* (*New China's Changing Diplomacy*) Vol. 4 (Beijing: Shijie zhishe chubanshe, 1996), pp. 7–34; Roderick MacFarquhar and Michael Schoenhals, *Mao's Last Revolution* (Cambridge: Belknap Harvard, 2006), pp. 320–3; Richard Wilson (ed.), *The President's Trip to China: A Pictorial Record of the Historic Journey to the People's Republic of China with Text by Members of the American Press Corps* (New York: Bantam, 1972); Stephen E. Ambrose, *Rise to Globalism: American Foreign Policy since 1938* (London: Penguin, 1988), pp. 245–7.

13   Liu and Liu, *Deng Xiaoping jishi*, pp. 686–689; Leng and Wang, *Deng Xiaoping nianpu 1975–1997*, pp. 498–503; David S.G. Goodman, *Beijing Street Voices: The Poetry and Politics of China's Democracy Movement* (London: Marion Boyars, 1981); Party History Research Centre, *A Chronology of Events (1919–1990)*, pp. 392–3, 397–8; Deng Xiaoping, *Selected Works, Vol. 2* (1975–82), pp. 166–195.

17. RETREATING TO ADVANCE: FROM THE GANG OF FOUR TO THE DEMOCRACY MOVEMENT (1980–92)

1   Zhao and Liu, *Deng Xiaoping de san luo san qi*, p. 237.

2   Ye, *Deng Xiaoping gaibian Zhongguo*, p. 442.

3   Cheng, *Chronology*, p. 76–84; Leng and Wang, *Deng Xiaoping nianpu 1975–1997*, pp. 669–73; Party History Research Centre, *A Chronology of Events (1919–1990)*, pp. 404–12; Ye, *Deng Xiaoping gaibian Zhongguo*, pp. 442–57.

4   Cheng, *Chronology*, p.79–80; Party History Research Centre, *A Chronology of Events (1919–1990)*, pp. 413, 415–16; Liu and Liu, *Deng Xiaoping jishi*, pp. 759–66.

5   Lieberthal, Kenneth G., *Governing China: From Revolution through Reform* (New York: Norton, 2004), p. 177.

6   Deng Xiaoping, 'Opening Speech at the Twelfth National Congress of the CPC', in *Selected Works, Vol. 2 (1975–1982)*, pp. 394–7; 'Speech at the First Plenary Session of the Central Advisory Commission of the Communist Party of China', 13 September 1982. Available at http://english.peopledaily.com.cn/dengxp/vol3/text/c1020.html (accessed 14 April 2014); Cheng, *Chronology*, p. 89; Party History Research Centre, *A Chronology of Events (1919–1990)*, pp. 393–5, 430–2; Liu and Liu, *Deng Xiaoping jishi*, pp. 804–15; Lieberthal, *Governing China: From Revolution through Reform*, p. 177; *Constitution of the People's Republic of China*, 1982. Available at http://english.people.com.cn/constitution/constitution.html (accessed 14 April 2014).

7   Yang Jisheng, *Zhongguo gaige niandai de zhengzhi douzheng* (*The Political Struggles of China's Reform Period*) (Hong Kong: Excellent Culture Press, 2004), pp. 18–25

8   Yang Jisheng, *Zhongguo gaige niandai de zhengzhi douzheng* (*The Political Struggles of China's Reform Period*), pp. 18–25; Yang Jisheng, *Mubei: yijiuwuba-yijiuliuer nian Zhongguo da jihuang jishi* (Hong Kong: Cosmos Books, 2010, 2 vols); Yang Jisheng, *Tombstone: The Untold Story of Mao's Great Famine* (London: Allen Lane, 2012); Han, *Hu Yaobang*; Zhao Ziyang, *Prisoner of the State: The Secret Journal of Zhao Ziyang* (London: Simon and Schuster, 2009); Li Honglin, *Zhongguo sixiang yundong shi* (*A History of Chinese Ideological Movements*) (Hong Kong: Cosmos Books, 2010 pp. 368–516; Wu, *Zhongguo zhizhengdang*, pp. 169–74, 175–83.

9   Zhao, *Prisoner of the State*, pp. 6, 8–14; Zhang Liang (compiler), Andrew Nathan and Perry Link (eds), *The Tiananmen Papers* (London: Little, Brown, 2001), pp. 175, 204–7, 354–63, 365, 368–70; Lowell Dittmer, 'Review Article', *China Quarterly*, 166 (June 2001), pp. 476–

83; Alfred Chan and Andrew Nathan, 'The *Tiananmen Papers* Revisited', *China Quarterly*, 177 (March 2004), pp. 190–214; Vogel, *Deng Xiaoping*, pp. 609–15, 616–39.

10   Party History Research Centre, *A Chronology of Events (1919–1990)*, p. 509.

11   Party History Research Centre, *A Chronology of Events (1919–1990)*, pp. 495–511.

12   Yang, *Zhongguo gaige niandai*, pp. 18–25; Han, *Hu Yaobang (1975–1982)*; Zhao, *Prisoner of the State*; Wu, *Zhongguo zhizhengdang*, pp. 169–74, 175–83.

18. SOUTHERN TOUR AND THE DENG LEGACY (1992–7)

1   Zhao and Liu, *Deng Xiaoping de san luo san qi*, p. 315.

2   Ibid., p. 355.

3   Liu and Liu, *Deng Xiaoping jishi*, p. 1071.

4   Leng and Wang, *Deng Xiaoping nianpu 1975–1997*, pp. 1334–41, 1341–6; Wu Songying, *Deng Xiaoping nanfang tanhua zhenqing shilu – jilu ren de jishu* (*Record of the Reality of Deng Xiaoping's Discussions in the South*) (Beijing: Renmin chubanshe, 2012); Niu Zhengwu, *Nanxingji: 1992 nian Deng Xiaoping nanfang tanhua quan jilu* (*Record of the Southern Tour: Complete Record of Deng Xiaoping's Discussions in the South*) (Guangzhou: Guangdong renmin chubanshe, 2012); Chen Kaizhi, *Qidian: Deng Xiaoping nanfang zhi xing* (*Starting Point: Deng Xiaoping's Journey to the South*) (Beijing: Zhongguo wenshi chubanshe, 2008); Party History Research Centre, *A Chronology of Events (1919–1990)*, p. 407; Joseph Fewsmith, *China since Tiananmen: The Politics of Transition* (Cambridge: Cambridge University Press, 2001), pp. 55–63; Zhu Rongji, *Zhu Rongji jianghua shilu* (Beijing: Renmin chubanshe, 2012); Zhu Rongji, *Zhu Rongji on the Record: The Road to Reform 1991–1997* (Beijing: Foreign Languages Press, 2013).

5   Jan van der Made, 'De dood van Deng Xiaoping: China's laatste "sterke man" overleden', *Het Parool* (20 February 1997); 'Deng Xiaoping begraven: subtiel protest op Tiananmen plein', (26 February 1997).

6   Author's discussions with sociologist Zhou Guansan, and other members of the Jiangsu Academy of Social Sciences, Nanjing, October 1983.

7   Priscilla Jiao, 'No great fanfare 20 years after tour' *South China Morning Post* (20 January 2012); Hu, *Zhongguo weishenme yao gaige*; Michael Dillon, 'China's Rulers: The Fifth Generation Takes Power (2012–13)', in Kerry Brown (ed.) *China and the EU in Context: Insights for Business and Investors*, (Palgrave Macmillan 2014) pp. 142–77.

BIBLIOGRAPHY

Constitution of the People's Republic of China (adopted 4 December 1982). Available at http://english.people.com.cn/constitution/constitution.html (accessed 14 April 2014).

'Les Schneider, Le Creusot: Une famille, une enterprise, une ville (1836–1960)', exhibition organised by the Réunion des Musées Nationaux and the Musée d'Orsay, 27 February–21 May 1995. (*Le petit journal des grandes expositions*, Hors série.)

Une page d'histoire: Découvrez comment la Chine est entrée dans l'histoire de Montargis. Montargis: Agglomération Montargoise et Rives du Loing. Available at www.agglo-montargoise.fr (accessed 14 April 2014).

Ambrose, Stephen E., *Rise to Globalism: American Foreign Policy since 1938* (London: Penguin, 1988).

Bachman, David, *Bureaucracy, Economy, and Leadership in China: The Institutional Origins of the Great Leap Forward* (Cambridge: Cambridge University Press, 1991).

Barman, Geneviève and Nicole Dulioust, 'Les années françaises de Deng Xiaoping', *Vingtième Siècle Revue d'Histoire*, 20 (1988), pp. 17–34.

Barrett, David D., *Dixie Mission: The United States Army Observer Group in Yenan, 1944* (Berkeley: University of California Centre for Chinese Studies, 1970).

Benton, Gregor, 'The "Second Wang Ming Line"', *China Quarterly*, 61 (March 1975), pp. 61–94.

—— *Mountain Fires: The Red Army's Three-Year War in South China, 1934–1938* (Berkeley: University of California Press, 1992).

Bukharin, N. and E. Preobrazhensky, *The ABC of Communism* (London: Penguin, 1969).

Chan, Alfred and Andrew Nathan, 'The *Tian'anmen Papers* Revisited', *China Quarterly*, 177 (March 2004), pp. 190–214.

Chassin, Lionel Max, *The Communist Conquest of China: A History of the Civil War 1945–9* (London: Weidenfeld and Nicolson, 1966).

Chen Guikang and Chun Tao, *Xiaogangcun de gushi* (*The Story of Xiaogang Village*) (Beijing: Huawen chubanshe, 2009).

Chen Kaizhi, *Qidian: Deng Xiaoping nanfang zhi xing* (*Starting Point: Deng Xiaoping's Journey to the South*) (Beijing: Zhongguo wenshi chubanshe, 2008).

Cheng Jin, *A Chronology of the People's Republic of China 1949–1984* (Beijing: Foreign Languages Press, 1986).

Cheng Zhongyuan, *Deng Xiaoping de ershisi ci tanhua* (*Twenty Conversations with Deng Xiaoping*) (Beijing: Renmin chubanshe, 2004), edited by 'Hu Qiaomu biography' Editorial Group.

Chi Hsin, *Teng Hsiao-ping – A Political Biography* (Hong Kong: Cosmos Books, 1978).

Deng Maomao, *Deng Xiaoping, My Father* (London: Harper Collins, 1995).

Deng Xiaoping 'Dangqian gangtie gongye bixu jiejue de jige wenti', *Deng Xiaoping wenxuan (1975–1982)*, pp. 8–11.

—— *Deng Xiaoping wenxuan 1975-1982 (Selected Works of Deng Xiaoping 1975-1982)* (Hong Kong: Renmin chubanshe and Sanlian, 1983).

—— *Selected Works of Deng Xiaoping, Volume 1 (1938–1965)* (Beijing: Foreign Languages Press, 1992).

—— *Selected Works of Deng Xiaoping, Volume 2 (1975–1982)* (Beijing: Foreign Languages Press, 1992).

—— *Selected Works of Deng Xiaoping, Volume 3 (1982–1992)* (Beijing: Foreign Languages Press, 1992).

Deutscher, Isaac, *Russia, China and the West: A Contemporary Chronicle 1953–1966* (London: Penguin, 1970).

Dillon, Michael, 'China's Rulers: The Fifth Generation Takes Power (2012–13)' in Kerry Brown (ed.) *China and the EU in Context: Insights for Business and Investors* (Palgrave Macmillan, 2014).

Dittmer, Lowell, 'Review Article', *China Quarterly*, 166 (June 2001), pp. 476–83.

Djilas, Milovan, *The New Class: An Analysis of the Communist System* (London: Unwin Books, 1957).

Dolven, Ben, 'Suzhou project: wounded pride', *Far Eastern Economic Review* (8 July 1999).

Domes, Jürgen, *The Internal Politics of China 1949–1972* (London: Hurst, 1973).

—— *Peng Te-huai: The Man and the Image* (London: Hurst, 1985).

Editorial Committee for 'Records of Deng Xiaoping's meetings with heads of state and journalists', *Deng Xiaoping yu waiguo shounao ji jizhe huitan lu (Records of Deng Xiaoping's meetings with heads of state and journalists)* (Beijing: Taihai Press, 2011).

Fallaci, Oriana, *Intervista con il Potere* (Milan: Rizzoli, 2009).

Fei Hsiao-tung, *Peasant Life in China* (London: Routledge and Kegan Paul, 1980/1939).

Fei Hsiao-tung and Chih-yi Chang, *Earthbound China: A Study of Rural Economy in Yunnan* (London: Routledge and Kegan Paul, 1948).

Ferrette, François, *La Véritable Histoire du Parti Communiste Français* (Paris: Demopolis, 2011).

Fewsmith, Joseph, *China since Tian'anmen: The Politics of Transition* (Cambridge: Cambridge University Press, 2001).

Finkelstein, David M. and Maryanne Kivlehan (ed.), *Chinese Leadership in the Twenty-First Century: The Rise of the Fourth Generation* (New York: M.E. Sharpe, 2002).

Frankland, Mark, *Khrushchev* (London: Penguin, 1966).

Gelder, Stuart, *The Chinese Communists* (London: Victor Gollancz, 1946).

Goodman, David S.G., *Beijing Street Voices: The Poetry and Politics of China's Democracy Movement* (London: Marion Boyars, 1981).

—— *Deng Xiaoping and the Chinese Revolution: A Political Biography* (London: Routledge, 1994).

Han Honghong, *Hu Yaobang zai lishi zhuanzhe guantou (1975–1982) (Hu Yaobang at a Turning Point in History (1975–1982))* (Beijing: Renmin chubanshe, 2009).

Hinton, Harold C., 'The Eighth Congress of the Chinese Communist Party', *Far Eastern Survey*, 26/1 (January 1957), pp. 1–8.

Hsiung, S.I., *The Life of Chiang Kai-shek* (London: Peter Davies, 1948).

Hu Deping, *Zhongguo weishenme yao gaige: siyi fuqin Hu Yaobang* (*Why China Needs Reform: Remembering my Father Hu Yaobang*) (Beijing: Renmin chubanshe, 2011).

Hu Qiaomu zhuan bianxiezu (ed.), *Deng Xiaoping de ershisi ci tanhua* (*Twenty-Four Conversations with Deng Xiaoping*) (Beijing: Renmin chubanshe, 2004).

Kampen, Thomas, *Mao Zedong, Zhou Enlai and the Evolution of the Chinese Communist Leadership* (Copenhagen: Nordic Institute of Asian Studies, 2000).

Kedward, Rod, *La Vie en bleu: France and the French since 1900* (London: Allen Lane, 2005).

Khanh, Huynh Kim, *Vietnamese Communism 1924–1945* (Ithaca and London: Cornell University Press, 1982).

Kuang Chen, Pan Liang (ed.) *Women de 1950 niandai (Our 1950s)* (Beijing: Zhongguo youyi chubangongsi, 2006).

Ladany, Laszlo, *The Communist Party of China and Marxism 1921–1985: A Self-Portrait* (London: Hurst, 1988).

Lee, Chae-Jin, *Zhou Enlai: The Early Years* (Stanford: Stanford University Press, 1994).

Leng Rong and Wang Zuoling (chief editors), *Deng Xiaoping nianpu 1975–1997* (*Chronicles of Deng Xiaoping 1975–1997*) (Beijing: Zhongyang wenxian chubanshe, 2004, two volumes).

Levine, Marilyn A., *The Found Generation: Chinese Communists in Europe During the Twenties* (Seattle: University of Washington Press, 1993).

Levine, Marilyn A. and Chen San-Ching 'Communist-Leftist control of the European Branch of the Guomindang, 1923–1927', *Modern China*, 22/1 (January 1996), pp. 62–92.

Li Honglin, *Zhongguo sixiang yundong shi* (*A History of Chinese Ideological Movements*) (Hong Kong: Cosmos Books, 2010).

Lieberthal, Kenneth G., *Governing China: From Revolution through Reform* (New York: Norton, 2004).

Lieberthal, Kenneth G. and Bruce J. Dickson, *A Research Guide to Central Party and Government Meetings in China: 1949–1986* (New York: M.E. Sharpe, 1989).

Liu Jianhua and Liu Li, *Deng Xiaoping jishi* (*Chronicle of the Life of Deng Xiaoping*) (Beijing: Zhongyang wenxian chubanshe, 2011, two volumes).

Liu Jintian and Zhang Airu, *Deng Xiaoping* (Hong Kong: Sanlian, 2003).

Liu Ying, 'Nanwang de sanbai liush jiu tian', *Liaowang* no. 41, (1986).

Lötveit, Trygve, *Chinese Communism 1931–1934: Experience in Civil Government* (Lund: Scandinavian Institute of Asian Studies, 1973).

Luo Guangbin and Yang Yiyan, *Hongyan* (Beijing: Zhongguo qingnian chubanshe, 2011/1961).

Ma Shexiang, *Qianzou: Mao Zedong 1965 nian chong shang Jinggangshan* (*Prelude: Mao Zedong's repeat ascent of Jinggangshan*) (Beijing: Contemporary China Press, 2007).

MacFarquhar, Roderick, *The Origins of the Cultural Revolution 1: Contradictions among the People 1956–7* (New York, Columbia University Press, 1974).

—— *The Origins of the Cultural Revolution 2: The Great Leap Forward* 1958–60 (Oxford: Oxford University Press, 1983).

MacFarquhar, Roderick, Timothy Cheek and Eugene Wu (eds) *The Secret Speeches of Chairman Mao: From the Hundred Flowers to the Great Leap Forward* (Cambridge MA: Harvard University Press, 1989).

MacFarquhar, Roderick and Michael Schoenhals, *Mao's Last Revolution* (Cambridge MA: Belknap Harvard, 2006).

Mao Zedong, *Mao Zedong xuanji* (*Selected Works*), Volume 5 (Beijing: Renmin chubanshe, 1977).

—— *Poems of Mao Tse-tung* (translated and edited by Wong Man) (Hong Kong: Eastern Horizon Press, 1966).

Mu Fu-sheng, *The Wilting of the Hundred Flowers: Free Thought in China Today* (London: Heinemann, 1962).

Niu Zhengwu, *Nanxingji: 1992 nian Deng Xiaoping nanfang tanhua quan jilu* (*Record of the Southern Tour: Complete Record of Deng Xiaopign's Discussions in the South*) (Guangzhou; Guangdong renmin chubanshe, 2012).

Party History Research Centre of the Central Committee of the Chinese Communist Party, *History of the Chinese Communist Party: A Chronology of Events (1919–1990)* (Beijing: Foreign Languages Press, 1991).

Price, Jane L., *Cadres, Commanders and Commissars: The Training of the Chinese Communist Leadership, 1920–1945* (Folkestone: Dawson, 1976).

Quinn-Judge, Sophie, *Ho Chi Minh: The Missing Years 1919–1941* (London: Hurst, 2003).

Saich, Tony, *The Rise to Power of the Chinese Communist Party* (New York: M.E. Sharpe, 1996).

Saich, Tony and Hans J. Van de Ven (eds), *New Perspectives on the Chinese Communist Revolution* (New York: M.E. Sharpe, 1997).

Salisbury, Harrison, *The Long March: The Untold Story* (London: Macmillan, 1985).

Schoenhals, Michael and Brewer S. Stone, 'More edited records: Liu Shaoqi on Peng Dehuai at the 7,000 Cadres Conference', CCP Research Newsletter No. 5 (1990).

Schram, Stuart (ed.) with Nancy Jane Hodes, *Mao's Road to Power: Revolutionary Writings 1912–1949* (New York: M. E. Sharpe, 1992).

Shambaugh, David, 'The Soldier and the State in China: The Political Work System in the People's Liberation Army', in Brian Hook (ed.) *The Individual and the State in China* (Oxford: Oxford University Press, 1996).

Shi Jian, *Gao Gang 'fandang' zhenxiang (The Truth about Gao Gang's anti-party activities)* (Hong Kong: Wenhua yishu chubanshe, 2008).

Shi Quanwei, *Shihua shishuo Deng Xiaoping (Straight Talking about Deng Xiaoping)* (Beijing: Zhongguo qingnian chubanshe, 2011, two volumes).

Tang Qinglin (ed.), *Huishou 1978: Lishi zai zheli zhuanzhe (Recollecting 1978: History Turned Here)* (Beijing: Renmin chubanshe, 2008).

Teiwes, Frederick C., *Politics at Mao's Court: Gao Gang and Party Factionalism in the Early 1950s* (New York: M.E. Sharpe, 1990).

Teiwes, Frederick C. and Warren Sun, *The End of the Maoist Era: Chinese Politics During the Twilight of the Cultural Revolution, 1972–1976* (Armonk, New York: M.E. Sharpe, 2008).

Tian Youru, *Zhongguo kang Ri genjudi fazhan shi (History of the Development of Resistance Bases in China's War of Resistance to Japan)* (Beijing: Renmin chubanshe, 1995).

Townsend, Peter, *China Phoenix: The Revolution in China* (London: Jonathan Cape, 1955).

Vogel, Ezra F., *Deng Xiaoping and the Transformation of China* (Cambridge, MA: Belknap Press at Harvard University Press, 2011).

Wang Shuzeng, *Jiefang zhanzheng (shang): 1945 8 yue–1948 9 yue (War of Liberation Volume 1: August 1945–September 1948)* (Beijing: Renmin chubanshe, 2011, two volumes).

Wang, Ting, *Chairman Hua: Leader of the Chinese Communists* (London: Hurst, 1980).

White, Theodore H. and Annalee Jacoby, *Thunder Out of China* (New York: Sloane, 1946).

Wilkinson, Endymion, *Chinese History: A Manual (Revised and Enlarged)* (Cambridge MA: Harvard-Yenching Institute, 2000).

Wilson, Richard (ed.), *The President's Trip to China: A Pictorial Record of the Historic Journey to the People's Republic of China with Text by Members of the American Press Corps* (New York: Bantam, 1972).

Wortzel, Larry M. and Robin D. S. Higham, *Dictionary of Contemporary Chinese Military History* (Santa Barbara: ABC-CLIO, 1999).

Wu Guoyou, *Zhonggong zhizhengdang jianshe shi (1978–2009) (History of the Construction of the Chinese Communist Party as a Ruling Party)* (Shenyang: Liaoning renmin chubanshe, 2011).

Wu Songying, *Deng Xiaoping nanfang tanhua zhenqing shilu – jilu ren de jishu* (*Record of the Reality of Deng Xiaoping's Discussions in the South*) (Beijing: Renmin chubanshe, 2012).

Xinhua (New China News Agency), no author, 'Ba qi huiyi (1927 nian) (7 August Upising 1927)', no date. Available at news.xinhuanet.com/ziliao/2003-01/20/content_697851.htm (last accessed 20 July 2014).

Xiong Xianghui, 'Dakai Zhong Mei guanxi de qianzou: 1969 nian siwei laoshuai dui guoji xingshi de yanjiu yu jianyi' ('The prelude to the opening of Sino–US relations: 1969 study of the international situation by four veteran commanders'), in *Xin Zhongguo waijiao fengyun* (*New China's Changing Diplomacy*) Vol. 4 (Beijing: Shijie zhishe chubanshe, 1996).

Yang Jisheng, *Zhongguo gaige niandai de zhengzhi douzheng* (*The Political Struggles of China's Reform Period*) (Hong Kong: Excellent Culture Press, 2004).

Yang Jisheng, *Mubei: yijiuwuba-yijiuliuer nian Zhongguo da jihuang jishi* (Hong Kong: Cosmos Books, 2010, two volumes).

Yang Jisheng, *Tombstone: The Untold Story of Mao's Great Famine* (London: Allen Lane, 2012).

Ye Xingqiu and Jiang Jingshi, *Faguo yizhan lao huagong jishi* (*Chinese Labourers in France During the First World War*) (Paris: Pacifica, 2010).

Ye Yonglie, *Deng Xiaoping gaibian Zhongguo: 1978 Zhongguo mingyun da zhuanzhe* (*Deng Xiaoping Changes China – 1978: Turning Point in China's Destiny*) (Nanchang: Jiangxi Renmin chubanshe, 2008).

Yu Boliu, *Weiren zhi jian: Mao Zedong yu Deng Xiaoping* (*Between Great Men: Mao Zedong and Deng Xiaoping*) (Nanchang: Jiangxi renmin chubanshe, 2011).

Yu Wei and Wu Zhifei, *Deng Xiaoping de zuihou ershi nian* (Beijing: Xinhua chubanshe, 2008).

Zhang Liang (compiler), Andrew Nathan and Perry Link (eds), *The Tian'anmen Papers* (London: Little, Brown, 2001).

Zhang Suhua, *Bianzhu: qiqianren dahui shimo (1962 nian 1 yue 11 ri – 2 yue 7 ri)* (*Critical Moment: Seven Thousand Cadres Conference 11 January to 7 February 1962*) (Beijing: Zhongguo qingnian chubanshe, 2006).

Zhao Xiaoguang and Liu Jie, *Deng Xiaoping de san luo san qi* (*The Three Falls and Three Rises of Deng Xiaoping*) (Shenyang: Liaoning renmin chubanshe (Liaoning People's Press), 2011).

Zhao Ziyang, *Prisoner of the State: The Secret Journal of Zhao Ziyang* (London: Simon and Schuster, 2009).

Zhong Wen and Wen Fu, *Deng Xiaoping waijiao fengcai shilu* (*Veritable Records of Deng Xiaoping's Elegant Diplomacy*) (Beijing: Renmin chubanshe, 2004).

Zhonggong Chongqing shiwei dang shi yanjiushi, *Zhongguo gongchandang Chongqing difang jianshi* (Chongqing: Chongqing chubanshe, 2006).

Zhonggong Chongqing shiwei dang shi yanjiushi, *Zhongguo gongchandang Chongqing lishi, diyi juan (1926–1949)* (Chongqing: Chongqing chubanshe, 2011).

Zhonggong Chongqing shiwei dang shi yanjiushi, *Zhongguo gongchandang lishi, di er juan (1949–1978) xiace* (*History of the Chinese Communist Party, Volume 2 (1949-1978), Part 2*) (Beijing: Zhonggong dangshi chubanshe, 2010).

Zhonggong Chongqing shiwei dang shi yanjiushi (ed.), *Jianguo yilai zhongyao wenxian xuanbian* (Beijing: Zhongyang wenxian chubanshe, 1994, Volumes 1–17).

Zhu Jiamu, *Wo suo zhidao de shiyi jie sanzhong quanhui* (*The Third Plenum of the Eleventh Central Committee That I Knew*) (Beijing: Dangdai Zhongguo chubanshe, 2009).

Zhu Rongji, *Zhu Rongji jianghua shilu* (Beijing: Renmin chubanshe, 2012).

Zhonggong Chongqing shiwei dang shi yanjiushi, *Zhu Rongji on the Record: The Road to Reform 1991–1997* (Beijing: Foreign Languages Press, 2013).

INDEX